Great Britain

Nations of the Modern World: Europe
edited by W. Rand Smith and Robin Remington

This series examines the nations of Europe as they adjust to a changing world order and move into the twenty-first century. Each volume is a detailed, analytical country case study of the political, economic, and social dynamics of a European state facing the challenges of the post–Cold War era. These challenges include changing values and rising expectations, the search for new political identities and avenues of participation, and growing opportunities for economic and political cooperation in the new Europe. Emerging policy issues such as the environment, immigration, refugees, and reordered national security priorities are evolving in contexts still strongly influenced by history, geography, and culture.

The former East European nations must cope with the legacies of communism as they attempt to make the transition to multiparty democracy and market economies amid intensifying national, ethnic, religious, and class divisions. West European nations confront the challenge of pursuing economic and political integration within the European Union while contending with problems of economic insecurity, budgetary stress, and voter alienation.

How European nations respond to these challenges individually and collectively will shape domestic and international politics in Europe for generations to come. By considering such common themes as political institutions, public policy, political movements, political economy, and domestic-foreign policy linkages, we believe the books in this series contribute to our understanding of the threads that bind this vital and rapidly evolving region.

Great Britain: Decline or Renewal?
Donley T. Studlar

Spain: Democracy Regained,
Second Edition, E. Ramón Arango

Denmark: A Troubled Welfare State,
Kenneth E. Miller

Portugal: From Monarchy to Pluralist Democracy,
Walter C. Opello, Jr.

FORTHCOMING

The Czech and Slovak Republics, Carol Leff

Albania, Elez Biberaj

Austria, Anton Pelinka

The Netherlands, Thomas R. Rochon

The Politics of Belgium, John Fitzmaurice

Ireland: The Challenge of Conflict and Change,
Second Edition, Richard B. Finnegan

Modern Greece, Keith R. Legg and John Roberts

France: Grandeur or Decline? W. Rand Smith

Germany, W. Donald Hancock and Henry Krisch

Italy, Patrick McCarthy

Switzerland, Ulrich Klöti

GREAT BRITAIN

BRITAIN

Decline or Renewal?

DONLEY T. STUDLAR

WestviewPress

A Division of HarperCollins*Publishers*

Nations of the Modern World: Europe

Copyright © 1996 by Westview Press, Inc., A Division of HarperCollins Publishers, Inc.

Published in 1996 in the United States of America by Westview Press, Inc., 5500 Central Avenue,
Boulder, Colorado 80301-2877, and in the United Kingdom by Westview Press, 12 Hid's Copse Road,
Cumnor Hill, Oxford OX2 9JJ

A CIP catalog record for this book is available from the Library of Congress.
ISBN 0-8133-1508-5; 0-8133-1509-3(pb)

The paper used in this publication meets the requirements of the American National Standard for
Permanence of Paper for Printed Library Materials Z39.48-1984.

10   9   8   7   6   5   4   3   2   1

Contents

List of Figures and Tables   xi
Acknowledgments   xiii
List of Acronyms   xv

1 INTRODUCTION: CONTINUITY AND CHANGE   1

The Importance of Britain, 1
Britain in the Modern World, 3
Conflict and Change in Britain, 4
The Policy Approach, 7
Outline of the Book, 12
Notes, 13

2 BRITAIN IN HISTORICAL AND GEOGRAPHICAL CONTEXT   16

Physical and Human Geography, 16
Economic and Social Development, 21
Demographics of the United Kingdom, 28
Feudalism, Industrialization, Urbanization, and Class, 31
Notes, 34

3 THE DEVELOPMENT OF POLITICAL INSTITUTIONS   36

From Absolutist to Constitutional Monarchy, 36
The Decline of Feudal Institutions: Monarchy and House of Lords, 37
The Decline and Survival of the House of Lords, 42
The Rise and Decline of the House of Commons, 43
The Rise and Rise of the Cabinet and Prime Minister, 51
The Civil Service: From Servants to Masters? 56

The Unitary State and Its Discontents, 59
The Judiciary—Supremacy of Law? 61
British Government in the Late Twentieth Century, 63
Notes, 63

4 POLITICAL FORCES: ORGANIZATIONS AND INDIVIDUALS

66

Elites and Masses, 66
Elites: Values, Value Change, and Socialization, 67
Mass Values, Socialization, and Value Change, 72
Mass Media as Linkage Mechanisms, 74
Interest Groups as Linkage Mechanisms, 79
Political Parties as Linkage Mechanisms, 85
Elections as Intermediary Institutions, 91
Elite Recruitment, 94
Summary, 97
Notes, 99

5 BRITISH FOREIGN POLICY: FROM GREAT POWER TO EUROPEAN PERIPHERY

105

The Policy Agenda, 107
Actors, 107
Policy Formation, Adoption, and Implementation, 111
Evaluation, 127
Notes, 129

6 ECONOMIC POLICY: FROM INDUSTRIAL GIANT TO BRITALY

132

The Agenda, 133
Actors, 134
Formation, Adoption, and Implementation, 136
Evaluation, 155
Notes, 160

7 SOCIAL WELFARE POLICY: FROM LEADER TO LAGGARD 165

The Agenda, 166
Actors, 168
Formation, Adoption, and Implementation, 170
Evaluation, 181
Notes, 184

8 SOCIAL REGULATORY POLICIES: FROM PUBLIC MORALITY TO SOCIAL PERMISSIVENESS 187

The Agenda, 188
Actors, 188
Formation, Adoption, and Implementation, 191
Evaluation, 206
Notes, 208

9 CHANGE AND INSTITUTIONAL ADAPTATION IN THE UNITED KINGDOM 212

Issues, 212
Institutions and Processes, 221
Conclusion, 224
Notes, 225

Further Reading   227
Bibliography   229
About the Book and Author 247
Index   249

Figures and Tables

FIGURES

Map of Great Britain   xvi

TABLES

4.1 Election Results in Britain, 1974–1992   86

6.1 Government Spending Categories as Percentage of Total
        Public Expenditures, 1978–1991   137
6.2 Comparative British Economic Performance   142
6.3 Privatization in Britain, 1979–1991   147

7.1 Social Security Benefits in Britain   179

Acknowledgments

THIS BOOK REPRESENTS a synthesis of twenty-five years spent studying British politics, during which time I have accumulated a large number of intellectual debts. My first formal course dealing with the United Kingdom was an undergraduate course on Western Europe at Texas Tech University in 1968, in which I learned about the country through the first edition of Richard Rose's book *Politics in England*. Subsequently I pursued graduate work on the subject at Indiana University, with dissertation guidance from James B. Christoph. The award of a fellowship from the National Defense Education Act, Title IV, sustained my graduate career. For the year I did field research for my Ph.D. dissertation on immigration policy in British electoral politics (1973), Richard Rose invited me to reside at the University of Strathclyde. My education was greatly enhanced by the faculty and graduate students there, as well as by the broader contacts residence in Glasgow allowed me. Over the years Chris and Marie Hewitt, whom I met there, have sensitized me to many issues, including British-Irish relations.

Soon after starting my first job at the University of Nebraska, I became a charter member of the British Politics Group (BPG), an academic organization based in the United States and devoted to the furtherance of scholarly study of the United Kingdom. Active involvement in this organization has enabled me to increase my knowledge and broaden my perspectives. I was fortunate enough to be awarded the first Samuel H. Beer dissertation prize given by the BPG. Professional association with the longtime executive secretary of the BPG, Jorgen Rasmussen of Iowa State University, has been an immensely rewarding experience. In 1994 I succeeded him as executive secretary.

Through the years at three other institutions of higher education in the United States—Centre College, Oklahoma State University, and West Virginia University—I have been afforded various opportunities to study Britain in greater depth. The libraries of these institutions, especially their interlibrary loan facilities, have been instrumental in clearing up problems. During a sabbatical year at the University of Warwick in 1983, I enjoyed the hospitality and assistance of one of the leading departments of political studies in the United Kingdom. Zig Layton-Henry and Jim Bulpitt were particularly helpful. Over the years my employers have also allowed me to test my ideas on students, mainly undergraduates, from widely divergent backgrounds.

During this twenty-five-year period, I have published a number of articles in scholarly journals on both sides of the Atlantic. Many of these have been collaborative efforts, and my coauthors on three continents deserve special thanks. They are Susan Welch, Ian McAllister, Zig Layton-Henry, Lee Sigelman, Richard Flickinger, and Alvaro Ascui. In addition, Jerold Waltman and I have coedited two volumes of original essays on Britain, one focusing on institutions, the other on social and economic policy. This volume expands the focus again. The theoretical focus of this book has been influenced by conversations with T. Alexander Smith of the University of Tennessee and Ray Tatalovich of Loyola University of Chicago.

This book would not have been written without the initiative of Susan McEachern at Westview Press or the series editor Rand Smith at Lake Forest College, without the suggestion of Jorgen Rasmussen, or without preliminary discussions with Chris Hewitt of the University of Maryland, Baltimore County. It would never have been completed without the indulgence of my wife, Susan Moyle Studlar, and of our children, Carl and Ross. Rand Smith and Chris Hewitt, along with Jeffrey Freyman of Transylvania University, Richard Flickinger of Wittenberg University, and Jerold Waltman of the University of Southern Mississippi, gave me expert critiques of the manuscript, in whole or in part. Julie Tennant typed the final version of the manuscript with her usual good humor and efficiency. I thank all of the above organizations and individuals and absolve them of any responsibility for remaining errors of omission or commission. Undoubtedly, I still have a lot to learn.

Donley T. Studlar
Morgantown, West Virginia

Acronyms

BPG	British Politics Group
EC	European Community
EU	European Union
G-7	Group of Seven
NATO	North Atlantic Treaty Organization
MPs	members of Parliament
BBC	British Broadcasting Corporation
IMF	International Monetary Fund
HMG	Her (or His) Majesty's Government
QCs	Queen's Counselors
NHS	National Health Service
ITV	Independent Television
NEDC	National Economic Development Council
TUC	Trades Union Congress
NUM	National Union of Mineworkers
NEC	National Executive Committee
SERPS	state earnings-related pension
GATT	General Agreement on Tariffs and Trade
COREPOR	Committee of Permanent Representatives
EFTA	European Free Trade Association
ERM	European Exchange Rate Mechanism
UDI	Unilateral Declaration of Independence
UN	United Nations
NICs	newly industrialized countries
VAT	value-added tax
GNP	gross national product
OPEC	Organization of Petroleum Exporting Countries
PSBR	public-sector borrowing requirement
LEAs	local education authorities
OASDI	Old Age, Survivors, and Disability Insurance
IRA	Irish Republican Army
AIDS	Acquired Immune Deficiency Syndrome

1

INTRODUCTION: CONTINUITY AND CHANGE

The Importance of Britain

Forty years ago, former United States Secretary of State Dean Acheson said that Britain had lost an empire and had not yet found a new role to play in the world. In many ways that statement remains true today. The former confidence of Britons of all political persuasions has been eroded, now replaced by confusion about what roles, foreign and domestic, the country should play. Has there been too much change or too little in British life in the past half century? Did Thatcherism produce a social revolution or did it leave things much the same as they were before? Published analyses conflict—and not on political or ideological grounds alone. It is the purpose of this book to explore the sources of the confusion about how to characterize contemporary British social and political life.

Despite its overall decline in importance in the world, Great Britain is probably still the foreign country about which citizens and students of the United States know the most. Some of the most common bonds between the two countries include the British settlement of America, the ease of communication through common language, close diplomatic relations, use of the British parliamentary model, and the frequent citation of Britain as an economic and foreign policy example for the United States.

Although the closest physical neighbors of the United States, Canada and Mexico, are largely ignored unless what they are doing impinges directly on the interests of the United States, both elite and mass opinion in America reflects British influence. At 9:00 P.M. eastern standard time on Sunday night, for instance, most cable television subscribers across the United States can view either

1

Masterpiece Theater on the Public Broadcasting System or *Question Time in the House of Commons* on C-SPAN. The personal problems of the monarchy are more often displayed on newsstands in the United States than are the personal problems of any U.S. leaders except the president. The author of a recent well-received journalistic survey of British culture and politics argues that, to a large degree, the elite public of the United States remains enamored of the country.[1]

Many people in the United States, then, know something about Britain. For many it is the repository of high culture and tradition, the origin of Western liberal democratic values, Christianity, and capitalism. For others its history embodies a warning about what can happen to a society that is class ridden, that relies too heavily on tradition, that does not adjust its economy to changing times, and that becomes too comfortable in its foreign leadership position.

Probably most citizens of the United States (and elsewhere) know less about Britain than they think they do. Of course, much remains the same in any country. But in the past half century, the United Kingdom has changed considerably, at least on the surface. For instance, Britain was recognized as the leading economic power in the world in the nineteenth century largely because of its espousal of industrialization and capitalism. Yet in the twentieth century many articles and books have been written arguing that what hampers Britain today is its continued embrace of its older, aristocratic traditions, which industrialization, urbanization, and capitalism did not overwhelm.[2] Further, in Britain church and state are united, both through the monarchy and through various kinds of state support of church activities, ranging from religious instruction in schools to Church of England bishops sitting in the House of Lords. Yet Britons are among the least devout people of "Christian" countries; indeed, one could consider Britain a thoroughly secular country.

Change has been particularly evident in the political and economic realms in recent decades. Since 1970, Britain has no longer had a conventional two-party system, except in Parliament. The world's first industrialized power has become the preeminent example of deindustrialization. What was once thought of (mistakenly) as a relatively homogenous society has been infused with multiracialism and multiculturalism, especially in urban areas. Parliamentary sovereignty has been compromised by membership in the European Community (EC), or European Union (EU), as it has also been called since 1991.

What has changed, then, and what has remained the same in Britain? What does the current balance of change portend for Britain's global role in the twenty-first century? In this volume, I examine the social, economic, and political dimensions of Britain's internal structure and external relations with focus on underlying explanations for continuity and change, especially concerning the trends of the last one-third of the twentieth century. History is examined selectively for its relevance to the contemporary situation of the country. The overriding question to be answered is this: Can Britain's institutions adapt successfully to the changes facing them in the remaining years of the twentieth century and beyond?

Britain in the Modern World

In 1962, *Anatomy of Britain*, by British journalist Anthony Sampson, became a touchstone for analysts of British society, economics, and politics.[3] With his access to political power brokers, Sampson was able to delineate a broad-based elite portrait of Britain in its Indian summer of postwar prosperity, through the country was troubled about the direction of its society and place in the world. His analysis of various social factors and attitudes and his questioning of the British capacity to adjust to new forces made Sampson's viewpoint symptomatic of what has come to be called the "decline of Britain" school, a body of thought that continues to flourish today.[4] By the 1990s, Sampson was still pessimistic about the direction of the United Kingdom, seeing the country as reluctant to become a full partner in the European Union and as having an overly centralized regime.[5]

This volume can be considered an attempt to continue this line of examination, though with a more focused political and academic content. No presumption of decline is made herein, as I examine British institutions and assess how well they are coping with the challenges put to them. The focus is on the post–World War II period, now a half-century old, a time period long enough to allow fair assessment. Britain has shared many political problems with West European countries and other advanced industrial countries elsewhere. These include problems of political identity, in the British case including the loyalties that some British citizens hold to such other political units as Wales, Scotland, Northern Ireland, the Irish Republic, and even the European Union. Although the United Kingdom is more frequently referred to as "deindustrialized" rather than "postindustrial," some of the characteristics associated with postindustrial society, such as shifting values and forms of political participation among the mass public, have also affected the country. Issues such as equal rights for women, race relations, and treatment of the environment have at times risen to the forefront of political debate alongside the more perennial ones of the economy, social welfare policy, national security, and foreign relations. In an increasingly aging society, the question of the trade-off between social welfare administered by the state and allowing sufficient market flexibility to free the economy to be competitive with world market forces has become increasingly acute. Voter volatility has made political parties less certain that their preferred solutions will appeal to their constituents.

If a country does not stand still, neither does its external environment. Britain continues to be a major actor, not only in Europe but on the world stage as well, through its leading role in such organizations as the Group of Seven (G-7) leading industrialized economies, the European Union (formerly the European Community), and the North Atlantic Treaty Organization (NATO). As Europe has changed over the years through greater economic integration and the collapse of the Soviet empire in the East, Britain has played a major role. The choices it makes in these areas, as well as in such other areas as development of information technology, will determine whether Britain can remain an influential actor in the twenty-first century. Britain has to adapt to a changing regional and international environment, but its choices will also influence, however modestly, the direction of those environments.

One overriding question in regard to the potential influence of the United Kingdom internationally is whether its position will be enhanced or diminished by the greater fluidity of international affairs observable since 1989, which presumably will continue. Arguably, the country's penchant for military strength and general solidarity with the United States helped maintain its international position during the Cold War despite its relative economic decline. How will the United Kingdom fare in a period in which alliances are in flux, military spending is in decline, the EU is enlarged and is perhaps more integrated politically as well as economically, and economic competitiveness is more important for international influence?

Britain has faced similar social, economic, and political challenges before. The innovative technology that led to the industrial revolution was one that Britain had to adapt to, as was the growth of liberalism (individual rights) and democracy (majority rule) as political movements. Internationally, the United Kingdom was able to move from the multipolar world of several major powers of the nineteenth and early twentieth centuries into the bipolar world of United States–Soviet competition after World War II. In fact, Britain is notable among countries for its capacity to adapt to changing circumstances while retaining many of its former characteristics.

Conflict and Change in Britain

Britain has often been viewed as an essentially stable society with conservative political institutions, albeit one that has been flexible enough to adapt when the social and political fabric seemed threatened. The British have avoided political revolution since the seventeenth century, for better or worse. Radicals have often become incorporated into the flexible framework of political institutions in the United Kingdom, becoming reformers. Thus Liberals, suffragettes, and Socialists became, in their fashion, defenders of a system that allowed them to reach at least some of their goals. This "aristocratic embrace" has been viewed with disdain by those immune to its seduction. Many go so far as to argue that what Britain needs is a genuine social revolution, for without that the necessary rearrangement of attitudes and institutions will never occur.

A key element in most accounts of how British society functions to disarm threats to its continuity is the flexibility of the unwritten English Constitution, first celebrated by Walter Bagehot in *The English Constitution* in the middle of the nineteenth century.[6] When threats become too severe from insurgent groups, the Constitution can be readily altered, either by majority vote of the House of Commons or by changing customs and conventions rather than formal laws. The monarchy can be changed from absolutist to constitutional. The House of Lords can be stripped of its capacity as a coequal branch of the legislature yet continue to be chosen by the most undemocratic means of any legislative chamber in a liberal democracy. The right to vote can be expanded to new groups, but in stages rather than all at once.

In short, the flexibility of British institutions means that in order to change policy, it is necessary first to convince enough of the governing elite that policy should be changed. If that can be done, any institutional barriers to change can normally be readily overcome. Policy change is frustrated when the elite is insufficiently convinced to make the necessary institutional adjustments. That was the case with the Labour government's attempt to introduce devolution (decentralization) for Scotland and Wales in the 1970s. Elite divisions within both parties have also been the major obstacle to full-scale British government acceptance of the demands of the European Union, making Britain an awkward partner for the other European countries over such issues as the Common Agricultural Policy, negotiation of the Maastricht Treaty for a more politically integrated European Community, and voting rights in the enlarged (fifteen-member) EU.

Even when demands for radical change threaten to overwhelm the system, the essential adaptable conservatism of the British elite comes to the fore. The most recent instance of this occurred in the 1970s and 1980s. As labor unrest and inflation surged, seemingly out of control, in the 1970s, expert opinion talked in alarmed tones of Britain's "ungovernability,"[7] the dangers of "elective dictatorships" through constitutionally unfettered major party control of the House of Commons through the executive,[8] and the problems of "adversary government" (reversing previous policies, as on trade union legislation in the 1970s) when the two major parties become more ideologically extreme.[9]

Yet after the Winter of Discontent in 1979, when disruptive strikes occurred all over Britain, the Conservatives under Margaret Thatcher were elected to deal with national problems. By allowing unemployment to rise in order to squeeze inflation out of the economy, they incurred not social revolution but enough calm to enable the government to proceed to do what was considered impossible in the previous decade, weakening the power of the trade unions through legislation. The type of accommodation to insurgent interests that the Thatcher government made was more attuned to the growing consumerism and individual rights orientation of the professionalized suburbs than to the collective power of the industrialized, urban trade unions. But by appealing to the membership of trade unions as individuals, and being able to retain power over a divided Labour opposition throughout the decade and into the 1990s, the Conservatives were able to defuse the threat to the stability of British political institutions without making major alterations in them. Today even the Labour Party seems to accept that these changes are permanent.

In the next decade, however, the United Kingdom is likely to face greater challenges from external rather than internal sources. Economic competition, especially in the tertiary (service) sector of information services through computers, is likely to be intense. As noted, the role of the European Union both as a political and an economic actor is an issue that generates immense conflict on the elite level in Britain. How much the United Kingdom will cooperate with the other states of the EU and how much it will resist the initiatives of the European Commission in particular will influence Britain's role not only in Europe, but in global political and economic arenas. Similarly, concern over the possible decline of the Anglo-American "special relationship," as well as opportunities for new alliances created by the breakup of the Soviet bloc, will make Britain's adjustment to its environment more challenging.

However, by refusing to face the problem of changing Britain's political institutions in fundamental ways, the Conservative governments may have left a legacy that will complicate the country's adjustment to its external challenges. With the European Union pressing for changes in British policy and increasingly taking over broader responsibilities in such areas as environmental policy, immigration, social policy, as well as trade policy, Britain is faced with decisions about not only how to deal with these particular issues but also how to adjust its institutions in order to best scrutinize and negotiate with the EU. However incoherently expressed by politicians, this is the issue that underlies the vitriolic Europhile-Europeskeptic dispute that at times has threatened to tear apart the Conservative Party, giving it an appearance of fractiousness more characteristic of the Labour Party.

The Conservatives have been able to postpone the debate over institutional change by concentrating on domestic economic policy, especially through deregulation and privatization, using the instruments of the central state to control their political opponents in the trade unions and local governments. But the politics of the twenty-first century is not likely to feature the long-term Conservative dominance that occurred after 1979. The opposition parties, be they Labour, Liberal, or nationalist, have an agenda of institutional reforms in mind, including devolution, a written bill of rights, abolition of the House of Lords, and proportional representation for electing members of Parliament (MPs). Although not all of these will necessarily be adopted, some of them will have to be addressed, even by a Conservative government. The likelihood of this confrontation arising is enhanced, not diminished, by the need for the United Kingdom to make adjustments in its international policy as well. In addition, changes in policy often lead to questions about changing institutions.

In the twentieth century, despite the ongoing symbol of parliamentary sovereignty, real political authority has resided in the executive sector of government. Now, that authority is being challenged institutionally on several fronts, ranging from populistic elements that want the executive and, indeed, Parliament to be more responsive to the will of the people between elections to those wanting more legal protections for individual citizens from big goverment. There are also the compromises to British sovereignty that have developed in the institutions and policies of the European Union. How will the traditional structures of British government cope with these challenges?

In summary, then, Britain has been institutionally a conservative but adaptive polity through the centuries. In the twentieth century, however, these proclivities have been insufficient to prevent, in comparison to other states, a relative loss of political and economic influence in the world, even though, over time, British prosperity is now greater than ever. Given this recent history, the question arises as to whether the adaptability of institutions and political culture can be judged adequate to meet the challenges, foreseen and unforeseen, of the twenty-first century. Certainly the long dominance of Conservative governments in Britain since 1979 has provided an opportunity for concerted change. Despite much controversy, both political and academic, the jury is still out on how well the Conservatives have managed to deal with fundamental, underlying problems in Britain. They were willing to change economically, at least in terms of the government's role in the economy, including certain aspects of social policy, but were less willing to change fundamental political institutions—what the British call "constitutional" change. Some commentators contend, however, that constitutional change does not matter because it cannot be shown to be directly connected to people's economic and social condition. Even on economic matters, however, it is not clear that the Conservative government was internationally minded enough to be able to provide a better base for maintaining even Britain's relative economic position. But this is not to argue that only the Conservative claims for fundamental change have been overdrawn. Somehow, the promised "white-hot technological revolution" of Harold Wilson's six-year Labour government in the 1960s was stillborn, which many argue was the beginning of the long-term popular disenchantment with the two-party system in Britain. The problems are not so much partisan ones as institutional or cultural ones. For all of the institutional flexibility that the unwritten British Constitution and parliamentary government provide, deeply rooted conservatism may be inadequate for the times. But countries, like individuals, that have been successful with certain forms of behavior are reluctant to change. In the rest of this book I examine whether evidence supports this argument for Britain.

The Policy Approach

Possibly the most succinct definition of public policy is "what governments choose to do and not to do".[10] Government is the administrative apparatus of the state, a legal entity that has sovereignty (final authority) over a given population and territory. A state has a regime, that is, a set of rules, written and unwritten, that are followed in how the affairs of state are conducted, no matter who is in charge at a particular time. Although much of policymaking may be removed from public sight and may affect parts of society in different ways, governments make policy for the whole society (public), not only a segment of it.

Public policy is broader than being just what governments do, however. As the struggles over public policy indicate, policy also concerns choices about what to do, and even what problems to address. If government chooses, either deliberately or by ignorance, not to address certain problems, that is public policy, too. This is what has come to be called the question of agenda setting and nondecisionmaking in public policy.[11] How do problems come to capture the public and decision-makers' consciousness? Why are some problems addressed and others ignored? What are the priorities among issues that government deals with?

In the British context, much of the historical argument about whether government has adequately dealt with public needs actually involves an implicit judgment about agenda setting. For instance, those who argue that the "aristocratic embrace" has inhibited Britain's ability to address its international economic competitiveness problems are saying, in effect, that the needs of the economy, especially those of industry, have been neglected in favor of concentration on maintaining the marriage of convenience between the aristocracy and capitalism, particularly as it manifested itself through the international financial capital sector of the British economy.[12] Similarly, Corelli Barnett, in a recent controversial interpretation of the postwar British experience,[13] has argued that British governments at the end of and after World War II made a fundamental mistake in concentrating policy emphasis and government resources on enhancing Britain's social welfare system rather than reforming and investing in education. However much one agrees with these particular interpretations, from the perspective of agenda setting proponents of this view are arguing that the problems government chooses to focus on, as well the ways government addresses these problems, can make a difference.

One-half of this book focuses directly on contemporary policy concerns. The theoretical perspectives evident in Chapters 4 through 8 and implicit elsewhere in the book stem from current public policy research. One such is the "history of public policy" approach, which in this case means examining the policy issues confronting British society and government at a particular time, as well as observing how the society, and particularly the government, responded.[14] Although I emphasize the actual debates and course of policy as it has been made in the United Kingdom, especially since World War II, I also use, in attenuated form, three related policy theories utilized by social scientists. The first, which serves as the organizing principle for these four chapters, is the "arenas of power" or "policy typologies" first developed by Theodore Lowi in his study of the United States and subsequently utilized by many others.[15] Policies are categorized into four broad areas: foreign policy, economic policy, social policy (also called social welfare policy), and social regulatory policy, which includes moral and constitutional issues. Obviously, as in all categorizations, there are some issues that are more difficult to place than others; thus, the classifications are not necessarily straightforward but in some cases are subject to judgment and debate. Nevertheless, on the whole I would argue that this is a meaningful categorization of public policies, not only in Britain but elsewhere as well. Lowi's classification, or some version of it, has been employed in the study of political systems in several advanced industrial democracies.[16] Unlike many studies, this one includes foreign as well as domestic policy, although it recognizes that the two are increasingly difficult to separate, especially in the context of the European Union and the Maastricht Treaty.[17] Increasingly, the term "intermestic" is used to describe issues, such as energy, having implications for both foreign and domestic policy.[18]

The second policy theory employed within the history of public policy approach is the "stages of public policy" perspective. Although the exact dimensions vary, policy analysts have in recent years delineated five such stages.[19] These are (1) problem indentification and agenda setting, (2) policy formulation and legitimation, (3) policy adoption, (4) policy implementation, and (5) policy evaluation. Problem identification and agenda setting refers to whatever problems policymakers deal with at a particular time. Policy formulation and legitimation means the consideration of alternative means of dealing with problems and the struggle to legitimize particular policy choices through the policy process. Policy adoption refers to the formal choice of policy made, usually through executive-legislative interaction. Policy implementation deals with the carrying out of policy through the bureaucracy. The final stage, policy evaluation, concerns the assessment of policy outcomes and consequences through various oversight mechanisms such as legislative committees, executive evaluations, and outside studies. Academic assessments are one form of policy evaluation.

In practice it is often difficult to differentiate among policy stages, and because of this some analysts have suggested different foci for public policy studies. Thus in the United States several studies have been organized around the concept of "advocacy coalitions,"[20] whearas the dominant concept in British policy studies has become "policy community" or "issue network" analysis,[21] which involves analysis of the government agencies and groups involved in an ongoing basis in particular policy sectors. Aside from their being largely metaphorical,[22] a major problem with both of these approaches is that they take the study of policy back toward intensive case studies of particular issues, groups, and sectors rather than being able to generalize across different policy areas. Thus the policy stages approach will be utilized in the relevant chapters. After introductory comments about how the subject matter in each chapter fits with policy categorizations (typologies), the policy agenda of the major general issues and potential issues in a particular area will be discussed. The political institutions that affect issue processing in the area will then be briefly outlined. In the fourth section of the policy chapters, the way policy has developed over the years in this area is considered. Finally, an evaluation of British policy performance assessing how well it has coped with policy problems will be presented.

The third related theory of policy analysis used in this book is to distinguish broadly between elite influence and mass influence on policy. In fact, Lowi's development of policy arenas occurred when he was attempting to determine whether policymaking in the United States was essentially pluralist or elitist. In other words, he asked whether policy was the outcome of group struggles among different sectors of the population or whether there was a cohesive group of elite actors who molded policy in their preferred direction consistently. There are different views on which elite actors are important. Lowi's reply was that the answer to this question depended on what policy area was being considered. Foreign policy, for instance, was more elitist than most domestic policy (if only considering the internal actors in each), but even within the latter, different patterns appeared in different types of issues. As noted above, after Lowi's first effort, the idea that influence varies by policy area has been taken up by a wide variety of scholars, including some who have attempted to relate issue types to the different institutional context of the United Kingdom.[23]

There is an ongoing debate about the relative merits of pluralism and elitism in the United Kingdom.[24] Especially important in this context are the concepts of "high politics and low politics"[25] and "liberal corporatism".[26] Jim Bulpitt has argued that British politicians have a characteristic "operational code," which leads them to focus on such "high politics" issues as foreign policy, economic development, and some social welfare policies at the central parliamentary level, largely leaving other "low politics" issues, such as education and race relations, to local government under normal circumstances. Advocates of the liberal corporatism perspective argue that British politics in the twentieth century developed a mode of operation in which there was a loose group of important institutionalized political actors that influenced most political decisions, at least until the rise of Mrs. Thatcher.[27] The power of corporatist groups depended on their importance in the economy and the significance of the economy for political officeholders. Thus business, organized labor, and the financial interests of the City of London have often been depicted as the main corporatist actors, along with the government.

This form of corporatism was "liberal" in contrast to the dictatorial corporatism under fascist regimes in Italy and Germany between the wars, in which the government exerted power over the economy by controlling the decisions of other groups in society. Under liberal corporatism, government was an important actor, though not all-important. Other major institutionalized centers of economic power also influenced the course of policy, but these were limited in number. Corporatism is one form of elitist analysis, although there are many others, including Marxism;[28] in Britain, the elite under corporatism is "the establishment," an interlinked upper-middle-class group of high-status worthies representing such traditional interests as the Church of England, the British Broadcasting Corporation (BBC), elite universities, military officers, newspaper proprietors, and landowners.[29] In liberal corporatism the groups that influence policy are limited in number and can wield influence only by achieving a strong position in the economy. Other groups, however many there may be and however much noise they may make, do not count for much in the final analysis because major decisions are made by consultation between government and the affected interests, often in secrecy.

There are other possible interpretations of the course of British public policy available. One is Mancur Olson's[30] celebrated theory of interest group sclerosis, whereby societies with large and powerful vested interests decline economically because of the power of such groups to protect their narrow interests at the expense of broader public concerns about maintaining economic competitiveness. Another widely cited view is Samuel Beer's[31] description of "pluralistic stagnation," in which, because of cultural developments toward selfishness, groups in Britain have become hindrances rather than aids to collective agreement on policy. Beer[32] had earlier described the rise of producer group interests in Britain and their increasing role in policymaking. Undoubtedly, there are more groups actively propounding policy positions today than ever before.[33] Both interest group sclerosis and pluralistic stagnation are general theories that do not rely on categorizing different issue areas, although they do tend to focus largely on economic policymaking.

Corporatism can readily fit with Bulpitt's theory of preferred elite statecraft. Similarly, Olson's theory of interest group sclerosis suggests movement from pluralism to elitism as some interest groups achieve a blocking position. Customary ways of making decisions by only taking seriously the arguments of certain actors can lead to ignoring some problems and relying on least-common-denominator policies that do not threaten the interests of the powerful. If the affected interests cannot agree on a policy approach, then policy deadlock occurs (ungovernability) or there is wavering from one policy direction to another (adversary politics). Beer's idea of pluralist stagnation is more congruent with pluralism, but after its own fashion it can also incorporate ungovernability and adversary politics. As Robert Putnam[34] has noted, elites exist in every society; it is important to ask, nonetheless, how diversified and open they are, not only in terms of who can enter but in their willingness to consider issues and positions raised by others.

All of these general categorizations of the British policy process, however, rely on the importance of institutions for policy development. Policy is molded by the behavior of individuals and groups in institutionalized contexts. Thus I relate policies to the institutional actors that are considered significant for policy formation in that area, and I also evaluate policy areas on the basis of their degree of elitism or pluralism, broadly considered. The importance of political institutions of various types for policy has recently been reaffirmed,[35] and Britain's long history of minimal institutional change is particularly conducive to understanding how this occurs. The overall theme of this book is geared to assess how well British political institutions, behavior, and public policy have coped with the challenges put to them by the domestic and international environment.

Nobody has been more critical of Britain's performance in these respects than some British analysts, who often speak in terms of the relative decline of the country from its former economic and international heights and who frequently condemn its leaders for being especially talented in managing decline without severe social disruption.[36] Others are less condemnatory, preferring to focus on the many areas in which Britain has continued to perform well, including those of political stability, absolute economic growth, and cultural excellence.[37] Although they take varying views on the desirability of the long rule of the Conservative Party since 1979, members of both groups have especially focused upon this as a test of how much Britain can change. Although I am attentive to the Conservative period of rule, the focus here is broader and considers the whole sweep of postwar British politics: How did the United Kingdom reach its present situation, and what prospects are there for further changes in its direction?

Outline of the Book

The rest of the book proceeds according to the criteria already set forth. In Chapter 2, the physical geography and a brief capsule history of Britain are presented, intended to set the country in both its spatial and historical configurations. In Chapter 3, British govermental institutions are likewise discussed, including an explanation of how they have evolved. The proximity of political institutions to formal policymaking is sufficiently important to justify a separate chapter. The fourth chapter concerns the role of mass and elite political behavior in channeling British policy responses. Thus such topics as political culture, on both the elite and mass levels, value change, and how elites and masses interact through such intermediary institutions (between the citizens and government) as elections, political parties, and interest groups will be examined.

The second part of the book, commencing with Chapter 5, provides a more specific policy focus. In Chapter 5, the changing contours of British foreign policy, including Britain's relationship to the European Community, NATO, the United States, the Commonwealth, and the states of the former Soviet bloc in Eastern Europe are considered. In addition, the implications of the end of the Cold War are assessed. In the sixth chapter, the broad sweep of British economic policy in the postwar period, including persistent macroeconomic and microeconomic pursuits and the role of Thatcherism in altering policies in this area is explored. Chapter 7 includes consideration of social welfare policy, which is designed to provide a minimum standard of living for individuals in straitened social circumstances through a combination of government transfer payments and direct provision of services. Chapter 8 deals with social regulatory policy, that is, rules concerning the regulation of social behavior among groups of people characterized by different races, nationalities, gender (including abortion), sexual orientation, and propensity for deviant behavior (crime and punishment).

Finally, the conclusion to the book presents a summary picture of Britain in the postwar period from a policy perspective, drawing conclusions on the utility of the various policy theories, exploring what adjustments the country might have to make in the near future, and assessing how well British institutions are prepared to cope with emerging policy challenges.

Notes

1. Richard Critchfield, *An American Looks at Britain* (New York: Doubleday Anchor Books, 1990).

2. Arthur Koestler, ed., *Suicide of a Nation?* (New York Macmillan, 1964); Michael Shanks, *The Stagnant Society* (Harmondsworth, England: Penguin Books, 1961); Max Nicholson, *The System: The Misgovernment of Modern Britain* (London: Hodder and Stoughton, 1967); Martin J. Wiener, *English Culture and the Decline of the Industrial Spirit, 1850–1980* (Cambridge: Cambridge University Press, 1981).

3. Anthony Sampson, *The Anatomy of Britain* (London: Hodder and Stoughton, 1962).

4. Koestler, *Suicide of a Nation?*; Shanks, *The Stagnant Society* Isaac Kramnick, ed., *Is Britain Dying?* (Ithaca: Cornell University Press, 1979); Bernard Nossiter, *Britain: A Future That Works* (Boston: Little, Brown and Company, 1978); William B. Gwyn and Richard Rose, eds., *Britain: Progress and Decline* (New Orleans: Tulane Studies in Political Science, 1980); Corelli Barnett, *The Audit of War* (London: Macmillan, 1986).

5. Anthony Sampson, *The Essential Anatomy of Britain* (New York: Harcourt Brace and Company, 1993).

6. Walter Bagehot, *The English Constitution* (London: Fontana, 1963).

7. Richard Rose, "Ungovernability: Is There Fire Behind the Smoke?" *Political Studies* 27, no. 3 (1979):351–370; Anthony King, "Overload: Problems of Governing in the 1970s," *Political Science* 23, no. 2 (1975):284–296; Robert Moss, *The Collapse of Democracy* (New Rochelle, N.Y.: Arlington House, 1976).

8. Lord Hailsham, *Elective Dictatorship* (London: British Broadcasting Corporation, 1976).

9. Samuel Finer, ed., *Adversary Politics and Electoral Reform* (London: Anthony Wigram, 1975).

10. Arnold Heidenheimer, Hugh Heclo, and Carolyn Teich Adams, *Comparative Public Policy*, 3d ed. (New York: St. Martin's Press, 1990).

11. Peter Bachrach and Morton Baratz, "The Two Faces of Power," *American Political Science Review* 56, no. 4 (1962):947–952.

12. Stephen Blank, "Britain: The Politics of Foreign Economic Policy, the Domestic Economy, and the Problem of Pluralistic Stagnation," *International Organization* 31, no. 4 (1977):673–721.

13. Corelli Barnett, *The Audit of War.*

14. Francis G. Castles, ed., *The Comparative History of Public Policy* (Cambridge: Polity Press, 1989).

15. T. Alexander Smith, *The Comparative Policy Process* (Santa Barbara, Ca.: ABC-Clio, 1975); Kenneth J. Meier, *Politics and Bureaucracy*, 3d ed. (Pacific Grove, Ca.: Brooks/Cole Publishing Company, 1993); Fred Frohock, *Public Policy: Scope and Logic* (Englewood Cliffs, N.J.: Prentice-Hall, 1979); Raymond Tatalovich and Byron W. Daynes, eds., *Social*

Regulatory Policy (Boulder: Westview Press, 1988); Randall B. Ripley and Grace Franklin, *Congress, the Bureaucracy, and Public Policy*, 5th ed. (Pacific Grove, Ca.: Brooks/Cole Publishing Company, 1991).

16. Smith, *The Comparative Policy Process*.

17. Peter Katzenstein, ed., *Between Power and Plenty* (Madison: University of Wisconsin Press, 1978); Robert O. Keohane, "The World Political Economy and the Crisis of Embedded Liberalism," in John Goldthorpe, ed., "Order and Conflict in Contemporary Capitalism" (Oxford: Clarendon Press, 1984).

18. John Spanier and Eric M. Uslaner, *American Foreign Policy Making and the Democratic Dilemmas*, 5th ed. (Pacific Grove, Ca.: Brooks/Cole Publishing Company, 1989).

19. Ripley and Franklin, *Congress, the Bureaucracy, and Public Policy;* Charles O. Jones, *An Introduction to the Study of Public Policy*, 3d ed. (Monterey, Ca.: Brooks/Cole Publishing Company, 1984); James Anderson, *Public Policymaking* (Boston: Houghton Mifflin Company, 1990).

20. Paul A. Sabatier and Hank C. Jenkins-Smith, eds., *Policy Change and Learning: An Advocacy Coalition Approach* (Boulder: Westview Press, 1993).

21. Hugh Heclo, "Issue Networks and the Executive Establishment," in Anthony King, ed., *The New American Political System* (Washington, D.C.: American Enterprise Institute, 1978); Grant A. Jordan, "Iron Triangles, Woolly Corporatism and Elastic Nets: Images of the Policy Process," *Journal of Public Policy* 1, no. 1 (1981):95–123; R.A.W. Rhodes, "Policy Networks: A British Perspective," *Journal of Theoretical Politics* 2, no. 2 (1990):293–317; David Marsh and R.A.W. Rhodes, eds., *Implementing Thatcherite Policies* (Buckingham: Open University Press, 1992); Keith Dowding, "Beyond Metaphor? Characteristic Explanation of Policy Networks" (paper presented at American Political Science Association Conference, New York, 1994).

22. Dowding, "Government at the Centre," in *Developments in British Politics* 4, ed. Patrick Dunleavy, Andrew Gamble, Ian Holliday, and Gillian Peele (New York: St. Martin's Press, 1993).

23. Smith, *The Comparative Policy Process;* Donley T. Studlar, "Elite Responsiveness or Elite Autonomy: British Immigration Policy Reconsidered," *Ethnic and Racial Studies* 3, no. 2 (1980):207–223; Christopher J. Hewitt, "Policy-making in Postwar Britain: A National-Level Test of Elitist and Pluralist Hypotheses," *British Journal of Political Science* 4, no. 2 (1974):187–216; Jim Bulpitt, *Territory and Power in the United Kingdom* (Manchester: Manchester University Press, 1983); Gary P. Freeman, "National Styles and Policy Sectors: Explaining Structured Variation," *Journal of Public Policy* 5, no. 4 (1985):467–496.

24. Philip Stanworth and Anthony Giddens, eds., *Elites and Power in British Society* (Cambridge: Cambridge University Press, 1974); Patrick Dunleavy and Brendan O'Leary, *Theories of the State* (London: Macmillan, 1987); A. P. Tant, *British Government: The Triumph of Elitism* (Brookfield, Vt.: Ashgate Publishers, 1993).

25. Bulpitt, *Territory and Power in the United Kingdom*.

26. Keith Middlemas, *Politics in Industrial Society* (London: Andre Deutsch, 1980).

27. Alan Cawson, *Corporatism and Political Theory* (Oxford: Basil Blackwell, 1986); Peter Jenkins, *Mrs. Thatcher's Revolution* (Cambridge: Harvard University Press, 1989); Peter Riddell, *The Thatcher Decade* (New York: Basil Blackwell, 1989).

28. Robert Alford and Roger Friedland, *Powers of Theory* (Cambridge: Cambridge University Press, 1985).

29. Hugh Thomas, *The Establishment* (London: Blond, 1959).

30. Mancur Olson, *The Rise and Decline of Nations* (New Haven: Yale University Press, 1982).

31. Samuel H. Beer, *Britain Against Itself* (New York: W. W. Norton Company, 1982).

32. Samuel H. Beer, *British Politics in the Collectivist Age* (New York: Random House, 1965).

33. Michael Rush, ed., *Parliament and Pressure Groups* (Oxford: Oxford University Press, 1990).

34. Robert D. Putnam, *The Comparative Study of Political Elites* (Englewood Cliffs, N.J.: Prentice Hall, 1976).

35. R. Kent Weaver and Bert A. Rockman, eds., *Do Institutions Matter? Government Capabilities in the United States and Abroad* (Washington, D.C.: Brookings Institution, 1993).

36. Sampson, *The Anatomy of Britain;* Nicholson, *The System: The Misgovernment of Modern Britain;* Barnett, *The Audit of War;* Sydney Pollard, *The Wasting of the British Economy,* 2d ed. (London: Macmillan, 1984).

37. Critchfield, *An American Looks at Britain;* Nossiter, *Britain: A Future That Works;* Gwyn and Rose, eds., *Britain: Progress and Decline.*

2

BRITAIN IN HISTORICAL AND GEOGRAPHICAL CONTEXT

Bᴿɪᴛᴀɪɴ ɪꜱ ᴀ ɢᴇᴏɢʀᴀᴘʜɪᴄᴀʟʟʏ ᴜɴᴜꜱᴜᴀʟ country. As has often been said, it is rare for an island to become as powerful and important as Britain has been for several centuries. Located just off the European continent, the British have always preferred to think of themselves as separate from the peoples of the continent, even though their fates were intimately bound together. This attitude still manifests itself today.

Physical and Human Geography

The specifics of British geography are well known. "Mainland" Britain (all territory except Northern Ireland) stretches about six hundred miles from north to south and no more than three hundred miles east to west. Overall, Britain's ninety-four thousand square miles makes it comparable in size to Oregon. Within that area, however, live over 57 million people, making Britain one of the most densely populated countries in Europe, second only to the Netherlands. The United Kingdom, composed of England, Scotland, Wales, and Northern Ireland, has the third-largest population in the European Union, after Germany and France. Over 90 percent of the population lives in urban areas. Conurbations, or continuous networks of urban communities, are a major feature of the landscape, especially in England. The major ones are listed on page xvi. All parts of the

United Kingdom are close to water, and there are several major seaports. The only country that it shares a border with is Ireland, along the three-hundred-mile contested divide separating Northern Ireland from the Republic of Ireland. Ireland was part of the United Kingdom until 1921, when the twenty-six counties in the southern part of the island seceded through treaty, leaving the six counties in the north, Northern Ireland or Ulster, as part of the United Kingdom. This division has been contested politically and militarily ever since. England, especially through the capital of London, located in the South on the Thames River, is the dominant part territorially, demographically, politically, economically, and culturally. England has 53 percent of the total land area of the country but 83 percent of the population. Scotland contains 32 percent of the land area but only 9 percent of the population. Wales has over 8 percent and 5 percent, respectively. Northern Ireland has less than 5 percent of the land area and less than 3 percent of the population, the latter being 1.5 million people.

The closest point to the continent on mainland Britain is located a mere twenty miles across the English Channel between Dover and Calais, France. It is often forgotten that the northern stretches of Britain, the Orkney and Shetland Islands, are Alpine in climate and closer to Norway than to any other country. Indeed, Britain shares North Sea oil with Norway. One reason for Britain's preoccupation with controlling Ireland, and even incorporating it within the United Kingdom, is the proximity of that island to Britain, only thirteen miles at its nearest point, between Northern Ireland and the Scottish coast.

Since 1921, then, the United Kingdom has consisted of four constituent parts, sometimes even called countries. They are not states or provinces because the United Kingdom is not a federal system. They have no inherent constitutional right to exist, and only one of them, Northern Ireland, has had a devolved (semi-autonomous) representative body, which lasted from 1921 until direct rule from London was imposed in 1972 in the wake of the revival of the "troubles." There are, however, ministerial offices for Wales, Scotland, and Northern Ireland in the British executive, which gives them a certain administrative autonomy, the exact dimensions of which depend on the government of the day.

These four constituent parts differ considerably not only in land area and population but also in economics, culture, and politics. England is most often confused with the whole of the United Kingdom because England dominates in all of these categories. The capital city, London, with its 7 million people, is the political, financial, commercial, and cultural center of the United Kingdom. Much of the industrialization that fueled British economic dominance, however, took place in the north of England.

Scotland has a large land area but a relatively small population. Above the two main cities of Glasgow and Edinburgh in the central lowlands, Scottish population becomes thin. From the second city of the empire in the nineteenth century when its shipbuilding industries were at their zenith, Glasgow has become a symbol of deindustrialization and urban decay, at least until replaced by Liverpool in

England in the latter part of the twentieth century. Furthermore, Scotland has its own legal and educational systems. Many laws applying in England and Wales are not automatically applicable in Scotland but may have to be passed by separate legislation by the British Parliament. Unlike England, where the Church of England (Episcopalian) dominates, in Scotland the major religious organization is the Church of Scotland (Presbyterian).

Wales is distinctive in several ways, even though it is the part of the United Kingdom and has had the longest union with England. The Welsh are famous for their coal production in the mountains (now much reduced), their nonconformist (largely Methodist and Baptist) chapels, their oratorical flair, choral music, and passions for rugby and education. Despite the fact that only about 20 percent of the population still speaks the Welsh language, the British government has funded a television channel largely devoted to the Welsh language, public services in Welsh, and education in the language. Because of the long union with England and the lack of economic resources that would support independence, there is less separatist feeling in Wales than in Scotland. Plaid Cymru, the Welsh nationalist party, is organized around defense and encouragement of the language, a minority position even within Wales. Ironically, it has been more successful in achieving its goals than the more popular and demanding Scottish Nationalist Party.[1]

The fourth part of the the United Kingdom is, of course, Northern Ireland, whose birth has been described above. For all of the publicity about sectarian division and violence in that part of Britain, it remains the smallest, poorest, and most remote part of the country. The Catholic share of the population has been gradually rising is now about 44 percent. Although the question of whether Northern Ireland belongs in the United Kingdom or Ireland dominates politics there, not all Catholics are Republicans wanting unification with Ireland.[2] But the mainland British parties have been unable to establish a foothold in Northern Ireland. Although partisan divisions exist within the two nationalist-religious communities, the "constitutional question" is still the principal basis of politics there.

For religious, security, and economic reasons, it has long been British policy to interfere when necessary in the affairs of continental Europe. In contrast to its own bastion on the British Isles (Great Britain and Ireland) and its empire, and later Commonwealth, across the ocean, however, Britain was never in a position to dominate the affairs of Europe, as, for instance, the United States and Soviet Union together were able to do in the 1945–1989 period. Thus Britain relied on temporary alliances with various powers, great and small, to accomplish its purposes. This led to its nineteenth-century reputation as "perfidious Albion," having no permanent friends, only permanent interests. The chief interest was for no single European country, be it Spain, France, Germany, or Russia, to dominate the continent. Britain stood in "splendid isolation," though not in the same sense as did the United States throughout much of the nineteenth and twentieth centuries.

Instead, it could afford to stand back from the European fray, watching for openings that would enhance its standing and forward its interests. But it did not have to join every dispute. Indeed, until the very precipice of World War I was reached, the Germans hoped that their major trading partner, and one that had a cousin of the Kaiser as monarch, would not throw its weight on the side of France and Russia. But such hopes were in vain.[3]

Physical separation from Europe has had other advantages. It made invasion difficult. The last successful invasion of Britain was by William of Saxony in A.D. 1066. Others have tried subsequently, notably Spain with its sixteenth-century armada, France at various times through Ireland, and Hitler's Germany in 1940–1941. But in each instance the invaders were rebuffed before making much progress inland. Even in the age of air power, Hitler's Luftwaffe could not soften British defenses sufficiently for Operation Sea Lion, as the invasion plan was called, to be put into operation. Subsequently, Britain has been under a nuclear umbrella, both its own and that of the United States through NATO.

Another obvious corollary to its separation from the migration waves and land armies of the continent was the opportunity for Britain to develop as a sea power. There were two aspects to this development—commercial and military. The commercial end allowed Britain to trade with far-flung areas of the world, many of which came under its stewardship either as formal colonies or as de facto protectorates (such as Egypt in the nineteenth century). Naval power was developed to protect both the island and its many explorers and trading vessels from incursions by unfriendly powers. Thus Britain became the supreme naval power in the world, a position that it maintained until the twentieth century. The mobility this afforded made Britain a formidable commercial and political competitor as well as a potent military adversary.

Back on the islands, separation from the continent also allowed the dominant group, the English, to come into eventual control of all of the British Isles. The story is a long one. There has been human habitation of the British Isles for approximately two hundred thousand years. The Celts came over peacefully from the European continent in the centuries before Christ, but an invasion by another Celtic tribe (the Belgics, or Britons) in 200 B.C. resulted in conflict. The Romans arrived in 55 B.C.

In the first centuries A.D., the fierce tribes settled in Britain gave the invading Romans a hard time, and eventually the latter withdrew from Britain in favor of the Angles and Saxons of northern Europe, with periodic invasions from other tribes from Scandinavia. The last epic incursion was the Norman conquest from France in 1066. After that, the groups blended together, although retaining somewhat distinct territories. In time, the English conquered the Welsh and Cornish peoples, as well as smaller groups, and established sway over the southern latitudes of the islands. Ireland and Scotland were more difficult.

Ever since the twelfth century the English had maintained a suzerainty over Ireland. Matters became more strained once Henry VIII separated from the

Roman Catholic Church, the strongly held faith of the Irish inhabitants, in the sixteenth century. Ireland became a matter of acute national security consideration for the British, especially for the Protestant monarchs and their supporters, because of fear that the Spanish or the French monarchs would attempt to penetrate the islands through their Irish coreligionists. The religious controversy over the throne in the sixteenth and seventeenth centuries intensified this fear, and with good reason. Thus firm control over Ireland became a sine qua non of British security policy.

This led to the attempts to pacify Ireland through the implantation of a Protestant colony, largely recruited from the Scottish population, in the seventeenth century. The repercussions of these actions are still heard three centuries later, in the form of the dispute between Catholics and Protestants in Northern Ireland over whether the province is to be a permanent part of the United Kingdom or the Irish Republic. Eventually in 1801 Ireland became a formal part of the United Kingdom of Great Britain and Ireland.

Before that, however, an equally contentious part of the islands had been incorporated into the United Kingdom. That was Scotland, which had a turbulent history of conflict with England. But through the royal succession, James IV, Protestant monarch of Scotland, also became James I of England upon the death of the childless Elizabeth I in 1603. Thus there emerged a peaceful unification of the two warring kingdoms, formalized in 1707 with the Act of Union, which dissolved the Scottish Parliament. From the middle of the eighteenth century until the middle of the twentieth century, the union was not seriously questioned. After the formal incorporation of Ireland in 1801, no alterations were made in the makeup of the United Kingdom until Irish secession in 1921.

The long and contentious British-Irish relationship has been the subject of many treatises. The Irish always chafed under British rule and were periodically rebellious. These rebellions, however, were never adequately supported and organized to enable them to succeed. Over the years, the proximate issues involved shifted from religion and national security toward economic, social, and political discrimination. Underlying all of these, however, was the constitutional question: Was Ireland to be subject to British rule from the Parliament in London?

In the late nineteenth century demands for home rule for Ireland became a major issue on the political agenda. This essentially implied a devolved government for Ireland, one with authority wide enough to make many decisions on its own without reference to the central parliament at Westminster. But in order for this to occur, a bill establishing home rule would have to be passed by both houses of Parliament, the House of Commons and the House of Lords, which at that time still had coequal legislative power.

The Irish members of Parliament offered to make common cause with any party willing to grant home rule. The two major parties of the time, the Liberals and the Conservatives, were suspicious of giving the poor and fractious Irish the chance to rule themselves. But eventually the Liberals under William Gladstone were willing to meet Irish demands. This fractured the Liberals, however, and, even when the House of Commons twice voted for Irish home rule, the House of Lords, dominated by a permanent Conservative majority, refused to agree. Thus the stalemate continued, poisoning British-Irish relations into the twentieth century.

Finally, after the weakening of the position of the House of Lords in 1911, home rule passed both houses of Parliament in 1913. By then, however, opposition and the threat of armed rebellion had arisen in the Protestant-dominated part of Ireland in the north, known as Ulster. The Ulster Unionists, as they called themselves, wanted to remain under the Parliament at Westminster, not under a Catholic-influenced government in Dublin.

The outbreak of World War I in 1914 further forestalled home rule. This eventually incited a civil war in Ireland against British rule, which was not quelled until a peace agreement was reached between the government of the United Kingdom, under David Lloyd George, and the Irish rebels in 1921.

Faced with the problem of what to do with armed Protestant population of the north, a compromise was reached. Sixteen of the twenty-two counties of Ireland, including three in Ulster, would become part of the politically independent and sovereign Irish state. Six counties in Ulster, heavily populated by Protestants, would remain in the United Kingdom. Northern Ireland was thus created, and the United Kingdom of Great Britain and Northern Ireland was born.

Economic and Social Development

Britain is not well endowed in natural resources, and the quality of its soil varies. Since the country is bathed by the Gulf Stream on its Western side, the weather may be rainy but not particularly harsh, allowing a long growing season. The problem of British agriculture has not been lack of productivity, but rather the large population that had to be fed. That led to the importation of foodstuffs from abroad, now constituting about one-third of the total. Fishing has been an important source of livelihood in many coastal areas. Britain has had excellent energy resources, ranging from numerous deposits of coal and iron ore to recent discoveries of petroleum and natural gas in the North Sea. The once-abundant forests of Britain have been logged so many times in the course of the centuries, especially during the Industrial Revolution, that the Forestry Commission has embarked on a program of reforestation in the twentieth century, but the country still has to import almost all of its wood products.

The United Kingdom was both a feudal-manorial society and the world's first industrialized country. Many of what are thought of as Britain's major characteristics, including the preoccupation with social class, stem from this heritage. The feudal structure was developed by the Normans after their arrival. As a feudal country, under the reign of monarchs and nobles, legal and ascriptive (from birth) social distinctions were endemic. As an island outpost, Britain was never under close control of continentally based forces, whether secular or religious. The major landowning group in the aristocracy, the barons, were relatively powerful, as indicated by their forcing King John to sign the Magna Carta at Runnymede in 1215. This document entrenched the principle of aristocratic consultation by the monarch in political affairs. Further, this set the foundation for the role of House of Lords and, later, the rising gentry, or lesser landowners, in the House of Commons to challenge the monarch when they were insufficiently consulted about major decisons, especially taxes. But in an agrarian economy, the nobles were even more powerful economically. Each landed estate, or manor, was, to a large degree, its own production and consumption unit. Towns were small, transportation was difficult, and trade was limited. Skilled artisans were organized into guilds to defend their rights and privileges against encroachment from outsiders, another foundation of the class system. Peasants were denied horizontal as well as vertical mobility. Life was, in the later words of Thomas Hobbes, "poor, nasty, brutish, and short." Primogeniture, the inheritance of the whole estate by the eldest son, meant that positions in the clergy and military had to be found for younger sons. There was little questioning of the status quo.

Although feudalism had begun to deteriorate earlier, the Renaissance, and especially the Reformation, finished the process by changing traditional society. Intellectual horizons were widened, at least for selected members of the elite. The sixteenth and seventeenth centuries saw a crisis of the old order develop. In 1534 Henry VIII broke with the Roman Catholic Church over the immediate issue of his divorce. His rejection of foreign Church authority over the lives of British subjects, including the monarch, however, resonates to this very day. Although a few barons resisted the split, most went along with it, and the Church of England became the handmaiden of the British state. The artistocratic elite was able to command the loyalties of the mass of people at the time.

More quietly, a few scientists and inventors began to have success with their experiments. These inventions, such as the steam engine and the spinning jenny, made power-driven machinery an essential part of the Industrial Revolution. These developments moved the economy of the United Kingdom from a predominantly agricultural one to an economy based on the existence of factories making secondary (finished) products through the application of science and mechanical engineering to primary (mineral) products. Textiles, iron making, and transportation were the three principal industries to develop in Britain in the eighteenth and nineteenth centuries. With industrialization came urbanization, aided by the enclosures of common land in the sixteenth and seventeenth centuries, which forced large numbers of peasants off the land. Agriculture, too, had become commercial, and landowners sought greater holdings in order to increase their sales and profits. Barrington Moore[4] argued that the uniqueness of the English Revolution of the seventeenth century was based on the rise of the gentry, a class that opposed royal patronage and prerogative in both countryside and city in the name of commerical advantage and individualism. In short, Britain fell into a commercial embrace, not the aristocratic embrace later posited as an explantion for its economic shortcomings. Industrialization and urbanization brought the rise of the middle class, originally factory owners, and the growing commercial and financial groups that came to serve the needs of the burgeoning cities, towns, and villages. The middle class was literally a middle group, between the traditional aristocracy and the peasants. The political implications of the rise of the middle class will be considered in Chapter 3. What is of concern here is the economic and social development of the country.

With industrialization under the aegis of a capitalist (private ownership) middle class came a further twist in the development of class relations in Britain. Legal rights, including the suffrage, were only gradually extended to insurgent groups, be they class, religious, nationality, gender, or age groups, from the eighteenth through the twentieth centuries. Thus some grievances, especially economically based ones, were allowed to fester for a considerable length of time before measures were taken to alleviate them. There were also substantial amounts of political violence involved, although these actions tended to be segmented rather than broadly based. Thus the characteristic British features of dissent and eventual incorporation of the dissenting groups into the system were developed.

In the nineteenth century, Karl Marx and Friedrich Engels saw the turmoil resulting from the Industrial Revolution in Britain as the precursor of the overthrow of capitalism and the establishment of communism. According to Marx and Engels, capitalist industrialization had released the bonds of productive capacity; life was no longer necessarily based on scarcity. The problem with capitalism, as with all previous economic and political systems, was that the elite refused to share wealth and power with the mass of the population despite the fact that the latter were ultimately the source of it. Transformation would come about only through revolution from below as the proletariat (the exploited masses) became more and more miserable and began to develop consciousness of themselves as a class. This class revolt and establishment of communism would occur first in the United Kingdom, according to Marx and Engels, because it was the leading capitalist state. Their development of communism as a theory was largely the product of their observations of British economic life in the nineteenth century, the conditions of which were also highlighted by Charles Dickens in several of his novels.

Instead of a Marxian future, however, Britain developed a characteristic pattern of class tensions but eventual class compromise on many issues. Workers were given the vote, harsh economic and socal conditions were ameliorated, and the welfare state developed. At the upper social class levels, observers refer to this phenomenon as the "aristocratic embrace." Capitalists became enamored of ancient institutions; thus the monarchy, the House of Lords, the established Church, and peerages were retained. Similarly, the proletariat turned out to be reformist rather than revolutionary, more influenced by Methodism than Marxism. As long as group privileges were maintained and advanced, broader social goals were dropped. In fact, much intraclass politics involves the maintenance of divisions, such as jurisdictional and "differentials" (in incomes) disputes among trade unionists. Thus Britain remains unusual in not having had a violent social revolution since at least the seventeenth century, if indeed the English Revolution even qualifies as such. Some analysts claim that this is not an unalloyed asset.[5]

The later nineteenth and early twentieth centuries were the times of Victorian optimism, named after Queen Victoria's long and mostly peaceful rule in 1837–1901. Britain was the world's preeminent industrial power, although after unification in 1871 Germany began to challenge Britain's economic supremacy. British diplomatic prestige was at its zenith as it managed to avoid combative entanglement in Europe's power struggles from the end of the Napoleonic Wars in 1815 until 1914. Instead, the United Kingdom looked outward, as building of the empire became a major preoccupation for economic, security, and cultural purposes. Although some territories had been acquired (and lost) earlier, imperialism became a source of pride and some controversy in the nineteenth century. The heroic civilizing mission of British imperialism, highlighted in the literary works of Rudyard Kipling, was taken seriously, however lacking in practice in some instances. By the early part of the twentieth century, British classrooms featured a map shaded in red for the British Empire, which extended over about 25 percent of the world's land area and 25 percent of the world's population. The empire extended to all continents of the globe with the exception of Antarctica, and included such major portions as Canada, Australia, the Indian subcontinent, much of eastern, central, and southern Africa, Egypt (de facto), portions of Southeast Asia (including concessions of terriorial control from China), and islands in the Caribbean Sea. Control over other territory, most important, over Palestine, was acquired from defeated Germany and the Ottoman Empire at the end of World War I.

The economic motivation for British overseas expansion was to provide a source of food and raw materials, the latter to be made into finished products in the United Kingdom. The security motivation was to provide outposts to protect British shipping lines and to deny potential foes such strategic points. Perhaps the most amazing feature of the empire was how few British people were involved in the administration of such a huge and far-flung enterprise. Military force was used sparingly. Once the natives began to take up arms against their masters, the British rarely put up resistance for very long before granting independence to the colony.

Some analysts argue that the seeds of British economic decline, relative economic decline to be sure, had already been sown by a failure to modernize British industry in the late nineteenth century.[6] After having had the advantage of being the first industrializer for a long time, Britain began to slide back toward its major rivals as their industrialization took hold with newer methods and machines. Furthermore, the controversial role of London as a world financial center began to play a part. Protecting Britain's overseas investments and the role of the pound sterling as a major international currency sometimes led British finance to favor projects other than those in industrial Britain.[7] But despite the economic competition, especially from Germany and the United States, for a time all of them prospered together.

World War I changed all that. The long war was damaging not only to Britain's social life, resources, and morale but also to its economic and diplomatic standing. By the end of the war many of the overseas resources had to be sold, especially to interests in the United States. The toll of World War, the civil war in Ireland, and rebuilding of domestic infrastructure was considerable. Then the Great Depression struck in 1929. As so often happens in times of crisis, Britain's economic policies became very conservative. It had previously been reluctant to leave the gold standard, and its policies in the Great Depression were counterexpansionist.[8]

While the old order stumbled domestically, military and political challenges multiplied abroad. Even though the empire (aside from Ireland) had remained united behind Britain in the first war, there were rumblings of discontent, especially from the Indian subcontinent, well before the second. By the Statute of Westminster in 1931, Britain had given legal self-rule to the older colonies dominated by European-descended settlers, such as Australia, Canada, and New Zealand. But the immediate challenges came from more economically and militarily insurgent countries in Europe and Asia. Britain and France, as the principal status quo powers in the world in the 1930s, with the United States, burdened by a great potential, standing in the background, faced a formidable opposition. Revived Germany, Japan, and Italy were clearly, to use the terms of international strategists, revisionist powers aiming to challenge the status quo established by the Treaty of Versailles, and in its own way, so was the Soviet Union under Joseph Stalin, although as a Communist he claimed to despise fascism. Thus it is no wonder that once the latter was neutralized by the Nazi-Soviet Pact in 1939, the status quo powers suffered a series of defeats, interrupted only by the Battle of Britain, until the Soviet Union, attacked by Hitler, joined their side in June 1941, followed six months later by the slumbering giant, the United States, after it was attacked by the Japanese at Pearl Harbor.

The price of victory was paid economically and diplomatically by what followed in the wake of the war. The empire came under challenge in many quarters from natives of the colonies demanding self-government, which resulted in independence for many countries far before political leaders in Britain had expected. The economy, at home and abroad, was in a shambles. Two wars, however victorious, in thirty years had taken their toll. A large financial loan on relatively stringent terms from the United States, followed by British withdrawal from various overseas military commitments starting with Greece in 1947, the need for the Marshall Plan, the devaluation of sterling in 1949, and problems with maintaining British access to Middle Eastern petroleum supplies in the 1950s, were also signs of economic difficulty.

For the last fifty years, what is usually termed the postwar period, the British economy has performed paradoxically. Aided by the Marshall Plan, which owed no small part to astute organizational efforts by the immediate postwar Labour government, the British economy recovered its overall prewar capacity earlier than most had predicted. Living standards began to rise as part of the "long boom" of the Western world, which lasted until the breakdown of the Bretton Woods international trade and monetary system and the petroleum supply shocks of the early 1970s. Much of the increased British productive capacity was utilized to provide more consumer goods for the population; for the first time, the United Kingdom entered the age of mass consumption. Ownership of refrigerators, televisions, washing machines, and even automobiles became the expectation of ordinary working-class people. The "social wage" of government-distributed benefits also aided consumers. Educational opportunities expanded.

Even given the sporadic economic growth that has occurred since the early 1970s, including the 1990s, with the highest unemployment level since the Great Depression, more people in Britain have been living better than ever before. But at the same time, the country's relative economic standing in the world, and in Europe, has consistently fallen. No longer is Britain an export giant; instead, its share of world trade has slid downward. Whenever its economic standing improved, the problem became one of buying too many imports, generating inflation, a drop in sterling's exchange value, and foreign trade deficits. Government policies to improve growth have often been succeeded in short order by other policies designed to stop inflation from getting out of control. This is the so-called stop-go cycle. British economic policy has therefore lacked consistency in being able to sell its own products domestically while also competing abroad.

The most traumatic events arising from the lack of British economic competitiveness have been three resisted sterling devaluations, in 1949, 1967, and 1992, and, most embarassingly, the necessity to resort to a loan from the International Monetary Fund (IMF) in 1976 in order to cope with its balance of payments problems. Despite Thatcherite monetary controls and balanced budgets through most of the 1980s, becoming self-sufficient in petroleum through the North Sea discoveries, and the gain to the public treasury by the selling of nationalized sectors of the economy, by the early 1990s Britain was suffering its deepest recession since the 1930s, and the deficit was rising. Neither the attempted cooperation with business and labor through the 1970s (corporatism)[9] nor the Thatcherite embrace of privatization and deregulation have managed to solve the problem to this point. The short-term prosperity of the British economy in the 1990s has relied on enticing Japanese firms to locate branch plants in the country.

The underlying reasons for this economic malaise have been endlessly analyzed. Some see the problem as inherent in early industrialization, having old plant and equipment that is not replaced, a condition aided by the encrustation of old interest groups, business, labor, and the financial sector, all of which act to protect their vested interests in the old ways.[10] Others see the problem as one of insufficient investment in industrial technology and education, particularly in scientific and business education.[11] It has often been pointed out that Britain seems to have lost the entrepreneurial spirit that came to the fore in the Industrial Revolution. Instead of competitive inventions, Britain generates Nobel Prize winners whose discoveries are made commercial by entrepreneurs in other countries. Several observers have attributed the relative economic decline to hostile business-labor relations, a manifestation of unsolved class tensions in society.[12] To some, the welfare state has also contributed to the desire to consume wealth without commensurate effort to produce wealth. For others, the problem is the aristocratic embrace; according to this view, economic productiveness in Britain has always rested on a fragile cultural shield. The successful entrepreneurs and their families would much rather enjoy the status of honors and acceptance into the social elite rather than keep on generating new products.[13]

Whatever the reasons, by the 1990s Britain's comparative economic standing was far below what it had been in the early twentieth century or even in the immediate post–World War II period. The two major losers of World War II, Germany and Japan, had rebuilt their economies from the ground up, and they now far outstrip Britain economically, especially in export markets. In 1992, Britain was seventh in the European Community in gross domestic product per capita, below Germany, France, Denmark, Luxembourg, the Netherlands, and Italy. Having an economy less productive than that of Italy is a particularly galling phenomenon for the British.

A principal ingredient of social relations since the industrial revolution, and a frequent target of critics searching for reasons for Britain's economic decline, has been the working class, more particularly as it has been incorporated in the trade union movement since the late nineteenth century. The development of a large segment of the population, until recently amounting to two-thirds of the total, with minimal education, income, and living amenities, led to a hardening of class relations and their manifestation in political life. There was much more rhetoric than genuine impulse to revolution in the British working class. The General Strike of 1926 was a failure, and in fact, the middle class has been much more loyal to the Conservative Party than was the working class to the Labour Party.[14]

Nevertheless, the struggle of the working class for legal recognition and economic concessions meant that the trade union movement was at best suspicious of business and government. The unions were fearful of government selling out its interests, even if the government was a Labour one. This wariness made economic competitiveness more difficult for a small country struggling in a changing international market. In contrast, labor-management-government cooperation, on various bases, in such countries as Sweden, West Germany, and Japan helped those nations' economies prosper to a larger degree.[15]

By the latter part of the twentieth century, however, the old industrial working class was both shrinking and fragmenting, symbolized by the failure of the coal miners' strike against the government in 1984–1985. Meanwhile, trade unions had grown in the middle-class service sectors of the economy, especially in the public sector.[16] The trade union movement, never highly centralized, became even more fragmented in its interests at the same time that it was losing public credibility from its failure to cooperate with the Labour Government in controlling inflation in the 1970s. This gave Mrs. Thatcher an opportunity to weaken the unions, which she did through the deindustrialization of the British economy in the early 1980s (the manufacturing base shrank 20 percent under the tight monetary policies of 1979–1981) and through later legislation subjecting them to greater legal regulations in relations with their members. The unions were no longer considered "an estate of the realm" as they had been in the 1960s and 1970s, when they often appeared to be more powerful than governments, leading to charges that Britain was "ungovernable".[17] Ironically, after the Conservative legislation was enacted to tame the unions in the 1980s, their standing with the public improved.

Another legacy of British economic development is the pattern of regional concentrations of enterprise and population distribution. London and the southeast, buoyed by excellent water connections to the Continent and the wider world, have remained financial and international trade centers, with a relatively prosperous population. Manufacturing, heavy industry, and coal mining were concentrated in other regions of the country, principally the Midlands and north of England, Wales, and Scotland. Agriculture and fishing have continued to be major employers in the eastern and southwestern parts of England, along with the upper reaches of Scotland. The decline of the manufacturing base in Britain has hit some regions disproportionately hard. There has been both out-migration and severe unemployment in these regions. Reflecting these tendencies, regions have shifted their political loyalties over the years. In 1955, Scotland had a majority of Conservative MPs; by the early 1990s, it was the most anti-Tory (anti-Conservative) sector of mainland Britain. There has been considerable controversy over whether regional political cultures exist independently of the economic and social status of the region, as well as over what role economic discontent plays in stirring up nationalist tensions in Wales and Scotland.[18]

Demographics of the United Kingdom

The population of the United Kingdom is not as ethnically homogeneous as is often claimed. Over the centuries Celts, Nordic invaders, Angles, Saxons, Normans, and others have blended into what today is called the Anglo-Saxon population. Despite there having been no successful invasion since 1066 A.D., however, there have been infusions of people resulting from selective migrations, especially in the nineteenth and twentieth centuries. The major migration in the nineteenth and early twentieth century consisted of Jews from Eastern Europe, fleeing pogroms in Poland and Russia. This led to a certain amount of antiforeigner agitation, especially as Jews settled in the East End of London. But in comparison to the traumatic anti-Jewish events later in the century in Europe, these episodes were relatively mild, and the East European Jewish population became integrated into society.[19] Similarly, Belgian refugees from the German invasion in World War I became accepted. A larger wave of refugees came from Poland as a result of the Nazi and Soviet invasions at the beginning of World War II. Irish immigration to the United Kingdom has never been controlled, for political reasons. However much the Irish may resent continued British control of Northern Ireland, Irish immigrants have traditionally looked to travel to urban areas in Britain for employment opportunities. Although such opportunities have shrunk in recent years, sections of such cities as Glasgow, Liverpool, and Birmingham remain identifiably Irish.[20]

By far the largest migration to the United Kingdom, at least in the short run, has been from the Asian subcontinent and the West Indies since the late 1940s. Like the Irish migration, this one was economic demand-driven. As the post–World War II British economy recovered and boomed, a labor shortage occurred. Under the laws obtaining at the time, any citizen of a Commonwealth country was entitled to come to Britain unchecked and would, upon entry, automatically become a citizen of the United Kingdom. Thus hundreds of thousands of migrants, mainly male, from the West Indies, India, and Pakistan (including parts that became Bangladesh, independent since 1971) came to the United Kingdom, especially to English cities, to take up manual and small tradespeople positions, which would earn them much better remuneration than was available in their home countries. Eventually, resentment against this wave of "colored immigration," as the British characterized it at the time, led to more restrictive immigration statutes. Yet today these colored immigrants and their descendants constitute approximately 5 percent of the population. Almost all of them are citizens of the United Kingdom, and they have made Britain, not without difficulty, a more multicultural and multireligious country than it previously was from European immigration. Salman Rushdie, for example, is a British citizen of Indian descent, and the bounty put on his head by the government of Iran for literary offenses against the Islamic faith has meant that the British government has had to protect him, not without protest from some of its own Muslim citizens.

Britain traditionally has been a country of emigration, not immigration. Britain's far-flung empire and trading opportunities abroad provided an opportunity for people dissatisfied with their prospects in the mother country to seek their fortunes elsewhere. Many did just that, either by settling in the colonies, providing the personnel for imperial and commercial exploits, or by migrating permanently to other countries. This provided a safety valve for the burgeoning population of Britain in the eighteenth and nineteenth centuries. But many of Britain's most talented people continue to settle abroad.

The history of population growth in the United Kingdom is an interesting one. In an agrarian society without modern sanitation and medical facilities, both birth and mortality rates were high. Then, as Britain began to industrialize and urbanize, the typical demographic transition occurred. Life expectancy lengthened—in an industrial society children became less valuable as economic contributors to the family—and eventually birth rates dropped. This was in contrast to Thomas Malthus's opinion in his famous *Essay on the Principle of Population* in 1798, in which he argued that the population was bound to increase geometrically while the food supply only increased arithmetically, making famine inevitable. In 1801, the population was less than 19 million in England, Wales, Scotland, and Ireland. By 1901, the population of the United Kingdom (still including Ireland) was less than 40 million. Longer life expectancies and some immigration since then have offset emigration and war to make the population now 57 million, a figure that has not substantially altered in the last two decades. Britain is approaching zero population growth.

In addition to urbanization and ethnicity, religion, age, education, and class are other important social attributes of a population. In the British context, religion has been declining for some time as both a social and political force. In the sixteenth and seventeenth centuries, religion played a preeminent role in social and political conflict. The identity of the United Kingdom as a Protestant state with a Protestant monarch was sealed in 1689 when Parliament invited William and Mary of Orange of the Netherlands to replace the "unreliable" Catholic monarch James II and in the first decade of the eighteenth century with the Succession to the Crown Act (1705) and the Regency Act (1707), which codified the principles of succession to the throne. Even today, in what we might call "post-Christian" Britain, where less than 10 percent of the population can be found in a place of worship in any given week, the monarch must profess the Protestant faith.

In the late nineteenth century, religion, at this time a matter of discord between adherents of the Church of England (Episcopalians) and dissenting Protestants, was still an important division in mainland Britain between supporters of the Liberals and Conservatives. But with increased urbanization, religion lost influence as a source of social cohesion and political organization. Formal religious occasions such as state investitures, marriages, and funerals are still impressive spectacles in the United Kingdom, but most people are only nominally believers, if that. A common "C of E" (Church of England) practice is to be baptized, married, and buried in the Church—but little else. Recent comparative figures on religious commitments show Britain to have only about one-half as many people who believe in life after death as does the United States, where over 80 percent profess such a belief. The monarch must be a member of the Church of England and upon coronation assumes the title of Defender of the Faith, yet in Scotland Presbyterianism is the established religion. Despite continued state influence over religion, in such acts as the prime minister choosing the archbishop of Canterbury and in having time set aside in schools for religious observation (not Anglican observation only), there has been increased questioning over whether the Church of England should remain established. Minority religions abound, including those such as Islam brought to the United Kingdom by recent immigrant groups. Jews number about one-fourth million, the second largest number in Western Europe. Both religious practice and political influence remain greater, of course, in Northern Ireland.

Britain has clearly become a secular society, and it has also become an aging one. What population growth there is largely comes from the younger minority groups of the population, such as the Irish and nonwhite immigrant descendants. As life expectancy has increased and birth control techniques have become more reliable, population increase has slowed and the population has aged. This puts additional pressure on social services, especially the health service. Overall, however, the population of the United Kingdom is not aging as rapidly as that of several other European countries.[21] Among other things, this is an economic advantage for the United Kingdom since, by current projections, there will be a better balance between the economically active and inactive sectors of the population in the years ahead than in such competitors as Germany and France.

Britain also shares another social characteristic with its European neighbors—that of a changing family structure. There are fewer marriages, more children born out of wedlock, and more divorces. But the British trends in these categories are not as high as those in several other European counties. For instance, Britain still has a relatively high marital rate, and there are proportionally more children born within wedlock in Britain.[22] Single-parent families are increasing, as is the number of women in the workforce. Overall, Britain has developed smaller and less stable households than previously. By European standards, moreover, the government provides relatively few child care services.

Feudalism, Industrialization, Urbanization, and Class

More generally, that prototypical (often stereotypical) British institution, social class, is changing, too. For instance, in the past twenty years coal mining has rapidly declined. Old industrial technologies such as shipbuilding, motor vehicle manufacture, and textiles have sharply declined or disappeared entirely, along with related industries. Unemployment has grown, but so have employment opportunities in service fields, ranging from banking and health to government bureaucracies and motorcycle courier businesses. In fact, service sector employment, broadly defined, now makes up some 60 percent of the British economy. Although trade union membership has declined overall, white-collar trade union membership has actually increased. Thus there are fewer classic members of the working class with most of the characteristics of a minimal education, housing rented from the local government council, a manual occupation, and a trade union card. Even though much of British social and political life still revolves around class differences, social class is much more complex today.

One of the complexities involves education. Traditionally education has been devalued for British society as a whole. It was thought to be a specialist preoccupation, not necessary either for large sections of the population, including part of the middle class and practically all of the working class. Only in 1870 were the first countrywide provisions for public education made. State-assisted education became state-supervised education in 1902.[23] Provision of free state schooling for all British citizens at the primary and secondary level has been a slow process, and it was not completed until the 1944 Education Act. Nevertheless, large portions of the better-off segments of society sent their children, especially boys, to private fee-paying (public, in British English) schools, starting usually at the tender age of five. The better public schools such as Eton and Harrow became the stuff of lore. The minor ones survived as best they could. Despite much leftist criticism of the disproportionate influence of the British public schools, they have continued to thrive and turn out a large number of influential people in the society, economy, and polity.

The state (public, in United States English) schools were further divided into an academic preparatory and a vocational mode, traditionally based on scores on standard tests at age eleven. Since almost all studies of childhood learning find that the early home environment is overwhelmingly important for this stage of education, it not surprising that well-off children tended to do better on the tests, even though the state academic preparatory schools (grammar schools) were open to all children of the requisite measured ability. Educational radicals, centered in the Labour party, argued for reorganizing the traditional British educational system into one more readily resembling that of the United States, involving a comprehensive rather than a streamed secondary education component. Finally, in 1965 they reached their goal with the adoption of "comprehensivization," meaning educating all state secondary school students under the same roof rather than in separate schools. Nevertheless, within the comprehensive school there are still often separate tracks for those academically gifted, as ascertained by standardized tests, and those deemed otherwise. The Conservative government's educational reform of 1988 attempted to make schools more responsive to parents and to the educational market, even in the state system, by allowing individual schools to opt out of the control by the local educational authority, the part of the local government system that has traditionally controlled the schools. Almost all of the school funds, however, come from central government in the form of grants to the local level.[24]

The United Kingdom has a healthy respect for educational "qualifications," usually in the form of certificates attesting to student achievement at certain standardized levels of performance. Most recently this has meant "O" (ordinary) and "A" (advanced) levels of performance in subjects at the end of secondary education. Sixth-form colleges of two years' work are the preferred form of preparation for higher education, and it usually takes a particular combination of A and O levels to qualify for a place in one of the institutions of higher education.

British higher education is world famous, but its reputation masks diverse realities and several problems. Oxford and Cambridge, often termed "Oxbridge," are the ancient, prestigious universities. Like all institutions except the University of Buckingham, they are public, not private, institutions, relying on the state for most of their funding. Although other universities such as London and Durham are also ancient, a major expansion of British higher education occurred in the

1960s to meet the demands of the baby-boom generation. This building of "plate-glass" universities was accompanied by the establishment of many polytechnics, supposedly more vocationally oriented institutions of higher education, and the Open University, allowing part-time study through correspondence. Labor Prime Minister Harold Wilson later claimed the latter as his proudest achievement.

Despite this expansion, British higher education has remained an elite calling. The percentage of young people in universities and other higher education institutions has stayed relatively low by European standards, at less than 20 percent. Institutions can remain selective because the number of places for students is limited by government declaration for each university and department. Each student accepted, however, is provided with a government "studentship," intended to pay most of the direct costs of education. The only students paying most of their own way in British higher education are foreign students. The corollary is that British students in regular universities, but not necessarily in other institutions of higher education, are full-time students. There are specialist teacher training colleges, arts institutes, and so forth. The universities are largely reserved for the traditional humanities, sciences, social sciences, and liberal professions.

The Conservative governments since 1979 have made many changes in higher education, over the complaints of the administrators and faculty in several instances. Universities have seen their funds restricted, their departments ranked on research and teaching status, and their practices questioned. The aim has been to create a more efficient government-funded operation by having universities establish closer working relationships with major employers in order to meet the demands of the economy. Polytechnics have been raised in status to be full-scale competitors of universities for students and government funds. Contrary to the aim of all British governments since the 1960s, however, the sciences have not risen appreciably in popularity as a field of study for students. English and Welsh universities require that students declare what in the U.S. would be called a "major" upon entrance in a three-year program, with a few exceptions for four-year programs such as law. Scottish universities pursue a regimen more recognizable to an audience in the United States—four years of study with the early years consisting of more general education.

The role of women in society has changed as well. The battle of the Brittish suffragettes in the early part of the twentieth century is well known. Less well known is the fact that when British women were finally allowed to vote, in 1918, it was only women of at least thirty years of age who could exercise the right to vote for a period of ten years. Only in 1928 did women acquire the vote on the same basis as men, at twenty-one years of age. To the surprise of those who looked to the suffrage movement to establish a new relationship between men and women, after gaining the vote such relations continued with little change. It was not until the second wave of feminism, beginning in the 1960s, that women effectively challenged their traditional roles in the workplace and society at large.[25] Increasing employment opportunities for women, the growth of single-parent families, and the emergence of other movements protesting social and political conditions around the world were some of the stimuli for the women's movement. Questioning of the sexual, social, economic, and political divisions of labor between men and women became more widely accepted. The reality of the situation remained, however, that women were disproportionately employed in part-time and clerical work, were paid much less than men, and still had the major responsibility for the home. Nevertheless, by the early 1990s, questions would be raised about why John Major did not appoint any women to his first cabinet after replacing Margaret Thatcher as Prime Minister.

In a variety of ways, then, the social structure of Britain has been changing over the years. But with constant population shifts caused by birth, death, internal migration, changing occupational structures, immigration, and emigration, these changes are often like the ocean, difficult to measure except from a distance. Fortunately, increasing attention has been devoted to documenting these changes and their implications for society.[26] More difficult problems arise when one attempts to link social changes with politics.

Notes

1. William L. Miller, *Electoral Dynamics in Britain Since 1918* (London: Macmillan, 1983).

2. Richard Rose, *Governing Without Consensus* (Boston: Beacon Press, 1969).

3. Paul Kennedy, *The Rise and Fall of the Great Powers* (New York: Random House, 1987).

4. Barrington Moore, *Social Origins of Dictatorship and Democracy* (Boston: Beacon Press, 1967).

5. Moore, *Social Origins of Dictatorship and Democracy.*

6. Martin J. Wiener, *English Culture and the Decline of the Industrial Spirit, 1850–1980* (Cambridge: Cambridge University Press, 1981).

7. Kennedy, *The Rise and Fall of the Great Powers;* Stephen Blank, "Britain: The Politics of Foreign Economic Policy, the Domestic Economy, and the Problem of Pluralistic Stagnation," *International Organization* 31, no. 4 (1977):673–721.

8. Dennis Kavanagh, "Crisis Management and Incremental Adaption in British Politics: The 1931 Crisis of the British Party System," in *Crisis, Choice, and Change,* ed. Gabriel A. Almond, Scott C. Flanagan, and Robert J. Mundt (Boston: Little, Brown and Company, 1973).

9. Alan Cawson, *Corporatism and Political Theory* (Oxford: Basil Blackwell, 1986); Central Office of Information, *Britain, 1994: An Official Handbook* (London: Her Majesty's Stationery Office, 1993).

10. Mancur Olson, *The Rise and Decline of Nations* (New Haven: Yale University Press, 1982).

11. Corelli Barnett, *The Audit of War* (London: Macmillan, 1986).

12. R. Emmett Tyrrell, ed. *The Future That Doesn't Work* (Garden City, N.Y.: Doubleday Books, 1977).

13. Wiener, *English Culture and the Decline of the Industrial Spirit, 1850–1980.*

14. Richard Rose, *Politics in England,* 2d ed. (Boston: Little, Brown and Company, 1974).

15. Peter Katzenstein, ed., *Between Power and Plenty* (Madison: University of Wisconsin Press, 1978).

16. Patrick Dunleavy, "The Urban Basis of Political Alignment: Social Class, Domestic Property Ownership and State Intervention in Consumption Processes," *British Journal of Political Science 9,* no. 4 (1979):409–443.

17. Richard Rose, "Ungovernability: Is There Fire Behind the Smoke?" *Political Studies* 27, no. 3 (1979):351–370; Anthony King, "Overload: Problem of Governing in the 1970s," *Political Studies* 23, no. 2 (1975):284–296.

18. R. J. Johnston, C. J. Pattie, and J. G. Allsopp, *A Nation Dividing?* (London: Longman, 1987); William L. Miller, "The De-Nationalisation of British Politics: The Re-emergence of the Periphery," in *Change in British Politics,* ed. Hugh Berrington (London: Frank Cass, 1984).

19. Geoffrey Alderman, *The Jewish Community in British Politics* (Oxford: Oxford University Press, 1983).

20. Ian McAllister and Donley T. Studlar, "The Electoral Geography of Immigrant Groups in Britain," *Electoral Studies* 3, no. 2 (1984):139–150.

21. B. Guy Peters, *European Politics Reconsidered* (New York: Holmes and Meier, 1991).

22. Chris Pierson, "Social Policy," in *Development in British Politics 4,* ed. Patrick Dunleavy, Andrew Gamble, Ian Holliday, and Gillian Peele (New York: St. Martin's Press, 1993).

23. François Bedarida, *A Social History of England, 1851–1975,* trans. A. S. Forster (New York: Methuen, 1979).

24. Geoff Whitty, "The Politics of the 1988 Education Reform Act," in *Developments in British Politics 3,* ed. Patrick Dunleavy, Andrew Gamble, and Gillian Peele (New York: St. Martin's Press, 1990).

25. Vicky Randall, *Women in Politics,* 2d ed. (Chicago: University of Chicago Press, 1987).

26. A. H. Halsey, *Change in British Society* (Oxford: Oxford University Press, 1982); Peter Catterall, ed., *Contemporary Britain: An Annual Review, 1990, 1991, and 1992* (New York: Basil Blackwell, 1990–1992).

3

THE DEVELOPMENT
OF POLITICAL
INSTITUTIONS

Political institutions in the United Kingdom are well recognized for
their gradual evolutionary development, with few sharp breaks from the past. With a
Constitution that is largely uncodified and relying in large measure on "custom and
convention," Britain has a unique capability for a democracy of altering its fundamental institutions by majority will of the House of Commons (parliamentary sovereignty). But there are drawbacks as well as advantages to this arrangement. Far
from making the Constitution subject to radical change, these procedures have
resulted in an emphasis on developing an elite consensus, normally across political
parties, for any major alterations. In the twentieth century, that has been broadened
to include at least a "permissive consensus" from the public as well. Furthermore,
change can become difficult, as the opponents, even within the party proposing
change, raise constitutional objections. In different ways, such bipartisan objections
played a large role in defeating both an attempted reform of the House of Lords in
the late 1960s and the devolution proposals of the 1970s. But formally, nonetheless,
there are few institutional obstacles to change, and in the long view, British politics
has changed its procedures considerably, even while retaining many of the same
institutions. Those developments are briefly surveyed in this chapter, and in the
next chapter the cultural obstacles to change are more carefully considered.

From Absolutist to Constitutional Monarchy

The journey of the United Kingdom from absolutism to democracy is well known
for its incremental nature. Gradually, from the Magna Carta in 1215 until the

nineteenth century, the power of the monarchy was compromised until it remained mainly as a potential residual check on partisan political conflict that threatened to paralyze the country. Similarly, the power of the aristocracy, originally a check on the monarchy, began to be perceived as a threat to the emergence of full democratic legal participatory rights in the nineteenth and twentieth centuries. Finally, in 1949 and 1958, the power of the House of Lords, especially that of the hereditary peers, was reduced to such a level that the next step, if ever taken, would be either to make it an elected chamber or to abolish it. Despite Britain's reputation for representative democracy, the liberal, individual rights component of "liberal democracy" developed at a much swifter pace than did the mass participation, democratic component. Indeed, a British historian has argued that Britain could not really be called a democracy until 1949, when the reduction of the delaying powers of the House of Lords to one year and the abolition of plural voting by business proprietors and university graduates meant that the country finally had achieved "one person, one vote." However, even after those measures were instituted, the size of electoral districts still varies considerably since geographical and historical factors are also taken into account in drawing constituency lines.[1]

As Bagehot[2] was one of the first to point out, the British constitution is not what it seems. Being largely unwritten, it is very flexible. Aided by an ongoing government obsession with secrecy and confidentiality, what are called "customs" and "conventions" change and often go unnoticed from outside until some enterprising journalist, academic, or politician no longer willing to play the game reveals how deep the changes are. Richard Crossman, who at various times followed all three occupations, is perhaps the twentieth-century exemplar of this phenomenon, and his arguments about the "presidentialization" of the British executive office and the confused direction of the Labour governments of the 1960s are still controversial.[3] In more recent times, the composition of cabinet committees was only revealed in 1993. Thus some changes in British governing institutions and practices can be marked by dates, others only by guesswork concerning when the changes occurred. The British capacity for incorporating changes in political institutions, including making major ones in their ruling power, with a minimum of violence and a maximum of continuity, has been much admired. As was noted in Chapter 2, however, some observers have suggested that this has not been an unmixed blessing. Furthermore, the political conflict over institutional change has often been protracted.

The Decline of Feudal Institutions: Monarchy and House of Lords

The power of the monarchy has slowly eroded over the past nine centuries. It is less often recognized, however, that the English monarchy was never as powerful as some of the continental monarchies. The Russian czar, for instance, had the capacity to exercise centralized control over even the aristocracy and to wield power over a huge land area. The British land area was considerably less, of course, and the power of the British monarch was always limited by the necessity to have the powerful landed aristocracy work with the Crown rather than against it.

Instead of a large and loyal bureacracy, as in several European countries, British monarchs relied on the legal system to dispense the "king's justice" throughout the land. Such justice, however, developed through common law interpretations and precedents and were not handed down from a central authority. As long as the monarch's touch was relatively light, this system worked well, aided by a feeling of nationalism and need for security against potential invaders from the continent. But when the monarchy acted without the consent of aristocratic and other organized interests, as occurred in the thirteenth and seventeenth centuries, then the result was the Magna Carta in the first instance and the political disruption of the English Civil War in the second. By the end of the second episode, with Parliament's invitation to William and Mary to assume the throne in 1689 on Parliament's terms, the dominance of the representatives of the people, however narrowly that term was defined, over the monarchy was assured.

Until the Middle Ages, domestic politics meant court politics, involving few players. With the expansion of learning and the growth of religious dissent in the fifteenth and sixteenth centuries, however, there was an increased, though still small, number of people sufficiently knowledgeable and powerful enough to have some influence. Even those prototypical absolutist monarchs, Henry VIII and Elizabeth I, were able to succeed because they drew upon wider loyalties than did their predecessors. Elizabeth in particular aroused English nationalistic sentiments against foreign interference, whether religious, political, or military. Her successor, James I, brought Scotland into the fold peacefully by inheriting both the English and Scottish crowns. But his successor, Charles I, ran afoul of parliamentary insistence on its taxing prerogatives, and the Civil War ensued. The sources of conflict in this unusual instance of protracted civil violence in Britain are still debated by historians; however, the war undeniably unleashed broader currents of dissent and dissatisfaction with political institutions than the narrow issue over which it commenced.

The rise and temporary triumph of Oliver Cromwell and his band of anti-monarchical religious dissenters resulted from these underlying currents. Not only was Charles I beheaded, but Britain became a Commonwealth, governed by Parliament and an executive council with Cromwell at its head. By the time of Cromwell's death in 1661, however, this particular version of government by committee (with Cromwell as a de facto monarch) had become so unsatifactory to the politically influential that Charles II was brought back for the Restoration. When his heir, James II, threatened to reimpose a strong monarchy and Catholicism upon Britain, the revulsion against him did not include abandoning the monarchy as an institution. But by the terms of the Bill of Rights of 1689 and the Act of Settlement of 1701, Parliament became consitutionally entrenched, even in written form, as the dominant branch of government. The monarch would be beholden for tenure of office on Parliament.

At the time, religion, not class, was the major social cleavage in British politics. Fueled by religious dissent not only against the Catholic Church but against High Church practices in general, the dissenters embraced individual conscience, individual rights, and elected representatives as better guarantees than established authority figures such as monarchs and churches. Thus in the latter part of the sixteenth century, John Locke and Richard Hooker engaged in their famous written dispute about the relative advantages of popular sovereignty versus absolutist monarchy, in the course of which Locke developed his version of the social contract theory of the state. The practical political outcome was a compromise. The Bill of Rights of 1689 entrenched the rights of Parliament against the monarch, not individual rights guarantees for British subjects. The Anglican Church continued to enjoy privileged status, even to the extent of being assured of control of the monarchy by the Act of Settlement. If Britain moved toward consitutional monarchy, it did not move very far toward popular sovereignty and constitutional guarantees for individuals. The ideas of John Locke, in fact, probably had far greater impact on the United States than on his native land.

Nevertheless, the result of the constitutional turmoil of the sixteenth and early seventeenth centuries was that the power of the monarch was much reduced, and Britain gradually began to move toward widened individual rights, the "liberties of Englishmen," accepted by ordinary statute of Parliament and custom rather than constitutional guarantee. Queen Anne in the early seventeeenth century was the last British monarch to veto an act of Parliament, although technically that right still exists. The monarch must proclaim every new law, in French no less, by signing it.

Negative liberty, in the sense of the basic rights to life, liberty, and property being assumed to be protected against arbitrary government actions, began to incorporate more and more people. Originally including Protestants only, these rights were gradually extended to other religious groups as well. Along with these individual rights came the right for dissenters, if they were of the right social status, to stand for Parliament. Eventually concern moved from individual liberties to rights of democratic participation and majority rule, that is, extension of the suffrage. But this did not occur until the nineteenth century and was only consummated in the twentieth.[4]

By the time of the American Revolution in 1776, the British monarchy had very little influence on the conduct of policy. Instead, policy was directed by His Majesty's Government (the king's ministers). For some years previously the monarch had consulted the Privy Council, a group of advisers chosen by the Monarch. But now, even though the Privy Council continued to exist as a more or less honorary organization, real power was exercised by a smaller group of advisers, the cabinet, which included the prime minister and was responsible to the Commons. The Commons was composed largely of a limited portion of the population, generally known as the gentry, meaning landowners without inherited titles.

The American revolutionaries, then, were fundamentally wrong in their analysis in the Declaration of Independence. George III was hardly to blame for the problems that the American colonies attributed to an unfeeling mother country. Instead, it was the British Parliament and government ministers who were to blame, but it made for a much better defense of the right of revolution and popular sovereignty to blame America's troubles on a despotic monarch rather than on a representative assembly. Under the theory of virtual representation, the American colonies were not treated any differently than the rest of the United Kingdom and colonies. Over the past four centuries monarchs have avoided coming into conflict with Parliament. When they have collided, the outcome has been a victory for Parliament, as in the case of the abdication of Edward VIII over his desire to marry an American divorcée, and, more recently, as with Queen Elizabeth II's agreement to pay taxes on her earnings. Despite the monarchy's cultivation of public approval through more media-conscious activities, the public fascination with monarchy, in Britain and abroad, does not extend to granting it a more powerful political role.

The political role of the constitutional monarchy today, then, is a relatively limited one. The monarch is the head of state and thus the representative of the whole of the British population, whatever their partisan views (even Republicans, in the sense of those who wish to replace the monarchy with an offical head of state elected or appointed in some fashion without the inheritance principle). The United Kingdom, like most European states, sees having a separate head of state as a focus for loyalty as a benefit, especially in times of partisan turmoil. As the symbolic head of the Commonwealth (although no longer the *British* Commonwealth), the monarch also serves as a symbol of broader loyalty for millions of people in the world, although the importance of this tie for the forty-nine politically independent and constitutionally varied member states of the Commonwealth should not be overrated. Unlike several others in Europe, the British monarch is not a "bicycle monarch," behaving largely like other citizens. Pomp and circumstance is still a large part of the British monarchy's appeal. Nevertheless, the loyalty of the population is strictly conditional on the monarchy's remaining "above the fray."

What are the monarch's constitutional duties? Briefly stated, they include the rights to be informed about matters of state and, if so desired, to give confidential advice to the prime minister on such matters. At least once per week when Parliament is in session, the prime minister of the day goes to Buckingham Palace to visit privately with the monarch. What they discuss is never revealed. Officially today, of course, it is HMG, Her Majesty's Government, and the queen lends her imprimatur to various government activities—naval battleships (Her Majesty's Ship), the postal service (the Royal Mail), and even the highest rank of legal representatives, barristers who become Queen's Counselors (QCs). But most of what is done in the queen's name is actually done by others. Her appointments, for instance, whether they be of the archbishop of Canterbury or those designated for the honors list (awards for distinguished service to the Crown, announced twice per year) are really decided by the prime minister. The queen, in effect, legitimizes these appointments, however controversial, with the British equivalent of the Good Housekeeping Seal of Approval. She also sends and receives ambassadors, proclaims recognition of various good causes, and makes goodwill tours both at home and abroad. As noted earlier, she also offically proclaims laws.

The queen also has several other duties that involve her in more significant public activities. Although the prime minister either chooses the date of the general election for all of the seats in the House of Commons within the five-year limit allowed or reports a defeat in a confidence vote in the House of Commons to the monarch, it is the queen who actually announces the dissolution of Parliament and the date of the general election in either case. The queen also opens a new session of Parliament, usually in November but also occasionally at other times, depending on the date of the election, with what is called the Queen's Speech, basically setting forth the legislative agenda of the government of the day (Her Majesty's Government) for the next session. This speech is only delivered by the queen; it is written by the prime minister and his or her cabinet. Although now more heavily leaked ahead of time than in the past, the Queen's Speech remains a great occasion of state, with the ceremonial horse-drawn passage of the queen from Buckingham Palace to the House of Lords in the Palace of Westminster, the dispatch of Black Rod from the House of Lords to the House of Commons to summon the members to attend to the speech in the "House of Peers" (House of Lords). The brief delivery of the speech, followed by the formal withdrawal of the queen, leaving Parliament to debate the contents of the speech. At the end of each parliamentary session, the queen delivers a less celebrated pro-rogation speech commenting on what, from the government's point of view, Parliament has accomplished.

The monarch is not, however, devoid of all political power.[5] There still exists a residue of constitutional authority, which comes to the fore during consitutional crises of two sorts. The first, unlikely since the weakening of the powers of the House of Lords in 1949, is as a source of constititutional authority to break a deadlock between the two legislative chambers. Thus it took the willingness of King George V to create as many new peers of the realm as necessary to force the House of Lords to agree to the changes that weakened its powers in the early twentieth century. This was not an unprecedented example of the monarch siding with the Commons against a recalcitrant Lords in a major constitutional dispute.

A second type of constitutional crisis in which the monarch can still play a role involves the formation of a government when there is no overall majority party in the House of Commons. This occurred as a result of the February election in 1974, and, as long as the British party system remains a multiparty one in the electorate, as it has for the past two decades, it could occur again. In such circumstances the monarch can encourage parties to form a coalition government, or, in the final analysis, the monarch could appoint a minority government. As with many British high constitutional matters, the monarch's role is not firmly laid out. Thus the role of the monarch remains one of the most flexible parts of the British constitution. In general, as long as the monarch acts with public and parliamentary consent, he or she is on firm ground. Lacking one of these, especially parliamentary consent, places the monarch's position in jeopardy.

The Decline and Survival of the House of Lords

That other medieval hangover institution, the House of Lords, has also retained its outward demeanor while losing almost all of its substantive power in the twentieth century. That the House of Lords continues to exist at all in a country that is considered a representative democracy at the end of the twentieth century is astounding. There is no pretense of electing the members of the House of Peers. Instead, about three-fourths of its approximately 1,200 members (the number is not fixed) are hereditary peers, eldest sons who inherited their titles from their fathers. Many of these people never bother to show up at all; only a per diem travel allowance is allocated for service in the Lords. Since 1958 the smaller, but far more active, group—the remaining one-fourth—is made up of life peers, basically retired or defeated politicians and others in public life (trade union officials, for instance) who cannot pass on the title and seat to their heirs. The monarch appoints life peers based on the recommendations of the prime minister, who has the real power of choice. One might look upon the House of Lords as a retirement home for old politicians, although some of them, such as Lord Owen (former Labour foreign secretary and Social Democrat party leader) are old only in the sense that their time in the House of Commons is past. These people want to remain active in politics to some degree, and in fact some of them will be chosen to serve in a government of their party because governments need spokespersons in the Lords as well as the Commons. In the nineteenth century, Conservative prime ministers were sometimes chosen from the Lords, but this is unlikely to happen today. Similarly, the approximately twelve law lords and the twenty-six archbishops and bishops of the Church of England compose select groups that serve particular functions as well as the more general ones of the Lords. Serving in committees to hear cases, the law lords sit on the highest appellate court in the United Kingdom, although the court of Law Lords does not have the broad interpretive powers of the United States Supreme Court.

The House of Lords has little remaining authority, which is a far cry from its historical role in moderating the monarch, resisting home rule for Ireland, and defeating government budget proposals. Composed largely of Conservative peers until recently, the House of Lords was a particular irritant to Liberal governments in the late nineteenth and early twentieth centuries. When the Lords refused to accept the Liberal budget of 1909, a constitutional crisis of democracy in Britain occurred. Finally, under pressure from the king, the House of Lords agreed to legislation that limited its own power, which was further restricted in 1949. Now it is allowed only one year to deal with legislation passed by the Commons, with only one month for finance bills. If the Lords refuses to pass a bill within that time period in a form with which the Commons can agree, then the Commons can simply pass its version of the bill a second time, and the bill becomes law.

Thus the Lords has the power of delay and amendment, but it is not a fully coequal branch with the Commons. In fact, in the 1980s the Lords became a major center of opposition to several proposals of the Conservative government and offered hundreds of amendments to legislation.[6] In the final analysis, however, it could not defeat the legislation, except in the circumstances of an early dissolution of Parliament, which ends the legislature until a new House of Commons is elected. Even then, if the same party was returned to government, then the legislation could be reintroduced. The opposition to the Thatcher government in the House of Lords reflects that fact that the internal nature of the body has changed. Once incorporating a permanent Conservative majority, now the Lords has an increasingly nonpartisan atmosphere, with many members sitting as "cross-bench" peers rather than claiming a partisan coloration. Now Lady Thatcher herself sits as a life peer in the House of Lords.

The Lords has survived for two reasons. The first is that it has little power, which allows public toleration of such a nondemocratic body. The second is that there is no agreement among the parties about how to reform it. The Labour Party has made fumbling efforts to reform the Lords, and in 1968 it introduced legislation to alter its composition to make it more representative by allowing only life peers to vote and by phasing out hereditary peerages. The 1968 legislation was filibustered and never came to a vote; the opponents were an unusual combination of Conservative traditionalists, such as Enoch Powell, wishing to preserve the Lords as is, and Labour radicals, such as Michael Foot, who wanted complete abolition of the Lords and a unicameral parliament.[7] Subsequent Labour governments had more pressing economic and social concerns on their minds, although Labour in opposition has continued to call for abolition of the Lords.

The Rise and Decline of the House of Commons

British constitutional theory provides a preeminent position for the sole elected representative body of the whole British population, the House of Commons. In the twentieth century, however, constitutional theory has taken a back seat to increasing dominance of the House of Commons by its agent, the cabinet, and particularly the prime minister.[8]

Unlike the United States, where Locke's ideas on popular sovereignty made greater inroads, Britain has never had a populist democracy. At least once every five years, reduced from seven years earlier, the whole membership of the House of Commons must stand at a general election. The government formed from that House, based on whichever party or parties can command a majority of the members of Parliament to support it, continues until its term has expired, or until it is defeated on a vote of confidence by the House, or until the prime minister decides to ask the queen for a dissolution and "go to the country" for a renewed lease on life through election of a new Parliament. The electorate, then, does not form the government directly. The only voters who can cast their ballots directly for or against a prime ministerial candidate are those in that member's individual constituency who vote for or against having that member as their MP. The same goes for other cabinet ministers. This is the celebrated fusion of power between legislative and executive branches of government.[9] The electorate chooses the House of Commons (currently 651 members) in single-member districts through a plurality vote (whichever candidates receives the most votes wins the seat), and, based on those outcomes, the new House of Commons chooses the prime minister, who in turn chooses the other members of the government. These lines of accountability have several implications. First, the single-member district, simple plurality electoral system means that a plurality vote in the country can lead to a majority in the House of Commons. This is exactly what has happened time and again in Britain, particularly since the rise of multiparty electoral politics in the early 1970s. For example, in the four elections of 1979, 1983, 1987, and 1992, the Conservatives had overall majorities of between 21 and 144 seats in the House of Commons based on a static 42–43 percent of the popular vote. The split opposition and the single-member district electoral system allowed the Conservatives to form comfortable majorities based on a consistent minority vote from the electorate. The electoral system also transformed multiparty electoral politics into two-party parliamentary politics. The third partisan force, under the various titles of Liberals, Alliance of Liberals and Social Democracts, and Liberal Democrats, never received more than 4 percent of the seats in the House of Commons despite a vote ranging up to 26 percent in these elections.

Controversy rages over the value of the single-member district, simple plurality system. Adherents of the present British system argue that it provides strong, single-party government, with direct redress for constituent grievances to an individual MP and overall accountability of the government to the voters. On the opposite side are advocates of one form or another of proportional representation (allocating parliamentary seats more closely to votes through multimember districts), who argue that the current system wastes votes, ignores minority party concerns even when they persist, and allows a two-party duopoly on power unjustified by those parties' standing in the electorate. The important point is that the current line of authority moves from a plurality of voters to a majority of MPs and on up to the prime minister and cabinet.

Second, the parliamentary form of British democracy provides for few populistic devices. There are no provisions for recall or for formal initiative petitions by the public, nor are there mechanisms whereby the public can force an early election in an unpopular government. The issue of term limits has never been broached. Only in the last twenty-five years have any referendums been held, and these have been on a selected few topics chosen by the government—the border issue in Northern Ireland, Scottish and Welsh devolution, and membership in the European Community (after the fact, in 1975). Even then, these were technically advisory referendums only, that is, the government was not constitutionally bound to follow popular wishes (that would compromise parliamentary sovereignty), and the former two referendums were taken in only parts of the United Kingdom. The populist wedge in British politics is very thin indeed—and likely to remain so.[10]

The third implication of the lines of accountability in British politics is that the government is chosen de facto as a collective body by the House of Commons. As with many things in British politics, custom and convention prevail, hence the importance of elite socialization and behavior as discussed in Chapter 4. The House of Commons as a whole never actually votes for either the prime minister or the cabinet; one "emerges," based on mutual consent and informal counting of heads. If the government wins the vote taken after the Queen's Speech on its general lines of proposed policy, then that is considered parliamentary endorsement of it. The prime minister goes to "kiss hands" with the monarch and to be officially invested as the monarch's chief minister. But the voters, through electing (usually) a one-party majority in the House of Commons, are considered to have selected that party to lead them. The government includes a cabinet of approximately twenty (again, not a fixed number; the prime minister has broad powers to reorganize executive departments), plus noncabinet and junior ministers numbering a total of about 100. All government ministers also sit in either the House of Commons or Lords. The cabinet serves as the executive committee of the parliamentary majority in the House of Commons.

Government ministers and the shadow cabinet (organized critics) of Her Majesty's Loyal Opposition (the largest opposition party) are called "front-benchers." The rest of the MPs are backbenchers, and they sit accordingly in the House of Commons. The physical layout of the chamber has the government of the day to the right of the Speaker's table and all of the opposition parties, led by Her Majesty's Loyal Opposition, to the left of the Speaker, who acts as the umpire in recognizing speakers and conducting procedure.

Indirectly, the people are considered to have selected the government through the House of Commons; therefore, it is the government as a whole that must survive votes of confidence in the Commons, not individual ministers. In fact, all individual ministers, including the prime minister, are dispensable without a new general election being called. Personnel changes have occurred time and again through death, resignation, and cabinet reshuffles by the prime minister. Most notably, in 1990 the Conservative Party in the House of Commons replaced Margaret Thatcher as party leader and prime minister with John Major without having to go to the electorate for approval, despite goading by the Labour Party on this point. The British constitution is sufficiently flexible so that the new prime minister could have called a general election if he had wanted a popular vote of confidence. But under the doctrine of parliamentary sovereignty, why should he?

As the United Kingdom moved toward democracy in the nineteenth century, the position of the House of Commons as the representative of the people was strengthened. The suffrage was reformed gradually, first expanding in 1832, then again in 1867, 1884, 1918, and 1928. Multiple voting was eliminated in 1949, and, finally, the voting age was lowered to eighteen in 1969. It was not only women who gained the vote (in two stages) in 1918 and 1928; until 1918 there was not even universal male suffrage above the age of twenty-one. Instead, voting was based on the payment of local property taxes, which eliminated the poorest sections of the population. By the end of the nineteenth century, however, the electorate had become large enough for political parties to be actively organizing the voters into blocs, and the age of the independent MP not closely following a party whip was over.[11]

As with many original changes, the first extension of the franchise was more important for its symbolic value than for its substance. The Great Reform Act of 1832, much contested in passage, was designed to accommodate the growing middle class of factory owners into an electorate hitherto restricted to landowners. The effective expansion of the electorate was from 3 percent of the adult population to 5 percent, hardly revolutionary. The later franchise extensions, however, brought the broader middle class, the agricultural workers (still a large share of the population at the time), and the urban working class into the electorate. The major political parties of the time, the Tories (Conservatives) and the Liberals, formed mass organizations and began to organize their election campaigns more formally in order to turn the new voters into loyal party members. Nevertheless, until 1918 voters constituted only twenty-eight percent of the adult population.

Until then, parties in Parliament had been relatively loose organizations, groupings of like-minded individuals originating through legislative, not constituency, connections and frequently dissenting from their own leaders. But now parties attempted to appeal to the voters, for the first time truly a mass electorate, with formal positions, especially as set forward in campaign documents. The notion of an electoral mandate—approval by the voters of the majority party's platform—began to take shape. The corollary to this was that the MPs of a particular party were expected to vote together, especially on votes of confidence for a government. Thus, if an MP could not agree in the long run with most of his party's positions, then he should find a place in another party or start his own.

Party became a collective identity—what became referred to as "responsible party government." That meant that voters should know that no matter which individual candidate they voted for, that candidate's party stood for the same set of principles all over the country. Each party had a range of opinion within it, but for the most part these opinions were expressed in ways other than parliamentary votes. On the cabinet level, this idea was expressed as "collective responsibility," which meant that no government minister was supposed to express public dissent from a collectively set government policy.

Both of these traditions have been marginally eroded recently. Dissent from specific government policies, and from the official positions of opposition parties as well, has become more widespread.[12] Nevertheless, dissent from the official party position occurs on only a tiny minority of parliamentary votes and, by most conventional standards, unified party voting in the House of Commons is still remarkably high.[13] Similarly, the rule of collective responsibility has been hedged somewhat, and in the referendum campaign of 1975 on the European Community, it was formally lifted to allow Labour cabinet ministers who opposed the EC to express themselves publicly even though the government as a whole supported membership in the EC. The most important outcome from the incremental increase in allowable party dissent in recent years has been that the convention is no longer that a government will resign if defeated on a major piece of legislation; instead, a government must be defeated on an explicit vote of confidence. That was what happened to the Labour government in 1979, the first time that a government was evicted from office by the Commons since 1924. It was also this convention that allowed the Conservative government of John Major to survive the rebellion of some of its own party members against ratification of the Maastricht Treaty of the EC in 1993. When put to the test, Conservative MPs would not join with opposition parties to bring down the government.

In addition to generalized belief in party loyalty, other mechanisms reinforce party discipline in the House of Commons. Parties have formal meetings of members only to air positions and reach common ground. Party leaders also have rewards and sanctions at their disposal. If an MP has the ambition to achieve a leadership position, either in opposition or in government, it is best not to offend the party leaders too often. Parties have members designated as official party whips to communicate between leaders and ordinary MPs. An official party order—also called, confusingly, a whip—sets forth the party position on how a member is expected to vote on an issue. The number of lines beneath the order, from one to three, indicates how important it is for the member to be present and voting the proper way. Members who consistently defy instructions from the leaders about how to vote may find their official membership of the parliamentary party in jeopardy. Since rebels who have the party whip removed (the third meaning, membership of the parliamentary party) are seldom reelected, this is a serious disincentive to pushing parliamentary dissent too far. Thus all the incentives in the British parliamentary party process push the MP toward party loyalty.

The organizational procedures of the House of Commons further insure that it will be a register for party preferences, especially those expressed by the executive, rather than a body made up of independent members. Since the early twentieth century, the government of the day has controlled approximately 75 percent of parliamentary time, with the official opposition controlling about 20 percent, leaving only 5 percent for the individual backbench members acting in their own capacity. If necessary, the government can usually impose a "guillotine" on the procedures, that is, limit discussion. Parliament, especially the House of Commons, prides itself on thorough airing of issues, usually in general debate or in the Committee of the Whole. But the government sets the agenda for discussssion, controls parliamentary time, and, through the party whips and party loyalty, usually controls a voting majority when it needs to. Legislation is rarely altered significantly from what the government has proposed.

As has been noted, the most controversial and difficult issues for a government to get through the House of Commons are those that divide its own party, particularly the front bench from a significant segment of its backbenchers.[14] Some of these may even be withdrawn before coming to a vote, thereby avoiding a damaging public party split. Ever since the decline of the Liberals in the 1920s, it has been an axiom of British politics that a disunited party is not an electorally appealing party. The Labour Party in the 1980s further affirmed the axiom through its divisions. Prominent divisive intraparty issues include the Labour government's strike legislation of 1968, the Scottish and Welsh devolution legislation of the late 1970s, Mrs. Thatcher's poll tax (community charge) bill of 1989, and the Maastricht Treaty on the European Community. In fact, the European Community has been an issue that has persistently divided both Labour and the Conservative Parties since the early 1970s.[15]

There are four formal and two informal functions of the House of Commons. The four formal procedures include passing legislation, finance and budgeting, serving as an electoral college, and providing oversight. The two informal functions are electoral campaigning and political recruitment. For reasons outlined previously, the formal legislative process is less significant than it appears. Most legislation is accepted as the government prepares it after consultation with the affected interests. As already noted, there are exceptional circumstances in which the House can alter or even defeat legislation, but these instances are rare.

The legislative process is not the obstacle course that it is in separation of powers systems or sometimes in multiparty coalition governments. Instead, the government controls the process, as previously discussed, and also controls information. Compared to the extensive bureaucratic sources of the executive branch, the legislature is poorly equipped. Bills go to generalist committees, not specialist committees. Legislative staff assistants are few and are often shared among MPs. There are no special staffs for committees. Thus the generalist MP with few resources is faced with government bills on which ministers are able to draw expertise from various quarters to help them. Is it any wonder that MPs often rely on their political party headquarters for information, where there is at least a staff willing to help them. The House of Commons also has a library, but again without large-scale, specialist staff assistance.

The formal legislative procedures in Parliament are as follows: (1) First Reading, the introduction of the bill and some debate on general principles; (2)

Second Reading, in which the issues in the bill are actually joined; (3) referral to a committee, which may be the Committee of the Whole House on important measures to allow as many MPs as possible to have their say; (4) the Report stage from the committee, including any amendments the committee has added; and finally, (5) Third Reading. Second Reading and committee consideration are the critical stages in ascertaining party positions, government resolve, and the direction of the legislation. Richard Rose[16] has found that, for all of the discussion of British politics becoming more ideologically driven and adversarial since the 1970s, a large amount of legislation is not even contested by opposition parties at Second Reading. Even before the formal legislative process, British governments may signal their intentions through the issuance of green papers, which are discussion documents about an issue that the government may legislate on, and white papers, which indicate more firmly the lines of policy the government will follow in its legislation.

Although some time is set aside for private members' bills, or legislation proposed by individual members without government endorsement, it is usually insufficient for a bill to go through all the stages of the process. Furthermore, private members lack the technical resources for drafting legislation that the government possesses through the civil service. Nevertheless, private members' legislation, aided by a government willing to allow sufficient parliamentary time for its consideration, has been instrumental in some social policy areas, as is shown in Chapter 8.

Normal legislative procedures favor the government, and those for finance bills do so even more. The government's presentation of the budget is a major occasion, awaited and attended to by all politically alert people. One reason it is so important is that, unlike in the United States, the executive budget will be the effective budget of the country. No amendments to the finance bill are accepted, and the budget will be voted through in relatively short order, with only a limited power of delay in the House of Lords. Thus the debate becomes one about the government's economic policy and whether it is the appropriate one for the country's needs.

In the third formal function, the House of Commons serves an the electoral college, although this term is not used in Britain. Nevertheless, by registering the popular preferences of the public and having a government formed on the basis of which party leaders can command a majority in the Commons, the House is serving an electoral college function. Furthermore, the House retains the right to remove the government from office through a successful resolution of "no confidence," although, as pointed out earlier, this procedure is rare.

The fourth formal function, oversight, is one in which the House of Commons performs in several ways. The first is through Question Time, a period set aside for government ministers, including the prime minister, to appear before the whole House to answer questions about their performance, their policies, and the management of government affairs. As those who have watched this activity can attest, most of the speeches in Question Time actually involve partisan point making rather than dispassionate investigations into government performance. Leading questions, either pro- or antigovernment, and short, snappy answers are favored, with much partisan snickering, braying, and other interruptions. When Question Time was first broadcast (before telecasting), the British public was aghast that their representatives would behave this way. But it is part of the culture of the House of Commons to behave rowdily. Impartial observers have expressed skepticism about whether oversight of the government through Question Time really serves its intended purpose, although written questions may receive somewhat more careful and thoughtful responses.[17]

A second major form of oversight by the House of Commons is a relatively recent one: the institution of Select Committees to investigate the affairs of particular ministerial departments. After being attempted on a limited basis for over a decade, a full set of Select Committees, organized around the same functions as government departments, was established in 1979. Although their powers to command information from the civil service are limited, they have been able to scrutinize the workings of government departments more carefully than has previously been the case. Government ministers now have to answer to these committees as well as to the whole House for their actions, and there is more chance for sustained interaction with legislators who have built some expertise in the subject. Nevertheless, these committtees do not have any more staff assistance than the rest of the House of Commons, and their reports are often ignored. They have exclusively oversight functions rather than legislative ones, meaning that unlike U.S. congressional committees, they do not consider bills.[18]

General debate can also serve the oversight function. The most common means of doing this is through adjournment debates, in which broad policy issues are debated at the end of the legislative day. The government is forced to defend and explain its policies in a particular area, and the opposition parties and individual MPs can stake out their own positions on the issues.

The two informal functions of the House of Commons are to serve as a continuous election campaign and to act as a socialization and recruitment mechanism for political party leaders and government ministers. If the government has what might be called a "working majority" of seats, that is, one in which it would take more than a few absentees and dissenters to defeat the government, then the opposition parties are not likely to be effective in amending legislation or getting the government to change its course of action. But what they can do is attempt to embarrass the government and build up their own records, with a view to the next general election. Of course, all they know is that it will occur within five years after the previous one, but the tendency has been for a government with a working majority to try to govern for at least four years. Thus the aim is to build a record for the party in Parliament that it can run on in the next election. This function was especially evident in 1991–1992, when everybody knew the government had to call the general election by June 1992. The parliamentary run-up to the election became known as the "long campaign."

The other informal function—the making of party leaders and government ministers—is discussed in the next chapter. Here it is worth noting that Parliament, especially the House of Commons, is the central agency of elite political socialization in the United Kingdom.[19] One becomes a party leader and embarks on a ministerial career by serving in the House of Commons, and normally, in fact, there is a substantial apprenticeship on the backbenches. Thus one has to impress one's peers and superiors in the Commons in order to rise to higher decisionmaking positions. Unlike in other systems, there is rarely lateral entry to top party leadership and political executive positions through service in other levels of government, private organizations, or civil service positions.

Thus Parliament remains crucial to the governing of the United Kingdom in several ways, but its days as the dominant institution are over, despite the constitutional fiction of parliamentary sovereignty. An increasing population, along with the growing complexity of society, has made governing more of a specialist profession, and, aside from the institution of Select Committees, Parliament has resolutely refused to specialize in terms of legislative procedures and staff assistance. The flexibility of the British constitution has meant that, under most circumstances, governments with an adequate majority can count on party loyalty in the House of Commons to carry their preferences into law.

The Rise and Rise of the Cabinet and Prime Minister

The cabinet, as the center of the political executive, is the principal power source of British government in the late twentieth century. The political executive refers to those parts of the executive branch that have positions appointed on the basis of partisan political considerations, as opposed to the bureaucracy or civil service, which relies most heavily on meritocratic criteria. The role of the civil service will be considered later in this chapter.

The prime minister appoints a government of approximately 100 people, all of whom also serve in Parliament, either in the Commons (most of them) or the Lords (a few). Thus at any time from one-quarter to one-third of the majority party in the House of Commons is serving in a government post. The most powerful part of the government is the cabinet, a group of about twenty ministers who head the most important departments. The prime minister has broad authority to rearrange executive departments as well as to shuffle the personnel of the political executive. A few departments, however, have consistently remained preeminent, particularly the Treasury, Foreign Office (now Foreign and Commonwealth Office), and Home Office, a large department with broad authority in domestic affairs, including law and order. As the domestic responsibilities of government departments have expanded in the twentieth century, the number, size, and importance of such departments have increased in relation to their more foreign-oriented counterparts. But with the accession of the United Kingdom to the European Community, even ostensibly domestic departments have considerable international duties, as described in Chapter 5.

Ambitious young MPs aim to become junior ministers if their party is in government or to become opposition spokespersons if their party is not in government. From either of these positions, they are poised to rise to senior positions if their party forms the government. Most ministerial careers are thwarted at some point, of course, but a chosen few manage to serve in senior positions, sometimes in several of them. Former Labour Prime Minister James Callaghan was the only person in the twentieth century to serve in the four most senior positions: prime minister, chancellor of the Exchequer (Treasury), foreign secretary, and home secretary. There is a lot of turnover of cabinet ministers in British government, but much of that turnover is lateral, that is, the same people move to other positions rather than resigning or being removed from executive office entirely.[20] With such high rotation in individual positions, some observers have questioned whether British government really puts a premium on administrative skills, especially on expertise in particular areas.[21]

Government ministers have three major responsibilities. First, they have individual ministerial responsibility for the administrative conduct of their departments. This form of accountability is what is being tested at Question Time, and more recently, in Select Committee hearings in the House of Commons. The convention of British government is that ministers get political credit or blame for what their departments do. But the development of the Next Steps program, as described later on, has changed the nature of individual ministerial responsibility by making ministers less accountable for the detailed activities within their departments. Individual ministers cannot be voted out of office by the House of Commons, but they can be put under pressure to resign, and they can be removed by the prime minister for any reason. Civil servants are supposed to be "anonymous" in the sense that their contributions are judged within the executive, not in the public political arena. But as with several other conventions, at times this one has been stretched in recent years as bureaucrats have testified before Select Committees and become associated with leaks from executive secrecy.

The second major responsibility of a government minister is called collective responsibility. That means that once official government policy is decided, all members of the government (but not necessarily backbench MPs of the majority party in Parliament) are expected to support the policy publicly, that is, in all public statements on the topic. If a minister cannot support the policy in this fashion, he or she is supposed to resign the ministerial position and return to the backbenches. The logic behind this is that the government should be united in its responsibility to the House of Commons for policy.

The third duty of government ministers is that of parliamentary responsibility, shared with all other members of the House of Commons or Lords. Government ministers are thus not excused from the ordinary duties of elected representatives, including voting, debating, and dealing with the grievances of constituents. Senior government ministers are also allowed to have a junior MP appointed as their individual parliamentary private secretary to handle many of their relations with other members of their parliamentary party.[22] In practice, ministers must retain the confidence of their party as well as that of the prime minister and other members of the cabinet.[23]

Although much is done in the name of the cabinet, as a body the cabinet does not meet often, only once or twice per week for a few hours, and decisions are often not thoroughly discussed. In short, the cabinet as a whole more resembles a ratifying body. Until very recently, the actual workings of the cabinet were encased in such secrecy that little was known. But the revealing memoirs of some politicians, including the diaries of both Richard Crossman and Barbara Castle, the release of cabinet papers under the thirty-year rule, and the delineation of cabinet committees by Prime Minister John Major in 1992 have shed some light on the subject. Although major decisions may be taken in the cabinet itself, most decisions are actually made by cabinet committees, within departments, or by the prime minister in consultation, often informal, with a select group of cabinet ministers.

Furthermore, the cabinet is dependent on the civil servants within the departments for preparation of an issue, including policy options, and implementation of whatever policy the executive, and in some cases Parliament, decides. Government policymaking often involves conflict between ministers who head major spending departments and the efforts of those departments, especially the Treasury, which aim to keep expenditures within bounds in the interest of overall economic policy. As minister for Education and Science in the Edward Heath government of the early 1970s, Margaret Thatcher was a spending minister; later as prime minister, she was considerably less sympathetic to increased expenditures. Within cabinet meetings, as with many executive sessions, electoral democracy is inoperable. The prime minister sets the agenda through control of the Cabinet Office, a small body of civil servants that organizes the meetings, and through the power of summing up the discussion and conclusions of the meeting. Thus the conduct of Cabinet meetings is weighted toward the power of the prime minister. But if several senior ministers feel strongly enough about opposing the prime minister on an issue, then their views may carry the day. This is what happened to Harold Wilson in 1969 over the Industrial Relations Bill. Above all, prime ministers want to avoid pushing their cabinets into such a row that it would split the party and damage chances for it to retain power.

The cabinet is so powerful because, in addition to its usual procedural dominance of Parliament, constitutionally it has broad authority over many policy areas. By issuing executive orders, known either as Orders in Council (exercising powers belonging to the monarch as part of the Royal Prerogative) or Statutory Instruments (delegated legislation allowed through broad grants of authority from Parliament), the cabinet can often make policy without consulting

Parliament at all.[24] Such actions may be subjected to parliamentary criticism, however, through such procedures as scrutiny of Statutory Instruments, Question Time, or adjournment debates. In the area of foreign policy, for instance, there is no need for Parliament to declare war, pass resolutions, or even to approve treaties. The prime minister and cabinet, in the name of the executive, have authority derived from their role as the monarch's ministers to declare what foreign policy actions are needed for the safety of the realm. Nevertheless, most of these decisions are the subjects of parliamentary discussion.

The role of the prime minister is particularly ambiguous. It is derived from the older tradition of the monarch appointing ministers as advisers; eventually these ministers had to seek the support of Parliament to serve as well, thus giving them a two-sided responsibility. Identifiable governments were formed, with one minister taking the lead, and eventually the monarch's discretion in appointments faded to selecting someone who could command support of a majority (if possible) of the House of Commons. The prime minister became head of government, and, in effect, the chief executive of the country. Nevertheless, there are few statutory descriptions of the prime minister's duties and limits. Thus, even in the flexible British Constitution, the office of prime minister is extraordinarily malleable in formal conception.

There has been an ongoing debate for many years about the presidentialization of British politics. The ultimate question, whatever the conventions, is whether the British prime minister really has powers similar to those of the President of the United States.[25] Because the executive is still so shrouded in secrecy, it is difficult to come up with a definitive answer. Those who argue for presidentialization think that the cabinet as a collective body has lost power to the prime minister over the years largely through prime ministerial control of the cabinet agenda and the civil service and because of the role of the media in personalizing the office. Those who reject the case contend that prime ministers' powers of apppointment are very limited, and they still must retain the confidence of the cabinet and, indeed, the whole parliamentary party. The long career of Margaret Thatcher and the circumstances of her ouster as prime minister have only added fuel to this debate.[26]

The broad powers of secrecy of the British executive are often invoked to keep Parliament as well as the public uninformed about what is transpiring. Despite the existence of Question Time and Select Committees, many times members of Parliament do not know the right questions to ask or the government may claim that national security considerations prevent giving answers. This is clearly the case with regard to questioning about security and intelligence services, some of which are not even established on a statutory basis, leaving Parliament with few tools for gathering information. Until the 1990s, it was not publicly known who headed these agencies, and their budgets are still largely secret. MI5 and its extension, Special Branch, are concerned with domestic security, functions performed by the Federal Bureau of Investigation in the United States. MI 6 (Secret Service) is the British equivalent of the U.S. Central Intelligence Agency, responsible for intelligence abroad. The Government Communications Headquarters at Cheltenham is the electronic arm of intelligence work, similar to the National Security Agency in the United States. There are also military intelligence agencies. Security considerations have even precluded legislative discussion on many aspects of energy policy, especially in regard to nuclear matters. Even when the right question is asked, evasive answers may be supplied.

Restrictive laws of libel and slander make people think twice or more about publishing or publicly repeating information that may be difficult to prove if contested. But the underlying reason for the failure to inform Parliament on many matters is that there is a culture of executive secrecy in Whitehall (the common reference for the bureaucracy, so named for the street in London on which several government ministries sit), reinforced by laws with strict sanctions for violators. Section Two of the 1911 Official Secrets Act is a broad legal blanket that allows prosecution for the unauthorized release of information by a minister or civil servant.[27] Thus the level of government leaks from disgruntled officials is relatively low although it has increased over the years. The most famous cases in which the government attempted to suppress information surrounded the posthumous publication of the Crossman diaries of the former Labour MP and cabinet minister and the publication of *Spycatcher,* in which a former British secret service agent living in Australia published material on his career. The fact that these prosecutions were unsuccessful has not led to a broader interpretation of the public's "right to know." Every government bill proposing reform of the laws of secrecy, when closely scrutinized, winds up being as restrictive, or even more so, than the current law. The same goes for laws on freedom of the press.

Britain has an official organized opposition called the shadow cabinet, which, although not part of the government or the bureaucracy, plays the role of questioning government ministers about policy and the performance of their departments.[28] The members of the shadow cabinet are the recognized leaders of Her Majesty's Loyal Opposition, the party with the second-largest number of seats in the House of Commons. The party leader of Her Majesty's Loyal Opposition actually receives a small salary from the government for playing this role. The members of the shadow cabinet receive no privileged access to government information, but they do have pride of place in debating government bills and general policy issues. If a party is out of power, membership in the shadow cabinet is a recognition of one's senior status in the party. Although shadow ministers often become the senior minister for the department they are shadowing upon their party's assuming power, this is not inevitable.

The role of the cabinet, then, is an amalgam of responsibility to Parliament and the inheritance of the broad sweep of executive authority from a powerful monarchy. There is sufficient flexibility in the institutional practices to allow for variations from government to government, depending on the style of the prime minister and the personal and political dynamics occurring among the individuals involved. Because of the lack of precise constitutional interpretations of responsibility and authority, an accretion of accustomed practices has built up. Governments of all political stripes have resisted intrusions on their powers from Parliament, the press, and the public.

The Civil Service: From Servants to Masters?

The British civil service is both famed and blamed worldwide. It is famed for its impartiality, lack of corruption, and generalized competence. It is blamed, however, for its elitism, conservatism, amateurism, and secrecy. Constitutionally, it is supposed to be the guardian of the permanent interests and information of the state and to be responsive to whichever political party is in charge of the government. The party receives credit or blame for what the government does, whereas the bureaucracy remains protected from political criticism, neutral civil servants supposedly giving better advice to their governors. In practice, the charge is often made, especially by politicians of the Left, that there is a "secret constitution"[29] by which the bureaucracy actually rules Britain through its control of information and manipulation of government ministers. Such views have been popularly presented in the successful transatlantic television series *Yes, Minister* and *Yes, Prime Minister*. These charges are inherently difficult to demonstrate, especially as they involve a conspiracy of omission and silence as well as commission of such behavior. But there is little doubt that there is an esprit de corps among the civil service that is based upon the notion that the civil service often understands the long-term interests of the country better than partisan politicians do.

The rationale for the standing of the civil service in Britain stems from some of the same sources as noted earlier for the standing of the cabinet, namely, the limited intrusion of popular and partisan pressures into performance of the duties of state, which were once the monarch's duties. In comparison to the government of the United States, in which the president appoints some three thousand officials, in Britain such appointments are strictly limited. Even the highest appointments the prime minister can make—the members of the cabinet—are constrained by the necessity of appointing people who serve in Parliament and are members of the majority party or parties in the House of Commons. Beyond the very highest levels of the executive, the prime minister has few appointment powers. There are bishops of the Church of England to appoint, of course, but here again the short list is limited by the Church. Honors, including peerages in the House of Lords, are bestowed by the prime minister, but their future political import is limited.

The prime minister has a Cabinet Office, ostensibly responsible to the cabinet as a whole, to oversee the overall coordination of the executive, but this office is staffed by civil servants, not by outside political appointees. There is also the prime minister's Private Office, again made up of bureaucrats. This small group of one-half dozen, headed by the principal private secretary, largely provides a liaison with departments as well as secretarial assistance. Communications functions for the prime minister are coordinated by another bureaucratic body, the press secretary and his staff of ten. The prime minister also has a Political Office staffed by two or three political appointees who are responsible for relations with the party organization. For a decade, there also existed the Central Policy Review Staff, empowered to review government policies and programs broadly and to recommend changes to the prime minister. Staffed by the civil service, it also employed outside consultants. But the Conservatives thought that it was too independent of political direction, and in 1983 it was abolished.[30]

Although specialist political and policy advisers have been increasing in British government, they still are nowhere near the numbers in the United States.[31] Over the past twenty years, the prime minister has had a Policy Unit of political advisers in Downing Street, ranging in number from four to thirteen, and other cabinet ministers have been allowed one or two such advisers. The prime minister has also had special advisers on occasion. Some of these appointments have led to controversy, as when Sir Alan Walters, economic adviser to Mrs. Thatcher, was accused by the resigning chancellor of the Exchequer, Nigel Lawson, of exercising too much influence over economic policy. The lack of politically appointed officials in the bureaucracy reduces the problem of making patronage appointments, but it leaves the administrative culture of Whitehall in place. Governments can also employ Royal Commissions of prominent people appointed with specific terms of reference to investigate and make recommendations on particular problems, with the government free to accept or ignore their advice. But the publicity these commissions often generate for their efforts led recent Conservative governments to avoid them in favor of the better controlled advice of the civil service and party bureaucracies.

Conservatives have not been so enamored, however, of the so-called quangos, or quasi-autonomous nongovernmental organizations, which multiplied in the 1960s and 1970s. Despite purported independence of the government, they are almost entirely government financed. These bodies perform two functions: one is to offer advice to citizens and governments, the other is to provide expertise in administration and disbursement of government funds for such activities as the arts, education, and manpower training. Quangos, not staffed by civil servants, provide government at arms length in specialized areas, at the cost of blurring lines of political responsibility. Although the Conservatives were eager to develop executive agencies to provide for administration by contract in the Next Steps program, to be described shortly, they vowed to cut back on quangos, arguing that such bodies often acted in the name of the government without clear lines of accountability to ministers and departments. Mrs. Thatcher was suspicious of quangos as part of the interventionist "corporatist" mentality, but they can also be viewed as an essentially pluralist institution, designed to allow different interests to exercise influence within government. The success of the attack on quangos is questionable. Within the civil service, appointment and promotion procedures have been revised several times, starting with the Northcote-Trevelyan Report in the nineteenth century, which set forth the basics of the meritocratic system that has been in place to the present day. In the mid-1960s, there was a flurry of interest in civil service reform, culminating in the Fulton Report, which attempted to broaden civil service recruitment and to standardize different administrative grades of civil servants.

Nevertheless, the British civil service is still disproportionately made up of humanities and social studies graduates of Oxford and Cambridge, recruited at an early age and serving as career bureaucracts. The highest ranking civil servant in each department is the permanent secretary, who serves as the chief policy adviser to the minister. The most notable performers often receive an honor upon their retirement.

Continuation and promotion in the civil service is based upon internal evaluations. Promotions to the top level of the administrative class, which involve major policy advice and management of departments as lieutenants to the few political ministers in the department, are made by the prime minister. But again the choices are limited to those eligible to serve in those capacities. Under Mrs. Thatcher's Conservative governments there was concern about the political reliability of high civil servants in implementing what she saw as her radical reforms, especially involving shedding government responsibilities in several economic and social areas. From the point of view of her critics, the problem was one of potential "politicization" of the high levels of the civil service, a violation of the traditional distinction between politicians and bureaucrats.[32] Under recent Conservative governments, the total number of employees in the civil service has shrunk significantly.

The role of the bureaucracy in British governance remains controversial. The growth of government responsibility for services to the public in the twentieth century, a trend which Mrs. Thatcher was able to stymie but not reverse to any appreciable degree, has led to an increase both in the number of bureaucrats and in the complexity of their coordination. The basic fairness, sense of competence, and political neutrality of the civil service is balanced against the charges of its narrow social base, lack of scientific and economic expertise, and resistance to change. The cult of administrative secrecy, designed to provide political responsibility to those few publicly visible for making policy, is a much more problematic benefit when government is so large and complex.

The major recourse that a citizen has for redress of grievances against the bureaucracy remains through the members of the House of Commons. For the past twenty-five years there has been an ombudsman (parliamentary commissioner) to investigate citizen complaints over treatment by government officials, but as the name suggests, it requires a member of Parliament to stimulate an investigation and to pursue the case with the bureaucracy. In short, unlike in some other countries, the ombudsman has only limited investigatory powers. The level of discontent with government delays and arbitrary behavior is indicated by the fact that John Major made the Citizen's Charter (not a bill of rights, but essentially a listing of consumers' rights to efficient government services) a centerpiece of his administration. Nevertheless, more serious questions about administrative malfeasance remain the preserve of MPs, who are often ill-informed about what the government is actually doing.

The Conservative government under Margaret Thatcher and John Major began to implement a program called Next Steps for the civil service. Although the full implications are still unclear, one aim seems to be to separate policy from administration by developing an internal market for the contracting out of services, similar to those developed previously in the education and health sectors of government, as noted in Chapter 7. That is, central government departments offer contracts for projects for various sectors of the bureaucracy or private groups to carry out. Thus the higher levels of the civil service (core departments) are to be policy advisers and the lower levels semiautonomous agencies (executive agencies) responsible for the administration of policy. Such a change in usual British administrative practices has considerable implications for the doctrine of individual ministerial responsibility; heads of executive agencies, in fact, now appear before the parliamentary Select Committees to answer questions within limits set by their ministers. Even though Next Steps has spread widely, its implementation has been uneven among departments.[33]

The military makes up a large portion of the bureaucracy, an often neglected fact. The military, especially the navy, has played a large role in implementation of British foreign policy up to the present. It often goes unrecognized how martial a society the United Kingdom is, both in its history and in its patterns of public spending. Yet the British military, as a professional service, has readily submitted itself to civilian dominance, especially in the twentieth century. There has been a notable absence of military-based revolts against civilian rulers, and the military leadership has rarely served as a recruiting grounds for political leadership, outside of the declining tradition of ex-officers serving as Conservative backbench MPs. Based on the British tradition of the younger sons of the aristocracy going into military service, officers seem to know their place, and in turn they have been given extensive responsibilities by political leaders. More recently, there has been discontent expressed about the disbandment of renowned military units as part of reductions after the Cold War. But the bulk of the population, even of the male population, has not had to serve since the end of conscription in 1958.

The Unitary State and Its Discontents

Although it is a small country in land area, the United Kingdom contains a diverse population. The tradition of monarchy, combined with concerns about national security against nearby enemies, parliamentary sovereignty, and a largely unwritten constitution have led to a continuing emphasis on the importance of maintaining central authority in the British state. Although devolution, or the granting of power to lower levels, has been discussed from time to time, central-ization has heretofore won out. This is true even for implemented cases of devo-lution, notably for Northern Ireland and for local governments, with the abolition of the Greater London Council and other county councils in 1986. In both cases a more direct form of central control was substituted for local structures when the center perceived that the political repercussions of maintaining the lower levels as they were would be too great. That is the operating principle of the unitary state—devolution when politically and, especially, administratively convenient, with a reversion to centralization when political forces dictate. Under parliamen-tary sovereignty, all it takes to reverse decentralist moves is a simple majority vote in the House of Commons, with the attendant procedures in the House of Lords.

There is an inbred fear of entrenching decentralization in the constitution of the United Kingdom either through guarantees to lower levels or by establishing a federal principle. The proposals for devolution to Scotland and Wales in the 1970s were some of the most controversial legislation of their time because of the fear that, once established, devolved institutions would serve as a "slippery slope" or "thin edge of the wedge" leading to further weakening of central authority, per-haps even to the breakup of the United Kingdom.[34] Furthermore, there was no proposal for a general, United Kingdom–wide decentralization that would include English regions.

Local government structures have been revised periodically by central legisla-tion, and local government depends on central government allocations for most of its finance. Moreover, local government is a key actor in policy implementa-tion, especially in such areas as education and housing. There are also regional levels of central government organizations, such as health authorities. Currently the local government structures vary in the different parts of the United Kingdom, with that of England being particularly complicated in terms of levels of government and responsibilities, even after the abolition of the metropolitan county councils in 1986.[35] The 1990s have again witnessed government attempts to "rationalize" local government structure. Although local government council-lors are elected periodically, the low turnout has led to charges of unrepresenta-tiveness, and ultimately the powers and finances of local government are subject to central government authorization. This has led to repeated rows, especially since the 1970s,[36] as central government, particularly under the Conservatives, has attempted to control local government spending. The most famous case is the central government changing of the local tax system from one based on property taxes ("the rates") to one based on a flat head tax (the poll tax or community charge) not based on ability to pay. The controversy over this change in the tax structure was a major contributing factor to the Conservative Party's eventual dis-enchantment with Margaret Thatcher in 1990.

Periodically the Labour Party has embraced decentralist proposals, for instance, in the 1920s, then again with the Scottish and Welsh devolution legislation of the 1970s, and, most recently, with it embracing Scottish devolution again in the 1990.[37] Local socialism has been extolled as an option in times of Labour opposition status in Parliament.[38] The problem with this is that Labour decentralist tendencies have always involved more partisanship than principle. They are particularly popular when Labour loses control of the central government and retreats to its regional redoubts. The competition of Scottish and Welsh nationalism in those areas also involves Labour in a bidding war for voters. Decentralist pledges are often forgotten or compromised, however, when Labour comes to power. The urge for uniform treatment of citizens according to an equal standard has been a more compelling urge for a socialist party. The Conservative party, with few exceptions, tends to stand by its centralist, British nationalist past.

Even though there are local differences in service delivery in the United Kingdom, for instance, in the length of waiting lists for surgery in the National Health Service (NHS) and in the availability of state-provided educational facilities, the maintenance of central authority through Parliament and the executive continues. Constitutional flexibility allows the establishment of central government ministries for certain areas, for instance, as with the offices concerned with Welsh, Scottish, and Northern Ireland affairs, but this constitutional flexibility is unlikely to be stretched far enough to develop a full-fledged program of decentralization in the United Kingdom.[39]

The Judiciary—Supremacy of Law?

The role of the judiciary in Britain is limited but important. In fact, there are three separate legal systems in the United Kingdom, those of England and Wales, Scotland, and Northern Ireland. Laws and legal practices are similar among the three systems. As in any liberal democracy, judicial independence is important in allowing the judiciary to apply the law to individual cases without political interference from the other branches of government. This was enshrined in the Act of Settlement in 1701, which made it impossible to remove judges except by application to the monarch by both houses of Parliament.[40] Although judicial independence is upheld in the United Kingdom, as an institution, the judiciary is, in fact, fused with the executive and legislature. The highest appellate court is the Law Lords, which determines disputed points of law. The Law Lords (officially Lords of Appeal in Ordinary) are a group of ten to twelve judges with extensive legal experience who are appointed as life peers to the House of Lords particularly to deal with legal matters, usually organized into panels of five judges. The state's chief legal officer, the lord chancellor, is simultaneously a member of the government (cabinet minister), the legislature, where he presides over the Lords, and the judiciary, where he supervises the Law Lords. All judges are appointed by the monarch upon recommendation of the prime minister and the lord chancellor, who may consult other members of the judiciary. Parliament is not part of the appointment process. Appointed judges, especially for the Law Lords, come from an extremely narrow background of elite education and are conservative in interpreting the law.[41] They can be removed only for misbehavior, which almost never occurs, and often serve until the retirement age of seventy-five.

The British judiciary does not have the formal power of judicial review, that is, being able to determine the constitutionality of acts of the legislature and executive. Thus it is not, in a political sense, a coequal branch of government. Courts do have the power to declare acts of the government ultra vires, meaning that the government has acted outside the laws as Parliament has made them. The government can cope with this, however, by getting Parliament to pass a law making the behavior legal. Parliament can also pass ex post facto laws, or, as they are called in Britain, "retrospective legislation." Thus parliamentary sovereignty is preserved. Nevertheless, recent decades have witnessed increased judicial activism and even claims for judicial review creeping into the British judicial system.[42]

In matters pertaining to the European Union, there is formal power of judicial review, whereby British citizens can challenge their own government as having acted outside European Community law and can have their case heard by the European Court of Justice. Britain is also a signatory to the European Convention on Human Rights, which means it is subject to a court in Strasbourg set up to hear appeals from the highest court within the member countries about violations of the principles. The court has found the United Kingdom breaking the convention more frequently than any other country,[43] but British judges are still reluctant to enforce the convention.

The structure of British courts is extensive, ranging from the Magistrates' courts, which deal with misdemeanors and are ruled over by unpaid citizen volunteers, to the House of Lords sitting in its judicial capacity. The British judiciary works within the common law tradition, derived from the case-by-case basis on which the king's justice was dispensed in local areas in the Middle Ages. Precedent is important in judicial decisionmaking, as is legal acknowledgment of Parliamentary sovereignty. The British judiciary does qualify as an independent judiciary, however, because it does not take orders from any other branch. Several appellate decisions in the early 1990s overturning convictions of people claimed to have been involved with Irish terrorism may have damaged the British reputation for fairness in the substance of the original verdict, but such decisions do illustrate judicial independence.

The British judiciary is renowned for its fairness. Nevertheless, recent changes in judicial procedures, such as limiting the right to silence in the courtroom and the use of internment without trial for suspected terrorists in Northern Ireland, have added to older controversies surrounding the judiciary, principally its narrow class base of recruitment. Judges are selected from those who practice the law, and serving on the bench is normally considered the capstone of an attorney's career. Solicitors, the branch of lawyers who deal with clients in first instance, are rarely selected; most judgeships go to barristers, the attorneys who argue cases in court. For most people, however, the British judiciary remains a conservative (not necessarily Conservative) bedrock of the political system.

British Government in the Late Twentieth Century

Parliamentary government in Britain today, then, is a combination of ancient institutions adapted to modern practices and purposes. Institutional change is often discussed in Britain, but despite the powers of the House of Commons to change the Constitution by simple majority rule, such changes are few and are usually incremental. Even "radical" governments such as those of Labour in the immediate postwar period, Wilson in the 1960s, and Thatcher in the 1980s pursued few institutional changes, and those were mainly tinkering. There have been modest changes made in eligibility for suffrage, eligibility for and powers of the House of Lords, civil service recruitment and structure, devolution and local government, and House of Commons procedures since World War II. The most politically conflictual of these issues were the institution of direct rule for Northern Ireland in 1972 and the debate over devolution for Scotland and Wales later in that decade. The problems over the community charge (poll tax) had more to do with the policy embedded within it than with the structure of local government. This suggests that, fundamentally, successful politicians are satisfied with the system as it exists, preferring to focus their efforts on policy rather than on institutional change. Their political behavior is examined more directly in the next chapter.

Notes

1. John R. Hibbing and Samuel C. Patterson, "'Representing a Territory': Constituency-Boundaries for the British House of Commons of the 1980s," *Journal of Politics* 48, no. 4 (1986):992–1005; T. Phillip Wolf, "Seats for Cheats: Reapportionment in the House of Commons" (paper presented at American Political Science Association Conference, New York, 1978).

2. Walter Bagehot, *The English Constitution* (London: Fontana, 1963).

3. R.H.S. Crossman, *Diaries of a Cabinet Minister,* 3 vols. (London: Hamish Hamilton and Jonathan Cape, 1975, 1976, 1977); Richard Crossman, *The Myths of Cabinet Government* (Harvard: Harvard University Press, 1964).

4. T. H. Marshall, *Social Policy* (London: Hutchinson, 1965).

5. See David Butler and Anne Sloman, *British Political Facts, 1900–1979,* 5th ed. (New York: St. Martin's Press, 1980).

6. Donald Shell, *The House of Lords,* 2d ed. (Hemel Hempstead, England: Harvester Wheatsheaf, 1992).

7. Ronald Butt, *The Power of Parliament,* 2d ed. (London: Constable, 1969).

8. Anthony H. Birch, *The British System of Government,* 6th ed. (Boston: Allen and Unwin, 1983); Bagehot, *The English Constitution.*

9. Bagehot, *The English Constitution.*

10. Harry Lazer, "The Referendum and the British Constitution," in *Dilemmas of Change in British Politics*, ed. Donley T. Studlar and Jerold L. Waltman (London: Macmillan, 1984).

11. William Aydelotte, "Constituency Influence on the British House of Commons, 1841–1847," in *The History of Parliamentary Behavior*, ed. William Aydelotte (Princeton: Princeton University Press, 1977); Jorgen Rasmussen, "Is Parliament Revolting?" in *Dilemmas of Change in British Politics*, ed. Studlar and Waltman.

12. Philip Norton, *Dissension in the House of Commons, 1945–1974* (London: Macmillan, 1975); Philip Norton, *Dissension in the House of Commons, 1974–1979* (Oxford: Clarendon Press, 1980).

13. Richard Rose, "Still the Era of Party Government?" *Parliamentary Affairs* 26, no. 2 (1983):282–299.

14. Anthony King, "Modes of Executive-Legislative Relations: Great Britain, France, and West Germany," *Legislative Studies Quarterly* 1, no. 1 (1976):37–65.

15. Norton, *Dissension in the House of Commons, 1945–1974*; Norton, *Dissension in the House of Commons, 1974–1979.*

16. Rose, "Still the Era of Party Government?"

17. Mark Franklin and Philip Norton, eds., *Parliamentary Questions* (Oxford: Clarendon Press, 1993).

18. Gavin Drewry, ed., *The New Select Committees*, 2d ed. (Oxford: Clarendon Press, 1989); Michael Jogerst, *Reform in the Commons* (Lexington: University Press of Kentucky, 1992).

19. Donald D. Searing, "A Theory of Political Socialization," *British Journal of Political Science* 16, no. 3 (1986):341–376.

20. Martin Burch, "Prime Minister and Whitehall," in *Churchill to Major: The British Prime Ministership Since 1945*, ed. Donald Shell and Richard Hodder-Williams (London: Macmillan, 1995).

21. Richard Rose, *Politics in England*, 5th ed. (Boston: Little, Brown and Company, 1989).

22. Donald D. Searing, *Westminster's World* (Cambridge: Harvard University Press, 1994).

23. King, "Modes of Executive-Legislative Relations: Great Britain, France and West Germany."

24. R. M. Punnett, *British Government and Politics*, 5th ed. (Chicago: Dorsey Press, 1988).

25. Crossman, *The Myths of Cabinet Government*; Michael Foley, *The Rise of the British Presidency* (Manchester: Manchester University Press, 1993).

26. Shell and Hodder-Williams, *Churchill to Major: The British Prime Ministership Since 1945.*

27. Richard Rose, *Politics in England*, 5th ed.

28. R. M. Punnett, *Front-Bench Opposition* (New York: St. Martin's Press, 1973).

29. Brian Sedgemore, *The Secret Constitution* (London: Hodder and Stoughton, 1980).

30. Burch, "Prime Minister and Whitehall"; Colin Seymour-Ure, "Managing Media Relations: The Prime Minister and the Public," in *Churchill to Major: The British Prime Ministership Since 1945*, ed. Shell and Hodder-Williams.

31. Richard E. Neustadt, "Whitehouse and Whitehall," *Public Interest* 2, no. 1 (1966):55–69.

32. James B. Christoph, "Thatcher and Organizational Power" (paper presented at Midwest Political Science Association conference, Chicago, 1990).

33. Drewry, *The New Select Committees*; Keith Dowding, "Government at the Centre," in *Developments in British Politics 4*, ed. Patrick Dunleavy, Andrew Gamble, Ian Holliday, and Gillian Peele (New York: St. Martin's Press, 1993).

34. Vernon Bogdanor, *Devolution* (New York: Oxford University Press, 1979); Anthony H. Birch, *Political Integration and Disintegration in the British Isles* (Boston: Allen and Unwin, 1977); Tom Nairn, *The Breakup of Britain*, 2d ed. (London: New Left Books, 1981); Richard Rose, *The Territorial Dimension in Government* (Chatham, N.J.: Chatham House, 1982).

35. Tony Byrne, *Local Government in Britain*, 4th ed. (London: Penguin Books, 1988).

36. Douglas E. Ashford, "At the Pleasure of Parliament: The Politics of Local Reform in Britain," in *Dilemmas of Change in British Politics*, ed. Studlar and Waltman (London: Macmillan, 1984); *Implementing Thatcherite Policies*, ed. David Marsh and R.A.W. Rhodes (Buckingham: Open University Press, 1992).

37. L. J. Sharpe, "The Labor Party and the Geography of Inequality: A Puzzle," in *The Politics of the Labor Party*, ed. Dennis Kavanagh (London: Allen and Unwin, 1982).

38. Martin Loughlin, M. David Gelfand, and Ken Young, eds., *Half a Century of Municipal Decline, 1935–1985* (London: Allen and Unwin, 1985).

39. Rose, *The Territorial Dimension in Government*.

40. John Oakland, *British Civilization* (London: Routledge, 1989).

41. David Robertson, "Preserving Order and Administering Justice: Other Faces of Government in Britain," in *The Developing British Political System: The 1990s*, ed. Ian Budge and David McKay (New York: Longman, 1993).

42. Jerold L. Waltman, "Judicial Activism in England," in *Judicial Activism in Comparative Perspective*, ed. Kenneth M. Holland (New York: St. Martin's Press, 1991).

43. Anthony Sampson, *The Essential Anatomy of Britain* (New York: Harcourt Brace and Company, 1993).

4

POLITICAL FORCES: ORGANIZATIONS AND INDIVIDUALS

As NOTED IN CHAPTER 1, elitism and pluralism are two of the most prevalent theories that explain the distribution of power in society and how policy-making is carried out. A general review of mass and elite political behavior is needed before drawing conclusions about the applicability of these theories in later chapters. The behavioral perspective on politics can be contrasted with the institutional perspective offered in the previous chapter. Not all political activities are determined by the formal institutions of governing, especially in a system of constitutional flexibility such as Britain's. The study of political behavior involves examining informal interactions that are not captured in formal, constitutional descriptions of institutions and their implications. Some of this behavior occurs within and between institutions, some outside of the governing institutions. Matters usually considered under the concept of political behavior include non-governmental institutions such as political parties and interest groups, which influence the conduct of governmental affairs.

Elites and Masses

Although much of the study of political behavior involves mass politics, principally such topics as the study of elections and political cultures, elite political behavior merits attention as well.[1] Elites are defined simply as the few who hold major positions of political influence and power in a society. In that sense, an elite is an empirical concept. It is possible to say that every polity has an elite, without making any assumptions about the social or policy coherence of the elite.[2] It has been argued that elite political culture, that is, the values and attitudes of elites about how politics ought to work in a political system, has greater impact on the politics of a society than do the views of the usually more passive masses, even though there have been vastly more studies of masses than of elites.[3] The politics of elite-mass interactions involves such things as the study of representation and of how elites and masses view each other. In this chapter, I set forth general findings about both mass and elite political behavior in the United Kingdom in order to understand better the policy issues and decisions discussed later. I shall consider elite political behavior, including basic political values, the question of changing values (postmaterialism), elite socialization, and political recruitment to party, legislative, and political executive positions. Values, socialization, and, especially, electoral behavior will be considered for the masses. The more general question of how elites and masses interact in the political process will focus on the roles of political parties, elections, interest groups, and the mass media.

Elites: Values, Value Change, and Socialization

The values of British political elites vary considerably, although not always in expected ways. For instance, partisanship would be expected to be a major dividing line. Sometimes it is, but on matters ranging from what should be done about various social issues (capital punishment, immigration, abortion, homosexuality) to civil liberties[4] to preferred political style, there are both differences within partisan groupings and substantial differences between leaders and followers of the same partisanship.[5] Similarly, sometimes the views of political elites change with time and experience. For instance, Donald Searing has found that whatever partisan rhetoric indicates, almost all members of Parliament learn to support the fundamental parliamentary rules of the game.[6] This is obviously a pillar of support for the regime—a pillar largely attributable to the elite socialization of politicians as adults serving in that particular institution rather than being due to earlier experiences. After all, many members of the House of Commons, especially in the Labour party, made their initial reputations as leaders of extraparliamentary dissent movements and groups. What values, then, motivate elites, and how have these values changed?

How do elites acquire their values? Since the United Kingdom is a small island (actually parts of two islands) with similar educational practices throughout (abeit with significant local variations), one would expect this to be an impetus for shared values. Even more than most societies, however, elites in Britain share similar experiences, especially educational ones, from an early age. Since the educational system is stratified, with both significant private (fee-paying) and streamed public (state) wings, elites emerging from this system are likely to have a common background not only in class and educational status, but even in the school attended, whether it be a prominent private school such as Eton or Harrow or the same grammar school or sixth-form college (university preparatory school).

As noted in Chapter 2, a relatively small proportion of the eligible age population actually attends university, and, within even that restricted realm, Oxford and Cambridge have retained their prominence as educators of both members of Parliament and members of the cabinet, although somewhat more so on the Conservative side.[7] The "old school tie" is not a phrase without meaning even in the late twentieth century. Debates across the Speaker's Table in the House of Commons may, literally, be continuations of arguments among the same individuals that occurred years before in the Oxford Union or other academic settings. As Rose[8] has pointed out, most of the people receiving elite educations do not go into politics; thus the connection between educational background, as well as class and other relevant socioeconomic background indicators, is bound to be attenuated. Nevertheless, the fact that a large portion of the British political elite has been drawn not only from a restricted socioeconomic base but from an even narrower educational background has long been thought to be significant. But it may be more significant for basic political values than for issue opinions or partisanship.

What are the political values of the elite? In terms of their orientation to political institutions and practices, they are generally moderately reformist, believing strongly in the value of representative government through Parliament. They feel considerable pride in British political institutions and accomplishments and have no very pervasive wish to change the parliamentary form of government or other institutions in a fundamental way. Even in the wave of criticism of the monarchy over the tax issue and the activities of the royal heirs in the early 1990s, support for the monarchy as an institution remained high. There are few Republicans among even those members of the elite on the Left, and practically none on the Right. Although groups like Charter 88, with their explicit appeal for a written bill of rights in the United Kingdom, have some following, it is more remarkable that there is such limited support for even a bill of rights, much less a written constitution, among the British political elite. Tony Benn, an exception to many generalizations, is perceived as a left-wing extremist not only because of his policy positions but also because he persistently questions many of the accepted institutions of the regime, including the monarchy, the House of Lords, and the lack of a written constitution.[9]

Parliament is principally a "talking shop" about policy, and the socialization of the British political elite reinforces that tendency. British education and culture emphasizes verbal facility as an important attribute of social and political advancement.[10] Members of the broader elite who were interested in politics, often indicated by their readership of a "quality" as opposed to a "popular" newspaper (the *Guardian, Independent, Observer, Times, Telegraph* versus the *Mail, Sun, Express*), are often referred to as "the chattering classes." Again, questions have been raised about whether verbal facility is such a desirable trait in aspiring politicians, as opposed to, say, management skills or economic understanding. But from school through candidate selection procedures to the House of Commons, no matter whether an individual is in cabinet or opposition, front bench or backbench, major party or minor party, verbal skills are emphasized. The normal weapon against the government in Parliament is, after all, words, not the threat of defeat or procedural maneuvers.

Policy is another major dimension of British elite values. Politics should focus on policy, not constitutions, institutions (except administrative ones that are linked to policy), procedures, or legalities. In a system such as that of the United States, or to some degree that of France, political discussion often involves one or more of the other approaches to politics. Individual rights, institutional reform, using recondite procedures to gain one's ends, and the need to reinforce or amend the constitution are constant refrains. Examples include the term limits movement in the United States, the emphasis on civil liberties issues tied to the constitution there, and the constant consideration of changing the term of the president and the electoral system in France. Such discussions do not achieve the same prominence in Britain, although they have increased in importance in recent years.

Instead, political discussion usually centers on policy issues of broad interest to society, such as economics, even down to particular firms' performance and strikes, socieconomic matters emanating from the welfare state, and, usually in a nonpartisan mode, other social issues. Constitutional matters are avoided if possible, but if Parliament is forced to confront them, major conflict ensues, perhaps largely because the usual orienting mechanisms are absent. Issue avoidance is exemplified by the case of Northern Ireland. For almost fifty years the House of Commons had a rule forbidding discussion of Northern Ireland matters in the House because they were considered the realm of the devolved government set up at Stormont. Issue conflict was particularly pronounced in the case of Scottish and Welsh devolution, where the House of Commons, unusually, forced the government to accept terms for a referendum that led to the defeat of these issues and the downfall of the Labour government. Confident of their institutional basis and enjoying concentrated authority and responsibility in the cabinet, government ministers and their challengers focus on policy discussion and position taking. Thus aspiring politicians on the backbenches, and indeed outside Parliament, are also encouraged to define themselves by setting forth policy positions.

Bulpitt[11] has argued that the British political elite has an operational code, a long-term bias in elite political culture that is oriented toward certain issues as being "high politics" worthy of discussion in such arenas as Parliament, party meetings, the media, and the cabinet, whereas other issues are defined as "low politics," which are sloughed off when at all possible to local government, private members' bills and free votes, and routine administration. Included in high politics are matters of foreign policy, economics, and the welfare state. Low politics issues include many social issues as well as constitutional ones. Low politics issues manage to achieve a larger amount of attention from politicians when they arouse enough mass discontent, as race relations and immigration have sporadically done, or when they are joined with high politics issues, as in the community charge (poll tax) controversy. David Judge's[12] study of backbench opinion in the House of Commons has confirmed that even among this group "high politics" concerns dominate members' specialities.

Connected to the preference for policy discussion are certain other elite values, such as leadership, generalism, and collective welfare. The elite, many of whom are generalists themselves by education and work experience, value the well-rounded person who can deal with any issue. This quality is emphasized in those who manage to rise in the ranks of both the civil service and the parliamentary party. The lack of research personnel and facilities in Parliament, the failure to press for them, and the satisfaction with the current procedural mechanisms of the Commons, including Question Time and generalist committees to examine legislation, all point to the continuted premium put upon generalization. Party loyalty in Parliament, of course, means that there is less need for individual legislators to acquire expertise in order to examine legislation and to act as an opinion leader for other MPs.

Policy is usually debated in collective rather than particular terms. "Collective" means that not only a unified party position but also the interests of the country as a whole rather than a part of it are emphasized. The most famous formulation of this tendency was enunciated by Edmund Burke, who, in his Speech to the Electors of Bristol, not only extolled the value of the trustee role for a representative over that of an instructed delegate from his constituency but also argued that a representative should take a "national" viewpoint rather than a narrower group- or constituency-oriented one. These views are echoed in the contemporary values of members of Parliament,[13] although not among the public, which claims to want delegates as MPs.[14] Britain, of course, is a small country, with constituencies that are relatively small as well, averaging only slightly over fifty thousand voters per MP. Furthermore, British parliamentary recruitment practices encourage "carpetbagging," the selection as party parliamentary candidates of people who do not necessarily live in the constituency beforehand but instead have established a career elsewhere, often in a major city. Such practices further encourage a "national" viewpoint over a constituency, regional, or group perspective. The inability of legislators to change government budgets once the bill is presented to Parliament also limits how many particularistic, "distributive" benefits one can secure for the constituency or favored group.[15] Thus most interest groups prefer to operate through the executive rather than the legislative branch.

Obviously particularistic demands for group and constituency benefits still exist and are sometimes rewarded. Government projects are often built in the areas of party leaders, and in the 1960s and 1970s there was considerable emphasis put on regional development projects, moving jobs to where the people were rather than vice versa. One of the attempts to mollify discontent in Northern Ireland has been to build recreation and leisure facilities throughout the province. Nevertheless, the elite political culture in Britain is less likely to emphasize the benefits of government policy to particular groups than are the more locally minded elites of other countries, for instance, in France and the United States.

Connected to the collective and policy orientations is an elite proclivity for ideological discussion. Robert Putnam[16] has documented the fact that parliamentary elites tend to be ideological while also often recognizing the need for compromise. In Britain this is reflected by the twin phenomena of disputatious collective policy debate in Parliament and lack of organized voting opposition to government proposals.[17] In other words, the opposition parties may question the government's policies but often do not oppose them on final passage; this is not, obviously, because they have been amended to the oppostion's satisfaction. Instead, there is a willingness to lend legitimacy to government actions. When the intense debate over government laws on trade unions occurred in the early 1970s, there was concern about "adversary politics" and governments reversing their predecessor's laws.[18] Yet ideological opposition does not usually go this far. Nevertheless, the parties continue to discuss politics in ideological terms, especially in the broad socioeconomic sense of government interventions in the economy tied to class welfare.[19] Accompanying the idea of collective representation of national ideological positions is an elite disinclination to form coalition governments in the latter half of the twentieth century. In the first part of the century, in contrast, coalitions were common, as in both world wars and in the national government of 1929–1931.[20] As British politics became firmly two-party for the first twenty-five years after World War II, however, coalitions became both unnecessary and unpopular. The return of multiparty politics has not led to a similar revival of coalition inclinations, except among the smaller parties. Even the Lib-Lab pact of 1976–1979, which kept the Labour government in office after it had lost its majority in the House of Commons through by-elections, was limited to legislative matters, which meant that the Liberals did not share full responsibility for policy by joining in the cabinet. The lack of any party having a majority in 1974 threw all parties into confusion, and a similar prospect, not realized in 1992, was the occasion for much speculation about procedures.

The refusal to change the electoral system is often justified on the basis that coalitions would become the norm and responsibility for government policy to the electors would be blurred. The two big parties in Britain, including even a Labour party condemned to long-term opposition status in the 1980s and 1990s, have preferred to argue in terms of a direct line of responsibility from voters through the single-member district, simple plurality system to the House of Commons and the government. Collective policy concerns and ideological argumentation would also be blurred by a coalition arrangement. Chastened by its four consecutive electoral defeats, the Labour Party of the mid-1990s was contemplating the possibility of introducing a referendum on proportional representation if it ever achieved power again.

The final element of elite political values to be discussed is the concern for strong leadership, a value that is closely tied to those just considered. The leadership that is desired is collectively oriented as well as policy oriented. The struggle for political elite positions in Britain, whether it involves nominations for parliamentary candidacies, cabinet positions, or a party leadership, is couched in policy and collective terms rather than in personal ones. Personal attacks on one's opponents for their backgrounds and nonpolitical beliefs are rare. However spirited the contest for positions might be, once the candidate or leader is chosen, then the party unites behind that person, at least outwardly.

Leaders are, of course, questioned and sometimes deposed, as Mrs. Thatcher was in 1990. Parties do change direction, as Labour did in the early 1980s amid charges that the previous leadership had compromised the beliefs of party activists too often when it had governed the country in the 1970s. But these were leadership controversies tied to policy disputes. Perceived policy failure and electoral failure are the two criteria most likely to lead to leadership controversy and competition, and there is never a shortage of potential contenders for powerful positions. But strong leadership that is successful for the party and the country is a valued commodity in Britain. Leaders do not have to be responsive to public opinion. They can lead and expect both party followers and the general public to follow if their leadership is perceived to be firm and successful. That, along with a divided opposition, was the secret of Mrs. Thatcher's success. Polls show that she was never a beloved figure among the public, and her policy appeal even among the parliamentary party was always limited.[21]

Has there been significant value change among the elite? There has been a lot of discussion about value change in the masses[22] but very little about such changes in the political elite.[23] Yet elites, being more educated and generally more knowledgeable about what is going on in the world, are more likely to change their values faster than masses. Although the question of elite value change remains to be investigated in Britain, it is evident that recent elites have been steadfast in their opinions about the importance of such issues as the economy, social class, and the welfare state. Studies of elite attitudes indicate that, if anything, British elites think more in terms of the importance of social class in politics than do British masses.[24] Furthermore, there is no indication that Mrs. Thatcher's anticorporatist and proprivatization policies and rhetoric for over a decade have had any bearing on elite attitudes on these issues, even within her own party.[25]

Mass Values, Socialization, and Value Change

Much more is known about mass political values in Britain than about elite values. Britain was one of the five countries included in the pioneering study of political values conducted by Gabriel Almond and Sidney Verba,[26] and many studies have been done of mass political values, attitudes, and opinions. The availability of a continous series of British Election Studies from 1963 onward and the widespead use of social survey techniques in Britain has allowed analyses of changes in British values and opinions over time to be performed. If there is a dearth of material on changing elite values, there is an overwhelming amount of data amassed on examining the question of mass value change.

British mass values were originally lauded as having the right mixture of participant and subject orientations to qualify as what Almond and Verba called a "civic culture," one in which elites were allowed to govern with a minimum of mass input most of the time but one in which the citizenry did feel it could do something about injustices and in which there were channels available, principally through elections for representatives, for mass input. This was a prototypical conception of what critics called the "elitist theory of democracy" or "democratic elitism,"[27] in which the mass potential for participation, rather than their actual participation, was emphasized. Joseph Schumpeter[28] had earlier contended that the major function of elections, especially in the United Kingdom, was simply to offer a choice between competing teams of leaders.

Does Britain, then, still have a civic culture? On the one hand, there is a considerable amount of leeway given to political leaders, both in the flexibility of the British Constitution and in the desire for having "strong leaders"[29] who can protect and advance the interests of the country. On the other hand, there has been a considerable falling away of the electorate from the two major parties, Conservative and Labour, since 1970. Whereas the two major parties formerly garnered over 90 percent of the two-party vote, in recent elections they have gained between 70 and 80 percent of the vote, with the rest going to the Liberals and their Social Democratic cohorts in the short-lived alliance and to nationalist groups of various vintages in Scotland, Wales, and Northern Ireland. But does this weakening of the two-party hold on the electorate betoken a shift of mass values, or does it merely reflect popular disappointment with the two major parties' policy achievements in office?

Evidence points to the latter interpretation. In the many studies of value change in postindustrial societies, Britain often appears to be an exceptional case; mass political values appear to have changed less than in many other advanced industrial democracies.[30] There is also less generational change occurring in Britain, and such change is usually associated with a growing preference for "postmaterialist" values like environmental consciousness, minority rights, and expanding civil liberties.[31] Furthermore, studies of British public opinion over time have indicated surprisingly little change in basic political attitudes, despite the rise to power of Thatcherite Conservatism.[32]

Nevertheless, partisan forms of mass participation have declined, as evidenced by declining membership figures for political parties, and direct action forms of participation have increased, often organized around particular issues.[33] Political participation beyond voting is still the province of only a small group of people.[34]

In general, British mass opinion is moderate rather than extremist.[35] Nationalization has not been a popular policy since the 1960s, and privatization, while supported, did not win large popular accolades in the 1980s either. The trade unions were under suspicion long before the Conservative governments of the

1980s made legislative inroads on their power.[36] The welfare state is supported, as Rose[37] has indicated, with "two cheers." On other social issues, public opinion is often more conservative than leadership opinion.[38] In the realm of political institutions as well, mass opinion tends to support the status quo, though not entirely uncritically. There is a willingness to try electoral reform, for instance, and qualified support for the monarchy.[39] But like the political elite, the mass public tends to think in terms of policy goals and changes rather than institutional reform. Unlike the elite, however, the masses do not tend to think in ideological terms of large numbers of connected issues.[40]

The major political socialization agents in Britain are the familiar ones of family, school, religion, peers, and mass media. Religion has declined as a socialization mechanism, and so, too, has social class. Even family political socialization, once thought to be powerful, has been shown to be of limited influence, largely because of the lack of communication of political values from parent to child.[41] Peer socialization is difficult to measure. Despite much effort expended on investigating the impact of the mass media, generalizations are difficult to make. There is a plethora of media sources in Britain, and to a degree they each speak to self-selected audiences. Citizens can choose to ignore the political content of media or choose their media because they like its political content.

Political socialization research has fallen into disfavor in recent years as its assumptions of long-term carryover effects have been questioned. As Richard Rose and Ian McAllister[42] have pointed out, the major partisan, electoral, and policy disruptions of British politics in the past twenty-five years have occured without a demonstrable major change in the socialization experiences of the mass public. The implications of particular generational experiences for mass political behavior are often difficult to trace. The premier examination of generational attitudinal differences in British politics predicted that Labour was about to move into an electorally dominant position—just at the point at which its support went into a twenty-five year tailspin.[43] Thus the importance of particular socialization processes for adult political values and behavior remains questionable.

Mass Media as Linkage Mechanisms

The role of mass media in affecting both elite and mass political behavior in Britain is a subject of considerable controversy. Unlike the United States, where conservative commentators have made an issue of the media's alleged eastern liberal bias and orientation toward the trendy, in Britain it is the Left that has complained about the rightward tilt of major media, especially the newspapers. In order to understand their contentions, one must understand that print, broadcast, and telecast media in Britain are all organized on a countrywide basis, although there are a few minor regional variations in programming. Until the rise of cable, which as of now penetrates into relatively few British households, television was exclusively the province of four channels, two private and two public. A fifth channel is being planned.

The public stations, BBC-1 and BBC-2, are operated by public authorities that are separate from the government. Parliament sets the ground rules governing operation of the BBC, and the government appoints members of the Board of Governors, supposedly with a view toward the partisan balance of the body. Normally the corporation does not take orders from the government as to what programs to show or points of view to espouse, but increasingly the relationship between the government and the BBC has become contentious. There were a few incidents in recent years in which the Conservative government objected to BBC programs, especially on Northern Ireland, and in extreme instances the government even prevented their being shown on security grounds. The major revenue support for the BBC is through the licensing fee that every television owner must pay; noncompliers are subject to detection and fine by the "television police," who travel through residential neighborhoods monitoring signals with electronic devices. The British Broadcasting Corporation has always considered itself to be governed by its own understanding of what is good for the public to see and hear rather than by responding to mass popularity alone. Nevertheless, BBC-1 presents mainly mass-appeal programs, as does Independent Television (ITV), on the commercial side. BBC-2 and Channel Four (the second commercial outlet) favor more highbrow, what the British call "minority," programming (meaning for minority tastes, not necessarily for ethnic or racial minorities). Channel Four has achieved a particularly prominent position in recent years as a coproducer of British films for the international market, many of them with political themes although not always obvious ones.[44]

Aside from the commercials on the private channels, there is not a lot of observable difference between the presentations of public and private television programs in Britain. The government awards franchises to private companies that control private telecasting in different areas of the country, subject to competitive tender and the meeting of certain standards for religious and children's programming. Despite these similarities, the introduction of commercial television into Britain in the mid-1950s caused a famous political battle, pitting the interests of middle-class entrepreneurs against those with traditional views, who, encouraged by the BBC, advocated "good taste" and giving the masses what was supposedly beneficial for them rather than what they might want.[45] The controversy over commercial television split the ranks of the Conservative party in the House of Commons. In practice, however, the two types of television production and presentation have converged. If that convergence is less than what the purveyors of good taste and human improvement might hope for, it is still substantially more varied and instructional than the usual offerings on television in the United States, including cable. Huge audiences for mindless, repetitive entertainment and sporting events are not the sole goal. BBC News, including its overseas service, has a particularly strong reputation for fairness and good international reporting.

Radio has tended to follow similar trends as television, with tight government control over the medium as a monopoly giving way to greater variety of ownership patterns. Some of the BBC outlets are still more oriented toward traditional radio programming, for example, offering narrative fiction and information. Although a Royal Commission in the mid-1980s argued for increased privatization of television, and cable and other fiber-optic alternatives present challenges, thus far the traditional practices of television have prevailed. It will be difficult for the joint BBC-ITV oligopoly to hold, however, in the face of the growth of alternative sources of rapid information. Further commercializaion of television is expected in the 1990s.[46]

The major controversy about politically biased news, however, concerns British newspapers. Britons are avid news readers, and the geography and transportation patterns of the island allow for the existence of "national" newspapers, printed in London and distributed countrywide on a daily basis either in the morning or afternoon, although predominantly the former. Local newspapers are usually delivered in the afternoon. The London press, therefore, dominates both the mass and elite news readership, although less so in such areas as Scotland and Northern Ireland.

As in many other things British, however, the papers can be divided into those aiming for a popular, heavily working-class readership and those aimed at the middle class and above, a more educated audience. The popular papers are all in tabloid form, include short stories, and feature entertainment and gossip rather than hard news, especially neglecting background news on current problems. These are the biggest circulation papers, including the *Sun, Daily Mirror, Daily Mail, Daily Express, Daily Star,* and *Today.* They sell from .5 to 3.6 million copies per day, mainly to those on the lower end of the social-class scale.[47] There are also five Sunday popular papers, ranging in sales from 1.7 million to 4.7 million. All of these papers except the *Daily Mirror* and its Sunday counterpart have recently supported the Conservative party at election time, however critical they might be of the party between elections.

The so-called quality papers (or broadsheets) feature heavier doses of international news, broader domestic coverage, and less entertainment and gossip. These include the *Times, Daily Telegraph, Guardian, Independent, Financial Times,* and their Sunday counterparts, particularly the *Observer.* These papers have a substantially lower circulation, individually and collectively, than the popular papers (ranging from 300,000 to 1 million daily, with similar figures for Sunday) and appeal more to an upper- and middle-class readership.[48] Overall, they maintain a more balanced political perspective even though pro-Conservative sentiments dominate in this sector, too. There are also a wide variety of magazines for more specialized tastes, including political ones. The *Economist* is a world-famous newsweekly, which prefers to call itself a newspaper and is much admired for its coverage of world issues and its wit. Although it generally favors Conservative interests, it sits more on the left socially than economically. The *New Statesman and Society* is an amalgam of two older publications, both left-leaning. The *New Statesman* was a crusading journal of opinion; *New Society* was more academic and empirical in orientation, concentrating on social policy, broadly considered.

In general, British newspapers are much more explicitly value-laden than their counterparts in the United States. Their political values suffuse the treatment of news stories as well as editorials (or what the British call "leaders"). After World War II the political positions of the major papers were more balanced than in recent years. In the 1980s, newspaper ownership became concentrated in the hands of a few, mostly Conservative, owners, most famously Rupert Murdoch, the Australian-born tycoon. Although there continues to be academic controversy over whether newspapers shape the partisan views of their readers,[49] the one agreed finding on media effects is that they do shape the political agenda, especially for the masses, by focusing on particular political issues.[50] Thus some on the political left in Britain argue that issues and positions favorable to their interests are systematically underreported by the Conservative newspaper barons. This charge raises a host of questions, including ones on the relationship between ownership and editorial control, the values of reporters, and what media sources voters consume.

Despite the sensationalism of much of the popular press, the British media actually operate under both stringent laws and restrictive news reporting practices. Libel and slander laws are more broadly applicable in Britain than in the United States, where almost anything can be printed about a famous person without having to prove it in a court of law. In Britain, people often do sue the media, especially print media, for libel, and even the threat of such suits can have a chilling effect on what is printed. British academics have even been known to threaten each other with libel for what is printed, or about to be printed, in academic journals! The satirical weekly *Private Eye* has particularly suffered from the awarding of large amounts of money to those who have brought it to court. On the one hand, although the law on libel may serve to improve the accuracy of British journalism, it also acts to discourage investigative reporting and informed speculation about politics. On the other hand, it also protects the rights of defendants in criminal trials. The sensationalist reporting of crimes of violence that are before the courts in the United States are unknown in the United Kingdom, thus providing protection for the accused against "trial by press."

In addition to the libel and slander laws, British media must also cope with other restrictive laws and practices emanating from the government. As noted earlier, executive government is secret government in Britain. Early in the century, the D-notice system was developed to protect government information against exploitation by hostile powers. Essentially this system means that the press must not print information that the government declares is part of its defense preparations, however remote the connection may seem to be. The Official Secrets Act allows prosecution of offenders. Despite much criticism of this act and the fact that some violators have managed to circumvent it, the law still stands as a deterrent to those who leak and those who print government information.

Perhaps the practice that most restricts the British press, however, is not based in law. This is the use of the "lobby," whereby government officials give off-the-record briefings to selected correspondents. These not-for-attribution sessions can be used to float trial balloons, damage the reputations or positions of adversaries, and generally provide information without the responsibility for backing it up. Correspondents are loath to give up this practice, however, because it gives them entry to official sources.

Coverage of political campaigns in Britain differs considerably, according to type of media. Television is most closely controlled. No political advertising is permitted, not even on the commercial stations. Instead, the two traditional major parties, Conservative and Labour, are allocated an equal amount of television time in five broadcasts, with times chosen by the television channels, to present their own messages, sometimes on all four countrywide channels simultaneously. As their popularity has risen, the Liberal Democrats have been allotted four broadcasts rather than three. In general, the party broadcasts have become slicker and more professional over the years, moving from static presentations of the talking heads of party leaders to more sophisticated encomiums about the prime ministerial candidates. Controversial presentations sometimes raise issues in the campaign, such as the charges made about the girl having to wait for an ear operation from the National Health Service in 1992, an event dubbed "the war of Jennifer's ear". A similar pattern of equality and neutrality is maintained for radio. Television and radio outlets are supposed to maintain balance in their news coverage of the campaigns as well, which, despite some grousing from politicians, they are generally recognized as doing.

Newspapers, however, are another matter. As previously noted, British papers may favor one party, not only in their editorial columns but also in their news stories. Some of the tabloids have even claimed to be responsible for electoral victories by the Conservative Party. Although individual candidates are limited by law in their spending for elections, the central party organizations are not so restricted. This works primarily to the advantage of the Conservative Party and secondarily to the Labour Party, since each party is buoyed by large amounts of outside contributions, from business and trade unions, respectively. The Liberal Democrats have to depend on individual contributions, as do the minor parties. Both the parties and other groups interested in the outcome of the election can take out advertisements in the press, and the parties provide many other campaign publications as well. The relatively short electoral campaign, however, limits the amount of spending.

Election campaigns have traditionally been concerned with issues. More recently, however, they have become more like campaigns in the United States, emphasizing personalities of the leaders, smoothly staged rallies and television productions, and the horse-race aspects of the campaign. The latter has led public opinion polls to assume a larger role in the campaign. More of them are done with every election, and many newspaper front-page stories during the campaign feature poll results. This "saturation polling" shows no sign of abating, despite the embarrassment the polls received in 1992 when their predictions of the outcome proved to be seriously wrong.[51] Despite this fiasco, British polls have a good record in predicting electoral outcomes, at least when they are taken near the date of the election.[52] Some people have even contended that polls influence how people vote, but the evidence for this is tenuous at best.[53] Even if the publication of poll results were banned for part or all of the campaign, as is done in some countries, political parties would still make use of private polls.[54] The media, then, serve as both a major agent of political socialization and an intermediary institution in the political process. The media serve the double function of presenting information for mass and elite consumption and attempting to instruct both masss and elite audiences about how to interpret that information. The search for demonstrable media effects, however, has proven to be a difficult and controversial one. Many people choose their source of media, especially their newspaper, because they already agree with its political positions, which limits the number of people who could potentially have their political choices affected by the media. This assumes, of course, that politics is even an issue at all in media selection. As noted earlier, the principal role of the media is in agenda setting. Even here, however, in order to make a significant impression, a considerable amount of repetition is necessary. On topics unfamiliar to members of the political elite, such as Northern Ireland for British MPs, the media are important sources of information.[55] In general, though, increasing education and the growth of alternative sources of information through international networks have probably decreased the power of the domestic British media to influence even the agendas of either the political elite or the masses. Nevertheless, in a country of media consumers, the potential power of the media remains important.

Interest Groups as Linkage Mechanisms

The role of interest groups as linkage mechanisms in the British polity has also been much disputed. Some observers, unable to find interest groups soliciting favor with legislators as in the United States, suggested in the 1950s that interest groups had less influence in the United Kingdom. Supposedly the uniform party platforms and collective discipline of MPs gave little scope for interest-group influence, compared with the less centralized party operations and greater flexibility for the legislature in the United States. However, Samuel Finer, in *Anonymous Empire*,[56] discovered a large amount of interest-group activity, but much of it was focused on relations with the executive rather than the legislature. Since the formation of policy in the British executive is less subject to outside observation than is the legislature, it is easy to underestimate interest-group strength. Furthermore, interest groups may be used by the government to gather information and to generate consent for policies as well as to petition the government for changes in proposed or extant policies.

In fact, some interest groups in Britain have always had a preferential status with the government. Producer groups such as business, finance, and labor unions have often been consulted as a matter of course on legislation and regulations that apply to them. These consulations have sometimes been formalized by the advisory committees to government departments. Undoubtedly one of the most famous of these was the National Economic Development Council (NEDC), which existed for almost thirty years starting in the early 1960s.[57] The NEDC was a product of much more ambitious plans for economic planning and development, at the time shared by both the Harold Macmillan Conservative government and the opposition Labour Party; the NEDC evolved as a place for business and labor to meet with government officials on economic policy.

Not coincidentally, it was at about this time that explanations of interest-group influence in terms the theory of corporatism, with variants called neocorporatism and liberal corporatism, began to be heard. More traditional explanations of interest-group influence in representative democracies emphasized pluralism, the activity of many different groups competing for power and having variable influence on policy outcomes, depending on the issue. But under neocorporatism, even in a representative democracy, some interest groups were privileged in influence by their size, organization, and, above all, role in the economy. Thus in neocorporatism, some interest groups, especially material interest types such as big business and big labor, were partners with government in decisionmaking. Unlike traditional fascist-style corporatism, this did not mean that government could necessarily coordinate other interests as it liked. Even though the relationship was more evenhanded, it provided for only a very limited form of democracy. On the crucial issues, it was the big battalions that counted, despite whatever other interests might be saying.[58]

Theoretically, corporatism never claimed to fully account for every policy in British government, only for the major ones. Traditionally, interest groups (or lobbies, as they are often called in Britain) are divided into material and ideal interests.[59] Material interests have members with a perceived economic stake in the issues they pursue. Ideal interests, whose members, for the most part, do not have a material interest in the policy they are pursuing, instead, join the group to advocate their particular values, which they want to see endorsed by the state. Abortion, capital punishment, and environmental concerns are issues that attract people largely on a value basis rather than because they will benefit financially from the adoption of certain policies. Other interest groups, such as those advocating equality of treatment for women or homosexuals, are more difficult to classify but are probably closer to the ideal category because, in order to succeed, they need to win the sympathies of many who are not in a position to benefit materially from the adoption of such policies.

Interest groups obviously differ in many ways—in number of members, financial resources, organization, leadership, and access to policymakers, among others. Just as many texts on British public policy overlook policy on value issues decided by free votes in the House of Commons, so too have interest-group analysts tended to denigrate the power of ideal interest groups in favor of the larger, more numerous, more evident material interest groups, especially business, financial, and labor interests.

Indeed, authors of several of the most influential analyses of postwar British politics argued that, for better or worse, corporatism was the order of the day.[60] In their view, functional representation through groups had replaced representation through geographical constituencies and the House of Commons acting as the major avenue for the population to influence government. After all, interest groups were a form of concentrated public opinion. In an era of class politics, producer groups obviously had influence through the parties. But parties of whichever stripe also needed the cooperation of large interest groups in order to realize their goals, particularly the overriding goal of the postwar period, economic growth and prosperity. Thus partisan representation was supplemented by representation through advisory committees and other forms of consultation of the affected interests. Britain was thus placed in the neocorporatist mold. Big government required big interests to work with it, for their mutual benefit.

So powerful was this idea that it even came to be part of the conventional political wisdom. The Labour Party needed the confidence of business and finance in order to govern without excessive strains on the economy, such as a run on the pound sterling requiring either devaluation or the expenditure of resources in sterling's defense. The Conservatives were more assured of the cooperation of business and finance but needed to mollify the trade unions sufficiently to keep the economy running smoothly. What happened when corporatism did not work well was exemplified by the furor over the Labour government's introduction of the Trade Disputes Act in the late 1960s and the difficulties the Conservative government experienced over implementing its Industrial Relations Act in the early 1970s. Internal divisions in the Labour Party led to the withdrawal of the first bill, and conflict with the trade unions over the second led to the calling of the February 1974 general election, in which the goverment was not returned. Thus this question arose in the 1970s: Is Britain ungovernable? Many people saw the trade unions as more powerful than the government, be it Conservative or Labour. According to no less an authority than Mrs. Thatcher, corporatism was at the root of Britain's problems, and she claimed to set the face of her governments of the 1980s firmly against it. Corporatism had made the government too manipulable by organized interests, particularly those of the trade unions. Rather than responding to the brace of stiff competition, both business and labor had grown soft and uncompetitive by counting on the government to bail them out through subsidies and wage concessions when they made mistakes. Mrs. Thatcher's mission, stated many times, was to rid Britain of corporatist tendencies.

After Mrs. Thatcher had eliminated the National Economic Development Council, tamed the trade unions through legislation limiting their political activities, and relentlessly eliminated weak manufacturing firms, she claimed to have made major strides in eliminating corporatism from British public life. The threat still existed, however, since one of the charges against her presumptive successor as Conservative Party leader, Michael Heseltine, was that he was a "corporatist."

Nevertheless, some observers have questioned whether corporatism ever really existed in the United Kingdom. Corporatist designs there may have been, but corporatism requires much more than just attempts at consultation with major producer interests on issue after issue. It requires organized interests with strong central leadership able to make deals on behalf of their members with the government—and make them stick. Careful comparative examinations of the corporatist phenomenon have found the United Kingdom wanting in these respects, and, on a continuum of the phenomenon, have rated Britain as no more than "weakly corporatist."[61] If Britain was only weakly corporatist at best, then it is more understandable that Mrs. Thatcher and the Conservative governments could do what was thought impossible in the 1970s, namely govern the country without the consent of the trade union leadership.

Neither business nor the trade unions had the necessary organization and leadership to exercise strong corporatism. Business leadership was fragmented, and the Confederation of British Industry, the major organization, could not speak on behalf of a united membership. Indeed, after the losses inflicted on manufacturers by the tight monetary policies of the early Thatcher years, Mrs. Thatcher began to rely on a separate business organization, the Institute of Directors, for whatever policy advice she wanted from that sector of the economy.[62]

Similarly, the financial sector has always presented problems for the corporatist thesis. In the first place, the financial sector (or "the City," in British parlance, meaning the financial district in the London borough of the Cities of London and Westminster), has often been cited as a separate interest, one whose preference for foreign over domestic investment has been associated with Britain's loss of international economic competitiveness and inclination to defend the value of the pound sterling (and thus overseas investment values) even when this led to distortions of economic policy. But even the City may not have enough unity of purpose to be able to be a proper corporatist partner. Who is the spokesperson for the City? Indeed, one of the complaints of opposition parties is that the Bank of England is too dependent on political control of financial policy, unlike such independent central banks as the German Bundesbank and the United States Federal Reserve. Financial corporatist interests in British policymaking are undoubtedly important, but their independent influence is hard to assess.

The famous corporatist interest in Britain, however, and the one that constitutes the linchpin on which any theory of corporatism must be built, is the trade unions. Their collective influence over postwar Labour and Conservative governments, at least until the advent of Mrs. Thatcher, has rarely been doubted. But even in this case it is hard to discern anything other than weak corporatism. Even though the Trades Union Congress (TUC) exists as a coordinating body and union membership in the United Kingdom by the late 1970s numbered over one-half of the employed population, the TUC had no capacity to compel its member unions to obey its policy stands. Indeed, the autonomy of individual unions is a closely guarded prerogative, and union solidarity has always had to be manufactured under particular circumstances rather than being assumed to hold. Similarly, the ties that the trade unions as organizations have to the Labour Party, including large financial contributions, their guaranteed places on the National Executive Committee (NEC) of the party, block votes at party conferences, one-third of the votes for party leader, and, until 1993, automatic voting rights in the selection of parliamentary candidates at the constituency level, have not made them a neocorporate actor because of conflicting aims among trade unions. Indeed, it is common to speak of right-wing unions, usually those that back the status quo and the Labour leadership, and left-wing unions, which advocate change, usually involving confrontation of business or government, or both, through industrial action (strikes) and extraparliamentary demonstrations. Although at times in the 1970s and early 1980s it appeared that the left-wing unions were gaining the upper hand over traditional union cooperation with the Labour leadership, widespread unemployment and the laws restricting union political activities, such as secondary strikes and the calling of strikes without consulting the membership in a formal ballot, have seemingly quelled some of the more radical unions. Even the advent of a Labour government would probably not result in a major change in this regard.

If in the 1970s it sometimes seemed that the trade unions had more power than the government, that was a function of the weakness of purpose of the governments themselves and the increasing fragmentation of the electorate. In a period of inflation brought on by the Arab oil embargo against Western countries for supporting Israel in the 1973 Middle East War (before Britain's own North Sea oil resources came on stream), trade unions, especially those involved with energy production and transportation, were able to bend government to their will, aided by the lack of strong single-party majority governments from 1974 to 1979. But the fact remains that most unions in Britain have fundamentally been conservative (but not Conservative) in their views, attempting to preserve the old structure of heavy industry, with their eyes firmly fixed on long-standing class resentments about exploitation by owners. Unions have spread into white-collar sections of the economy to a much greater extent than in many countries. Even in the early 1990s, Britain had 37 percent of its working population unionized, versus 18 percent in the United States. Nevertheless, the union leadership was slow to grasp the implications of deindustrialization and an increasing tertiary, or service, sector of the economy. The result was temporary triumph but a long-term decline in influence, as electoral dealignment, a shrinking working class, and a government committed to controlling trade union behavior spent over a decade in office.

Nowhere is this more evident than in the reduced status of the National Union of Mineworkers (NUM), considered the most powerful of unions for its role in bringing down the Heath government and imposing huge losses on the economy by its strike in the winter of 1973–1974. But twenty years later, the NUM was a shadow of its former self. Even in 1973, the number of miners in the NUM had shrunk from 695,000 in 1955 to 250,000. With the onset in production of North Sea oil, which realized its first output in 1975, the production of coal became a less important source of energy in Britain.[63] Mrs. Thatcher backed down from a confrontation with the NUM in 1981, but by 1984–1985, backed by a large reserve supply of coal stocks, she refused to concede to the strike action of the NUM. By 1992–1993, there was the prospect, at first resisted by even Conservative MPs but later largely acquiesced to, of reducing the number of deep-pit coal mines run by British Coal from fifty to nineteen. The workforce had already shrunk to less than 50,000 miners by 1993. Thus the 1973–1974 work stoppage, far from being the harbinger of increased union power, marked its zenith, to be followed by sharp decline. Privatization of energy, utilities, and transportation sectors under recent Conservative governments have also shifted the onus for bargaining to the private sector.

"Free collective bargaining," which meant the right of trade unions to act unrestricted by law, has become passé. So, too has the much-vaunted "social contract" of the 1970s, whereby the unions agreed to bargain responsibly and hold wage demands down in return for the government controlling inflation and maintaining the "social wage," that is, the level of welfare state benefits available to the unemployed, disabled, and others disadvantaged by the economy. Union overreaching at the time of the 1978–1979 Winter of Discontent when the country suffered from prolonged and disruptive strikes in several different sectors, ended the notion of a social contract. This not only helped defeat the sitting Labour government in 1979 but also may have had a long-term deleterious effect on Labour's prospects. In subsequent elections, the Conservatives have used the Winter of Discontent as an alarm to warn against the return of a Labour government. Even though much of the current electorate was not of voting age at the time, the symbol of a social contract that did not work still has some significance. Thus it may be that the political influence of the trade unions in earlier years left them less capable of adjusting to the economic situation of the late twentieth century.

There is no doubt that interest groups remain important intermediary institutions in the United Kingdom. In fact, there have been an increasing number of interest groups employing "political consultants," or, lobbyists, over the past decade. But even the most powerful material interest groups, which include not only those mentioned above but also quieter organizations such as those representing agricultural interests,[64] have to excercise influence mainly through representation to an executive that has its own interests, commitments, and, most important, usually a voting majority in the House of Commons. Of increasing importance, however, are interests such as environmental interest groups, which are linked to international concerns, either through the European Community or through the globalization of problems. It may soon be impossible to determine which groups are principally British and which are part of a worldwide network, especially in the case of those representing international business and financial concerns. Karl Marx had it wrong; it has been business and finance that have realized their international common interests much more than workers have.

Ideal interest groups have a more difficult time exercising influence. If ideologically based, they are dependent on having a government of their particular persuasion in power, and even then, the executive may only adopt their positions very broadly, if at all. More specific issue-oriented ideal interest groups often have to work through Parliament rather than the executive, a considerable handicap since the government controls most of parliamentary time as well as the parliamentary agenda. If an interest group can secure cross-party support among MPs and have a sponsor who manages to secure a high place in the competition for private members' bills, it still needs a government willing to allow sufficient time for the bill to be debated before it has a chance to get legislation passed. Although the barriers are formidable, at times they have been surmounted, as in the cases of social welfare policies benefiting particular groups of handicapped people and, as is shown in Chapter 8, some social regulatory policies. Despite the hurdles for cause groups, they have multiplied in recent years as interest-group activity in Britain has become more detached from a partisan base. Much of their activity consists of extraparliamentary action such as marches and other forms of demonstration, which reached a crescendo over the poll tax in 1989 and 1990.

Considering the sheer number of active groups, the interest group constellation in contemporary Britain most closely resembles pluralism. This does not mean, however, that groups are equal or nearly equal in influencing policy. Interest groups may be important actors in general, whether one subscribes to either the pluralist or elitist arguments, but their power is circumscribed by the nature of the issue at hand, the power of the state, the willingness of governments to impose their own views, and, increasingly, international economic circumstances.

Political Parties as Linkage Mechanisms

Of the various institutions that link mass and elite, political parties are perhaps the most important. In order for political parties to be effective as linkage mechanisms, they must share enough of the values of the mass public to be able to persuade them that the party would be capable of governing in ways the public would find congenial. Although Britain is often thought of as a prototypical two-party system, in fact it has usually had more than two parties electing candidates to the House of Commons, especially from the Celtic fringe areas of Northern Ireland, Scotland, and Wales. The mainland British parties have never made much of an electoral impact in Northern Ireland, where several parties, most of them representing either the Catholic or Protestant sections of the community alone, get almost all of the vote.

But even in England itself, there have been substantial periods in which there was three-party, rather than two-party competition, at least at the electoral level. The single-member district, simple plurality electoral system, however, punishes parties unless they can concentrate their votes sufficiently to finish first in enough constituencies to secure a beachhead in the House of Commons. Thus, ironically, third parties with a broad appeal find it more difficult to get seats in the House of Commons than those with a narrower, regional appeal. In the two elections of 1983 and 1987, for instance, the Alliance of Liberals and Social Democrats received about 25 percent of the popular vote but less than 4 percent of the seats in the House of Commons, whereas the nationalist parties of the Celtic lands received 4 percent of the vote countrywide and yet also secured 3 percent of the seats (see Table 4.1).

Despite an electoral system that encourages but does not guarantee two-party dominance, the identity of the two major British parties has changed over the years. In the nineteenth and early twentieth centuries the two major competitors were the Liberals and the Conservatives. In fact, in the early twentieth century the Liberals were the dominant party.[65] But the enfranchisement of the working class and burgeoning expression of political grievances of a deprived class had already led to the nascent Labour Party winning some seats. The discouragement and suffering of World War I, party splits among the Liberals, and the increasing perception of Labour as a legitimate alternative led, in the 1920s, to Labour replacing the Liberals as the major alternative to the Conservatives on the left.[66] By 1924, Labour formed its first government, a minority one that did not last long.

TABLE 4.1   Election Results in Britain, 1974--1992

	February 1974		October 1974		1979		1983		1987		1992	
	% Votes	% Seats	% Votes	% Seats	% Votes	% Seats	% Votes	% Seats	% Votes	% Seats	% Votes	% Seats
Conservative	37.9	46.8	35.8	43.6	43.9	53.4	42.4	61.1	42.3	57.8	41.9	51.6
Labor	37.1	47.4	39.2	50.2	36.9	42.4	27.6	32.1	30.8	35.2	34.4	41.6
Liberal	19.3	2.2	18.3	2.0	13.8	1.7	25.4	3.5	22.6	3.4	17.5	3.1
Others	5.7	3.6	6.7	4.1	4.4	2.5	4.6	3.2	4.3 ·	3.6	5.9	3.7
Seats	635		635		635		650		650		650	
Turnout	78.7%		72.8%		76.0%		72.7%		75.3%		77.7%	

Source: *Times Guide to the House of Commons,* various years

But the Liberals did not completely disappear, either from the electorate or from the House of Commons. Beginning with strong by-election (special election) showings in the late 1950s, they began to make a comeback. As both major parties proved themselves incapable of meeting all of the expectations they had raised about increasing economic prosperity and a "white-hot technological revolution" in the 1960s, the Liberals began to attract more support as an alternative to voter-perceived performance failures by the other parties. Better financial support allowed the party to field more candidates. In the February election of 1974, called by the Conservative government in the wake of the miners' strike on the issue of "who rules Britain?" the Liberals surged to 18 percent of the vote, and as the "third force" with a Liberal base, whatever their name (Alliance, Liberal Democrats), they have not fallen below 14 percent in the five elections since then.

The Liberals were boosted in the early 1980s by internal turmoil in the Labour Party. Leftist groups within the Labour Party blamed the party leadership for not implementing a true Socialist program when in government in the 1970s, which led to the defection of four former Labour cabinet ministers. In turn, those ex-ministers became the leaders of the new Social Democratic Party, a party that had a program similar enough to the Liberals' program to form an electoral Alliance, that is, an agreement between them to run only one candidate per district. Even this could not get them over the third-party electoral barrier, but they came close in the two elections of 1983 and 1987. After the election of 1987, the Alliance fragmented, but from the ruins of the Liberals and Social Democrats arose the newly named Liberal Democrats, who took most of the members and supporters of the two former parties.

Labour has been in a difficult position for some time. The last time it received over 40 percent of the vote was in the election of 1970, which it lost. The decline of the manufacturing sector in the United Kingdom has meant that Labour's industrial working-class base has shrunk. Even more worrisome, it has also lost many of the votes it used to receive from citizens who remain in the working class. The economic problems of Labour governments in the 1960s and 1970s, along with internal left-right conflict within the party, convinced many voters that Labour was incapable of governing effectively.[67] By the early 1990s, Labour appeared to have beaten off the Liberal Democratic threat to its position as the major party of the Left, but it had not yet recovered a sufficient share of the electorate to be able to dislodge even a vulnerable Conservative government and campaign in the general election of 1992. But if the Conservatives were able to rule since 1979 more because of a split opposition rather than their own policy successes, then Labour might also be able to benefit from continued Conservative problems and eventually regain power.

Despite the rise of Labour as a major challenger to the Conservatives and the great potential that a large industrial working class offered as an electoral base for such a party, governments dominated in whole or in large part by Conservatives have ruled Britain for well over one-half of the twentieth century. In general, the

Conservative Party has been pragmatic and adaptable, willing to jettison its former ideological positions if they proved to be unpopular or unworkable. Thus Conservative reluctance to intervene in the economy, rearm adequately in the face of the rise of fascism, embrace the welfare state, initiate decolonization, and enter the European Community was replaced when it became untenable. Despite ideological spasms, leadership quarrels, and periods of governmental ineffectiveness, the overriding aim of the Conservative Party has been to win office. When crises arise in the party, the pragmatic, office-seeking tendency usually wins out, in the long run if not in the short run. No substantial group of MPs has split from the Conservatives in the twentieth century, which reaffirms the view that the Conservative Party is made up of political tendencies, not more cohesive factions.[68]

In contrast, other parties are more faction ridden. As already noted, the Liberals fell from power at least partially because leadership and issue controversies stemming from World War I became too intense for them to remain a unified party. More recently, part of the Social Democratic Party refused to amalgamate with the Liberals in the new Liberal Democratic Party. Similarly, factional fighting between left and right wings has periodically plagued Labour, including the late 1950s–early 1960s conflict over whether a nationalization pledge should remain part of the party's constitution, an ongoing debate about the political role of trade unions and industrial policy in the late 1960s and throughout the 1970s, and the more recent controversy about the direction of the party, which led to the formation of the Social Democrats as a largely right-wing Labour rump.

Labour believes in internal democracy and fights its battles in public view. Basically, the conflict has been between those who take the traditional socialism (nationalization, welfare state, international cooperation) written into the party's 1918 constitution seriously as a goal and those who qualify their socialist commitment with a desire to do what is necessary to compromise with political reality and retain office. The latter tendency is called "labourism," in that it emphasizes the party's commitment to the welfare of the working class, especially the trade unions affiliated with the party, who continue to play a large role in party finance and organization.[69] The more committed Socialists are often middle-class radicals who take ideas seriously and think that the party should, too. Ironically, it is often the middle-class activists, themselves relatively comfortable economically, who want to continue the class struggle and overturn or seriously modify British capitalism.[70]

Party divisions are often reflected in the organizational structure of the parties. All of the major parties maintain party headquarters (central offices) in London. The chairperson of the Conservative Party is nominated by the party leader, and the staff of party headquarters is normally respectful of what the leader and the rest of the parliamentary party desire. The parliamentary party caucus chooses the leader. Thus the party as an organization is deferential to the parliamentary wing of the party. Although the Conservatives hold an annual party conference, as do the other parties, in order to discuss policy and rally the troops, it is rare for a Conservative conference to defy the party leadership by passing resolutions it objects to. Even when the leadership is divided, these divisions do not publicly permeate the ranks of the party.

In contrast to the Conservatives, the Labour Party organization and conference often display party divisions. Since 1981, the Labour leader and deputy leader are no longer chosen by members of Parliament exclusively but instead by an electoral college made up of three groups: (1) affiliated trade unions, (2) members of the parliamentary party and European Labour MPs, and (3) dues-paying constituency members. Each of these groups now has one-third of the votes. Even though the Labour leader always comes from the House of Commons, the leader has to generate a broader base of support within the party. After the sudden death of John Smith in 1994, these three groups chose Tony Blair as party leader and John Prescott as deputy leader. Blair and Prescott both received a majority of the vote for these positions in all three sections of the party, although this was not required.

The Labour Party organization is also not at the leader's beck and call. Formally, it is led by a twenty-three-member National Executive Committee, which chooses the executive secretary of the party to run the day-to-day operations of the organization. The NEC has reserved places for trade unionists and women to be chosen by their cohorts within the party. The party conference chooses the rest of the NEC, and the choices are often an index of which groups hold sway, however temporarily, in the party. The NEC is supposed to draw up the party program and in general be responsive to the annual party conference. There have been several occasions in which party leaders have clashed with the NEC over policy, especially since the party leader ultimately determines what will appear in the party election manifesto.

Labour Party leaders have also had their problems with the party conference, which is the final authority on general party policy. Again, the various factions of the Labour Party often take part in policy disputes aired publicly at the conference. Unlike the Conservatives, the Labour Party conference has frequently differed with its leaders on policy directions, usually espousing a more left-wing direction than leaders prefer. The conference participants are party activists, who are more likely to be committed Socialists than the average Labour Party member, much less the electorate as a whole.[71] Trade unions can also employ their bloc votes at party conferences, thus making it important for leaders to cultivate their support. Although the policymaking power of the Labour Party conference has been questioned,[72] its capacity to dramatize existing party divisions is unrivaled. Although its conference usually receives less attention, the Liberal Democrats and their predecessors have also often had controversy over policy erupt at their meetings between a more left-wing membership and a more moderate leadership.

The dominance in government enjoyed by the Conservative Party is not due solely to its pragmatism and adaptable nature. It has become evident that, in many ways, Britain is a "conservative nation," and that on many value questions the Conservatives share outlooks with the country as a whole better than Labour does.[73] In addition to lacking a strong class or institutional support base, the Liberals are handicapped by mass perceptions of inexperience, vagueness, and factionalism.[74] A medieval carryover of deference to one's betters was once thought to be the engine of Conservative electoral success,[75] but the reality is more prosaic. The Conservatives stand for a strong British posture in the world, traditional pride in British institutions, and a willingess to adapt to changing circumstances. They could not have held office as long as they have in the twentieth century without these values appealing to large sections of the working class as well as to those in the middle class. In that sense the British population has been essentially moderate in its desire for change. Even in periods of government perceived as "radical"—primarily the immediate postwar Labour government under Clement Attlee and Mrs. Thatcher's Conservative governments of the 1980s—some changes were foreshadowed by previous governments (the Beveridge Report outlining the postwar welfare state was developed under the wartime coalition government led by Winston Churchill; monetarism as an economic policy was begun under the Labour government after the 1976 IMF crisis), and the changes proceeded under a "permissive consensus" from the public.[76] The refusal of Labour to propose sweeping reform of British institutions is a further indication of the conservative nature of the country. Labour is sometimes willing to be radical in policy, but aside from its periodic thrusts at the House of Lords and devolution, it has rarely been willing to propose major institutional reform. Its long period of opposition, however, has now made Labour more willing to consider such proposals.

The British party system has fluctuated more than is often realized. A two-party system based on class politics may have been a goal of many politicians in the twentieth century, but it has never been fully implemented. Nationalist tendencies and the institutional remains of the once-powerful Liberal Party formed the basis for a resurgence of multipartyism in the electorate in the latter part of the twentieth century, even if parliamentary debate remained largely two-party. When the consensus politics of Butskellism (a term coined by the *Economist* to refer to the similar economic polices of Conservative Chancellor of the Exchequer R.A.B. Butler and Labour Chancellor Hugh Gaitskell) did not produce the prosperity promised after World War II, the two major parties began to search for alternatives, and this led to more extreme policies and an emphasis on the politics of class conflict, at least as it appeared to the electorate. This allowed other parties to make inroads into the electorate, even if their direct influence on government has been slight.[77]

British parties do not claim to represent every majoritarian desire of the public. There has always been an emphasis on strong leadership and on the parties presenting their plans for government as a package to the voters in elections. The results, although often interpreted in terms of an electoral mandate by the winners, are far from that.[78] For one thing, voters may not agree with their chosen party across the whole range of issues or may be ignorant of party positions. For another, although parties may differ on some issues, they take similar positions on others. Even some of their differences cannot readily be discerned by voters as conflicting positions. For instance, the following are some party positions taken in the 1992 election manifestos.[79]

European Bank and Currency

Conservative: We will not accept the imposition of a single currency and establishing a European central bank would remove national control of economic policy.

Labour: A European central bank would be needed if there were monetary union, but it should be accountable to finance ministers of the twelve countries.

Liberal Democrat: Our immediate priorities are economic and monetary union, including, in due course, an independent European central bank and a single currency.

Coal

Conservative: We will privatize British Coal, but plans are still at the preparatory stage.

Labour: We will secure the future of the coal industry by the development of clean-burn technology.

Liberal Democrat: We would see to reducing the use of coal—a heavy emitter of carbon dioxide.

Pensions

Conservative: We will protect the basic state retirement pension against inflation.

Labour: We will increase the pension by at least £5 for a single person and £8 for a couple and thereafter in line with earnings or prices, whichever is higher.

Liberal Democrat: We will raise the pension by £5 and £8, restore the link with earnings and abolish SERPS, the state earnings-related pension.

As Patrick Dunleavy[80] has pointed out, the British party system was the model for Schumpeter's idea of democratic elections as choices of teams of elites, without particular policy content in the choices of voters. As such, the parties receive consent to govern, as interpreted by the electoral institutions of the country.

Elections as Intermediary Institutions

Several of the the most salient features of British elections have already been noted, such as the electoral system, patterns of party competition over the years, and the rise of class and decline of religion as influences. Candidate selection by the parties will be discussed later. It is also useful, however, to consider some of the formalities of elections.

A general election is the only chance the electorate as a whole has to influence who the leaders of the central government will be. Since the House of Commons acts to choose the prime minister and government, at best the electorate can only exercise indirect influence by choosing which parties in which proportions will be represented in the House. It is up to the parties to choose the candidates for the individual constituencies, but all of the candidates contest the election under the party manifesto, the set of principles and promises the party makes for the campaign. Thus the stated policy positions of candidates for the same party will show few differences, and, even in an era in which individual candidates are considered to be worth more votes than they were previously, most of the variation in votes candidates receive is attributable to party factors rather than to candidate characteristics.[81] Basically, candidates are part of a team, and as the campaigns have become increasingly focused on the personalities of the party leaders, voters are aware of the fact that their vote for a party candidate is, in effect, a vote for that party to form the government.

British electoral campaigns are among the shortest in liberal democracies. The campaign commences with the prime minister asking the monarch for a dissolution of Parliament, which the monarch invariably grants. Although there may be a "phony campaign" leading up to an expected election, especially as the five-year limit of a parliamentary term nears the end, the formal campaign is usually only about one month in duration, and voting always takes place on a Thursday. As noted earlier, expenditures are limited, and increasingly the campaign has been waged in the media, especially on television. Voting is done by traditional paper ballot, and the results are announced alphabetically by candidate's name, with all candidates standing behind the chief electoral officer. Candidates receiving less than one-eighth of the votes in the constituency forfeit the financial deposit for their candidacy, which acts to discourage frivolous candidacies. Average turnout has been around 75 percent of the electorate in recent elections, although the electoral register on which this figure is based may vary in how current it is, depending on when the election is held. Once per year, the government attempts to enroll all who meet the eligibility requirements for voting.

Redistricting of seats for elections occurs approximately every fifteen years. With 651 seats, the United Kingdom has one of the larger lower houses in the world, but it has been even more populous in the past. Although MPs represent approximately 75,000 electors on average, there is considerable variation in the constituencies, which varied between 23,000 and 101,000 in 1992. This is partly because traditional boundaries of local government districts, for instance, tend to be observed when possible rather than aiming for close numerical equality among districts. Furthermore, Scotland and Wales are overrepresented according to strictly numerical criteria. There is a nonpartisan Boundary Commission (actually four commissions, one for each part of the United Kingdom) responsible for adjusting constituency boundaries every 10–15 years, but the legislation necessary to implement the changes must be presented to Parliament by the government.[82] At times when an election is approaching, a government may decide to push or delay Boundary Commission recommendations in Parliament because of expected seat gains or losses. For instance, the Labour government of 1969 delayed implementation of the report until after the 1970 election. Labour is particularly vulnerable to losing seats due to redistricting because its members tend to come from inner-city areas that lose population over time. Major redistributions occurred after the elections of 1945, 1951, 1970, 1979, and 1992.

Although there will be further discussion of the importance of issues in the policy chapters, to come in general there has been found to be a high degree of economic voting in the United Kingdom, with the exception of Northern Ireland.[83] Other issues wax and wane; for instance, there is some evidence that immigration was important in 1970, and defense in 1987.[84] Partisan loyalties obviously carry over from one election to the next, and there is evidence that regional loyalties may have become more important, though in a somewhat erratic fashion.[85] Few people make the direct switch from Conservative to Labour or vice versa; instead, abstention and voting for other parties, especially the Liberal Democrats, acts as a halfway house and safety valve for those discontented with their previous commitment. This is shown by the fact that the Liberal Democrats are the second-favorite party to the Conservatives in many middle-class constituencies in recent elections. The specific image of competence that parties develop in the time between elections and that they project in an election campaign can also be important. In general, as the British electorate has become more educated, it has lost its class and partisan blinders, becoming more open to judging the performance of governments and the promises of other parties. Thus performance and issues have become more important in voting outcomes, and earlier political socialization, less important.[86] Parental and class loyalties have lessened in favor of instrumentalism, meaning how voters assess the parties' performance. One indication of these tendencies is that despite the British penchant for economic voting, party popularity is now much less tied to aggregate economic indicators, especially unemployment, than was the case in the immediate postwar years.

Labour has suffered most from the increasing fluidity of voters in modern Britain. The decline of manufacturing and extractive industries, social mobility through education, and the spreading of middle-class lifestyles have weakened traditional working-class communities, the bulwark of Labour support. Although overall class-related voting has declined,[87] Labour still draws disproportionate support from areas of concentrated working-class residents in the United Kingdom.[88]

Modern British elections are almost completely free of charges of corruption, and they do provide choices of leaders and policy. Turnout has remained high, but the past two decades have shown a persistent disjuncture between voters' choices and representation of the parties in the House of Commons. Even after the long tenure of the Conservatives, principally under Mrs. Thatcher, the question remains: How much difference do parties and elections make in how the country is governed?[89] This issue is examined in subsequent chapters.

Elite Recruitment

One of the most important aspects of political behavior in any country is elite recruitment, that is, how people rise to leadership positions. In Britain there has been considerable scholarly attention devoted to this issue because socioeconomically the elite is very unrepresentative of the population it serves, both in terms of origin and current occupation.[90] Although attorneys do not dominate the ranks of members of Parliament as they do in legislatures in the United States, for instance, Conservatives are solidly middle-class business and professional men of middle-class origin, with an Oxbridge elite in the party leadership. Despite a much larger working-class contingent in the Commons, largely from trade union sponsorship, Labour also has a middle-class leadership, although one more likely to have a teaching or journalism background and a "redbrick" university background. It is much more difficult to assess the dynamics of how leaders are recruited. Nevertheless, recently there have been more investigations of the procedures and the pool of candidates used by political parties for nomination to parliamentary seats,[91] as well as of the characteristics of party members.[92] Because of the recent leadership embroglios in all three major partisan groupings, attention has also been focused on how the party leaders are selected, and there have been some changes in procedures.[93]

In all major parties, parliamentary candidate selection is an elaborate process involving the listing and encouragement of eligibles by the central party organization, but usually the ultimate selection is made by the local constituency organization. In order to take part in that selection, one must be a paid-up dues-paying member of the political party, and possibly even active enough in the organization to win a place on the Local Management Committee of the party. The idea in Britain is that the parties select the candidates, and then the voters choose among the candidates that the parties offer at the general election.

Within the parties, both Labour and the Liberal Democrats have attempted to democratize their selection process both in terms of the diversity of candidates selected and by allowing more party members to participate in the selection. These changes came about in the wake of complaints that left-wing activists unrepresentative of local opinion seized control of several Labour parties in the early 1980s and nominated candidates of their liking. Until changed by the Labour Party Conference of 1993, affiliated trade unions had voting privileges for their members in candidate selection without the members individually having to join the constituency party. The Conservatives have not changed their formal procedures in recent years, although Central Office has encouraged the adoption of women and nonwhite candidates by local constituency parties. The Liberal Democrats, however, require that at least one woman be on the shortlist (the finalists) of candidates for a nomination where women are in the contest, and Labour now has a similar provision.[94] Labour has been plagued with the question of whether to allow "black sections" as an organized group within the party that would be allowed to nominate black candidates for constituency shortlists. Black sections have not been formally recognized, and, although Labour nominates more nonwhites for parliamentary seats than any other party, such nominations have not increased appreciably in recent elections.[95] Also, few nonwhite members of Parliament have been elected. The number of women candidates, on the other hand, has multiplied in all three major parties, and Labour in particular has been able to increase its proportion of women MPs considerably. After the 1992 election, women composed almost 10 percent of the House of Commons, double their percentage of a decade previously. Jill Hills[96] has contended that women's child-care responsibilities inhibit their entering the competition for parliamentary seats, because in local government their numbers now approach 20 percent of the councillors. Certainly there is intense competition for "safe seats," in which, based on previous patterns of party loyalty, a nominee could expect to be elected. With countrywide competition for a local party nomination possible, it is not surprising that the members of the "chattering classes" with urban cosmopolitan connections, usually white, middle-aged, middle-class professionals, are advantaged. In the mid-1990s, some Labour constituency parties began to take "positive discrimination" steps to develop shortlists of parliamentary candidates composed exclusively of blacks and women, but such procedures, even if successful, are not likely to spread widely because of the fear of an electoral backlash.

Turnover of members of Parliament is minimal, averaging about 20 percent over the postwar period.[97] Most turnover is due to death and retirement rather than to lack of renomination by the constituency party or defeat in a general election. In fact, the number of marginal seats, the crucial ones at stake in an election, have shrunk over the years[98] as both Conservative and Labour parties have built up redoubts of safe seats in particular areas of the country—suburban or urban, rising tertiary or declining industrial. The Liberal Democrats are often the principal challengers to the Conservatives in the former seats. Once ensconced in a safe seat, a member of Parliament can normally look forward to a long career at Westminster.

The argument has been made that parties in Parliament have become more ideological partially because of differences in recruitment.[99] Thrusting businessmen have replaced Tory lords of the manor on one side, and teachers and journalists have replaced trade union officials on the Labour benches. But it has been difficult to connect such change to ideological differences.[100] Overall, MPs are still recruited from a relatively narrow section of the population. They usually have extensive experience within their political parties, sometimes even on the national level. Given the "old school ties" nature of British politics, many of them have known each other, even from across ideological and partisan divides, since private (public) school, university, or local government experience. Thus the socialization channels accustom new recruits to know what to expect and weed out most rene- gades and rebels. Those who do succeed in becoming legislators are what some observers would call "licensed critics." This may be one of the secrets of political stability in a system in which the formal procedures of the system could allow, and even encourage, instability.

An even more select group are party leaders, both those in the cabinet and on the front bench opposition. If election to Parliament is rare for aspirants, even fewer are chosen for leadership positions, and many of those do not have long careers in that position. Even fewer reach the top of the "greasy pole," as Disraeli called it. The party leadership group is even more likely to be composed of mid- dle-aged, elite-educated, middle-class white males than is the parliamentary party. Although women increasingly have been promoted to leadership positions, especially in the Labour Party, they have not reached the top ranks—Exchequer, Foreign Affairs, and Home Office—in anywhere near their proportions in the party. Especially in the Labour Party, there is a dearth of people with management experience chosen except for those who have local government experience. Although some promising younger members may be tapped for junior positions almost upon their entry into the House of Commons, it normally takes several years, and several elections, for a member to rise to a senior ministerial or front bench opposition position. The advantage that an ambitious MP has is that he or she is already part of the eligible pool for leadership since positions have to be filled from within Parliament, and mostly from the Commons. But it still takes the right combination of intellectual acumen, popular appeal, support from one's colleagues, speaking ability, and, above all, standing in the eyes of the party leader in order to be selected for an office or a shadow position. Once in, the same abili- ties must be cultivated. The leader's choice is constrained not only by the formal pool of eligibles but also by the fact that some people are too important within the parliamentary party to be left out of the cabinet or shadow cabinet.

The preeminent position, of course, is that of parliamentary party leader, which makes one the actual or potential prime minister. Few reach this pinnacle. Not only is there only one position, but turnover is rare. Most party leaders hold on to the position for some time, perhaps through several elections if they are successful in forming the government after some of them. Thus, when the time for a change in leadership occurs, a politician must be well positioned to mount a challenge. This usually means having had a substantial tenure of more than a decade (at a minimum) in the House of Commons, in addition to major minis- terial or opposition front bench experience and broad support in the parliamen- tary party. In the twentieth century, the average prime minister has served over fifteen years in the House of Commons before becoming even a party leader. Recently, however, there has been a tendency for the parties to select younger, less experienced leaders. When chosen party leader in 1990, John Major had been an MP only since 1979, but he had held positions as a junior minister of Social Security, chief secretary of the Treasury, foreign secretary, and chancellor of the Exchequer. When chosen party leader in 1994, Tony Blair had been an MP since 1983 and had held the positions of shadow spokesman on treasury and economic affairs, shadow spokesman on trade and industry, chief opposition spokesman on energy, chief opposition spokesman on employment, and shadow home secretary. The three parties now choose their party leaders by radically different methods. The Conservatives are the most traditional in having only Conservative MPs vote for the leader, but the ballot structure is complicated, with more than a simple majority required on either the first or second ballot. This aided the anti-Thatcher dissidents in 1990, when she fell two votes short of election on the first ballot. Since the early 1980s, the Labour Party has elected its leader through an electoral college in which MPs have only a minority of votes. The other two elements are the affiliated trade unions and the constituency parties. Although the party leader must be a member of Parliament, the leader is not necessarily the one the parliamentary party would have chosen. The Liberal Democrats elect their leader by a postal ballot of all paid-up members of the party in the country. Unlike many political systems, party leaders who step down, either voluntarily or by being defeated for reelection to the position, may continue to serve in Parliament, even in other party spokesperson positions. Most frequently, they serve as backbench MPs for a decent interval before becoming a life peer in the House of Lords.

Summary

The overriding implication of this chapter is that, for better or worse, the stability of British politics is largely due to how the institutions, including the political parties, channel both elite and mass behavior in ways that do not fundamentally challenge the existing assumptions about how politics should work. In order to rise into the political elite, a long apprenticeship of party and parliamentary work is necessary, which few survive. Turnover is low, especially in the higher positions, which further inhibits innovation. Thus, by the time anybody becomes a member, even a junior member, of the British political elite, he or she has been thoroughly socialized into the parliament-centered and rhetorically based, British nationalist and class politics-oriented elite political culture. Radicals may flourish for a time, especially in such lower levels of parties as local government, parliamentary constituency parties, and even occasionally on the backbenches of the House of Commons, but it is difficult for them to attain the higher reaches of the party, especially in the House of Commons or cabinet, in large enough numbers to control overall direction of the party, especially when it is in government. The few radicals in ministerial positions have revealed more of their frustrations there than their accomplishments.[101]

This relatively conservative (in the institutional, not in the ideological sense) elite view is reinforced by a mass electorate that also has a distaste for radical solutions. The consistency of mass values and public opinion is matched by its essentially moderate and gradualist orientation. Both nationalization and privatization of the economy have been elite initiatives supported by a permissive consensus of the population, not demanded by them. The General Strike of 1926, for all of its mythology, was a failure. The widespread work stoppages of the Winter of Discontent in 1979 not only harmed Labour's electoral chances later that year, but their invocation continued to help the Conservatives even more than a decade later. Still, the public never became enamored of full-blooded Thatcherism.

In many ways the last one-quarter of the twentieth century has seen the elites, especially in the Labour and Conservative Parties, become more ideological while the masses have remained moderate and centrist, as shown by the rise of the Liberals, Alliance, and Liberal Democrats as an electoral force. When Labour moved back to the center under Neil Kinnock in the late 1980s and early 1990s, it once again became possible to think of a Labour government.[102] The two big parties remain more attached to the politics of class than are the masses. But as Richard Rose and Derek Urwin[103] point out, class politics can be compromised in terms of material shares, whereas with the politics of nationalism or other value-laden politics such as religion or culture this is more difficult to do. Northern Ireland exceptionalism, in which moderate politics are difficult and class-based politics impossible, highlights the mainland tendencies. Not insignificantly, the British population has consistently wanted the government to suppress the provisional Irish Republican Army (IRA) and then leave.[104] Northern Ireland is, in the popular British view, too different from the rest of the country to sustain the connection.

Agitation for populist devices such as the referendum, initiative, recall, and term limits is rarely heard in Britain.[105] Even calls for the referendum are usually attached to debate over a particular issue, such as the European Community, devolution, or capital punishment. Thus the British population remains generally satisfied with the workings of British political institutions and does not desire radical institutional reform. Nevertheless, there has been a declining public confidence in politicians and political institutions in recent years, paralleling, even if not reaching the depths of, institutional questioning in other countries.[106] The elite still has broad scope for institutional change, but only rarely is there sufficient consensus to seize it. Even relatively modest reforms such as changing the House of Lords or devolution are difficult to implement, despite the lack of both constitutional and popular impediments to them. Even when the outcomes of the British political process are unsatisfactory to the participants, calls for massive overhaul of fundamental institutions are unlikely to be heeded, not least because politicians cannot confidently predict the consequences. But how well does this conservative process deal with policy issues facing it in the postwar period?

Notes

1. Russell J. Dalton, *Citizen Politics in Western Democracies* (Chatham, N.J.: Chatham House 1988).

2. Robert D. Putnam, *The Comparative Study of Political Elites* (Englewood Cliffs, N.J.: Prentice-Hall, 1976).

3. Putnam, *The Comparative Study of Political Elites;* Robert D. Putman, *The Beliefs of Politicians* (New Haven, Conn.: Yale University Press, 1973); Joel D. Aberbach, Robert D. Putnam, and Bert A. Rockman, *Bureaucrats and Politicians in Western Democracies* (Cambridge: Harvard University Press, 1981).

4. David Barnum and John L. Sullivan, "The Elusive Foundations of Political Freedom in Britain and the United States," *Journal of Politics* 52, no. 3 (August 1990):719–739.

5. Putnam, *The Comparative Study of Political Elites;* Putnam, *The Beliefs of Politicians;* Richard Rose, *Politics in England,* 2d ed. (Boston: Little, Brown and Company, 1974); Patrick Seyd and Paul Whiteley, *Labour's Grassroots* (Oxford: Clarendon Press. 1992).

6. Donald D. Searing, "A Theory of Political Socialization." *British Journal of Political Science* 16, no. 3 (1986):341–376.

7. W. L. Guttsman, *The British Political Elite* (London: MacGibbon, 1963); David Baker, Andrew Gamble, and Steve Ludlam, "More 'Classless' and Less 'Thatcherite': Conservative Ministers and New Conservative MPs After the 1992 Election," *Parliamentary Affairs* 45, no. 4 (1992):665–668.

8. Rose, *Politics in England.*

9. Tony Benn, *Office Without Power: Diaries 1968–1972* (London: Hutchinson, 1988).

10. Richard Critchfield, *An American Looks at Britain* (New York: Doubleday Anchor Books, 1990).

11. Jim Bulpitt, *Territory and Power in the United Kingdom* (Manchester: Manchester University Press, 1983).

12. David Judge, *Backbench Specialization in the House of Commons* (London: Heinemann, 1983).

13. Donald D. Searing, *Westminster's World* (Cambridge: Harvard University Press, 1994); Bruce Cain, John Ferejohn, and Morris Fiorina, *The Personal Vote* (Cambridge: Harvard University Press, 1987).

14. Philip Norton and David Wood, *Back from Westminster* (Lexington: University Press of Kentucky, 1993).

15. Theodore J. Lowi, "American Business, Public Policy, Case Studies, and Political Theory," *World Politics* 16, no. 4 (1964):677–715; Kenneth J. Meier, *Politics and Bureaucracy,* 3d ed. (Pacific Grove, Ca.: Brooks/Cole Publishing Company, 1993); T. Alexander Smith, *The Comparative Policy Process* (Santa Barbara, Ca.: ABC-Clio, 1975).

16. Putnam, *The Beliefs of Politicians.*

17. Richard Rose, "Still the Era of Party Government?" *Parliamentary Affairs* 26, no. 2 (1983):282–299.

18. Samuel Finer, ed., *Adversary Politics and Electoral Reform* (London: Anthony Wigram, 1975).

19. Ian Budge and Denis Farlie, *Explaining and Predicting Elections* (London: Allen and Unwin, 1983); Ian Budge, David Robertson, and David Hearl, eds., *Ideology, Strategy, and Party Change* (Cambridge: Cambridge University Press, 1987).

20. David Butler, *Governing Without a Majority* (London: Macmillan 1983).

21. Philip Norton, "'The Lady's Not for Turning,' but What About the Rest? Margaret Thatcher and the Conservative Party, 1979–89," *Parliamentary Affairs* 43, no. 1 (1990):41–58; Harold D. Clarke, William Mishler, and Paul F. Whiteley, "Recapturing the Falklands: Models of Conservative Popularity, 1979–1983," *British Journal of Political Science* 20, no. 1 (1990):63–81.

22. Dalton, *Citizen Politics in Western Democracies;* Ronald Inglehart, *The Silent Revolution* (Princeton: Princeton University Press, 1977); Ronald Inglehart, *Culture Shift* (Princeton: Princeton University Press, 1990).

23. Russell J. Dalton, "Political Parties and Political Participation: Party Supporters and Party Elites in Nine Nations," *Comparative Political Studies* 17, no. 2 (1985):267–299.

24. Dalton, "Political Parties and Political Participation: Party Supporters and Party Elites in Nine Nations"; Putnam, *The Beliefs of Politicians;* Seyd and Whiteley, *Labour's Grassroots;* Pippa Norris and Joni Lovenduski, "Women Candidates for Parliament: Transforming the Agenda?" *British Journal of Politial Science* 19, no. 1 (1989):106–115.

25. Norton, "'The Lady's Not for Turning,' but What About the Rest? Margaret Thatcher and the Conservative Party, 1979–89;" Jack Brand, *British Parliamentary Parties* (Oxford: Clarendon Press, 1992).

26. Gabriel Almond and Sidney Verba, *The Civic Culture* (Princeton: Princeton University Press, 1963).

27. Peter Bachrach and Morton Baratz, "The Two Faces of Power," *American Political Science Review* 56, no. 4 (1962):947–952.

28. Joseph Schumpeter, *Capitalism, Socialism, and Democracy,* 3d ed. (New York: Harper Colophon Books, 1962).

29. Mark Abrams and Richard Rose, *Must Labour Lose?* (London: Penguin Books, 1960).

30. Inglehart, *The Silent Revolution;* Inglehart, *Culture Shift;* Alan Marsh, "The Silent Revolution, Value Priorities, and the Quality of Life in Britain," *American Political Science Review* 69, no. 1 (1975):21–30.

31. E. Gene Frankland, "Does Green Politics Have a Future in Britain? An American Perspective," in *Green Politics One,* ed. Wolfgang Rudig (Edinburgh: Edinburgh University Press, 1990).

32. Ivor Crewe, "Has the Electorate Become Thatcherite?" in *Thatcherism,* ed. Robert Skidelsky (London: Chatto and Windus, 1988); Ian McAllister and Donley T. Studlar, "Popular Versus Elite Views of Privatization: The Case of Britain," *Journal of Public Policy* 9, no. 1 (1989):157–178; Anthony Heath, Roger Jowell, John Curtice, Geoff Evans, Julia Field, and Sharon Witherspoon, *Understanding Political Change* (Oxford: Pergamon Press, 1991); Richard Rose, *Ordinary People in Public Policy* (Newbury Park, Ca.: Sage Publication, 1989).

33. Samuel H. Barnes et al. *Political Action* (London: Sage Publication, 1979); Inglehart, *Culture Shift.*

34. Geraint Parry, George Moyser, and Neil Day, *Political Participation in Britain* (Cambridge: Cambridge University Press, 1992).

35. Richard Rose, "Inheritance Before Choice in Public Policy," *Journal of Theoretical Politics* 2, no. 2 (1990):263–291.

36. David Butler and Donald E. Stokes, *Political Change in Britain,* 2d ed. (New York: St. Martin's Press, 1974).

37. Rose, "Inheritance Before Choice in Public Policy."

38. Rose, *Politics in England*, 2d ed.

39. Donley T. Studlar and Ian McAllister, "Protest and Survive? Alliance Support in the 1983 British General Election," *Political Studies* 35, no. 1 (1987): 39–60; Richard Rose and Dennis Kavanagh, "The Monarchy in Contemporary Political Culture," *Comparative Politics* 8, no. 4 (1976):548–576.

40. Butler and Stokes, *Political Change in Britain;* Donley T. Studlar and Susan Welch, "Mass Attitudes on Political Issues in Britain," *Comparative Political Studies* 14, no. 3 (1981):327–355; Studlar and McAllister, "Protest and Survive? Alliance Support in the 1983 British General Election."

41. Richard Rose and Ian McAllister, *The Loyalties of Voters* (London: Sage Publication, 1990).

42. Rose and McAllister, *The Loyalties of Voters.*

43. Butler and Stokes, *Political Change in Britain.*

44. Lester Friedman, ed., *British Cinema and Thatcherism* (Minneapolis: University of Minnesota Press, 1993).

45. H. W. Wilson, *Pressure Group* (London: Secker and Warburg, 1961).

46. Kenneth Newton, "Do People Read Everything They Believe in Newspapers? Newspapers and Voters in the 1983 and 1987 Elections," in *British Elections and Parties Yearbook 1991*, ed. Ivor Crewe, Pippa Norris, David Denver and David Broughton (London: Harvester Wheatsheaf, 1992).

47. Martin Harrop and Margaret Scammell, "A Tabloid War," in *The British General Election of 1992*, ed. David Butler and Dennis Kavanagh (New York: St. Martin's Press, 1992).

48. Harrop and Scammell, "A Tabloid War."

49. Butler and Stokes, *Political Change in Britain;* William L. Miller, *Media and Voters* (Oxford: Clarendon Press, 1991); Newton, "Do People Read Everything They Believe in the Papers? Newspapers and Voters in the 1983 and 1987 Elections."

50. Maxwell E. McCombs and Donald L. Shaw, "The Agenda-Setting Function of the Mass Media," *Public Opinion Quarterly* 36, no. 2 (1972):176–187; Shelly D. Day Crynes, "Agenda-Setting on Ethnic Issues: An Analysis of British Policy Towards Northern Ireland, 1968–1972" (master's thesis, Oklahoma State University, 1993).

51. Ivor Crewe, "A Nation of Liars? Opinion Polls and the 1992 Election," *Parliamentary Affairs* 45, no. 4 (1992): 475–495.

52. Robert M. Worcester, ed., *Public Opinion Polling: An International Review* (New York: St. Martin's Press, 1983).

53. Ian McAllister and Donley T. Studlar, "Bandwagon, Underdog, or Projection? Opinion Polls and Electoral Choice in Britain, 1979–87," *Journal of Politics* 53, no. 3 (1991):720–741.

54. Dennis Kavanagh, "Opinion Polls and Elections," in David Butler, Howard Penniman, and Austin Ranney, *Democracy at the Polls*, (Washington, D.C.: American Enterprise Institute for Public Policy Research, 1981).

55. Crynes, "Agenda-Setting on Ethnic Issues: An Analysis of British Policy Towards Northern Ireland, 1968–1972."

56. Samuel Finer, *Pressure Group Politics* (London: Pall Mall Press, 1958).

57. Martin Harrop, ed., *Power and Policy in Liberal Democracies* (Cambridge: Cambridge University Press, 1992).

58. Philippe Schmitter, "Still the Century of Corporatism?" *Review of Politics* 36, no. 1 (1974):85–131; Alan Cawson, *Corporatism and Political Theory* (Oxford: Basil Blackwell, 1986); Central Office of Information, *Britain, 1994: An Official Handbook* (London: Her Majesty's Stationery Office, 1993); Keith Middlemas, *Politics in Industrial Society* (London: Andre Deustch, 1980).

59. Anthony H. Birch, *The British System of Government,* 6th ed. (Boston: Allen and Unwin, 1983).

60. Samuel H. Beer, *British Politics in the Collectivist Age* (New York: Random House, 1965); Samuel H. Beer, *Britain Against Itself* (New York: Norton, 1982); Mancur Olson, *The Rise and Decline of Nations* (New Haven: Yale University Press, 1982); Middlemas, *Politics in Industrial Society.*

61. Schmitter, "Still the Century of Corporatism?"; Jurg Steiner, *European Politics,* 2d ed. (New York: Longman, 1991).

62. Harrop, *Power and Policy in Liberal Democracies.*

63. Joseph R. Rudolph, Jr., "Energy Policy in the United States and Britain," in *Political Economy: Public Policies in the United States and Britain,* ed. Jerold L. Waltman and Donley T. Studlar (Jackson: University Press of Mississippi, 1987).

64. Roland J. Pennock, "Agricultural Subsidies in England and America," *American Political Science Review* 56, no. 3 (1962):621–633; Peter Self and Herbert Storing, *The State and the Farmer,* 2d ed. (London: Allen and Unwin, 1971).

65. George Dangerfield, *The Strange Death of Liberal England* (New York: H. Smith and R. Haas, 1935).

66. Butler and Stokes, *Political Change in Britain;* Chris Cook, *A Short History of the Liberal Party, 1900–1984,* 2d ed. (London: Macmillan, 1984).

67. Bo Sarlvik and Ivor Crewe, *Decade of Dealignment* (Cambridge: Cambridge University Press, 1983); Anthony Heath, Rogert Jowell, and John Curtice, *How Britain Votes* (Oxford: Pergamon Press, 1985).

68. Richard Rose, *Do Parties Make a Difference?* (Chatham, N.J.: Chatham House, 1980).

69. Paul Webb, *Trade Unions and the British Electorate* (Aldershot, England: Dartmouth, 1992).

70. Seyd and Whiteley, *Labour's Grassroots;* Paul Whiteley, *The Labour Party in Crisis* (New York: Methuen, 1983).

71. Louis Minkin, *The Labour Party Conference,* 2nd ed. (Manchester: Manchester University Press, 1980); Whiteley, *The Labour Party in Crisis.*

72. Robert T. McKenzie, *British Political Parties,* 2d ed. (New York: St. Martin's Press, 1963).

73. Andrew Gamble, *The Conservative Nation* (London: Routledge, 1974).

74. Sarlvik and Crewe, *Decade of Dealignment.*

75. Robert T. McKenzie and Alan Silver, *Angels in Marble* (Chicago: University of Chicago Press, 1968).

76. Angus Campbell, Philip Converse, Warren Miller, and Donald Stokes, *The American Voter* (New York: Wiley, 1961); George H. Gallup, *The Gallup International Public Opinion Polls, Great Britain, 1937–1975,* Volume 1, 1937–1964, Volume 2, 1965–1975 (New York: Greenwood Press, 1976); George Gallup, *The International Gallup Polls: Public Opinion 1978* (Wilmington, Del.: Scholarly Resources, 1980); McAllister and Studlar, "Popular Versus Elite Views of Privatization: The Case of Britain."

77. Ivor Crewe, Bo Sarlvik, and James E. Alt, "Partisan Dealignment in Britain, 1964–74," *British Journal of Political Science* 7, no. 1 (1977):129–190; Studlar and McAllister, "Protest and Survive? Alliance Support in the 1983 British General Election."

78. Birch, *The British System of Government.*

79. David McKie, ed., *The Election: A Voter's Guide* (London: Fourth Estate, 1992).

80. Patrick Dunleavy, "Democracy in Britain: A Health Check for the 1990s," in *British Elections and Parties Yearbook 1991,* ed. Ivor Crewe, Pippa Norris, David Denver, and David Broughton (Hemel Hempstead, England: Harvester Wheatsheaf, 1992).

81. Cain, Ferejohn and Fiorina, *The Personal Vote.*

82. T. Philip Wolf, "Seats for Cheats: Reapportionment in the House of Commons" (paper presented at American Political Science Assocation Conference, New York, 1978); John R. Hibbing and Samuel C. Patterson, "'Representing a Territory': Constituency Boundaries for the British House of Commons of the 1980s," *Journal of Politics* 48, no. 4 (1986):992–1005.

83. Michael S. Lewis-Beck, *Economics and Elections* (Ann Arbor: University of Michigan Press, 1988); Helmut Norpoth, *Confidence Regained: Economics, Mrs. Thatcher, and the British Voter* (Ann Arbor: University of Michigan Press, 1992).

84. Donley T. Studlar, "Policy Voting in Britain: The Colored Immigration Issue in the British General Elections of 1964, 1968, and 1970," *American Political Science Review* 72, no. 1 (1978):46–64; William L. Miller, "What Was the Profit in Following the Crowd? The Effectivieness of Party Strategies on Immigration and Devolution," *British Journal of Political Science* 11, no. 1 (1981):15–38; Heath et al., *Understanding Political Change.*

85. R. J. Johnston, C. J. Pattie and J. G. Allsopp, *A Nation Dividing?* (London: Longman, 1987); McAllister and Studlar, "Bandwagon, Underdog, or Projection? Opinion Polls and Electoral Choice in Britain, 1979–87."

86. Rose and McAllister, *The Loyalties of Voters.*

87. Mark Franklin, *The Decline of Class Voting in Britain* (Oxford: Oxford University Press, 1985).

88. William L. Miller, *Electoral Dynamics in Britain Since 1918* (London: Macmillan, 1977).

89. Anthony King, "The Rise of the Career Politician in Britain—and Its Consequences," *British Journal of Political Science* 11, no. 2 (1981):249–285; Rose, *Do Parties Make a Difference?*; Brian Hogwood, *Trends in British Public Policy* (Buckingham: Open University Press, 1992).

90. W. L. Guttsman, *The British Political Elite* (London: MacGibbon, 1963); Baker, Gamble, and Ludlam, "More 'Classless' and Less 'Thatcherite': Convervative Ministers and New Conservative MPs After the 1992 Election."

91. Austin Ranney, *Pathways to Parliament* (Madison: University of Wisconsin Press, 1965); Pippa Norris and Joni Lovenduski, *Political Representation and Recruitment* (Cambridge: Cambridge University Press, 1994).

92. Seyd and Whiteley, *Labour's Grassroots;* Paul Whiteley, Patrick Seyd, Jeremy Richardson, and Paul Bissell, "Thatcher and the Conservative Party," *Political Studies* 42, no. 2 (1994):185–203.

93. David Kogan and Maurice Kogan, *The Battle for the Labour Party* (London: Fontana, 1982); Norton, "'The Lady's Not for Turning,' but What About the Rest? Margaret Thatcher and the Conservative Party, 1979–1989."

94. Norris and Lovenduski, *Political Representation and Recruitment.*

95. Norris and Lovenduski, *Political Representation and Recruitment.*

96. Jill Hills, "Lifestyle Constraints on Formal Political Participation: Why So Few Women Local Government Councillors in Britain," *Electoral Studies* 2, no. 1 (1983):39–52.

97. Norris and Lovenduski, *Political Representation and Recruitment.*

98. John Curtice and Michael Steed, "Electoral Choice and the Production of Government in the United Kingdom: The Changing Operation of the Electoral System Since 1955," *British Journal of Political Science* 12, no. 2 (1982):249–298.

99. King, "The Rise of the Career Politician in Britain–and Its Consequences."

100. Martin Burch and Michael Moran, "The Changing British Political Elite, 1945–1983: MPs and Cabinet Ministers," *Parliamentary Affairs* 38, no. 1 (1985):1–15; Norton, "'The Lady's Not for Turning,' but What About the Rest? Margaret Thatcher and the Conservative Party, 1979–89."

101. Tony Benn, *Office Without Power: Diaries 1968–1972.*

102. Colin Hughes and Patrick Wintour, *Labour Rebuilt: The New Model Party* (London: Fourth Estate, 1991).

103. Richard Rose and Derek W. Urwin, "Social Cohension, Political Parties and Strains in Regimes," *Comparative Political Studies* 2, no. 1 (1969):7–67.

104. Richard Rose, Ian McAllister, and Peter Mair, *Is There a Concurring Majority about Northern Ireland?* University of Strathclyde Studies in Public Policy No. 22 (Glasgow, 1978).

105. Henry Lazer, "The Referendum and the British Consitution," in *Dilemmas of Change in British Politics,* ed. Donley T. Studlar and Jerold L. Waltman (London: Macmillan, 1984).

106. John R. Baker, Linda L. M. Bennett, Stephen E. Bennett, and Richard S. Flickinger, "Looking at Legislatures: Citizens' Knowledge and Perceptions of Legislatures in Canada, Great Britain, and the United States" (paper presented at International Political Science Association Conference, Berlin, Germany, 1994).

5

BRITISH FOREIGN POLICY: FROM GREAT POWER TO EUROPEAN PERIPHERY

Pᴇʀʜᴀᴘs ᴛʜᴇ ꜰɪʀsᴛ ɪssᴜᴇ ᴛʜᴀᴛ people think about in assessing Britain's policy performance in the postwar period is foreign policy. This is natural enough since Britain was one of the victors of World War II and has always heavily emphasized foreign policy. As a small island with limited natural resources, potentially threatened by more populous, more resource-rich neighbors on the continent of Europe, and in the age of air power, threatened from even further abroad, Britain has developed much of its national identity around the successful execution of foreign policy aims. The zenith of its power, of course, was in the late nineteenth and early twentieth centuries, when it controlled vast overseas territories and was generally considered the preeminent economic and foreign policy power in the world. That was an unnatural situation for a small island, and it was bound to change.

The effects of economic competition and participation in two world wars, which consumed vast quantities of resources, human and material, have left Britain with the status of what is usually termed a "middle-range" power, with extensive diplomatic commitments elsewhere, from Hong Kong to the Falklands. Britain still holds a permanent seat on the Security Council of the United Nations and is a major player in such international organizations as the European Union, NATO, the IMF, the General Agreement on Tariffs and Trade (GATT) (largely through the EU), and the G-7 leading industrialized economies, as well as the

Commonwealth. Even after several defense cutbacks, Britain still has extensive security interests.

The purpose of this chapter is neither to analyze Britain's descent from the status of a great power[1] nor to provide a detailed survey of contemporary aspects of foreign policy.[2] Instead, I assess how the British policy process has dealt with some of the major foreign policy issues facing the country in the postwar world. After outlining the foreign policy agenda, I analyze how the British policy process has functioned in formulating foreign policy, what the outcomes have been, how goals and performance have matched, and whose views are reflected in the outcomes. This is an area, of course, in which all of the relevant actors are not internal, which makes conclusions more tentative. Nevertheless, the analysis will follow the same pattern as succeeding chapters, working through discussion of agenda, actors, process (formation, adoption, and implementation), and evaluation.

Although the distinction between foreign policy and domestic policy has been increasingly eroded for all countries, there still remain important differences. This makes foreign policy more difficult to analyze in terms of policy process generalities.[3] The multitude of outside actors, including nongovernmental bodies as well as international organizations and states, and the variety of interactions that this generates for any particular country presents problems for explanation. Thus policy process theories are usually more persuasive about grouping policies on the domestic level, where there are a finite number of actors who tend to interact with each other in reasonably predictable ways over time. In contrast, every country is presented with foreign policy "crises," in which major decisions must be made within a short period of time, often with little guidance from past events.[4] Furthermore, there is greater secrecy in foreign policy formulation, on national security grounds, even in the most open polities. Although I recognize these problems, I nevertheless attempt to develop a general analysis of British foreign policy as an issue area by examining a few major areas of policy, especially in the postwar era.

A popular method of analyzing British foreign policy is to hearken back to Winston Churchill's "three circles" concept of how Britain should exercise influence internationally: (1) globally through the Commonwealth, (2) regionally through European cooperation, and (3) transatlantically through the Anglo-American "special relationship."[5] I prefer to consider the first two of these as policy areas but consider the third one to be defense policy more generally. Much of the Anglo-American special relationship has been concerned with defense matters and will be touched upon here, but it will also be incorporated in the other policy areas when it is relevant.

What policies will be considered? As in Chapters 6, 7, and 8, which concern policymaking as well, a few broad policy areas are selected within which to focus on more specific issues. In the case of foreign policy, these are (1) the European Community (or European Union as it is also called), including the decision to join it, the referendum campaign in 1975 on continued British membership, and subsequent developments concerning Britain's relations with the Union and its institutions; (2) the end of empire, or decolonization, including the more specific problems of India, Suez, Rhodesia (renamed Zimbabwe upon independence), South Africa, the Falklands, and relations with the Commonwealth; and (3) defense and security concerns, including the level of defense spending, relations with the United States, membership in such organizations as NATO, and Britain's development, retention, and modernization of nuclear weapons. This should provide both a suitably broad range of issues and a variety of temporal perspectives.

The Policy Agenda

The broad policy agenda of British foreign policy has not changed greatly over the postwar period. It has always been to maintain as much British influence on affairs elsewhere in the world as possible. For historical reasons already delineated, Britain has considered a strong foreign policy essential to its domestic prosperity and security. To leave its far-flung foreign policy concerns in the hands of others would be to invite a reduced status in the world, endangerment of its domestic prosperity, and perhaps even, as in 1940, the threat of foreign conquest. As a practioner of realpolitik, however, the United Kingdom was not interested in pursuing foreign policy goals at all costs. A mixture of diplomatic, economic, and military instruments was used, depending on the specific goal and its importance in the overall scheme of British foreign policy at the time. If the costs became too great, as in fighting the American revolutionaries in the late eighteenth century, then Britain withdrew in the interests of preserving its power elsewhere in the world. Thus the general postwar policy goal is clear, but more specific goals shifted as ingredients in the overall view. The key question, are, given the foreign policy status of the United Kingdom in 1945, is this: As a battered but victorious combatant in World War II, how successfully has the country managed to maintain its relative position in the world, and at what cost?

Some policymakers doubtless hoped for Britain to reclaim its previous status as in international affairs, but it was questionable whether it still occupied that role even before World War II. Britain was not the dominant power, even on the European continent, after World War I, and given developments elswhere in the world, especially the economic and military power of the United States, which was relatively unbruised by the two world wars, Britain had little practical hope of reasserting its pre–World War I position. But it had reasonable expectations of seeing its valor in World War II rewarded with a stable position as a major player in the postwar world. How did the country go about attempting to achieve that?

Actors

The foreign policy actors in the British policy process are relatively restricted compared to other policy arenas. As noted previously, even the role of Parliament is limited. The sovereign power of the executive is considered to cover a broad range of foreign policy. The government can commit the country to war or treaties with minimal consultation with Parliament if it so desires. In practice, major decisions such as joining the European Union, going to war in the Falklands, and negotiating the Maastricht Treaty are subjected to parliamentary debate and, in the case of European Union business, to parliamentary ratification. But the original decisions to develop nuclear weapons were made without informing the House of Commons until years later. Members of Parliament are free to raise issues as they want in adjournment debates at the close of the parliamentary day; thus, major foreign policy issues are often aired there. In the case of European Union issues, it has always been considered a fundamental compromise with the sovereignty of the British Parliament for the United Kingdom to be a member of the Union. Parliament therefore has somewhat greater capacity for involvement in these decisions than in most areas of foreign policy. Nevertheless, the relevant committee in the House of Lords has emerged as a closer overseer of European legislation than the Committee on European Secondary Legislation in the House of Commons (Scrutiny Committee). Governments have preferred to keep the negotiating power on EU legislation to themselves as much as possible.[6]

The executive, both in its political and bureaucratic wings, is heavily involved in all foreign policy decisions. Although cabinet committees, especially the Defense and Overseas Policy Committee, are thought to be important actors in the formulation of policy, little is known about how they function. The major departments currently concerned are the Foreign and Commonwealth Office, Defense, and Treasury. As economic matters have become more important in international concerns, the influence of the Treasury has expanded. Historically, there were several different offices responsible for imperial and commonwealth affairs, and in wartime, responsibilities shift to some degree. Governments rarely campaign for office on anything other than general, vague platforms on foreign affairs.[7] Since foreign policy is subject to many external influences, it requires constant adjustment, and most parties think it best not to give too many hostages to fortune by making rash promises in election campaigns. The presumption is also that governments enjoy a permissive consensus from the public in such matters since information and opinion on foreign matters is generally low.[8] Public opinion polls rarely ask "background" questions on foreign affairs to ascertain knowledge. Only rarely are foreign policy problems rated by respondents as the "most important problem" the country faces, and even in these cases their tenure in this position tends to be short. A few long-running foreign policy issues, however, such as the costs and benefits of membership in the European Community and British relations with the United States, have been the subject of enough surveys to be able to ascertain trends.[9]

In the absence of a large section of the public that is both engaged and opinionated on foreign policy questions, interest groups have room to flourish. Although there are groups devoted to every possible foreign issue organized in London, most of them are small, and their influence is questionable. It is probably the famed caution of the British Foreign Office rather than the political influence of pressure groups that is responsible for most foreign policy decisions. Interest groups usually lack a strong legislative input into foreign policy decisionmaking and are thus often limited to lobbying the executive. On European Union matters, interest groups can attempt to influence the British negotiating position through the government as well as by lobbying the EU more directly.[10] Since the European Union has incorporated regional and local governments into its policy implementation network, some of these governments have established their own lobbyists in Brussels.[11] Political parties are reluctant to incorporate many foreign policy planks in their platforms for fear of alienating other groups, which is too little benefit in terms of votes. The problems that antinuclear stances have brought for the Labour party illustrate well why "glittering generalities" reign in most areas of foreign policy during election campaigns. But foreign policy concerns do animate various pressure groups on the political extremes, such as the Campaign for Nuclear Disarmament and the League of Empire Loyalists. Often mass demonstrations, especially by left-wingers opposed to the policies adopted, are a feature of dissent. However, such protests are often a sign of weakness rather than strength in terms of influence on the institutional decisionmaking process.

The media are active in foreign policy crises but otherwise reflect rather than mold public opinion by concentrating their attention elsewhere. Television in particular, however, does have a stream of programs dealing with world trouble spots, although the implications for British foreign policy are not necessarily developed. The judiciary takes only a small role in British foreign policy in rendering decisions about how people suspected of terrorism related to the conflict in Northern Ireland are to be treated. In fact, the British judiciary, as well as the British House of Commons, can be overruled by the European Court of Justice on matters relating to Britain's European Union obligations. Thus the domestic actors involved in foreign policy, despite its considerable implications and far-flung geography, are relatively few.

European Union institutions can now be considered established actors in British foreign poliicy as well. These institutions have constantly evolved, and, with the prospects of more new members and the scheduled Intergovernmental Conference of 1996, they will doubtless continue to do so. As of the mid-1990s, they were exerting increasing influence over British policy, especially in economic decisionmaking. The major institutions of the EU are the European Council, the Council of Ministers, the European Commission, the European Parliament, the European Court of Justice, the Presidency of the Council of Ministers, and the Committee of Permanent Representatives (COREPOR). The ultimate ongoing political authority in the Union, even if it is not recognized in formal constitutional documents, is the biannual meeting of the European Council, a summit of heads of government of the member countries. It is in this forum that the most difficult problems of the Community are worked out, such as Mrs. Thatcher's demands for a budgetary rebate for Britain. In formal terms, the highest authority empowered to make decisions on behalf of the Union is the Council of Ministers, composed of cabinet ministers from each of the member states and operating on the basis of a system of weighted voting, with larger states having more votes. Which cabinet ministers are involved depends on what the topics for decision are.

Although the Council of Ministers is supposed to make policy, the European Commission is responsible both for developing and carrying out policy. The European Commission, composed of three elements, acts as the executive of the Union for most purposes and represents the organization as a whole rather than the countries from which its members come. As of 1994, there were seventeen commissioners in the twelve-member EU, with larger states having two commissioners each and smaller states one each. The commissioners are, in effect, the heads of departments of the EU. They oversee policy development and implementation in their assigned areas of responsibility. The Council of Ministers decides how to divide the commissioners' portfolios among the countries, and the government of each country nominates two people to act as the commissioners allotted to it. Britain has traditionally had one Labour and one Conservative to act as its commissioners, and they are to act for the welfare of the Union as a whole, not the United Kingdom or their party. Commissioners serve four-year terms and can be ousted as a group by a vote of the European Parliament.

At the pinnacle of the European Commission stands the president of the European Union, chosen by the heads of government of the member countries for a five-year term, with the agreement of the European Parliament. This person is usually a prestigious senior politician with a history of achievement in his or her country, but again the responsibility of the position is to look after the interests of the whole Union. Among other things, the president acts as the spokesperson for the Union. The third element of the commission includes the bureaucrats of the EU, sometimes referred to as "Eurocrats," numbering over ten thousand, plus staff. These people are international civil servants and key advisers and policy implementers within the organization.

Until recently the European Parliament had a secondary role in the Union. In 1994 some 567 members sat in the Parliament in Strasbourg; British members number eighty-seven. The overall number will grow with enlargement. Direct elections for the European Parliament occur every five years; the latest was in June 1994. European elections have been plagued by decreasing voter turnout. Traditionally, the European Parliament had relatively few legislative powers; now there are more areas of "codecision," whereby the Parliament has limited or full veto power, as a result of the Single European Act and the Maastricht Treaty, but it still cannot initiate legislation. In other words, even with enhanced powers, the Parliament remains very much a reactive body. If the "democratic deficit" of the EU is to be cured, then a more substantial operating role for the European Parliament is imperative, as are better links between the institution and citizens of

the individual countries. But Britain has been wary of allowing such developments for fear of undermining the role of governments through the Council of
Ministers.

The European Court of Justice is actually the institution that more directly
compromises British sovereignty. The court, made up of one member from each
country, is empowered to hear cases and make decisions binding on members
concerning European Union law, whether such cases are brought by governments,
individuals, or groups. Thus Britain has sometimes been found to be in violation
of EU law and told by the court to correct its practices. Even if British courts do
not have full power of judicial review, the European Court of Justice does, at least
within the restricted areas heretofore covered by the European Union.

The presidency of the Council of Ministers rotates among the member countries on a six-month basis. It involves mainly the capacity to set the agenda for
discussion in the council within that time period, and possibly beyond if the
issues are considered significant enough. The Committee of Permanent
Representatives consists of the ambassadorial team from each country sent to
represent that country's interests at the European Union's headquarters in
Brussels, Belgium. Since other representatives of individual member governments, such as the prime minister and cabinet ministers, spend most of their time
at home, these people, consisting of envoys from both the Foreign and
Commonwealth Offices and other civil servants on temporary assignment from
their departments, do much of the negotiating for Britain with representatives of
the European Commission.

Policy Formation, Adoption, and Implementation

European Union

Britain's role in the European Union is an issue that has moved over the years
from an almost exclusively elite concern to one that has engaged broader sections
of the population. Yet the survey evidence indicates that the EU is not an issue of
abiding concern to most of the public. It remains the only issue subject to a countrywide referendum in the British political experience. There have been calls for
further referendums, but opinion about the community has tended to fluctuate
widely over the years.[12]

The decision not to join the European Union, or European Community, upon
its formation in 1957 was essentially an executive decision made by the
Conservative government of Harold Macmillan. The decision did not generate a
lot of controversy at the time. Most British leaders thought that relying on established trade patterns within the Commonwealth and with the United States was a
more reliable way of generating economic growth than the relatively untried
methods of the newly formed Community of France, West Germany, Italy,

Belgium, the Netherlands, and Luxembourg. Furthermore, the British have traditionally been leery of any commitments involving a compromise on sovereignty
over their own affairs, especially those dealing with economic matters. The overriding political goal of some of the founders, that of developing a United States of
Europe, also made the British wary of the EU. This was not a mere free trade
agreement; indeed Britain became a founding member of the European Free
Trade Association (EFTA) shortly after the origin of the EU. Instead, joining the
EU involved, at least in principle, a commitment to allow the organization to
make decisions over certain limited areas of economic policy, including agricultural and trade (a common external tariff against nonmember states, for
instance). In short, the European Union was designed to have at least a degree of
"supranational" or "suprastate" power; individual states were not to retain veto
power over all measures. They did, however, retain the ultimate sovereignty of
withdrawing from the organization if they found its obligations too onerous. The
British elite of both major parties at the time found such a commitment too compromising, especially coming from continental countries that had often been
viewed with suspicion in the past. The Commonwealth as an economic and
diplomatic community and the Anglo-American special relationship were the
preferred alternatives, along with EFTA.

By the early 1960s, the strength of the European Community as a trading bloc,
compared with the lesser economic performance of the United Kingdom and the
reluctance of Commonwealth members to accept the British lead on many matters, made entry more attractive. Furthermore, the United States encouraged it.
First, the Conservative government under Harold Macmillan, and later in the
decade, the Labour government of Harold Wilson made unsuccessful attempts to
enter, falling afoul of a French veto of its application each time. The French, especially President Charles de Gaulle, feared a strong British presence in an organization in which France, along with West Germany, had heretofore played the leading roles. De Gaulle also thought that the British were too tied to United States
interests. Public opinion surveys at the time indicated that the public was not
especially interested in the arguments over British membership in the
Community. Elite opinion, although divided, was generally favorable.[13]

When the Conservatives returned to office, somewhat unexpectedly, in 1970,
Edward Heath, who as a Conservative minister had negotiated with the EC for
British entry in the early 1960s, became prime minister. He was committed to taking Britain into the European Community, and with De Gaulle gone from the
scene in France, this was finally accomplished through negotiations ending in
1972. Interestingly enough, France had a referendum on British membership, but
Britain did not. The opposition Labour party, under Harold Wilson, argued that
Heath had not negotiated favorable terms, and many Conservatives were bothered by the sovereignty question and the fear that the Community would come to
dominate British economic and foreign policy decisonmaking. Thus debates in
the House of Commons on the treaty were rancorous, with split votes in both

major parties.[14] Mass opinion, too, was split, though not on party lines.[15] The Liberals were united in favor of EC participation, a position they have maintained throughout the ensuing years.

Maintenance of British membership on the terms renegotiated by the Wilson Labour government was approved by a 2–1 margin in the 1975 referendum, despite continued intraparty dissension on the issue.[16] The referendum was not demanded by the population but by the political elite. With the issue continuing to split both of the two big parties, Prime Minister Harold Wilson found a way to proclaim an improved arrangement over what the Conservatives had negotiated, to avoid a permanent division within his own party and to allow dissidents, including those in the cabinet, to test their claim that the population was not enamored of the EU. Thus the referendum served the need of the political elite for a signal from the public, preferably a definitive signal, to end their intraparty bickering over the issue. Even though the vote was decisive, by the early 1980s the Labour party was again racked with controversy over the issue. Two decades later Prime Minister John Major resisted calls from an array of opinion leaders, including the *Economist* and Lady Thatcher, for a referendum on the Maastricht Treaty for enlarging the scope of European Community competence. The debate will doubtless be renewed when the European Intergovernmental Conference on consitutional issues takes place in 1996.

With a large contingent of moderates within the Labour Party moving to set up their own party (the Social Democrats) in 1981, leftists suspicious of the "capitalists' club" in the Community gained control of Labour. Anything that hindered a potential Labour government from full control of the British economy was viewed with suspicion. Unlike their continental counterparts, British socialists have tended to look skeptically at movements for greater European integration, as Labour Party splits and shifts over the EU issue suggest. In the 1983 election campaign, Labour ran on a platform of withdrawal from the European Community, a position that had to be rethought in view of the devastating defeat (only 28 percent of the popular vote, with many Labour candidates thrown into third place in their constituencies) that the party suffered. By the early 1990s, with moderates once again leading the party, Labour was proclaiming a greater Euro-enthusiasm than the Conservatives under Mrs. Thatcher and Mr. Major, although such a posture did not preclude them from voting against the approval of the Maastricht Treaty when it was presented to Parliament, ostensibly because of the British exclusion from the Social Chapter, which provides minimum benefits and guarantees for workers. The suspicion remains that Labour, like much of the rest of Britain, is a reluctant European.

The Conservative Party has generally been more consistently committed to the Union, though not without a significant dissident group within it opposed to further European integration. Once in the European Community, Britain, especially under the Conservative government of Margaret Thatcher, constantly complained about its relative budgetary contributions. With its small agricultural sector, Britain did not benefit greatly from the Common Agricultural Policy of the EC, which accounted for well over one-half of the EC budget. Furthermore, the fact that other economies were growing more than Britain's led to the British league-standing in economic prosperity falling within the community. Mrs. Thatcher argued that the British budgetary contribution was too large, and in 1984 she secured an annual refund. This mollified Conservative qualms for a while, but later on, further problems appeared.

In the mid-1980s, the European Community began to move toward greater integration. The Conservative government agreed to the Single European Act of 1985, promising free movement of goods, services, finance (capital), and people (labor) by the end of 1992, because these provisions were in line with the government's preferences for lowering barriers to international trade. Although this act gave the European Commission and European Parliament enhanced powers, it also left implementation of the act largely to the individual governments. Britain is generally considered one of the countries most compliant in implementation of the Single European Act and other EU policies, although there have been notable exceptions, such as in environmental policy. As with all European Union legislation, complete realization of goals was not reached by the target date, but significant progress was made.

The Thatcher government was more resistant to schemes to establish the European Monetary Union, starting with the question of whether Britain should join the European Exchange Rate Mechanism (ERM), which was an optional arrangement linking European currencies together in such a way that the members were pledged not to alter their mutual exchange rates beyond a certain level. Although the arrangement was not a compulsory one for EC members, both West Germany (after 1990, unified Germany) and France had agreed. After resisting joining the ERM for several years because of the erosion of British control over its own exchange rate and monetary policy that the institution represented, in 1989 the Conservative government finally joined. The rate agreed for the pound sterling in relation to other currencies, particularly the dominant deutsche mark, struck many critics as too high. On September 15, 1992, Britain suffered Black Wednesday, in which massive selling of sterling by international financiers eventually led to Britain leaving the ERM. This caused recriminations between Britain and Germany over the relative blame for this situation between the two countries. Britain had a weak economy and high unemployment, whereas the independent German Bundesbank, ever fearful of inflation in its economy because of vast government spending on the newly incorporated eastern regions, had high interest rates. Thus the temptation was for international investors to put their money in Germany, to the detriment of the economic prospects of other members of the Community. This whole episode reinforced British suspicions about the utility of the Community, especially with a united Germany as its economic engine, having almost one-third of the total annual production of the EC. It also complicated consideration of the Maastricht Treaty.

The Maastricht Treaty, negotiated in December 1991, promised to deepen the integration of the Community. In addition to the major goals of creating a common European bank by 1997 and a common European currency by 1999, it enhanced European "competencies" in such areas as foreign policy, defense policy, and social policy.[17] On social policy, Britain was allowed to avoid committing itself to a limitation on working hours that the other eleven countries had agreed upon.

Even before the treaty was negotiated, a major debate in the House of Commons revealed severe party divisions, especially within the governing Conservatives, over what Britain's negotiation position should be and how far it should go to meet the demands of its European partners. Then the events of 1992, including the initial narrow referendum defeat of the treaty in Denmark (reversed in 1993) and its equally narrow endorsement in France, in addition to continuing turmoil over the relative value of different European currencies, created further doubts. Those less enamored of the EU argued for "subsidiarity," that is, allowing the lowest possible level of government—the individual states—to deal with most problems rather than automatically assuming that they required central coordination from the European Community. Another argument advanced was that rather than having central regulations for every member, the EC should adopt something more like a "cafeteria" approach, with members grouping themselves according to how much they wanted to be committed to particular policies. This was considered especially desirable in view of the pending membership of several other countries, including most of the remaining EFTA members and some of the developing democracies in Eastern Europe. Doubts were particularly voiced about German dominance of a central bank and currency, especially in the wake of the failure of the ERM to maintain currency stability among its members, a situation that was exacerbated in 1993. Thus the Conservative Party wobbled again on how committed it wanted to be to supranational integration schemes, and the opposition took advantage of this to prolong the debate over the Maastricht Treaty in the House of Commons. This made some Conservative dissidents go so far as to vote against their own government, again showing the depth of feeling within the party over this issue. Another group, led by a former editor of the *Times,* took up the issue of whether Parliament had the power to commit the United Kingdom to this degree of compromise of its own sovereignty without a referendum to the Law Lords, but later withdrew the case. But the public continued to be unmoved.[18]

In summary, then, Britain's activity within the European Community has been a long-running issue in British politics, and in several ways it has been a rather unusual one. Clearly the agenda has been set by elites, not by masses or by particular interest groups. There has been a persistent division within the elite, however, over how much authority Britain should allow the European Community to exercise. There have been those "little Englanders" in both major parties who have wanted Britain either to stay out, withdraw, or keep its commitment minimal. In the Labour Party this has usually involved leftists who want the power to have

Britain operate its own socialist economic policy, including nationalization when thought necessary, with little concern for its European partners. In recent years, however, some trade unions and others have seen the EU, especially through its Social Chapter, acting as a potential counterweight to domestic Conservative governments hostile to the extension of collective benefits in the United Kingdom. In the Conservative Party, the issues have usually been political rather than economic. In both cases, they reveal interesting tendencies in elite ideology. The leadership of both parties has, in general, wavered in the face of backbench carping about Europe, although some leaders (Edward Heath and Margaret Thatcher) have been more consistent in their very different positions. The Liberals and their moderate successor parties, as well as the small nationalist parties of the Celtic fringe, have been more consistently favorable toward the Community because they have looked to it to help legitimize some of their preferred plans, such as proportional representation, devolution, and regional aid. Despite all of the big party divisions over Europe, the public has never viewed the issue in quite the same intense terms. Only rarely has it rated Europe as a major political issue. The public has tended to take its cues from the party leaders, bespeaking no deep commitment in either direction toward Europe.

One of the unusual features of this issue has been that, despite being largely, although not exclusively, a foreign policy issue, it has generated major institutional variations in the normal British political process. The only countrywide referendum so far was called on the European Community, and collective responsibility of the cabinet was dropped for the duration of the referendum campaign. Various votes on the European Community, both on the original entry terms and on subsequent matters stimulated by the Community, have been a major source of intraparty parliamentary dissent in the House of Commons.[19] Nevertheless, policy formulation and legitimation have remained very much in elite hands as well, with little pressure from public opinion, individual constituencies, or interest groups. Once decisions have been made, and despite its reputation as a reluctant European, Britain has been one of the countries foremost in implementing EC policies. Thus membership in the European Community has been an issue that has seen a permanent intraparty elite split and serious constitutionally and economically related wrangles, but not one that has animated the mass public. Turnout for European parliamentary elections, for instance, has been far below that of general elections.[20]

As the European Union has "deepened" as an organization, the implications of British membership for policy areas such as foreign and socioeconomic policy have grown, although they have not necessarily become clear. EU policy in these areas has been voluntaristic rather than compulsory. Britain is compelled to discuss these topics and defend its positions in meetings of the Council of Ministers, but so far it has not had to adopt any policies it opposes. As noted, Parliament has not followed up its general discussions of EU policy with careful examination of proposed EU legislation. The British institution with the greatest amount of involvement with the Community is the civil service, which represents Britain in Brussels through the United Kingdom Permanent Representation to the European Communities. Members of the civil service there come from various departments, serving two-year terms on leave. They form the working groups of the Committee of Permanent Representatives, a major policy-development group for the EU. Thus the British role in the European Union has remained largely an executive function, one that contributes to complaints about the "democratic deficit" of the EU.[21]

In the wake of the attempts at greater integration of the European Union in the 1980s and 1990s and enlargement of the organization in the 1990s, the United Kingdom's policy dilemma over the EU has become intensified, and promises no relief. What should the trade-off between "deepening" and "widening" be? How far should Britain cooperate with the EU in its ever-increasing (if erratically so) policy competencies, even in fiscal policy? What are the costs and benefits of such actions, in terms of Britain's freedom of economic, diplomatic, and defense maneuverability? Does the United Kingdom really see itself as a part of a common European enterprise, or is it determined to maintain its independent decisionmaking capacity? These problems will demand attention, whoever rules the country.

Decolonization

Like the issue of European Community membership, the issue of decolonization and its aftermath seems to have engaged elite opinion vigorously but has had relatively little impact on mass opinion. The decolonization issue has differed, however, in that intraparty voting divisions in the House of Commons were not a usual feature. Whatever their internal debates, both major parties were able to present a united public front on most decolonization concerns. In a sense, the decolonization issue can be considered "normal politics" in Britain, at least according to Rose's[22] criteria. There was a good deal of posturing and criticism across the parliamentary benches, but in office the two parties' performance was not dissimilar. Both disengaged from colonial rule at a relatively swift pace, certainly much faster than was anticipated before World War II, but they also encountered some intractable problems, which they tended to approach with caution rather than force. Thus, for all of the partisan rhetoric, performance in office was similar.

The Labour Party promised independence for India in its campaign in the general election of 1945. Although there is no evidence that this was a massive vote-winning issue, under the British notion of an electoral mandate for the winning party's platform the Labour government proceeded to implement this pledge. The contrast with the Conservatives at the time could hardly have been sharper, since the Conservative leader, Winston Churchill, had opposed Indian independence. Extricating Britain from involvement in its vast colonial possessions abroad, however, proved to be a complex and bloody business, as the warfare between Hindus and Muslims over the division of the Raj into India and Pakistan demonstrated. The pattern was repeated, although not on so vast a scale, in

Palestine, Cyprus, Malaysia, Rhodesia (Zimbabwe), and elsewhere. By and large, however, the British avoided the entrenched conflict against insurgent peoples that characterized the extrications of other European imperial powers, most notably the French in Vietnam and Algeria.

Even though Labour made noises about being the anti-imperialist party sympathetic to the equality demands of dependent peoples and the Conservatives were considered the leading imperialist party through long historical inclination, their performances in office were not dissimilar. Neither was really prepared for the rapid pace of decolonization, especially in Africa. Labour criticized the Conservative government's creation of the Central African Federation in 1953, which amalgamated blacks with the white settlers of Rhodesia, but the independence of the first African state, the Gold Coast (renamed Ghana) in 1957 was followed by the release of several others, notably Nigeria, in 1960. For all of the publicity given to the Mau Mau uprising in Kenya, less than one hundred people were killed.

The greatest difficulties came where there had been an appreciable number of white settlers long resident in the country, as in South Africa. The locus classicus was Rhodesia, where the whites refused British attempts to negotiate independence on the basis of equality with the local black population and made a Unilateral Declaration of Independence (UDI) in 1964. Subsequent British governments of both major parties "talked tough" about not allowing this to stand; however, following United Nations sanctions on the renegade republic, they were often criticized, ironically, by the Left for not using force. But it was the Conservatives under Mrs. Thatcher who were finally able to negotiate a settlement of the issue in 1979, ensuring black majority rule for the newly named country of Zimbabwe.

Among the elite, there was a broad consensus on wanting peaceful resolution of decolonization conflicts and incorporation of the newly independent states into the Commonwealth, which was looked upon as a developing arena not only for trade enhancement but also for continuing British political influence in the world. Until 1962, the United Kingdom maintained an immigration policy oriented toward that end, whereby any citizen of an independent Commonwealth country had the untrammeled right to travel to the mother country and automatically assume the full rights of a British citizen upon entry. This condition held despite the opportunity in 1948 to enact a more restrictive British citizenship when the issue had to be reconsidered in light of Canada's new citizenship law. The Commonwealth Immigrants Act of 1962, which for the first time put limits on immigration from the new Commonwealth, meaning the newly independent states in Asia, Africa, and the Americas, was symbolic of how the earlier British elite hopes for the Commonwealth were being dashed. The domestic race-related aspects of immigration will be considered in Chapter 8.

The independent states of the Commonwealth, which eventually grew to number nearly fifty members, proved to be neither a vast market nor an arena for the exercise of British international influence. Although these states continued to be important trading partners for the United Kingdom, especially in the supply of agricultural products, and constituted a sterling area with the value of their currencies dependent on that of the British pound, their economies did not grow to an extent that allowed them collectively to compete with the developed economies of the United States and Western Europe as partners in secondary (manufacturing) and tertiary (services) trade. Canada and Australia were exceptions to a degree, but the size of their economies was limited by their small populations. After 1957, Britain quickly found that being outside the common external tariff of the six countries in the European Community more than outweighed the economic benefits of Commonwealth trade. Not all of the advantages of favorable prices for Commonwealth agricultural prices were lost upon entering the EC in 1973, especially because of the negotiation of the Lomé Convention, a major trade agreement between the community and a group of Third World countries. But the British choice was still clear—to take either the economic benefits of the European Community, including its controversial Common Agricultural Policy, or the traditional cheap food and minerals policy from the Commonwealth. Even before its formal entrance into the European Union, Britain's trade with those countries had surpassed that with the Commonwealth, and the two trends have continued relentlessly in opposite directions subsequently.[23]

Politically, the Commonwealth countries proved to be awkward partners. The old Commonwealth of Australia, New Zealand, and Canada was rapidly outnumbered by the new Commonwealth of newly independent states. Despite the adoption of parliamentary institutions, many of the new states quickly turned into one-party dictatorships, often espousing various brands of Marxism. Ethnic resentments often led to disaster, as in Nigeria and Uganda. As their numbers swelled in the United Nations (UN), the newly independent states formed part of the Third World majority in the General Assembly that voiced its criticism of various Western economic and political positions as "neo-imperialism." The United Kingdom, like its two Western compatriots on the Security Council, found itself casting an increasing number of vetos there. As economic growth became stalled, many newly independent Commonwealth countries joined in the demands for a New International Economic Order, one in which Third World countries would gain more favorable economic terms through enhanced influence in the World Bank, international price supports for agricultural products, easier loans, and other policies favorable to technologically underdeveloped debtor countries. British overseas aid has never reached the UN goal of 0.7 percent of gross national product, and under recent Conservative governments aid has been reduced.

The continuing racial apartheid in South Africa, a former British colony, was a particular flashpoint for Commonwealth conflict. After South Africa left the Commonwealth in 1959, the venue of discussion moved to the United Nations. But South African policies, and especially its political and military activities elsewhere in southern Africa, such as Rhodesia, Angola, and Mozambique, continued to plague the quadrennial meetings of Commonwealth prime ministers as well. Other countries pressed Britain to do more—economically, politically, and militarily—to remedy racial discrimination and its offshoots elsewhere in southern Africa. British governments were anxious to limit their involvement to moral condemnation. The one clearly mutually satisfying outcome of this political engagement was the negotiation of independence for Rhodesia (Zimbabwe) on the basis of black majority rule in 1979–1980. Even this did not quiet Commonwealth criticism of British policies. By the 1990s, even Australia was questioning whether it wanted to retain the monarchy as a symbol of its ties to Britain. Republics could still remain in the Commonwealth, but the organization had long ceased being the instrument of British policy that elites had hoped it would be. Ironically, after South Africa achieved black majority rule in 1994, it reapplied to join the Commonwealth.

There were a variety of interest groups organized around the promotion of perceived British interests in relation to Commonwealth countries, but only rarely were any of them particularly influential on the course of policy. Larger questions of foreign policy and what international commitments could be sustained, economically and militarily, dominated decisionmaking in this area. The public was a passive actor. For all of the claims made about a strong British international presence being linked to British nationalism and sense of purpose, there is precious little evidence that the public saw either the maintenance of strong British leadership in the Commonwealth or any particular Commonwealth problems as crucial to Britain's future. Suez and the Falklands are cases in point.

More books have been written about Suez than any other British postwar foreign policy imbroglio.[24] It has been widely viewed as Britain's last attempt to assert itself as having an independent foreign policy worthy of a great power. This was one instance in which the government's position was vigorously opposed by both opposition parties of the time, Labour and the Liberals. Yet it was not the public or opposition criticism that forced the Conservatives to change policy; it was economic and political pressure from the United Kingdom's most important ally, the United States.

Briefly, the United Kingdom had unofficially dominated Egypt since 1882, even though Egypt had never formally been incorporated into the empire. After the overthrow of the corrupt King Farouk by military officers in 1952, the new Egyptian nationalist government increasingly came into conflict with Britain over the latter's control of the Suez canal. Finally, in 1956 Colonel Gamal Abdel Nasser, the Egyptian leader, announced that he was going to nationalize the canal in order to realize enough revenue to build the Aswan High Dam on the Nile River after the United States had canceled its loan for the project. Rather than resisting directly on their own, the British hatched a three-way scheme with France (under a Socialist government) and Israel, both of which were also concerned about Egyptian unreliability in managing this important international waterway. Israel technically was still in a state of war with Egypt over the latter's invasion in an attempt to quash Israeli independence in 1948. Thus, in 1952 when Israel attacked Egypt, France and Britain acted to "protect" the Suez Canal from the encroaching conflict by rushing troops there and fighting the Egyptians, too. The major problem with this strategy was that apparently none of the three attackers had bothered to consult with their major ally, the United States. Although the United States was also wary of Egyptian nationalism, it did not wish to be perceived as endorsing a resurgence of European imperialism, especially in view of the Soviet invasion of Hungary at the same time. Thus the United States refused to support the European invaders' currencies when they came under pressure in the international market. Lacking the diplomatic and economic backing of the United States, the invaders were forced to settle for an armistice on the ground within a few days, to be followed by an eventual withdrawal.

The lessons about British policy in an increasingly anti-imperialist world were several. To begin with, the use of large-scale military force was not necessarily desirable either in achieving its goal or in generating an overwhelming endorsement from the citizenry. Instead, in addition to the partisan controversy there was also a division of public opinion on the issue, although a majority of the public supported the government.[25] But with a secure majority in the House of Commons and no general election needed for several years, the Conservative government could have carried out its policy of force, had it not been concerned about its standing with the United States and its international economic condition. Ultimately international, not domestic, considerations dominated government decisionmaking. Domestically, the government suffered no long-term effects from its retreat, but the invasion itself alienated much of Commonwealth opinion about British methods of dealing with its former colonies. The prime minister, Anthony Eden, was soon replaced, ostensibly on health grounds, by Harold Macmillan, but by 1959 the Conservatives managed to win a third consecutive term with an increased majority of seats in the House of Commons, largely on the issue of increased economic prosperity. Domestic policy moved the voters; foreign policy did not.

As Christopher Hewitt[26] has pointed out, interest groups in foreign policy crises are usually caught unaware, and the premium put on rapid decisionmaking limits their influence. In the cases of both Suez and the Falklands, however, there was a long-term buildup to a crisis, and there were established interest groups, especially those interested in maintaining a strong British role. But there is no indication that these groups, or indeed the generally pro-Arab Foreign Office, had much influence on the decision to use force in Suez. As discussed further on, the role of interest groups and their backbench allies in the Conservative Party is more controversial in the Falklands decision. In the Suez case, however, even though the political elite was split on partisan grounds, the government, meaning the cabinet led by the prime minister, was able to pursue its preferred policy until it became limited by international, not domestic, factors. Dissident Conservative back-benchers who wanted a more diplomatic approach encountered difficulties with their local constituency parties.[27]

The Conservative government's decision to retake the Falklands Islands after Argentina invaded them in 1982 has several surface dissimilarities to the Suez case, but the processes of decisionmaking also have some underlying similarities. If anything, the Argentinian invasion was even more of a surprise than the Israeli invasion of Egypt since the issue had been on the back burner of foreign policy for some time. The Falklands, or Malvinas, as they are called by Argentina, had only 1,600 people, practically all of them British-descended, although, after the 1981 British Nationality Act, they were not able to claim a right to British citizen-ship. The Defense Department was trying to cut expenditures by putting naval warships into mothballs; some of these had to be rejuventated for the Falklands battle. For some time, diplomats had been urging a resolution to the long-standing British-Argentinian dispute over sovereignty in the Falklands. But when the Argentinians took matters into their own hands in March 1982, the British elite and public responded as one. The opposition parties supported the Con-servative government's decision to resist the aggression with force, as did the pub-lic. This was fundamentally a British decision, although there was a great deal of diplomatic effort put forward to make sure that the United States and the European Community in particular supported the decision. The retaking of the Falklands was successful in its objectives, and as such, some analysts have argued that the operation restored the public's pride in Britain as an international actor and was largely responsible for the overwhelming Conservative electoral victory in 1983.[28] Mrs. Thatcher became identified as a leader who carried through on her convictions both abroad and at home.

The argument has been made that the Falklanders were able to prevent a settle-ment of the dispute that would give Argentina some share of sovereignty by lob-bying backbenchers in the House of Commons, particularly when the Labour government under James Callaghan sounded out opinion on such a solution in the late 1970s.[29] Yet as in the case of Suez, scattered backbench opinion is not usu-ally important in foreign affairs situations, especially crises. In other situations involving the threat or use of force in the extended empire, such as in Iran in 1951,[30] as well as in Malaysia, Aden, and various imbroglios in Africa, backbench opinion in one or both parties has counted for little. Why would it, along with interest representation from the Falklanders, be considered so important here?

If credibility can be given to the interest group–backbench influence argument, its importance lies in the low priority the government attached to the issue. The Falklands was never an issue of high priority to the Foreign Office or to the polit-ical elite, generally. It amounted to part of the "winding up of empire" problem, which has remnants all over the globe.[31] With such few people and resources, involving a country that Britain did not ordinarily have crucial dealings with, the Falklands had considerably less importance than, say, the dispute over Gibraltar with Spain or over Hong Kong with China. If the government had decided to pursue a negotiated settlement in the late 1970s, it could probably have readily overcome any interest group–inspired backbench dissent. But the issue was not considered important enough to pursue, given the press of other concerns. When the issue became a crisis with the Argentine invasion, the government still had the capacity to make a negotiated settlement, as efforts in this direction were carried on especially by the secretary-general of the United Nations. But Mrs. Thatcher carried through her combative policy to the end, to military victory.

The lessons from these episodes in decolonization, a major part of British foreign policy in the postwar world, indicate a great deal of domestic freedom of decision for the government. The public normally is more concerned with domestic issues, especially economic ones; imperial glory and world standing are not major issues. Depending on the situation, various British governments have pursued both accommodation and resistance to demands for independence and territorial concessions by Third World leaders, with no particular ill effects as far as public opinion was concerned. Beneath the foreign policy bombast in the House of Commons and the media, there has usually also been underlying partisan agreement on the general direction of policy, as measured by actual votes in the House of Commons. Parliamentary dissenters have been few, usually limited to right-wing Conservatives and left-wing Labour, often voting together for different reasons.[32] The decision to resist an Egyptian takeover by invading the Suez Canal Zone was somewhat different than the norm in that both partisan disagreement and a major split in public opinion occurred. But neither prevented the government from pursuing its own policy and, when that policy failed to reach its objectives and was abandoned, there were no negative electoral effects. The constraints on policy were foreign, not domestic. As Lowi[33] argued in his seminal study linking policy issues to the pluralism-elitism debate, in foreign policy, elitism is the norm. This may be even more true in the United Kingdom than in the United States.

Defense and Security

One of the paradoxes of politics in the United Kingdom is that, although the nation is widely perceived as a substantial welfare state in the United States, it has retained a formidable defense force and defense budget even as its influence abroad has declined. In percentage terms, British defense spending has traditionally been the highest in NATO except for the United States; until the early 1990s, it was above 5 percent of gross national product. As the Cold War ended, it had shrunk to 4 percent and is projected to be even lower in the next few years. As an island state, Britain has maintained defense and security as paramount concerns. Cutbacks have occurred but not to the same extent they have in other countries.

There has been a surprising degree of agreement, at least in office, between the two major parties on defense matters. Labour has sometimes sounded skeptical of

United Kingdom defense commitments in opposition, particularly over the development and retention of nuclear weapons, but in office Labour has been a staunch supporter of alliance commitments and defense spending, much to the disgust of its left wing. In fact, the basic defense posture of the United Kingdom was a product of the Attlee Labour government. Even as it withdrew, largely on economic grounds, from its extensive overseas commitments in such places as the Middle East and Greece, it endorsed the role of the United States in stepping into these power vacuums. It became evident that the international power structure of the postwar world would be bipolar. Furthermore, led by the foreign secretary, Ernest Bevin, the Labour government took an active role in developing the Western defense posture as the Soviet threat became evident. The first fruits of this inclination were the Brussels Pact among the United Kingdom, France, Belgium, the Netherlands, and Luxembourg, followed by the founding of the North Atlantic Treaty Organization in 1949. NATO is a collective defense organization, in which an attack on any of its members would be considered an attack on all. Unlike the European Community, Britain was present at the creation of the major Western security alliance and has continued to contribute substantially to both political decisions and force commitments.

NATO eventually grew to seventeen members, stretching from Canada to Turkey, but its area of geographic focus was the United States and Western Europe. Many analysts consider NATO to be, in effect, a guarantee by the United States of involvement in European defense against outside aggression. By committing its troops and nuclear weapons to European security, the United States was establishing a sphere of influence to counter the gains of the other emergent power after World War II, the Soviet Union. In return, it received defense contributions from the other members of NATO although the United States made the major troop and spending commitments and retained most of the decision making capacity.

The United Kingdom was a key actor in developing NATO as part of its more general defense policy, characterized as the Anglo-American special relationship. As an extension of the strong relationship developed between the two countries during World War II, Britain was eager to have the United States permanently involved in the defense of Western Europe in the postwar period. Thus Britain was willing to back the United States elsewhere in the world, as it did in the Korean War, and was generally more sympathetic to United States security and foreign policy initiatives than other European countries. By maintaining its own substantial contribution to NATO in troops and spending, the United Kingdom was able to keep the ear of the most powerful country in the world. Even though Britain's nuclear deterrent was billed as "independent," Britain was the only country to which the United States was willing to sell its nuclear delivery systems.[34] More generally, Britain attempted to work, whenever possible, in conjunction with the United States in security matters. Until recently, this was more feasible in Europe than elsewhere.

Even under the uncertain Western security arrangements in the wake of the collapse of communism, Britain continues to be a major actor. Conservative governments have continued to support a strong NATO and the U.S. presence in Europe. After the collapse of communism in Eastern Europe, however, NATO's mission has become uncertain. Former Communist regimes, including the Soviet Union itself, are now tied to NATO through consultation agreements. Moving NATO from collective defense to other goals has proven elusive and, like the EU, its members have also been unable to agree on an effective policy toward the conflict generated by the breakup of Yugoslavia. Other countries feel the need to include Britain in any non-NATO defense structure that might be developed, for example, by working through the West European Union, another international intergovernmental organization. In any common defense policy of the European Community, Britain will be expected to play an important role. As discussed in the section on imperial and Commonwealth affairs, on occasion Britain has also projected its force capability into areas further afield, most significantly in Suez, the Falkland Islands, and later as part of the operation against Iraq's invasion of Kuwait. The situation in the Falklands shifted British defense spending substantially, moving it from a scheduled rundown of the navy to a long-term commitment to protect the Falkland Islanders. "Fortress Falklands" is an expensive policy. Nevertheless, the defense budget has gradually shrunk, ebbing from 8 percent of gross national product in the 1950s to 4 percent today. In the 1950s, Britain made a concerted effort to remain a major power in international security affairs. The British developed their own nuclear weapons in executive secrecy under both the Labour and Conservative governments, making them the third-ranked nuclear power in the world after the United States and the Soviet Union. The pattern of executive secrecy was repeated by a Labour government when it developed plans to buy the next generation of nuclear weapons (Trident) in the late 1970s. By the latter part of the 1950s, there were concerted attempts to economize on defense spending. Ironically enough, development of nuclear capacity made this possible because the possession of a few nuclear weapons as a threat was much cheaper than maintenance of a large standing military force. Conscription was ended in 1958.

Not everybody was happy with these nuclear developments. The Campaign for Nuclear Disarmament conducted its first significant marches in 1959, as public concern mounted over the issue of the effects of nuclear weapons testing and tension between the United States and the Soviet Union increased. It was the nuclear weapons of the United States, after all, that were the ultimate NATO deterrent to Soviet aggression. In a nuclear exchange, the United Kingdom was unlikely to remain unscathed.

The Conservative government under Harold Macmillan was instrumental in negotiations leading to the Nuclear Test Ban Treaty of 1962, which committed signatories to no above-ground tests, and the Nuclear Nonproliferation Treaty of 1964, a multilateral agreement limiting nuclear weapons to those states already possessing them. Even though Britain had its own nuclear weapons, as delivery systems moved from bombers to rockets and submarines, the country became dependent on the United States for the technology for these systems, which both tied the weapons more closely to NATO and increased the subordinate role of Britain to the United States.[35] Even as defense commitments "east of Suez" were cut back in the late 1960s, the reliance on nuclear weapons as a major part of Britain's defense posture in Western Europe continued. Britain also contributed its share of troops to the major Western defense point in West Germany.

In most of the struggles of the Cold War, Britain came down firmly on the side of the United States, even while a minority of the public remained skeptical of the United States.[36] Some right-wingers in the Conservative Party lamented the loss of Britain's world leadership role and reacted as "little Englanders," wanting to determine the country's foreign commitments from London. Similarly, some left-wingers in the Labour Party saw British policy toward the Soviet Union and other Communist countries as too belligerent. But these groups remained small minorities. The broad center, in both public and parliamentary terms, supported the Atlantic Alliance, NATO, and the possession of an independent nuclear force.[37]

After the split of the Social Democrats from Labour in 1981, the left wing of Labour became more influential on policy than ever before. Labour pledged itself to unilateral disarmament in nuclear weapons in the 1983 and 1987 general elections, positions that did not generate a positive response in the public.[38] By 1992, Labour had repositioned itself to be in favor of "multilateral, negotiated disarmament." For a while in the early 1980s, the British adoption of NATO's two-track strategy for meeting the Soviet forward-based nuclear threat, which was negotiating on the one hand, while, on the other hand, placing NATO's short-range missiles in various European countries, including Britain, provoked a revival of the Campaign for Nuclear Disarmament. But when the chips were down, Britain accepted the missiles.

In the various other confrontations of the Cold War in Europe—in Berlin, Hungary, Czechoslovakia, and Poland—Britain lined up solidly with the United States and its NATO partners as well. It was less supportive, militarily and politically, of the United States in Cold War confrontations in other parts of the world, especially after Suez showed that Britain could not always count on reciprocal backing from the United States. Britain viewed some of these struggles, such as Vietnam, as distractions from the principal concern, Soviet policy in Europe. Given their dissimilar experiences with the rest of the world, it is not particularly surprising that the United Kingdom and the United States would differ somewhat in their approaches to events in Asia and Latin America. In Africa, however, they tended to reinforce each other, being generally more accommodating to white minority regimes in Rhodesia and South Africa than most Third World countries would have liked. Similarly, the United States backed Britain's position in the Falklands despite considerable pressure from Latin Americanists to tilt toward Argentina, and Britain was a principal contributor to the United States–led force under United Nations auspices that rebuffed Iraq's seizure of Kuwait in 1991.

Margaret Thatcher took some credit for helping to end the Cold War through the collapse of communism. After all, she earned her sobriquet—the Iron Lady—from the Soviets for her firmness in negotiations in the early 1980s. She was also impressed by an early meeting with Mikhail Gorbachev after he became Soviet leader, saying he was a man with whom the West could deal. The complexities of foreign policy make it difficult to sort out definitively where the credit should be given for the end of communism, but there is no doubt that, for better or worse (and economically, if not politically, it was often for the worse), the British were on the front lines of confrontation, and, under both Labour and Conservative governments, they rarely blinked.

Evaluation

As noted previously, foreign and defense policy are, in constitutional terms, primarily executive functions in the United Kingdom. The monarch has the formal role as head of the Commonwealth and exchanges goodwill visits with dignitaries from other states. Major defense commitments, such as the building of the British atomic bomb in the early 1950s and the decision to build a new generation of nuclear missiles for submarines in the late 1970s, have often been made in secret, with little or no parliamentary, much less public, input. Similarly, foreign policy is largely in the hands of the executive. Major commitments involving a certain amount of constitutional revision, such as the treaty making Britain a member of the European Community or the Maastricht Treaty, are submitted for parliamentary approval, but most foreign policy becomes a matter for debate through parliamentary adjournment motions and prime minister's Question Time rather than through legislation laid before Parliament.

In short, in the United Kingdom foreign policy is clearly an elitist policy area, and the public does not take that much interest in it. Despite claims that Britain's fall from great power status has had a deleterious effect on public pride, evidence of any effect on public opinion from foreign policy, traditionally considered, is difficult to find. This is a classic instance of what some analysts have labeled a "permissive consensus." As long as the executive is successful, it has wide scope for initiatives and, indeed, secrecy. Despite considerable interpartisan debate over foreign policy matters, once in office the broad middle sector of elite opinion on foreign policy, preferring engagement with the rest of the world, maintenance of the Anglo-American and Atlantic Alliances, and use of military force if deemed necessary, has carried the day. Many foreign policy matters have not even generated that amount of debate.

During the twentieth century, Britain has declined from being a great power and has become a middle power—and has even seen its status shrink within that designation. Although British leaders are skillful at diplomacy and in the coordination and selective use of military force, Britain has been unable to arrest strategic weaknesses arising from its small territorial base (a particular handicap in an age of air and missile power) and its declining position in the world economy. Britain simply did not have the economic productiveness to enable it to maintain its former international standing when challenged by more populous, better-endowed, and more economically resourceful newcomers. It is instructive to compare its situation to that of the other island middle power in the Pacific, Japan. While the Japanese prospered economically but shrank from assuming major roles in defense and foreign policy more generally, during the same years Britain relied on its military commitments and diplomatic skills to maintain its position in the world but lagged in economic growth. By the 1990s, however, Japan was being urged by other countries to assume a foreign policy and defense posture commensurate with its economic role in the world, whereas Britain's foreign policy position was widely considered to be beyond its economic status. Although the institutions of the United Nations are difficult to change, there have been movements to give Japan and Germany seats on the Security Council. Few question the United Kingdom's possession of a seat, but in a Security Council with broadened membership, its influence would probably shrink even more proportionately than the number of members would indicate.

Aside from the shifting international environment and relative economic decline, a third factor contributing to postwar policy problems, especially at the end of the twentieth century, is the confused British attitude toward Europe.[39] As noted, this debate has heretofore occurred largely at the elite level, and it divides both the Labour and Conservative Parties. In foreign policy terms, the debate is over how Britain can best retain even its middle power position in the world, whether by cooperating wholeheartedly with the rest of the European Union or by maintaining its aloofness in the interest of following more closely its own definition of what is in its national interest. A European Union led by Germany is a disturbing thought to many foreign policymakers in Britain, as is the plethora of problems arising from the removal of the Soviet Union as the dominant factor in Eastern Europe. Would greater incorporation into a more federalist Europe lead to Britain becoming a small, niche power, losing even its current status, or would its standing be enhanced by being one of the more powerful members of an upsurgent organization? In the wake of the end of the Cold War, with defense commitments being reduced and prospects for greater social and foreign policy cooperation in the European Union looming, the urgency for an answer to this question becomes greater. Nevertheless, the European Union remains primarily an economic organization, and Britain's postwar economic performance, both out of and within the EU, is troubling.

More generally, Paul Kennedy,[40] in a widely read historical analysis of the problems of great powers, has cited "imperial overstretch" as a major factor in the United Kingdom's decline both diplomatically and economically. According to Kennedy, Britain in the nineteenth and twentieth centuries provides a good example of a country whose worldwide commitments, exacerbated by the effects of the world wars, led to neglect and decline of its domestic economic base. In short, the attempt to maintain and extend international influence, fundamentally, are distractions not easily resisted and are fatal to a country's longer-term power prospects. Nevertheless, Kennedy sees Britain as having managed its decline relatively well, compared to other falling great powers. Although this is an attractive theory, it is difficult to confirm, given the vast range of other possible factors that have been cited as contributing to Britain's problems in the twentieth century. It is difficult enough to evaluate these factors in the economic realm alone, as shown in the next chapter.

Notes

1. F.E.S. Northedge, *Descent from Power: British Foreign Policy, 1945–73* (London: Allen and Unwin, 1974); Paul Kennedy, *The Rise and Fall of the Great Powers* (New York: Random House, 1987).

2. Peter Byrd, ed., *British Foreign Policy Under Thatcher* (Oxford: Philip Allan, 1988); Peter Byrd, ed., *British Defence Policy: Thatcher and Beyond* (London: Philip Allan, 1991); David Goldsworthy, *Colonial Issues in British Politics, 1945–1961* (Oxford: Clarendon Press, 1971); John Darwin, *Britain and Decolonization: The Retreat from Empire in the Postwar World* (New York: St. Martin's Press, 1988); Michael Dockrill, *British Defence Since 1945.* (Oxford: Basil Blackwell, 1988); Lawrence H. Freedman and Michael Clarke, eds., *Britain in the World* (Cambridge: Cambridge University Press, 1991); Stephen George, *Britain and European Integration Since 1945* (New York: Basil Blackwell, 1991).

3. Randall B. Ripley and Grace Franklin, *Congress, the Bureaucracy and Public Policy,* 5th ed. (Pacific Grove, Ca.: Brooks/Cole Publishing Company, 1991); R. Kent Weaver and Bert A. Rockman, eds., *Do Institutions Matter? Government Capabilities in the United States and Abroad* (Washington, D.C.: Brookings Institution, 1993); Theodore J. Lowi, "American Business, Public Policy, Case Studies, and Political Theory," *World Politics* 16, no. 4 (1964):677–715; T. Alexander Smith, *The Comparative Policy Process* (Santa Barbara, Ca.: ABC-Clio, 1975); John Spanier and Eric M. Uslaner, *American Foreign Policy Making and the Democratic Dilemmas,* 5th ed. (Pacific Grove, Ca.: Brooks/Cole Publishing Company, 1989).

4. Richard E. Neustadt and Ernest R. May, *Thinking in Time* (New York: Free Press, 1986).

5. Brian C. White, "British Foreign Policy: Tradition and Change," in *Foreign Policy in World Politics,* 8th ed., ed. Ray C. Macridis (Englewood Cliffs, N.J.: Prentice Hall, 1992); David Sanders, "Relations with Outside Governments: Foreign and Military Policy," in *The Developing British Political System: The 1990s?* ed. Ian Budge and David McKay (New York: Longman, 1993).

6. Emil Kirchner, "A Third Level of Government: Britain in the European Community," in *The Developing British Political System,* ed. Ian Budge and David McKay (London: Longman, 1994).

7. Ian Budge and Denis Farlie, *Explaining and Predicting Elections* (London: Allen and Unwin, 1983); Ian Budge, David Robertson, and David Hearl, eds., *Ideology, Strategy, and Party Change* (Cambridge: Cambridge University Press, 1987).

8. Ivor Crewe, "Britain: Two and a Half Cheers for the Atlantic Alliance," in *The Public and Atlantic Defense,* ed. Gregory Flynn and Hans Rattinger (Lanham, Md.: Rowman and Littlefield, 1985).

9. Jorgen Rasmussen and James M. McCormick, "British Mass Perceptions of the Anglo-American Special Relationship," *Political Science Quarterly* 108, no. 3 (1993):515–541; Richard S. Flickinger, "British Political Parties and Public Attitudes Toward the European Community: Leading, Following or Getting Out of the Way?" in David Broughton, *British Parties and Elections Yearbook, 1994*, ed. David Broughton, David Farrell, David Denver, and Colin Rallings (London: Frank Cass, 1994).

10. Sanders, "Relations with Outside Governments: Foreign and Military Policy"; Neil Nugent, "The European Dimension," in *Developments in British Politics* 4, ed. Patrick Dunleavy, Andrew Gamble, Ian Holliday, and Gillian Peele (New York: St. Martin's Press, 1993).

11. Nugent, "The European Dimension."

12. Russell J. Dalton and Robert Duval, "The Political Environment and Foreign Policy Opinions: British Attitudes Toward European Integration, 1972–1979," *British Journal of Political Science* 16, no. 1 (1986):113–134; Flickinger, "British Political Parties and the European Community: Leading, Following or Getting Out of the Way?"

13. Flickinger, "British Political Parties and Public Attitudes Toward the European Community: Leading, Following or Getting Out of the Way?"

14. Philip Norton, *Dissension in the House of Commons, 1945–1974* (London: Macmillan, 1975).

15. Flickinger, "British Political Parties and Public Attitudes Toward the European Community: Leading, Following or Getting Out of the Way?"

16. David Butler and Uwe Kitzinger, *The 1975 Referendum* (London: Macmillan, 1976).

17. Nugent, "The European Dimension."

18. Flickinger, "British Political Parties and Public Attitudes Toward the European Community: Leading, Following or Getting Out of the Way?"

19. Norton, *Dissension in the House of Commons, 1945–1974*; Philip Norton, *Dissension in the House of Commons, 1974–1979* (Oxford: Clarendon Press, 1980).

20. Richard S. Flickinger and Donley T. Studlar, "The Disappearing Voters? Exploring Declining Turnout in Western European Elections," *West European Politics* 15, no. 1 (1992):1–16.

21. Kirchner, "A Third Level of Government: Britain in the European Community."

22. Richard Rose, "Still the Era of Party Government?" *Parliamentary Affairs* 26, no. 2 (1983):282–299.

23. Sanders, "Relations with Outside Governments: Foreign and Military Policy."

24. Hugh Thomas, *The Suez Affair* (London: Weidenfeld and Nicolson, 1966).

25. Leon Epstein, *British Politics in the Suez Crisis* (London: Allen and Unwin, 1964).

26. Christopher J. Hewitt, "The Power Structure of Britain" (Ph.D. diss., Brown University, 1970).

27. Epstein, *British Politics in the Suez Crisis.*

28. Ivor Crewe, "How Labour Was Trounced All Around," *Guardian,* 14 June, 1983; Harold D. Clarke, William Mishler, and Paul F. Whiteley, "Recapturing the Falklands: Models of Conservative Popularity, 1979–1983," *British Journal of Political Science* 20, no. 1 (1990):63–81; David Sanders, Hugh Ward, David Marsh, and Tony Fletcher, "Government Popularity and the Falklands War: A Reassessment," *British Journal of Political Science* 17, no. 3 (1987):281–313.

29. Max Hastings and Simon Jenkins, *The Battle for the Falklands* (London: Michael Joseph, 1983).

30. Christopher J. Hewitt, "Policy-making in Postwar Britain: A National-Level Test of Elitist and Pluralist Hypotheses," *British Journal of Political Science* 4, no. 2 (1974):187–216.

31. Jan Morris, *Farewell the Trumpets* (New York: Oxford University Press, 1990).

32. Hewitt, "Policy-making in Postwar Britain: A National-Level Test of Elitist and Pluralist Hypotheses"; Norton, *Dissension in the House of Commons, 1945–1974;* Norton, *Dissension in the House of Commons, 1974–1979.*

33. Theodore J. Lowi, "American Business, Public Policy, Case Studies, and Political Theory."

34. Sanders, "Relations with Outside Governments: Foreign and Military Policy."

35. Richard E. Neustadt, *Alliance Politics* (New York: Columbia University Press, 1970).

36. Rasmussen and McCormick, "British Mass Perception of the Anglo-American Special Relationship."

37. Crewe, "Britain: Two and a Half Cheers for the Atlantic Alliance."

38. Crewe, "How Labour Was Trounced All Around"; Anthony Heath, Roger Jowell, John Curtice, Geoff Evans, Julia Field, and Sharon Witherspoon, *Understanding Political Change* (Oxford: Pergamon Press, 1991).

39. John H. P. Williams, "Britain and the European Community: Maverick or Insider?" (paper presented at British Politics Group/American Political Science Association conference, Washington, D.C., 1993).

40. Kennedy, *The Rise and Fall of the Great Powers.*

6

ECONOMIC POLICY: FROM INDUSTRIAL GIANT TO BRITALY

MuCH OF POLITICS, ESPECIALLY IN modern times, is concerned with economic matters. This is often the major policy area on which government performance is judged, both by commentators and the public. The most common policy classifications concentrate on economic policies within their categories, sometimes ignoring other policy areas. For instance, Lowi's[1] schema, which classifies by distributive, redistributive, and regulatory categories, is almost exclusively concerned with different processes for making economic policy, leaving some room for social welfare policy. In T. Alexander Smith's[2] typology, economic policy is included in distributive, redistributive, and sectoral fragmentation policies, but he does add emotive symbolic policies. Even Randall Ripley and Grace Franklin's[3] policy classification creates more categories for domestic economic policy than for foreign policy.

As is indicated by these varying categories, economic policy can take different forms in the policy process, ranging from the highly contentious and divisive (redistributive) to the small-scale and largely ignored (distributive). There is actually considerable agreement on many economic goals, especially macroeconomic ones, but differences arise in how to reach these goals. Political discussion in other economic areas, such as in the nationalization-privatization arena, involves more fundamental differences in goals as well as means. Thus, even within the realm of economic policy, there is room for variation in how the policy process functions and in which actors are more influential. In this chapter, some of the more important economic policies in British politics are examined.

Increasingly, however, economic policy for all countries has been moving away from being a principally domestic concern, becoming largely international in scope. Both trade and finance are subject more than ever before to the vagaries of forces outside the state, including those of multinational companies, international financiers, other countries, and international organizations. As Wyn Grant[4] has pointed out, British governments are still judged on their economic performance, even as they become progressively less in control of the country's economic fate.

The Agenda

Economic policy has dominated British political life for most of the twentieth century. The only other contender for that preeminent place, at least on the "high politics" agenda, has been foreign policy. As noted in the previous chapter, especially since World War II, the decline of British external influence has made foreign policy less important, at least as part of the mandatory agenda.[5] Economic policy is always part of the mandatory agenda, and the debate over what to do and how to do it has dominated Parliament and government.

In the United Kingdom, economic policy is both a position and a valence issue, that is, an issue with agreed-on goals. As a valence issue, everybody wants the economy to do "better," as measured in various ways, and wants groups and individuals in the society to share in that improvement. To a considerable degree governments are judged by the electorate on valence economic criteria, however vague. When compared to the United States, France, Germany, and Italy, Britain ranks highest in economic voting, meaning that citizens vote primarily on the basis of their evaluations of the economy.[6] Certainly the amount of time governments have spent calculating and defending economic policy indicates an overwhelming concern not only with management of the economy but also with the electoral implications of this management. Multiparty competition in the 1970s–1990s, however, has blunted some of the effects of drawing direct economic comparisons between Labour and the Conservatives. Indeed, one popular hypothesis is that the overriding reason for the rise of multiparty competition was that both Labour and the Conservatives, based on their performance in office over the immediate post–World War II period, were judged to be inadequate by large segments of the population.[7]

But in Britain economic policy is also a position issue, that is, one on which parties offer differing viewpoints both about goals and concerning what is to be done to achieve them. This is, of course, classic British class politics. The Labour Party as a whole has always been ambivalent about capitalism. It has embedded in its party constitution the famous Clause IV, establishing socialism as a goal for the greatest collective benefit. The particular version of socialism that Labour has articulated and implemented is that of nationalization of basic industries for the greater public benefit of all the people, starting with "the commanding heights of industry" in the 1940s. Later nationalizations, and even the goal itself, have generated tremendous conflict within the party.[8] It has been shown that, at least since the 1960s, the British public has not been enamored of the idea of nationalization.[9] The impact of the extensive policy of privatization by the Conservative governments under Mrs. Thatcher may have ended any further Labour dreams of extensive nationalization.[10] Nevertheless, Labour will doubtless continue to claim that it is pursuing "socialism," in the sense of paying greater attention to government measures for the collective economic and social welfare of the country, however attenuated its "socialist" component may have become.

During the twentieth century, the Conservatives, by contrast, have always defended capitalism and the private sector. Even though the degree of this advocacy has varied—and paternalist Conservatives were quite willing to implement government ownership and subsidies—the dominant strain of Conservative policy has been to preserve the essentially capitalist nature of the economy, even (or especially) in times of crisis. The policies of Mrs. Thatcher were not entirely unprecedented,[11] although their scope has been.

If what to do in economic policy is the basic material of partisan conflict, it is also clearly a place where domestic and foreign policy meet. Britain has for centuries been a trading country, and its economy is heavily dependent not only on foreign trade per se but also on the exchange rates of currencies and the strength of the pound sterling against other currencies. The value of sterling drives foreign trade in certain directions. Almost one-half of the country's total economic activity is attributable to foreign trade.[12] The European Union is an important component of this. Britain's trade with countries of the EU has risen from 10 percent of the total in 1950 to almost 60 percent in the 1990s. Britain is also an active member of GATT, which sets world trade policy. In short, due to its economic circumstances Britain has been for some time, an "open polity." To a large degree British economic policy has always been foreign policy, and vice versa, but this tendency has become even greater as Britain's capacity to exert power over its own economic destiny, foreign and domestic, has declined. The continuing dilemma of British membership of the European Community is the most evident sign of the tension that prevails between the desire for political (decisionmaking) self-sufficiency and the exigencies of economic interdependence. Both domestic and foreign pressures on economic policy and the implications thereof are considered here, with concentrating on the domestic dimension of the British role, however constrained by outside forces.

Actors

As in other countries, the institutional apparatus of the British state with some responsibility for the conduct of economic policy is a fairly elaborate one. Key actors are the cabinet and prime ministerial advisers, the Treasury, the Bank of England, and "the City of London," the group of international financiers (banks, insurance companies, and other large investors) headquartered in an east central section of London. The European Union is an increasingly important actor. If Britain maintains full participation in the EU and if the planned development of a central bank and a common currency goes more or less according to form, the EU will obtain greater control of British macroeconomic policy through the financial sector. But Black Wednesday of September 1992, showed that Britain could not even maintain its membership in the European Monetary System, which regulates the range of variation within which participating countries' currencies can fluctuate. Secondary institutional actors in the British political economy include other government departments such as Trade and Industry,[13] Environment (with considerable control over local government spending and grants), the Scottish Office, Welsh Office, and Northern Ireland Office, as well as Energy (when it has existed as a separate department), Employment, Defense, Education and Science, Transportation, and other "spending" departments, chief among them being Health, and Social Services. Such nongovernmental actors as the trade unions, the Confederation of British Industry, and other sectoral groups are important, too, but if the recent extended period of Conservative governance has demonstrated anything, it is that a government committed to its own economic purposes can ignore pressure from internal interest groups if it chooses to do so. Although Parliament must officially approve the budget and major economic initiatives, that body is mainly a forum for debate rather than a major actor. Only rarely will a government with a safe majority bow to parliamentary pressure, and that occurs when the pressure involves its own backbenchers rather than the opposition parties alone. Parties attempt to develop coherent policies on economic matters both for electoral and governing purposes, but the conditions under which they find themselves competing and governing, both domestically and internationally, often change these.

The role of the City of London as one of the three major centers of international finance (Japan and the United States are the others) has given it an important place in economic policy considerations, which some have argued has been detrimental to the domestic political economy as a whole and to manufacturing in particular. The Treasury, headed by the cabinet officer with the quaint name of the chancellor of the Exchequer, is the major government economic department. It has the combined powers of the Treasury, the Office of Management and Budget, and the Council of Economic Advisers in the United States. In addition, at times it has had overall responsibility for the civil service, that is, for assignments, discipline, and promotions within the bureaucracy. Treasury ministers, led by the chancellor of the Exchequer, have closely watched responsibility for setting general British macroeconomic policy. The Treasury has generally been viewed as an agency for economic conservatism, attempting, with considerable success, to oppose plans for increased outlays by the "spending departments."[14]

In this effort the Treasury has usually been considered in league with both the City and the Bank of England, which has overall responsibility for monetary policy through its control of the currency supply and interest rates. The Bank of England, however, is not a strongly independent central bank, such as those in Germany and the United States. The Labour government nationalized the Bank of England in 1946, and ever since, the government ultimately has been able to control the policies of the bank, especially in regard to interest rates. Thus government officials often announce increases and decreases in interest rates once they decide to employ this tool of macroeconomic policy, though some scholars maintain that the bank does have a degree of independence in representing the interests of financial markets, which makes it more than the handmaiden of the government.[15] As previously noted, increasingly, the United Kingdom has lost the power to determine its own economic policy to strong outside forces, of which the European Union is only the most obvious.

Formation, Adoption, and Implementation

Macroeconomics

Economists conventionally divide their subject into two large categories, microeconomics—the behavior of individual firms and sectors, and macroeconomics—the behavior of the economy as a whole. Policies can similarly be divided into microeconomic policies, or those that are primarily concerned with affecting the behavior of particular firms or sectors, and macroeconomic policies, those that are aimed at affecting the aggregate economy without being directed at particular sectors of it. Even if the actions of government are mainly of one sort, of course, they may have particular consequences for the other category of policy as well. Trade-union reform, for instance, is microeconomic because it is directed at one particular factor of production, but changes in laws governing trade unions may also have consequences, and indeed are intended to, for the whole economy, at least in the long run. It may also be ambiguous as to whether a policy belongs in the macroeconomic or microeconomic policy area. Tax policy, for instance, can be considered macroeconomic if there is a general tax increase or tax reduction designed to affect the overall economy. It can be considered microeconomic, however, if it concerns changing the tax code to encourage or discourage certain forms of economic endeavor or certain sectors of the economy (see Table 6.1).

Although governments have always been concerned with management of the economy to some degree, this responsibility has broadened as government expenditures and intervention into society has increased in the twentieth century. Despite Mrs. Thatcher's fondness for the analogy to the household budget, the government budget is not the same. It has broader social, economic, and political purposes. Two of the major goals in the Twentieth Century have been to support the basic needs of the population in the form of social spending, that is, managing the welfare state, and to affect aggregate demand in the economy. The latter purpose especially developed under the influence of Keynesian economics, named

TABLE 6.1   Government Spending Categories as Percentage of Total Public Expenditures, 1978--1991

	Average	Real Change
Defense	12.0	% +17.1
Overseas services and aid	1.4	0.0
Agriculture, fisheries, food, and forestry	1.7	+12.5
Trade and industry, energy, and employment	5.5	-26.8
Employment and training	2.0	+16.0
Transport	4.3	+5.7
Housing	4.0	-50.5
Other environmental services	3.9	+10.9
Law, order, and protection services	4.7	+79.7
Education and science	13.8	+14.4
Arts and libraries (National heritage)	0.6	+44.4
Health and personal social services	15.4	+41.2
Health	14.0	+40.2
Social security	29.0	+77.1
Miscellaneous	3.4	+6.4
TOTAL:		+26.2

Source: David McKie, ed. The Election: A Voter's Guide (London: Fourth Estate, 1992)

after the Cambridge professor, Liberal political adviser, and sometime civil servant John Maynard Keynes.

Keynesian economic theory revolutionized modern macroeconomics. Designed to save capitalism when it was under theoretical attack from Marxism, under practical attack from communism and fascism, and being challenged by post–World War I recovery and the Great Depression, Keynes argued that there was no natural, inevitable return to an economic equilibrium of supply and demand once the swings of inflation and depression had played themselves out. Instead, government could use its two main macroeconomic powers, fiscal and monetary, to prod the economy in the desired direction, depending on the circumstances. This is called countercylical demand management. Fiscal policy, the politics of taxing and spending, was the main tool because it would affect aggregate demand for goods and services in the appropriate ways. The principal Keynesian remedies for economic ills were (1) increased general levels of taxation and running a budget surplus when the economy was moving into inflation, or (2) deficit spending through tax cuts or increased government spending when the economy was suffering from recession or depression. Monetary policy, or government manipulation of the money supply either directly through currency transactions or indirectly through raising and lowering interest rates, was a secondary tool in the Keynesian perspective.[16]

Although other countries, such as Sweden and the United States, used Keynesian policies, sometimes unwittingly, to increase aggregate demand during the Great Depression, the United Kingdom did not.[17] After World War II, however, Keynesian policies gradually came to be adopted.[18] In the heyday of the "long boom" in Western economies, which lasted from the late 1940s until the early 1970s, Keynesianism was hailed as the solution to the problems of capitalism. Some observers even thought that government could fine-tune the economy to avoid anything other than minor fluctuations in the rising prosperity evident thoughout the Western world in those decades. By 1956, Labour politician and theoretician Anthony Crosland wrote that distribution, rather than production, would be the major question facing Western economies and socialist parties in the future.[19] In the wake of certain events of global economic importance—the United States disengaging the dollar from gold, the disruption of petroleum flow to the West by the Arab producing countries in 1973, the rise of newly industrialized countries (NICs) as competitive industrial producers, and various financially speculative disruptions of international trade patterns—constantly rising economic prosperity has disappeared. Futhermore, confidence in Keynesian economics as a solution to the recurrent trade-cycle problems of capitalism has been damaged by the onset of inflation and higher unemployment occurring simultaneously (stagflation).[20]

It was not until the early 1980s, however, that an alternative to Keynesian policies was explicitly espoused by a British government. Mrs. Thatcher came into office in 1979, trumpeting the superiority of monetarism as an economic policy. Under monetarism, as most fully developed by Professor Milton Friedman of the University of Chicago,[21] monetary policy becomes the major macroeconomic tool, replacing fiscal policy. Theoretically, according to monetarists, if the monetary supply is adequately controlled, then all the rest of the economic indicators will fall into place, without the necessity of implementing a whole range of other macroeconomic and microeconomic policies. Although Mrs. Thatcher and her economic team at the Treasury were never complete monetarists—and indeed they expended considerable energy altering microeconomic policy—nowhere else was the monetarist view so rigidly followed, at least for a time.[22]

Many observers argue, however, that monetarism actually was the underlying British macroeconomic policy after 1976 under the Labour government of James Callaghan, when the country's inflation and debts forced it to secure a loan from the International Monetary Fund. The "conditionality" imposed by the IMF made it necessary for the Labour government to cut public spending and control the monetary supply more rigorously.[23]

Mrs. Thatcher's Conservative government, however, pursued monetarism explicitly as the solution to Britain's macroeconomic difficulties. The results in her first two years were horrendous, with 20 percent of the manufacturing sector being eliminated, unemployment burgeoning to 13 percent, and economic growth coming to a standstill. Government spending did not drop as she had hoped, because of the large amount of social spending necessary to support those out of work. Inflation was suppressed, however, and after 1981 the economy improved until it went into a prolonged slump, the worst since the Great Depression, in 1990. The monetary targets, however, became redefined several times, until by the end of the decade monetarism was no longer the explicit policy of the government. Thus, at the very least, monetarism in practice did not become the panacea for Britain's economic ills as some had predicted.[24]

A sympathetic article in the *Economist*[25] on the political economy of Prime Minister Margaret Thatcher and U.S. President Ronald Reagan argued that the former's principal economic achievements lay in microeconomics rather than macroeconomics, especially by freeing the "supply side" from government and trade unions' restrictive practices. This is not to be confused with the supply-side policies followed by the Reagan administration, in which freeing the supply side (producers) from government restrictions and lowering taxes was supposed to generate a booming capitalist economy. It did, for a time, but also produced record budget deficits. Reagan reduced taxes and increased spending for defense and mandated social programs. Thatcher, however, increased taxes in the process of shifting from direct (income) to indirect value-added taxation (VAT) while cutting government spending, largely through cutbacks in subsidy programs and privatization of nationalized industries.

What economic goals are microeconomic, and especially macroeconomic, policies supposed to reach? Jim Tomlinson[26] has suggested that post–World War II British policy has had four major goals, with different emphases at various times. They are (1) full employment, (2) low rates of inflation, (3) stable exchange rates and balance of payments, and (4) economic growth. Sydney Pollard,[27] in a withering critique of the failure of postwar British governments to keep up with other industrialized countries in investment and growth, listed a total of ten goals. The tools used in attempts to achieve these goals include the two major macroeconomic ones, fiscal and monetary policy, and such others as exchange rate controls, trade and tariff policies, industrial relations (trade-union) policies, labor market policies (including education, training, and minimum wages), nationalization or privatization, taxation, industrial and regional policy (economic aids to private sector companies), regulation or deregulation, and wage and price controls (incomes policies). Different governments had different priorities and used different tools to try to achieve these goals, even in the course of their own tenure in office.

Partly in reaction to the Great Depression, full employment was a highly rated goal throughout the long boom. In the 1950s, a labor shortage led to the immigration of thousands of workers from the West Indies, India, and Pakistan (including the portion that became Bangladesh in 1971), thus changing the social and cultural face of Britain forever. In the 1960s, it was considered electoral suicide for a governing party to have unemployment reach even 5 percent of the workforce. But in the 1980s and early 1990s, double and almost triple that percentage unemployed did not result in electoral defeats for the Conservative governments.

Instead, low inflation became enshrined as the major economic policy goal. There had been earlier signs of this goal in the voluntary wage and price controls initiated by the Attlee government in 1949 and the Wilson government in the late 1960s. Nevertheless, anti-inflation policies began in earnest under Conservative Prime Minister Edward Heath in the early 1970s, when, in contrast to his party's espousal of freeing the private sector when in opposition, his government initiated statutory wage and price controls (incomes policies). The successor Labour government of Harold Wilson tried to revert to a voluntary basis for wage controls with the trade unions, but eventually the arrangement broke down, leading to the strikes of the Winter of Discontent of 1978–1979 and the Labour defeat in the general election of 1979. Under the following Conservative governments, low inflation was acclaimed as their greatest macroeconomic policy success.

A stable exchange rate and balance of payments has proven to be one of the most difficult goals for British governments to achieve. This has led to perhaps the major policy dilemma of post–World War II governments, stop-go trade policies. The problem has been that whenever Britain has had an expanding economy, there has emerged a tendency for too many goods to be imported, leading to deficits in balance of trade (goods and services) and balance of payments (a broader measure including loans, grants, military and tourist spending, and international currency flows). Deficits in one or both of these measures lead to downward pressure on the pound, as Britain is judged by international financiers to be consuming beyond its capacity to produce in return. This pressure has led to formal devaluations of the pound sterling in 1949, 1967, and 1992, the final devaluation occuring through withdrawal from the European Exchange Rate Mechanism, a device for regulating the ratios of the European Community members within it. Furthermore, since the institution of floating rather than fixed exchange rates (with the exception of voluntary ones, such as the ERM) in 1972, the exchange rate of the pound has effectively been devalued several times (but also revalued) by the operations of the currency market.

British policymakers have been obsessed with protecting the value of the pound, and every episode of devaluation has been both resisted and resented as a sign of British economic weakness when it has occurred. The international financial interests of the City of London are an important—some would argue too important—concern of the government. Some analysts of the economic and political decline of Britain have argued that overseas investments have played too influential a role in British policymaking, to the detriment of domestic manufacturing, both in terms of lack of domestic investment and in the activities designed to keep the pound high, which does not help exporters.[28] The British share of international manufacturing trade exports has progressively declined in the twentieth century, especially in the postwar period. In the course of forty years (1950–1990), Britain's share of world manufacturing trade shrank from 26 percent to 9 percent.[29] Once the workshop of the world, Britain retains few of its formerly dominant industries, such as textiles, shipbuilding, motor vehicles, and iron and steel. In the mid-1980s, the United Kingdom incurred its first deficit in trade in manufactured goods in over two centuries, indicating the depths to which British manufacturing had sunk during the early tight money policies of the Thatcher government. Today Britain offers services, especially cultural and financial ones, and a large, trained workforce to attract international companies. Irrespective of whether concerted attempts to protect overseas investments and the value of sterling have been warranted, however, the stability of exchange rates has been a problem for Britain, one that assumed an increasing importance in the post–World War II environment.

The fourth policy goal of postwar British economic policy, economic growth, has been the most doggedly pursued but also the most frustrating to achieve. By historical standards Britain has done well in the postwar period, with a gross national product (GNP) per capita rising in real terms from $2,000 (having almost doubled since 1890) in 1950 to $14,570 in 1989.[30] But growth has been bumpy, especially since the oil shocks of the early 1970s. Furthermore, ever since the early 1960s, Britain has been concerned with its falling ranking according to many economic indicators of the world's leading industrialized countries. In 1890, its per capita GNP was first among European countries; by 1990, it ranked fifteenth in the world, behind eleven European countries as well as Japan, the United States, and Canada.[31] During the Heath government in the early 1970s, Lord Rothschild, head of the Central Policy Review staff, alarmed cabinet ministers by reporting that at current rates of economic growth, compounded, the United Kingdom would fall below Italy in gross domestic product per capita.[32] By the 1990s, Britain had reached this position. When discussion turns, as it often does, to British decline, what is usually meant is comparative economic decline[33] (see Table 6.2).

For a time after World War II, the engine of growth fueled British economic recovery. The Marshall Plan was instrumental in this recovery. Labour Foreign Secretary Ernest Bevin took a leading role in organizing the recipients of United States aid. Despite the end of the lend-lease program from the United States upon the termination of the European conflict, the unfavorable terms of the American loan of 1946, and some severe winters, by the end of the 1940s economic growth began to take hold in the United Kingdom. Although rationing did not end completely until 1955, from 1948 on various wartime controls were progressively eliminated. It is often forgotten, at least in the United States, that the Marshall Plan was such a success in rebuilding the economies of wartorn Europe that it was terminated ahead of schedule.

The Conservative governments of the 1950s rode the rising prosperity and secure position of Britain within NATO and the Atlantic Alliance to three consecutive election victories and very nearly to a fourth in 1964. The prototypical cartoon of the period was one in which Prime Minister Harold Macmillan, after the

TABLE 6.2   Comparative British Economic Performance

Average Real GDP Growth, 1967--1993

United Kingdom	1.9%
G-7	2.7%
European Community	2.3%
OECD Europe	2.3%
Total OECD	2.7%

Average Unemployment Rates (Standarized), 1973--1992

United Kingdom	7.8%
G-7	6.0%
European Community (except Greece, Luxembourg, and Denmark)	7.7%
Total OECD (17 countries)	6.6%

Average Government Spending, Percentage of Nominal GDP, 1978--1993

United Kingdom	42.2%
G-7	35.6%
OECD (19 countries)	39.0%

Average Government Financial Balances, Percentage of Nominal GDP, 1978--1993

United Kingdom	-2.9%
G-7	-2.9%
OECD	-3.1%

Source: OECD Outlook (Paris: OECD, 1993)

third consecutive electoral triumph in 1959, was depicted as addressing the durable consumer goods (a washing machine, a refrigerator, an auto, a TV) "seated" in the chairs around him: "Well, Gentlemen, together we have fought the good fight."[34] Even though the stop-go problem reared its head at awkward intervals and British economic growth was below the European norm, for most people the 1950s and 1960s were a period of continuous rising prosperity. Immigrants had to be imported to do lower manual and service jobs because of labor shortages, and Britain was confident enough about its economic prospects to reject the prospect of joining the Common Market at its inception in 1957. The age of mass consumption, which commenced in the United States in the 1920s, finally arrived in Britain in the 1950s. Consumer durables such as refrigerators, televisions, and washing machines became commonplace, to be followed in due course by the telephone and the automobile.

These were also the years characterized by what the *Economist* called "Butskellism," a fundamental similarity of views between the governing Conservative and opposition Labour front benches, personified by the chancellor of the Exchequer, R.A.B. Butler, and the shadow chancellor, Hugh Gaitskell. The engine of growth seemingly had been harnessed according to Keynesian principles, and the partisan argument concerned mainly which group could better manage the machinery. At this point, conduct of the economy had become a strongly valence issue rather than a position issue. Even if Gaitskell, after becoming Labour leader, could not persuade his party to change Clause IV of the party constitution, wherein nationalization was promised, such commitments did not figure highly in practical electoral or policy concerns.

When anxieties arose in the early 1960s over Britain's comparative economic performance, the victorious Labour Party promised not socialism but a "white-hot technological revolution" to lead British economic growth forward. Performance, however, was not up to this standard. Stop-go continued, problems with the trade unions increased under governments of both major stripes, and the international financial dislocations of the early 1970s harmed British economic growth prospects. The latter included the end of fixed exchange rates, two dollar devaluations, the end of the fixed dollar-gold exchange rate, the rise of NICs, and the embargo of petroleum supplies by the Organization of Petroleum Exporting Countries (OPEC) against Western consuming countries as political pressure for their support of Israel in the Middle East War of 1973. With an economy heavily dependent on international trade, the United Kingdom suffered disproportionately from these occurrences. Even the development of North Sea oil later in the decade did not ameliorate the underlying problems of productivity and overconsumption in the British economy.

By the mid-1970s, Britain was widely considered to be "ungovernable," largely on economic grounds. Inflation was double-digit, unemployment was growing, the two major parties were becoming more ideologically divided about what economic policies to follow to reclaim prosperity, and budget deficit problems mounted until the Labour government was forced to go to the International Monetary Fund for a loan, accepting the conditionality terms on which the IMF offered the loan. This was not only a major economic defeat for the government, but it also marked the beginning of a move toward the discipline of monetary targets and cutting government spending, which the later Conservative government formalized.

Margaret Thatcher's attitude toward economic growth was to treat it as an important but secondary target. The versions of monetarism that she propounded, particularly in her early years in office, officially jettisoned all four of the major postwar economic policy goals in favor of a concentration on targets for monetary growth and "cash limits" for government spending programs. If the monetary supply could be controlled, according to this perspective, then the other economic policy goals would fall appropriately in line. In reality, the government began to hedge on the monetarist doctrine because of other considerations, and by the mid-1980s monetarism was dropped as a guiding doctrine. Meanwhile, the definition of the monetary target to aim for had changed several times in the course of the Conservative governments. Furthermore, although the government refused to induce stimuli to the economy in the earlier period, when the high value for sterling because of North Sea oil simply compounded problems of

British international competitiveness, it later showed similar tendencies to previous governments by cutting taxes and increasing spending when an election approached. Inflation was pretty well controlled, but the growth swings of the British economy became even more severe under the Conservatives in the 1980s and 1990s than they had been previously. As previously noted, by the early 1990s Britain was in its most severe economic slump since the depression, although it slowly began to recover in the mid-1990s.

With a three-party system in the electorate, however, the Conservatives suffered no electoral punishment for the problems of the economy. They continued to draw 42–43 percent of the vote for four consecutive elections in 1979–1992. Labour, on the other hand, wavered in its alternative economic policy, promising a major program of nationalization and withdrawal from the European Community in 1983; greater attention to health, social services, and the unemployed in 1987; and government spending to stimulate the economy in 1992. The folk memory of the Winter of Discontent, however, acted to discredit Labour's plans. However bad economic matters were under the Conservatives, a lingering suspicion persisted that they might be worse under Labour. Thus Labour was unable to turn its seeming advantages on the economy into a voting edge successful enough to reclaim control of the government. British political economy no longer moved according to the underlying currents of the 1960s. In fact, some observers credited the decline of the two-party system electorally to disenchantment of the voters with both parties, stemming from the policy failures of the 1960s.[35]

Microeconomics

Although all the ramifications of economic policy cannot be covered here, some attention must be paid to policy in specific sectors, that is, microeconomic policy. Policy is important in four areas in the postwar period: industrial policy, including the politics of nationalization and privatization; policy toward the trade unions; taxation; and the nexus between energy, environmental, and transportation policy. Fortunately, other policy areas within the general realm of economic policy have been widely covered elsewhere.[36]

Industrial Policy. Industrial policy has been a controversial area of economic policy throughout most of the postwar period. Industrial policy refers to direct government aid to certain economic sectors, with the aim of long-term improvement in the supply capacity of the economy. This occurs primarily through subsidies, partial ownership, or even complete ownership of the industry. Government can aid an economic sector by other means as well, for instance through tax breaks (tax expenditures), regional aid policies that buttress the prospects of particular economic sectors, and laws protecting economic sectors through regulations, tariffs, and quotas on foreign products or services. All governments intervene in at least some of these ways, but sometimes industrial policy refers only to an explicit, planned, coordinated program of intervention. Nationalization and privatization are the two ends of the continuum of industrial policy.[37]

Contrary to much popular belief, the Attlee government was not the first to nationalize privately owned enterprises. Despite the strength of laissez-faire capitalism (let the economy alone) in Victorian Britain, some nationalizations and subsidies, even under Conservative governments, had already occurred, as with the British Broadcasting Corporation, for instance.[38] There was nothing like wartime shortages and exigencies, however, to concentrate the minds of politicians on the supply deficiencies of certain sectors under private ownership—the railroads, for instance. Labour first espoused nationalization as a major means of implementing socialism in 1918, although the party was never in government long enough before 1945 to do much about it. The Attlee government, however, came into office with explicit plans for taking the "commanding heights of industry" into public ownership. The justification for this was that these were the essential industries of the country, too important to the welfare of the whole population to allow them to continue to be run for the private profit of the owners. Accordingly, these industries—iron and steel, natural gas, petroleum, electricity, shipbuilding, coal, railroads, road haulage, and airlines—were duly nationalized in the first postwar Labour government. Although the Conservatives opposed many of these nationalizations at the time,[39] when they regained office in the 1950s they were unwilling to denationalize anything except iron and steel and road haulage. Thus industrial policy in the form of nationalization became an accepted part of British political economy, as did subsidies, including a large dose of regional development aid to induce people to stay in certain areas of the country rather than having them migrate to other areas. Only iron and steel became a political football as the partisan color of governments changed, and Labour promised no new large nationalizations during the years of Butskellism. As noted, in 1960, Labour leader Hugh Gaitskell even proposed to abolish the clause of the party constitution pledging itself to nationalization. New Labour leader Tony Blair proposed a similar move in 1994.

As far as can be determined from surveys, however, nationalization was never an especially popular policy, particularly as it moved beyond the core industries and services. In their surveys of the 1960s, David Butler and Donald Stokes[40] found that even Labour supporters were not promoting more nationalizations. Most of the British public at the time was pretty well satisfied with the balance of nationalization and privatization as it stood. However, in reaction to the perceived economic failures of the 1960s Labour government, the left wing of the party pushed its agenda for greater public control of the economy. Through its control of the party's National Executive Committee, the Left managed to commit the party on paper, especially through the party program for 1973, to an extensive series of nationalizations of major companies. The Labour governments of the 1970s were reluctant to put these commitments into practice, leaving them subject to further battering from the left wing in the intraparty struggles of the early 1980s. The Labour governments did, however, have a cabinet-level ministry for industry, headed by the redoubtable left-wing leader Tony Benn, that dispersed both regional aid and subsidies to encourage particular economic sectors. The results of these attempts at a concerted industrial policy were controversial.

The promised extensive Labour nationalizations of the 1983 Party Manifesto ("the longest suicide note in history," as one party wag dubbed the document) never came about, of course, and subsequently Labour adjusted its industrial policy sufficiently under its "modernization strategy" to accommodate largely to the 1980s Conservative privatizations. Greater public investment, selective subsidies, and even selective renationalizations are possible under a future Labour government, but the more likely policy is greater emphasis on regulation of private monopolies. There is unlikely to be a great surge toward increased nationalization.

In the 1980s, industrial policy ran in the other direction, or some would say, was virtually abandoned, meaning that under Margaret Thatcher the emphasis was on privatization and deregulation, not nationalization and regulation. Again, elite political debate has run ahead of popular opinion since there has never been an overwhelming public endorsement of the Conservatives' privatization plans and, indeed, the public was suspicious of the more difficult and controversial plans, such as those for coal and rail that commenced in the third Thatcher term and continued beyond.[41] The longer privatization ran, the less support it generated. Nevertheless, starting not with specific pledges in the 1979 election manifesto but with the popular success of the selling of council houses at huge discounts to the sitting occupiers, the 1980s Conservative governments pushed forward a privatization boom that had not only countrywide but international implications. Many expressed reservations, and they emanated not only from the expected opposition quarters but also from traditional state-oriented Conservatives such as Lord Stockdale (Harold Macmillan), who protested against "selling the family silver," as well as from other observers who questioned whether turning public monopolies into private monopolies would have a major long-term economic benefit. The Conservatives plunged ahead, on a large scale, the culmination of the project being the gradual privatization of coal and railroads in the mid-1990s (see Table 6.3).

The debate over industrial policy, including nationalization-privatization, has been principally an elite debate. The more extreme wings of the two major parties, the Left in the Labour party and the Right in the Conservatives, have periodically been able to push their parties into adopting strong positions on industrial policy, largely as a reaction to perceived economic or political failure of more moderate policies. But the push has come from somewhat different sources, from the leadership of the Conservatives in the 1980s but from the persistent left-wing rank and file in Labour. Large sections of both major parties, as well as the leadership of the other parties, have remained moderate on industrial policy, or perhaps only inconsistent and ad hoc in their attitudes, as shown by the minimal denationalizations under the Conservatives prior to 1979 and the resistance of Labour leaders toward large-scale programs of nationalization beyond those of the

TABLE 6.3   Privatization in Britain, 1979--1991

Economic Sector	Date Initiated
British Petroleum	1979
British Aerospeace	1981
Cable and Wireless	1981
Amersham International	1982
National Freight Corporation	1982
Britoil	1982
Associated British Ports	1983
Enterprise Oil	1984
Sealink	1984
Jaguar	1984
British Telecom	1984
British Shipbuilders Warship Yard	1984--1985
British Gas	1986
British Airways	1987
Royal Ordnance	1987
Rolls Royce	1987
British Airports Authority	1987
Rover	1988
British Steel	1988
10 Water Corporations	1989
Electricity Corps. Distributors	1990
Electricity Corps. Power Generators	1990--1991

Source: Nicholas Zahariadis *Markets, States and Public Policy: Privatization in Britain and France* (Ann Arbor: University of Michigan Press, 1995)

immediate postwar period. The public has moved much less than the parties, with the large central mass sector being satisfied with things as they are in almost all circumstances. Public opinion has been permissive, not a strong constraint on elite initiatives in either direction, except insofar as Labour election losses often temporarily inhibit further nationalization pledges. The nationalization–free enterprise issue has been such a fundamental part of the class-politics partisan debate in British politics for such a long time that it is difficult to conceive of it ever entirely disappearing. The public is not terribly interested, but the more ideological elites, at all levels of the two major parties, are. For instance, even surveys that find that Labour Party activists are not as extreme as commonly portrayed have discovered that the middle-class Socialists who make up the bulk of the party are significantly more prone to favor nationalization than are Labour voters.[42] The ever-more-interconnected capitalist economies of the European Community are often considered a force working against greater nationalization, even with the regulatory predilections of the European Commission. But as long as economic difficulties remain a periodic feature of the British political landscape, the temptation to offer policy options further toward the extreme, left or right, will exist.

Policy Toward Trade Unions. Intimately connected with the industrial policy question is the fate of the trade unions, a second microeconomic policy area worth exploring. Britain is unusual among industrialized countries in maintaining the close link—organizationally, financially, and in memberships—between the organized trade-union movement and a single political party, in this case the appropriately named Labour Party. The maintenance of these links, the espousal of nationalization as a major commitment by the Labour Party since 1918, and the continuation of class-politics rhetoric and emphases by the two major parties, even after clear indications from the voters in the past twenty-five years that they are not enamored of the politics of class,[43] have made government policy toward the trade unions, as well as many other associated economic and socioeoconomic policies, a critical issue in Britain.

In fact, in the 1970s the argument was frequently heard that Labour was the natural party of government because only that party could make deals with the trade unions, collectively and individually. But as union membership has declined, become more middle-class, and more popularly suspect because of the activities of unions in the 1970s, particularly during the Winter of Discontent in 1979, the strong influence of the trade unions on government policy has declined precipitously. In 1974, the coal miners could force a three-day workweek and compel the Conservative government to call a general election, which the government did not win (although neither did Labour); in 1981, Margaret Thatcher's Conservative government compromised with the coal miners rather than confront them, but by 1985 she was able to break the coal miners' strike. Similarly, in 1968 the unions could defeat via intraparty politics the Labour government proposal to put limits on strike activity; in the early 1970s, the efforts of the Conservative government under Edward Heath to control union behavior through legislation were greeted with widespread defiance and repeal of the measures by the succeeding Labour government. Nevertheless, by the 1980s the unions were able to mount no effective opposition to Conservative government legislation far more radical than anything previously proposed; in fact, the Labour Party has now become reconciled to most of that legislation. What the Conservative governments were able to impose entails, among other measures, (1) officially supervised balloting of trade-union members for union elections, strike votes, and the establishment or renewal of political action funds, (2) no legal immunities for the closed shop, and (3) outlawing secondary actions. In short, the government has attempted to make the trade unions more internally democratic and to remove some of their legal protections. More generally, it is agreed that the Conservatives' goal has been to weaken the collective economic and political power of trade unions.[44]

Although the unions are no longer a dominant power wielder in British society, Britain is still a highly unionized society. The long experience of the industrial revolution, and the location of that industrial revolution primarily in a few places, largely in the north of England, facilitated collective organization. More recently, unions have spread into middle-class ranks as well. Even with the fall of union membership in the face of higher unemployment and greater legal restrictions on their activities in the 1980s and 1990s, union membership still constitutes about 40 percent of total economically active employees, versus 18 percent in the United States.[45] But this is a reduction of over 10 percent during the Conservatives' reign, and considering the higher levels of unemployment obtaining, total union membership has fallen by about one-third in that period.

In Britain union membership usually comes with an "attitude" as well. The class privileges of the rich and well born, the huddling together of early factory workers in horrible working and living conditions (as Marx, Engels, Dickens, George Orwell, and others have described over the years), mass unemployment between the two world wars, and the long refusal of the rulers to recognize workers' rights and even to give workers the vote has led to massive class resentment and the view that workers give forth effort only grudgingly and must use the political process to protect themselves from exploitation. "I'm all right, Jack" was a phrase developed in the 1950s to describe union obstructionist behavior and ingrained social conservatism, a conservatism based on the espousal of "free collective bargaining" with few legal restrictions on what unions could do in its pursuit. Hence the struggle first against the efforts of the Wilson Labour government, and later, against the Heath Conservative government's attempts to control that behavior.

Even though public opinion surveys conducted as long ago as Butler and Stokes's in the 1950s[46] showed that the public overall was not especially enamored of trade unions, their crucial role in the economic production process, their relatively high level of membership and organization, and their strong ties to the Labour Party gave them a powerful position in the 1960s and 1970s, even as the industrial base on which they relied went into decline. In the famously graphic phrase of Ernest Bevin, trade-union leader and Labour Foreign Secretary in the Attlee governments, "The Labour Party grew out of the bowels of the trade union movement." But contrary to much public impression abroad and also to much British academic discussion about corporatism, British trade unions were never, as an economic element, highly centralized. The Trades Union Congress was not much more than a holding body. Real power lay in the individual unions themselves, especially in those unions that could claim a large membership, an important economic role, and a leadership with considerable discretion in taking positions without necessarily consulting its mass membership at major turns. Much of the union activity was concerned with jurisdictional disputes and maintaining differential wage structures among various unions rather than with activity directed specifically against management or the government of the day.

The system worked well for the unions as long as economic prosperity was rising and labor was scarce. But more and more, the system of free collective bargaining led to abuses, which became only too prominent in the 1970s. With the arrival of the Conservative government under Margaret Thatcher in 1979, a tougher approach toward the unions appeared, one that in microeconomic terms was concerned with freeing the supply side of production from unnecessary constraints. Out went the specified goal of low unemployment. Indeed, unemployment rose to theretofore unimagined postwar levels, and between 1979 and 1981 the United Kingdom lost fully 20 percent of its manufacturing capacity, thus further undercutting the union base. The Conservative government moved gingerly at first in enacting legislation that restricted union activities, as it did in dealing with union demands in the then-large public sector (before privatization), but further legislation aimed at the unions was progressively introduced and passed as the Conservatives continued to rule.

Whether the unions could make a comeback and recover their economic clout and political power under a Labour government is an interesting question. The role of the trade unions has changed somewhat within the Labour Party, since their role in choice of the leader was enhanced in an alliance with the left wing of the party in 1981. Under the modernization strategy, pursued throughout the latter 1980s and into the 1990s, the role of the individual member is enhanced and the role of groups, in both local constituency associations and central party affairs, is reduced. In short, the Labour Party has attempted to distance its image from being too closely tied to the trade unions. Nevertheless, even in the wake of Conservative limits on union political funds, the trade unions continue to be the largest financial supporters of the party, and trade union–sponsored members of Parliament, even if reduced in numbers, still exist in the party.[47] The unions themselves now have a more middle-class profile than previously, although the consequences of this change have not yet been studied.

Dunleavy[48] has postulated a "consumption cleavage" approach, in which he argues that those groups heavily dependent on the public sector (pensioners, the poor, council-house tenants, trade-union members, government employees) will behave differently than those whose consumption of jobs, housing, and income derives largely from private sources. Although such views have been taken up by several commentators,[49] the main problem with this provocative thesis is that it lacks independent empirical support.[50] As long as Britain remains constrained by high unemployment and increasing international competitive claims, especially regional ones within the European Community, a return to the heights of trade-union power experienced in the 1960s and 1970s remains unlikely. But the unions may benefit from any British adherence to the social policies of the European Union, which is one reason they have been resisted by the Conservative government.[51]

Energy and Environment. The third microeconomic sector worthy of extended attention is policy development on energy and the environment, which also intersects with transportation and agricultural policy. From its days as an imperial power, the United Kingdom has held energy policy as a high priority. Unlike some other countries, Britain does have some domestic sources of energy, notably coal and, since the 1970s, a large share of the North Sea oil and gas fields. But with a large population and a small land area, at times it has had to supplement these resources by gaining access to energy sources elsewhere, including petroleum in the Middle East, coal and natural gas from abroad, and more recently, development of nuclear energy. As a major energy importer (as well as importer of foodstuffs), government choices about energy sources and usage have been crucial to their development.

Joseph Rudolph[52] has referred to the United Kingdom as pursuing a "four fuels" policy, relying to some degree on coal, natural gas, electricity (generated from various sources, including nuclear), and petroleum. Little effort is expended on distinguishing among sources of power, to the chagrin of environmentalists. The balance of the four fuels has varied over the years, however, as supplies became more abundant or more restricted and as governments chose to empha-size certain areas of energy. The relatively abundant supply of coal, and the growth of a large workforce to mine it, made coal a natural choice in earlier years. But once petroleum came on line in the twentieth century as a major propellant of sea fleets and domestic transportation, both public and private, the need for petroleum supplies became paramount. This stimulated Britain's interest in the Middle East, especially after World War I, complementing earlier interests there primarily in the Suez Canal as a passageway to British imperial holdings in India and the Far East. Britain remained embroiled in the politics of the Arab peninsula and Iran after the war, largely because of the availability of the principal fuel of the twentieth century.

As the coal stocks of Britain became more expensive to mine, the search con-tinued for other sources of fuel. Increasing amounts of coal were imported from abroad. Nuclear energy was developed in Britain beginning in the 1950s. In fact, the initial British research into nuclear power, in conjunction with developing Britain's independent atomic bomb, was done by both the Attlee Labour and Churchill Conservative governments in complete secrecy from Parliament as well as the public in the early 1950s. Even today, nuclear matters are almost com-pletely hidden from Parliament and the public. In 1957, some years after the fact, it was revealed that there had been a major accident at the Windscale nuclear facility that released more radiation into the atmosphere than the later accident at Three Mile Island, Pennsylvania. Even in the face of declining stocks of coal and the example of other countries such as nearby France investing heavily in nuclear facilities, Britain has been reluctant to rely too much on nuclear energy for its domestic supplies. Nevertheless, there has been controversy about British encouragement of nuclear capacity, including concerns about its cost and safety. Despite encouragement from the Conservative government, by the 1990s nuclear power accounted for less than 10 percent of British energy production, far below the three other sources. The costs of nuclear production of electricity, revealed by the privatization of electricity in 1986, made many investors hesitant to back it.[53]

The discovery of large stocks of petroleum and natural gas in the North Sea off the coast of Scotland helped fuel demands of the Scottish Nationalist Party for independence in the 1970s ("It's Scotland's oil.") The exploitation of these reserves, which are shared with Norway, has made Britain a major oil exporter over the last two decades. This bonanza has also provided a major tax source for the government. Considerable controversy has ensued over concern that the Conservative government may not have made the best use of this depletable resource for investment in Britain's long-term future. Now on its downward slope of exploitation, at least in known reserves, this resource will become a declining part of the country's economic and tax base. What will Britain have to show for its window of petroleum opportunity early in the twenty-first century?

Consideration of energy, of course, leads naturally to the question of transportation, since much of any energy resource is utilized for this purpose. Wind, water (through an extensive system of canals and steam-powered railroads), and animal locomotion have given way over the years to the faster forms of travel offered by diesel and electric-powered locomotives and subways, diesel-driven ships, and gasoline-powered motor vehicles and airplanes. As noted above, the search for reliable sources of petroleum, the key fuel of the twentieth century, has led British foreign policy into various far-flung enterprises, only to have petroleum discovered on its doorstep in the middle of the twentieth century. Until well into the twentieth century, the fundamental thinking of British policymakers about transportation was collectivist, in the sense that the emphasis was on finding means for moving people in groups, largely through public transportation. Individual automobiles were for the elite few in a largely urbanized society, but even small villages had the railroad, and eventually, the bus. By the standards of the United States, Britain still has a considerable public transportation network, with many more train and bus services between small locations. Nevertheless, there has been a transportation revolution in Britain in the twentieth century, especially in the period since World War II. The growth in population and increased availability of disposable income has provided a mass market for private automobiles where none existed before. In 1955, for instance, only a minority of the British adult population could afford a privately owned automobile; by 1990, fully 65 percent had the means to own one. Perhaps an even more startling statistic is that by 1990 71 percent of the members of the Labour Party, the party of the public sector according to Dunleavy, had their own automobile.[54] More highways have been built to accommodate this trend, though whether as cause or consequence is debatable. At the same time, there have been persistent cutbacks and increases in price in rail service, starting with the Beeching reforms of the early 1960s.[55] As in the health service, British governments of all stripes have been accused of insufficient investment in public transportation.

Nevertheless, the conservationist lobby has remained strong enough to prevent the wholesale paving and rearrangement of the country in the interests of the automobile. Such projects as a ring road around London and the third London airport have been frustrated by conservationist and environmentalist resistance, and the policy of having green belts around urban areas has been maintained.[56] A large program of road building begun under the Conservative government was subjected to criticism from several quarters. In short, in transportation as in other areas, such as industrialization, the British attitude toward modern technology has remained fundamentally ambivalent.

As in several other countries, environmental concerns and agricultural interests have impinged on each other. British agriculture, despite the relatively few people directly engaged in the enterprise, has continued to be politically influential with governments of all political complexions.[57] This may be due partly to the aristocratic agrarian tradition in Britain, partly to the persistent desire of British governments to avoid dependence on imported foodstuffs as much as possible, and partly to the boost to British agriculture given in both market and subsidy terms by membership of the European Community. Whatever the confluence of circumstances, British agriculture has become markedly more mechanized and efficient in the postwar period; it now produces 80 percent of foodstuffs consumed by the domestic market, the largest proportion in over a century.[58] Its efficiency, in fact, in part explains why British governments, principally Mrs. Thatcher's, have been so militantly opposed to the huge subsidies of the Common Agricultural Policy of the European Community, which largely go to less efficient, larger producers in other European countries. In comparative terms, Britain as a whole benefited very little from these subsidies because its agricultural sector is so small and so efficient. Thus it was quite obvious that Britain, as a highly industrialized and urbanized society, was largely contributing to the welfare of the agricultural sector in other EC countries.[59]

Despite its hallowed political status, British agricultural policy has been under attack for being environmentally destructive. Britain, like other industrialized countries, has seen the rise of environmental groups and environmental consciousness over the past two decades. Although often considered a laggard in both postmaterialist values[60] and organized green politics,[61] Britain, including the Conservative governments of Mrs. Thatcher and Mr. Major, has developed greater environmental proclivities sporadically over the past decade. But both public and governmental attention to environmental concerns have been inconsistent. John McCormick[62] attributes the rise and fall of environmentalism on the public agenda to the relative economic conditions in the country. On the governmental level, even though Britain has been willing to deal domestically with some environmental issues, it has lacked overall coordination, and in recent years, has been subject to much enforcement from the European Union on environmental policy. The Single European Act mandated greater environmental coordination in its attempt to remove barriers to the market among EU members.

Ironically, until the 1960s the United Kingdom could be considered a leader in environmentally sensitive policies.[63] Public control over land and conservation of environmental resources were important parts of the Socialist agenda, embodied in legislation during the immediate postwar Labour government. In the 1950s, Britain took action to cope with the problems of water pollution by cleaning up the Thames and addressed air pollution through the Smoke Abatement Act of 1956.[64] Despite a government department called Environment, created in the early 1970s, responsibility for the environment largely rested with local government, housing, and planning the "built" environment. Responsibility for environmental enforcement has been scattered among several departments and agencies, most notably the Ministry of Agriculture, Fisheries, and Food. No general requirement for environmental impact statements has been necessary, and public inquiries into the environmental consequences of major projects have been limited. Indeed, the Channel Tunnel project was passed through Parliament as a special bill not requiring public inquiries, which might have delayed its completion.[65] The government has permitted solid-waste disposal procedures held in disfavor elsewhere, the ocean has been treated as an all-purpose dumping ground, and the acid-rain problem was ignored for a long period. Problems such as these led Britain to gain a reputation as the "dirty man of Europe" in the 1980s. But under pressure from the European Union and the sudden upsurge of the Green Party in the European elections of 1989, the Conservative government became particularly active on international environmental issues, including protection of the ozone layer and concern about the greenhouse effect.[66] As long as the priorities of British governments of all types remain largely economic, however, it is questionable how dedicated governments will be to dealing with environmental problems.

Taxation. One area of both macro- and microeconomic policy with which British governments love to tinker is taxation. Announcement by the chancellor of the Exchequer of the government's budget each year is an eagerly awaited public event, not least for what will be revealed about tax rates. Unlike the United States government, the British government presents a unified budget, in which government revenues and spending are clearly set out. Much informed commentary surrounds the likely effects of various tax schemes. Again unlike the United States system, there is heavy reliance on central taxation; indeed, central government has even exerted control over local government's capacity to tax, as well as providing most of the income on which local government relies.[67] But like the United States, Britain relies on a combination of personal and corporate income tax, sales tax, and social insurance taxes.[68] The sales tax takes the form of a value-added tax, levied at each level of manufacture of a good and collected from the consumer as part of the purchase price when the good is sold. Products are differently "value-rated," by the government, and some of the VAT money goes to the European Union by collective agreement of the members. Recent Conservative governments have made lower taxation a touchstone of their attempt to generate a more market-based economy. Despite these avowals and legislation, a recent survey of tax policy in Sweden, the United States, and Britain found that Britain had the least coherent tax system.[69] Apparently tinkering with the tax codes is more reflective of symbolic adversary politics than it is of a systematic approach to taxation fueled by a particular philosophy. Some would see the conservative, incremental hand of the Treasury behind this.

Britain has never ranked particularly high in overall tax burdens among industrialized countries.[70] When the Conservatives came into office in 1979, they began lowering income tax rates, but they replaced this revenue loss with the imposition of VAT. Thanks to revenue from North Sea oil and privatization sales, the public-sector borrowing requirement (PSBR) dropped and eventually, public-sector spending was reduced as the economy began to grow. But by the 1990s, revenue from the North Sea was reduced, there were few government assets left to sell, economic recession was succeeded by slow growth again, and social security spending had relentlessly increased. This led to a substantial deficit, the massive tax increase of 1994, and discussion of a return to "selectivity" in social insurance benefits.

Evaluation

Management of economic policy in the United Kingdom is obviously a large and complex task, taking up much government time, personnel, and expenditure. In its various manifestations it is always high on the governmental and public agenda, although the exact dimensions of concern differ from time to time. Nevertheless, macroeconomic policy and much of microeconomic policy qualifies as a recurrent item on both agendas, and it is always likely to be so. It is instructive that even so dominant a figure as Margaret Thatcher was unable to shift the terms of the economic debate as much as she set out to do upon becoming prime minister. The consensus is that by the middle of her second term she had abandoned monetarism and was instead focusing government policy on the traditional macroeconomic targets. A preelection boom was engineered for the run-up to the 1987 general election, and subsequently Britain went into a deep recession, the worst since the Great Depression. For all of Mrs. Thatcher's changes in microeconomic policy in areas such as taxation, privatization, and labor policy,[71] the results of macroeconomic policy in Britain in the early 1990s remained suspiciously similar to what had previously been the case—a boom-and-bust cycle heavily dependent on international trade and financial conditions. There was abundant discussion of Britain becoming not so much a postindustrial country as a deindustrialized one. In the European Community, Britain has declined to seventh position in gross domestic product per capita in the early 1990s, and it is also ranks lowest among the G-7 countries. In 1962, the United Kingdom had the fifth-highest gross domestic product per capita in the world; by the early 1990s, it had sunk to sixteenth place.[72] In world exports, the British share has slipped from 10 percent of the total in 1939 to less than 5 percent. Pollard[73] has indicted all postwar British governments for having wasted the assets of Britain's economic position at the end of World War II by not targeting domestic investment in manufacturing, in contrast to the practices of almost all other industrialized democracies. By implication he has rejected the thesis of Martin Wiener[74] that Britain has been an anti-industrial culture for a longer period of time. Whatever the causes, relative decline has continued unabated.

Different economic sectors and regions have experienced widely varying results from economic policy. Until the early 1990s, the south of England enjoyed a boom from computer technology, London's status as a financial and entertainment center, and rising prices for real estate, whereas the traditional manufacturing centers in England and Scotland suffered, as did the coal mining regions of Wales and elsewhere. But in the early 1990s, the collapse in property prices and the fall in the value of sterling against foreign currencies affected the southeast, too, to the detriment of the Conservatives in the 1992 election.

After the rage for privatization and deregulating the supply side in the 1980s, the 1990s have seen a limited resurgence of industrial policy, which Mrs. Thatcher considered "corporatism." The more precise notion is that large corporate institutions—trade unions, economic sectors, and government—work together through collective decisionmaking in order to try to bring about improved economic prospects for the country as a whole.[75] For all of the discussion of this term in the British context, particularly in the attempts of government to direct economic planning and investment and arrange binding agreements with the trade unions in the 1960s and 1970s,[76] the British version of corporatism has always been a weak one, a "liberal corporatism."[77] There is not enough coordination among various business and labor groups to allow binding agreements to be made. Furthermore, the British government has traditionally had a penchant for a hands-off attitude toward large sections of the economy, if not as compared to the United States, certainly in comparison to continental European countries.[78] Strong corporatism has been more prevalent and more successful in smaller European countries—Austria, Sweden, and Norway—where the economic health of the whole country is crucially dependent on the efficient production of a few exports and where the corporate structures are centralized enough to be able to be reliable bargaining partners.[79] Whatever continuities there are in British economic policy exist largely because of factors other than a corporatist mentality and structures. Is British economic policy, considered as a whole, pluralist or elitist? Many of the macroeconomic goals are valence issues, with disagreement occurring over the means of achieving them and over what tradeoffs should occur rather than over whether they should be achieved. Even recent Conservative governments at their most monetarist would not fundamentally dissent from that. Microeconomic goals are much more frequently matters of partisan and group disagreement, however, with the long-term nationalization-privatization dispute being the most prominent. In government rather than in opposition, however, even microeconomic policy differences have been less vast than the overheated partisan rhetoric would suggest.

In the 1970s, when the two-party system in the electorate began to falter and ideological debate replaced Butskellism between the two major parties, the idea of "adversary politics" arose.[80] Supposedly the more ideologically-inclined Conservative and Labour governments shifted policy, especially economic policy, back and forth as they came into office. Sven Steinmo's[81] research on tax policy has indicated that there is some credence for the adversary politics thesis. Rose,[82] however, has argued that party behavior in office, and even party behavior in Parliament on such matters as Second Readings of government bills, has been much less adversarial than popularly thought, even in the contentious 1970s. In short, there is a strong case for continuity in British economic policy, based on such factors as the constraints of Britain's international position, traditional policy preferences of major sectors of the economy, and the standard operating procedures of British government, including the civil service.[83] Even the Labour innovations of the 1940s and the Conservative ones of the 1980s seem, in retrospect, less revolutionary than either their proponents hoped or their opponents feared. Although the Conservatives would not have nationalized so extensively in the 1940s and Labour would not have restricted trade union operations as much as the Conservatives in the 1980s, the inclination of both, at least in the short term, has been to continue broadly the policies of their opponents. British economic policy in the twentieth century has operated within a fairly narrow band of opinion, particularly on the macroeconomic level. In 1931, the leaders of the Labour Party abandoned their party in favor of collaboration with the Conservatives in a national government rather than defying economic orthodoxy about budget deficits, as interpreted by international bankers. The British government was slow to take up Keynesian economics, despite its British origin.[84]

Unlike Keynes, however, those who would take the British political economy outside that narrow range have generally been frustrated in both the short and long run. As in the case of Tony Benn, that has not stilled their dissent, especially on the opposition benches, but party policies in opposition and the same party's policies in government have often been at odds. In short, adversarial postures and even policies in some areas may occur for a while, but when in government, parties have not used their position of "elective dictatorship" under the British constitution to impose radically different economic policies in most instances. Economic policy rhetoric may often sound redistributive, but in fact British economic policymaking has usually been regulative (sectorally fragmented) in character.[85]

The public has tended to be a permissive actor in economic policy. It has endorsed the general goals of economic policy and not been overly concerned with the means that are used to obtain them. Parties have been relatively free to pursue those policies that they thought appropriate to the desired economic ends.

As far back as the 1960s, it was shown that a majority of Labour voters did not want any further nationalization, yet the Labour Party espoused nationalization in its programs.[86] Later, the Conservatives' program of privatization was not strongly endorsed by the public, but it was tolerated,[87] and it marginally aided the Conservatives' reelection prospects.[88]

The public is not concerned with the details of often obscure and esoteric economic policies. What it wants to see is delivery of the major macroeconomic goals. This is an instance of what V. O. Key[89] called the "broad dikes" of public opinion as a constraint upon government. Although governments usually have a permissive consensus to act economically as they see fit, the ultimate public constraint is the electoral one at the next general election. Governments think, with good reason, that the chief public policy factor affecting their chances for reelection is how well the economy performs.[90] Furthermore, in Britain as elsewhere, it is not so much people's individual economic circumstances that affect their voting behavior (pocketbook voting) as how well they think the economy as a whole is doing (sociotropic voting).[91]

But even the public opinion constraint of "success" in economic policy does not work as straightforwardly as it used to. Three-party competition in the electorate means that a party can win a plurality of votes and a majority of seats even though a majority of voters choose other parties. Furthermore, the dominant Conservative governments of the 1980s and 1990s managed to get a lot of mileage out of the proposition that however bad the economy was under their tutelage it would be even worse under the opposition, especially Labour. The legacy of the Winter of Discontent of 1979 still reared its head in the election of 1992. Regionalization and sectoralization of economic prospects have also worked against the simple "mandate" theory of economic voting. The state of the economy is still the principal issue of every general election, but assessing economic conditions has become more complex than in the past.

Even if the British policy process on economic policy is not fully corporatist, it could still be elitist. Many different economic interests are voiced, and several different government agencies and institutions, often with conflicting goals, attempt to realize the goals. Some sectors, such as finance, seem to get their way more often than others, such as manufacturing. The trade unions, once considered more powerful than the formal institutions for making economic policy, have declined as a factor in policymaking in recent years. Political parties may have internal conflicts over policy, but these seldom reach the level of intraparty dissent on the floor of the House of Commons. Even though opposition parties are often vitriolic in denouncing the economic policies of governments, they are prone to adopt similar policies themselves when they are in government. As studies of party programs in election campaigns have shown,[92] parties do not so much debate in election campaigns as talk past each other by emphasizing the issues most beneficial to them.

Under these circumstances, the repertoire of government policies to deal with the economy is limited. Even "Mrs. Thatcher's revolution"[93] had been under discussion for some time, especially when the Conservatives under her predecessor, Edward Heath, were in opposition in the late 1960s; then, the party platform was dubbed "Selsdon man" after a notable meeting of the party in Selsdon Park. Similarly, the program of the Attlee government after the war was less radical than it would have been if attempted between the two world wars. Six years of wartime coalition government, along with the need to rely on planning and government-directed endeavor both to win the war and reconstruct the peacetime economy, made those ideas widely shared. As a third example, monetarism began in 1976 under the Labour government as a response to the need for a loan from the International Monetary Fund. Thus the larger constraints on economic policy in Britain are not domestic, but international.

Despite the various attempts to generate continuous and widely shared economic prosperity in the United Kingdom, the results, in comparative terms, must be judged to be uniformly disappointing. Britain remains a small country, strongly tied to the international economy, but with no firmly held beachheads in international production that would allow it to regain its former status as a leading world economy. Indeed, given developments over the past one hundred years, the safest bet is that under leftist or rightist, interventionist or market-oriented governments, its position relative to other countries will continue to fall. The next group of challengers may come from the Newly Industrialized Countries, especially in Asia. A famous study of the country's economic prospects[94] argued that Britain's underlying problem was one of productivity, deeply embedded in its social structure. Economic growth could not be sustained because its appearance only led to a surge in imports, declining trade balances, and decline of sterling—the infamous stop-go cycle. A long-term change in the supply-side of the British economy was necessary to correct this. Despite the decline of social class as a divide, greater freedom for managers over workers, and a concerted Conservative attack on supply-side rigidities over the past twenty years, these problems remain. The debate over the role of Britain in the European Union, which animates Labour as well as the Conservatives, can be viewed as another manifestation of the controversy over the proper economic and political strategy to pursue. Those who see immersion in the EU as the United Kingdom's best hope are, in effect, despairing that the country can ever really steer itself well on its own. It can grow—but not as much as its major competitors, and the list of such competitors is growing. Without adequate growth, social goals become harder to reach. In short, relative economic decline is inevitable unless Britain can be forced to be more efficient and disciplined, with social support, if necessary, lent by a stronger European Union. By the Conservative government's willingness to allow such formerly leading British industries as automobiles and steel to decline, as well as by its enthusiasm for the lowering of trade barriers in accordance with the EU's single market program, the leadership showed that it partially accepted this logic, though only partially. There was great reluctance to give up national economic decisionmaking en masse in the Maastricht Treaty, and the social goals of the Community are treated with suspicion. Similarly, a governing Labour Party would feel pressured by its left wing not to renounce fully the British capacity to develop its own economic policy in the interests of the "capitalists' club" of the EU, currently with the German Bundesbank as its financial center. The dangers of abdicating British responsibility for its own economic future are not to be underestimated. The British disease might be just as intractable under the guidance of a European Union macroeconomic policy as it has been under a domestic British one.

Nevertheless, the record of the past century, and especially of the past twenty-five years, remains. Britain has been able to grow, though not fast enough to maintain the status to which it had become accustomed. A variety of policies has been tried, to little avail in solving the long-term, or even the medium-term, problem of British productivity. The political culture and political institutions of the United Kingdom alone seem incapable of altering the course of relative British economic decline—and not for lack of trying. It may be time to try something different. But whether deep-seated traditions of British nationalism and suspicion of being too deeply involved with Europe will allow it is doubtful.

Notes

1. Theodore J. Lowi, "American Business, Public Policy, Case Studies, and Political Theory," *World Politics* 16, no. 4 (1964):677–715.

2. T. Alexander Smith, *The Comparative Policy Process* (Santa Barbara, Ca.: ABC-Clio, 1975).

3. Randall B. Ripley and Grace Franklin, *Congress, the Bureaucracy, and Public Policy*, 5th ed. (Pacific Grove, Ca.: Brooks/Cole Publishing Company, 1991).

4. Wyn Grant, *The Politics of Economic Policy* (London: Harvester Wheatsheaf, 1993).

5. Jack L. Walker, "Setting the Agenda in the U.S. Senate: A Theory of Problem Selection," *British Journal of Political Science* 7, no. 4 (1977):423–445.

6. Michael S. Lewis-Beck, *Economics and Elections* (Ann Arbor: University of Michigan Press, 1988).

7. James E. Alt, *The Politics of Economic Decline* (Cambridge: Cambridge University Press, 1979).

8. Robert T. McKenzie, *British Political Parties*, 2d ed. (New York: St. Martin's Press, 1963); Peter Jenkins, *Mrs. Thatcher's Revolution* (Cambridge: Harvard University Press, 1989).

9. David Butler and Donald E. Stokes, *Political Change in Britain*, 2d ed. (New York: St. Martin's Press, 1974); Ian McAllister and Donley T. Studlar, "Popular Versus Elite Views of Privatization: The Case of Britain." *Journal of Public Policy* 9, no. 1 (1989):157–178.

10. Colin Hughes and Patrick Wintour, *Labour Rebuilt: The New Model Party* (London: Fourth Estate, 1991).

11. James Cronin, "The Historical Margaret Thatcher," in *Margaret Thatcher: Prime Minister Indomitable*, ed. Juliet L. Thompson and Wayne Thompson (Boulder: Westview

Press, 1994); A. P. Tant, *British Government: The Triumph of Elitism* (Brookfield, Vt.: Ashgate Publishers, 1993).

12. Helen Milner, "Maintaining Commitments in Trade Policy," in *Do Institutions Matter?* ed. R. Kent Weaver and Bert A. Rockman (Washington D.C.: Brookings Institution, 1993).

13. This department was downgraded under the Conservatives, who reduced Britain's commitment to an industrial policy. See Stephen Wilks, "Economic Policy," in *Developments in British Politics* 4, ed. Patrick Dunleavy, Andrew Gamble, Ian Holliday, and Gillian Peele (New York: St. Martin's Press, 1993).

14. Samuel Brittan, *Steering the Economy* (Harmondsworth, England: Penguin Books, 1971).

15. Hugh Heclo and Aaron Wildavsky, *The Private Government of Public Money*, 2d ed. (London: Macmillan, 1981); Paul Mosley, "Economic Policy," in *Developments in British Politics* 2, ed. Henry Drucker, Patrick Dunleavy, Andrew Gamble, and Gillian Peele (New York: St. Martin's Press, 1988).

16. Peter Hall, ed., *The Political Power of Economic Ideas* (Princeton: Princeton University Press, 1989).

17. Dennis Kavanagh, "Crisis Management and Incremental Adaption in British Politics: The 1931 Crisis of the British Party System," in *Crisis, Choice, and Change*, ed. Gabriel A. Almond, Scott C. Flanagan and Robert J. Mundt (Boston: Little, Brown and Company, 1973).

18. Jim Tomlinson, *British Macroeconomic Policy Since 1940* (London: Croom Helm, 1985); Hall, *The Political Power of Economic Ideas.*

19. Anthony Crosland, *The Future of Socialism* (New York: Schocken Books, 1963).

20. B. Guy Peters, *European Politics Reconsidered* (New York: Holmes and Meier, 1991).

21. Milton Friedman, *Capitalism and Freedom* (Chicago: University of Chicago Press, 1962).

22. Paul Whiteley, "Economic Policy," in *Developments in British Politics* 3, ed. Patrick Dunleavy, Andrew Gamble, and Gillian Peele (New York: St. Martin's Press, 1990).

23. Kathleen Burk and Alec Cairncross, *Goodbye, Great Britain* (New Haven: Yale University Press, 1992).

24. Whiteley, "Economic Policy."

25. "Conservative Economics: Lord Wishful, Lady Rigorous," *Economist*, 24 October, 1987.

26. Tomlinson, *British Macroeconomic Policy Since 1940.*

27. Sydney Pollard, *The Wasting of the British Economy*, 2d ed. (London: Macmillan, 1984).

28. Stephen Blank, "Britain: The Politics of Foreign Economic Policy, the Domestic Economy, and the Problem of Pluralistic Stagnation," *International Organization* 31, no. 4 (1977):673–721; Pollard, *The Wasting of the British Economy.*

29. Grant, *The Politics of Economic Policy*, p. 14.

30. David McKie, ed., *The Election: A Voter's Guide* (London: Fourth Estate, 1992); Grant, *The Politics of Economic Policy*, p. 13.

31. Grant, *The Politics of Economic Policy*, pp. 12–13.

32. Grant, *The Politics of Economic Policy.*

33. Alan Sked and Chris Cook, *Post-War Britain*, 3d ed. (New York: Penguin Books, 1990); Pollard, *The Wasting of the British Economy;* Isaac Kramnick, ed., *Is Britain Dying?*

(Ithaca: Cornell University Press, 1979); William B. Gwyn and Richard Rose, eds., *Britain: Progress and Decline* (New Orleans: Tulane Studies in Political Science, 1980).

34. David Butler and Richard Rose, *The British General Election of 1959* (New York: St. Martin's Press, 1960).

35. Alt, *The Politics of Economic Decline;* Ian McAllister and Anthony Mughan, "Attitudes, Issues and Labor Party Decline in England, 1974–1979," *Comparative Political Studies* 18, no. 1 (1985):37–57.

36. Jerold L. Waltman and Donley T. Studlar, eds., *Political Economy: Public Policies in the United States and Britain* (Jackson: University Press of Mississippi, 1987); Paul Cloke, ed., *Policy and Change in Thatcher's Britain* (Oxford: Pergamon Press, 1992); Stephen P. Savage and Lynton Robins, eds., *Public Policy Under Thatcher* (New York: St. Martin's Press, 1990); David Marsh and R.A.W. Rhodes, eds., *Implementing Thatcherite Policies* (Buckingham: Open University Press, 1992); Peter Catterall, ed., *Contemporary Britain: An Annual Review, 1990, 1991, and 1992* (New York: Basil Blackwell, 1990–1992); McKie, *The Election: A Voter's Guide;* Dunleavy, Gamble, Holliday, and Peele, eds., *Developments in British Politics 4.*

37. Jeffrey B. Freyman, "Industrial Policy: Patterns of Convergence and Divergence," in *Political Economy: Public Policies in the United States and Britain,* ed. Waltman and Studlar.

38. Anthony King, "Ideas, Institutions, and the Policies of Government: A Comparative Analysis, Parts I and II," *British Journal of Political Science* 3, nos. 2 and 3 (1973):291–313, 409–423.

39. Richard Rose, *Do Parties Make a Difference?* (Chatham, N.J.: Chatham House, 1980).

40. Butler and Stokes, *Political Change in Britain.*

41. McAllister and Studlar, "Popular Versus Elite Views of Privatization: The Case of Britain."

42. Patrick Seyd and Paul Whiteley, *Labour's Grassroots* (Oxford: Clarendon Press, 1992).

43. Ivor Crewe, Bo Sarlvik, and James E. Alt, "Patrisan Dealignment in Britain, 1964–74," *British Journal of Political Science* 7, no. 1 (1977):129–190.

44. David Farnham, "Trade Union Policy, 1979–89: Restriction or Reform?" in *Public Policy Under Thatcher,* ed. Stephen P. Savage and Lynton Robins (New York: St. Martin's Press, 1990); David Marsh, "Industrial Relations," in *Implementing Thatcherite Policies,* ed. David Marsh and R.A.W. Rhodes (Buckingham: Open University Press, 1992); Ian Holliday, "Organized Interests After Thatcher," in *Developments in British Politics* 4, ed. Dunleavy, Gamble, Holliday, and Peele.

45. Marsh, "Industrial Relations."

46. Butler and Stokes, *Political Change in Britain;* Mark Abrams and Richard Rose, *Must Labour Lose?* (London: Penguin Books, 1960).

47. Paul Webb, *Trade Unions and the British Electorate* (Aldershot, England: Dartmouth, 1992); William D. Muller, *The Kept Men? The First Century of Trade Union Representation in the House of Commons, 1874–1975* (London: Harvester Press, 1977).

48. Patrick Dunleavy, "The Urban Basis of Political Alignment: Social Class, Domestic Property Ownership and State Intervention in Consumption Processes," *British Journal of Political Science* 9, no. 4 (1979):409–443.

49. Webb, *Trade Unions and the British Electorate.*

50. Mark N. Franklin and Ed Page, "A Critique of the Consumption Cleavage Approach in British Voting Studies," *Political Studies* 32, no. 4 (1984):521–536.

51. Farnham, "Trade Union Policy, 1979–89: Restriction or Reform?"

52. Joseph R. Rudolph, Jr., "Energy Policy in the United States and Britain," in *Political Economy: Public Policies in the United States and Britain,* ed. Waltman and Studlar.

53. McKie, *The Election: A Voter's Guide.*

54. Seyd and Whiteley, *Labour's Grassroots.*

55. Anthony Sampson, *The Anatomy of Britain Today* (New York: Harper Colophon Books, 1965).

56. Michael Rush, ed., *Parliament and Pressure Groups* (Oxford: Oxford University Press, 1990).

57. Peter Self and Herbert Storing, *The State and the Farmer,* 2d ed. (London: Allen and Unwin, 1971); Roland J. Pennock, "Agricultural Subsides in England and America," *American Political Science Review* 56, no. 3 (1962):621–633.

58. McKie, *The Election: A Voter's Guide.*

59. Hans J. Michelmann, "Britain and the European Community," in *Dilemmas of Change in British Politics,* ed. Donley T. Studlar and Jerold L. Waltman (London: Macmillan, 1983); Stephen George, *Britain and European Integration Since 1945* (New York: Basil Blackwell, 1991).

60. Ronald Inglehart, *Culture Shift* (Princeton: Princeton University Press, 1990).

61. Wolgang Rudig and Philip D. Lowe, "The Withered Greening of British Politics," *Political Studies* 34, no. 2 (1986):262–284; E. Gene Frankland, "Does Green Politics Have a Future in Britain? An American Perspective," in *Green Politics One,* ed. Wolfgang Rudig (Edinburgh: Edinburgh University Press, 1990).

62. John McCormick, "Environmental Politics," in *Developments in British Politics* 4, ed. Dunleavy, Gamble, Holliday and Peele.

63. David Vogel, "Representing Diffuse Interests in Environmental Policymaking," in *Do Institutions Matter?,* ed. Weaver and Rockman.

64. John B. Sanderson, "The National Smoke Abatement Society and the Clean Air Act," *Political Studies* 9, no. 2 (1961):236–253; McCormick, "Environmental Politics."

65. John Bradbeer, "Environmental Policy," in *Public Policy Under Thatcher,* ed. Stephen P. Savage and Lynton Robins, (New York: St. Martin's Press, 1990).

66. McCormick, "Environmental Politics."

67. Jerold L. Waltman, "Changing the Course of Tax Policy: Convergent in Intent, Divergent in Practice," in *Political Economy: Public Policies in the United States and Britain,* ed. Waltman and Studlar.

68. Richard Rose, *Understanding Big Government* (London: Sage Publications, 1984).

69. Sven Steinmo, *Taxation and Democracy* (New Haven: Yale University Press, 1994).

70. Arnold Heidenheimer, Hugh Heclo, and Carolyn Teich Adams, *Comparative Public Policy,* 3d ed. (New York: St. Martin's Press, 1990).

71. "Conservative Economics: Lord Wishful, Lady Rigorous."

72. Wilks, "Economic Policy."

73. Pollard, *The Wasting of the British Economy.*

74. Martin J. Wiener, *English Culture and the Decline of the Industrial Spirit, 1850–1980* (Cambridge: Cambridge University Press, 1981).

75. Philippe Schmitter, "Still the Century of Corporatism?" *Review of Politics* 36, no. 1 (1974):85–131; Alan Cawson, *Corporatism and Political Theory* (Oxford: Basil Blackwell, 1986). Central Office of Information, *Britain, 1994: An Offical Handbook* (London: Her Majesty's Stationery Office), Freyman, "Industrial Policy: Patterns of Convergence and Divergence."

76. Andrew Shonfield, *Modern Capitalism* (New York: Oxford University Press, 1965); Keith Middlemas, *Politics in Industrial Society* (London: Andre Deutsch, 1980).

77. Freyman, "Industrial Policy: Patterns of Convergence and Divergence"; Holliday, "Organized Interests After Thatcher."

78. Heidenheimer, Heclo, and Adams, *Comparative Public Policy.*

79. Jurg Steiner, *European Politics,* 2d ed. (New York: Longman, 1991); Peters, *European Politics Reconsidered.*

80. Samuel Finer, ed., *Adversary Politics and Electoral Reform* (London: Anthony Wigram, 1975).

81. Steinmo, *Taxation and Democracy.*

82. Rose, *Do Parties Make a Difference?*

83. Waltman and Studlar, eds., *Political Economy: Public Policy in the United States and Britain;* Jeremey Richardson, ed., *Policy Styles in Western Europe* (London: Allen and Unwin, 1982).

84. Hall, *The Political Power of Economic Ideas.*

85. Lowi, "American Business, Public Policy, Case Studies, and Political Theory"; Smith, *The Comparative Policy Process.*

86. Butler and Stokes, *Political Change in Britain;* Richard Rose, *Politics in England,* 2d ed. (Boston: Little, Brown and Company, 1974).

87. McAllister and Studlar, "Popular Versus Elite Views of Privatization: The Case of Britain."

88. Donley T. Studlar, Ian McAllister, and Alvaro Ascui, "Privatization and the British Electorate: Microeconomic Policies, Macroseconomic Evaluations and Party Support," *American Journal of Political Studies* 34, no. 4 (1990):1077–1101; Helmut Norpoth, *Confidence Regained: Economics, Mrs. Thatcher, and the British Voter* (Ann Arbor: University of Michigan Press, 1992); Pippa Norris, "Thatcher's Enterprise Society and Electoral Change," *West European Politics* 13, no. 1 (1990):63–78; Anthony Heath, Roger Jowell, and John Curtice, *How Britain Votes* (Oxford: Pergamon Press, 1985); Anthony Heath, Roger Jowell, John Curtice, Geoff Evans, Julia Field, and Sharon Witherspoon, *Understanding Political Change* (Oxford: Pergamon Press, 1991).

89. V. O. Key, *Public Opinion and American Democracy* (New York: Knopf, 1961).

90. Lewis-Beck, *Economics and Elections.*

91. Lewis-Beck, *Economics and Elections;* Studlar, McAllister, and Ascui, "Privatization and the British Electorate: Microeconomic Policies, Macroeconomic Evaluations and Party Support."

92. Ian Budge, David Robertson, and David Hearl, eds., *Ideology, Strategy, and Party Change* (Cambridge: Cambridge University Press, 1987); Richard Hofferbert and Ian Budge, "The Party Mandate and the Westminster Model: Election Programmes and Government Spending in Britain, 1945–1985," *British Journal of Political Science* 22, no. 1 (1992):151–182.

93. Philip Jenkins, *Intimate Enemies* (New York: Aldine De Gruyter, 1992).

94. Richard Caves and Lewis Krause, *Britain's Economic Performance* (Washington, D.C.: Brookings Institution, 1980).

7

SOCIAL WELFARE POLICY: FROM LEADER TO LAGGARD

Social welfare policy encompasses a broad array of British government policies. Often called "social policy,"[1] the more specific term "social welfare policy" is used here to distinguish it from the area of "social regulatory policy" to be discussed in Chapter 8. Social welfare policy refers to the use of the state as an income-transfer mechanism to provide services and monetary supplements to sectors of the population deemed by the government to deserve such assistance through their social circumstances and to provide basic social services for all citizens. Some of these services, such as those offered by the National Health Service, are provided to all of the public, and others, such as the public (or state-run) educational system and government-provided pensions, are provided to almost all of the population in a particular age group. A third category of social welfare, exemplified by programs such as those for unemployment insurance, public (council) housing, child benefit, and the Supplementary Benefit (formerly called National Assistance), is more selectively implemented, usually requiring what the British call a means test to qualify for benefits. Nevertheless, all of these programs involve the state use of material resources gathered principally through taxes to relieve social needs by disbursing funds and services to some group of people.

As a whole, social welfare policy is discussed by legislators and political parties more than any other issue except economic policy.[2] Such policies can be part of several of the policy categories devised by Lowi, Smith, and Ripley and Franklin. They are rarely redistributive in terms of their political process characteristics, except when some comprehensive programs are introduced, more frequently distributive or regulatory (sectoral fragmentation). Although there obviously are economic implications for almost all social welfare programs, that is, they cost money, at least in the short term, the economic aspects rarely dominate discussion of the policies. Instead, the focus is on the desirability of their social goals, their target populations, and their likelihood of success. In this chapter, some of the most important of these programs are reviewed.

The Agenda

Even though the growth of the welfare state is normally associated with the postwar period, first through the Attlee Labour government and later through Butskellism, in fact Britain has had a welfare state, at least in selective areas, since 1906.[3] At that time the Liberal government brought in a selective form of industrial accident insurance. This was followed by government-provided pensions, illness insurance, health insurance, and unemployment insurance, all started, although hardly comprehensively, by 1920.[4] Early British social welfare programs were focused on dealing with the problem of poverty, and to a large degree this orientation has carried over into the more comprehensive programs enacted later, usually through the provision of minimum benefit levels.[5] Postwar governments, of course, expanded the welfare state, notably through the establishment of the National Health Service in 1948, expansion of public housing, and creation of a number of categorical aid programs. Dunleavy[6] has argued that the retreat from empire provided vacant "policy space" that allowed social welfare programs to grow relatively unobtrusively, if incrementally, in the late 1950s and throughout the 1960s.

Overall, the agenda in postwar British social welfare policy has moved from one of "minimum benefits" for all to one of "selective benefits" to most.[7] Whereas the welfare state was once considered a basic ingredient of "social citizenship," complementing legal rights and voting equality,[8] in more recent times greater consideration has been given to the targeting of benefits rather than to maintaining all-inclusive benefits. Of course, some inclusive benefits, particularly those of the National Health Service, still exist, but even within the NHS, targeting occurs, especially through the limitation of expensive services to those most in a position to benefit from them. In general, even though the overall benefits of the British welfare state have risen, Britain has been moving down the ladder of advanced industrialized countries in terms of the generosity of its coverage. Earlier in the twentieth century, Britain was considered a leader in welfare state provision, but by the 1980s, careful observers considered it a laggard.[9] This situation is not due solely to post-1979 policies.

The key development in the British welfare state was the Beveridge Report in 1942. An all-party committee under the leadership of the Liberal William Beveridge recommended the establishment of a "national minimum" for all citizens, based largely on the insurance principle. Although the original benefits were not that generous, and as a Liberal, Beveridge did not envision an expansionist welfare state, the very fact that all citizens were entitled to them encouraged the notion of a "social citizenship," in which the state owed a duty to its citizens to provide for their basic needs. Some of these needs were comprehensively supplied, such as with the National Health Service. Others were more selective, based upon particular needs. Such selective needs, called in Britain "social security," have proliferated over the years, to the point where in the 1990s they have taken up about one-third of the government budget. Today there are not only pensions and unemployment insurance, but also the housing benefit, legal aid, mortgage interest payments for the unemployed, the invalidity benefit, child benefit, Supplementary Benefit, and others, all paid for out of National Insurance contributions collected from the employed. In the 1960s, requirements for drawing benefits were loosened, allowing more people to join the programs.[10] The National Health Service, public housing, and education are run as separate services and are not included in the social service budget. Together, all of these welfare state services account for two-thirds of British government spending in the 1990s; this proportion has been growing as the population ages, unemployment persists, and more single-parent households are formed.

The British mix of social welfare programs thus includes both social insurance and direct provision. Insurance involves contributions to the state, in return for which contributors become entitled to benefits when they enter a need category such as unemployment or old-age pension. Direct provision takes place when the state provides services, such as health care, housing, or education, on the basis of general taxation rather than using earmarked contributions for a particular purpose. In general, the limits on welfare expansion introduced by the Conservative governments under Thatcher and Major over the past two decades have involved moving the British welfare state from direct provision toward the European norm of insurance and selectivity.[11]

Even earlier than 1906, of course, the British government was involved in providing for public education through state-run and financed schools, ranging from primary to university, but on an extremely selective basis. As noted in Chapter 2, how well the state has performed its public policy role in education is a long-running controversy in Britain. But since 1884, there has been provision for state standards in education. There have been bursts of state activity in education policy, for instance in the early 1900s, again at the end of World War II, and at the higher education level in the 1960s. More recently in the 1980s, Conservative governments have changed the shape of both higher education, by altering government financing, and of lower education, by passing the Education Bill of 1988, both of which will be touched on later. The more general point here is that however reluctant some may be to think of education as part of social welfare policy there is a strong case to include it.[12] Even if the British have chosen to invest more of their social welfare policy resources in other areas, education policy certainly has broad social welfare goals as well.

In the rest of this chapter, I concentrate on the more expensive, more comprehensive programs, such as health, housing, education, and parts of what the British call "social security" (their term for social welfare, or what others would call income maintenance), including, for example, pensions and basic selective benefits. Again, the focus rests on which institutions are relevant to these policies; in a broad sense, on how policy has developed; and finally, on what can be concluded about the relative influence of pluralism and elitism on policy in this area in the United Kingdom.

Actors

The major institutions in the social welfare area include the traditional parliamentary ones, the House of Commons and the government it supports, abetted in the twentieth century by an expanded bureaucracy to administer the variety of programs. Despite the image of the United Kingdom as a centralized polity, local governments and regional administrations play a considerable role in administering several of these policies. Even under Mrs. Thatcher, social welfare policy is part of "high politics" and as such is embedded in party platforms, the queen's speeches, and government bills and announcements presented to the House of Commons. Social welfare policy affects almost everybody in the United Kingdom in a distributional sense and, however indirectly, also affects their pocketbooks.

The principal politically responsible actors within the governing party are the prime minister, the ministers responsible for Health, Social Security, Education and Science, and Environment (local government, especially housing), in addition to the ministers in charge of the Northern Ireland Office, the Scottish Office, and the Welsh Office, which deal with the relevant programs in those parts of the United Kingdom.[13] There have been periodic reorganizations, including renaming, of the government departments responsible for social welfare. Health, Social Security, Education and Science, and Environment are four of the largest government departments, both in terms of personnel and spending,[14] further demonstrating the premium that is put on these functions. For instance, social security expenditure of itself forms the largest share of the government budget, although almost all of the expenditure involves income transfers through the tax system rather than government purchases of goods and services. The National Health Service, on the other hand, employs more people than any government agency in Europe outside the military of the Commonwealth of Independent States.

Policies are developed within these ministries, often in consultation with affected interests and outside experts. Among the groups that influence social welfare policy are the various professional associations and unions working in this area, including social workers, teachers, and physicians. Academic experts have often played a substantial role as well. Mrs. Thatcher attempted to avoid the "Yes, Minister" syndrome by promoting civil servants she judged to be neutral in their advice rather than pushing government ministers toward particular political positions. She also attempted to limit outside consultations, especially with trade-union groups. Social welfare matters are complex, however, and a great deal of time and consultation is usually needed to develop them. Major changes are often floated in the form of green papers or white papers. The details, however, are very much in the hands of the ministries—governing politicians and bureaucrats. In fact, the author of one recent survey of this policy field[15] argued that ministers are largely unaccountable and can engage in policy change by stealth through administrative regulations, even to the extent of frustrating the intent of Parliament. In a system without a strong judiciary to settle executive-legislative disputes, it takes persistent legislative oversight to ascertain what is going on in the executive—oversight that the British House of Commons, despite its Select Committee system, has problems providing.

Once developed, policies are brought to the House of Commons for debate. In addition to the debates over specific legislation, social welfare matters are often the subject of written and oral questions and adjournment debates. In this area, not only do the opposition party leaders engage the government in debate but backbench members of Parliament also often specialize and raise concerns.[16] The government of the day rarely, however, suffers a defeat or even dissenting votes from its own party on social welfare matters, at least in overt terms. It may be amenable to changing or even abandoning its own policies under pressure from its own backbenchers if enough of them demur, as happened to some of the Conservative plans for higher education in the 1980s, but a government rarely gives in to opposition amendments. Thus social welfare matters are high politics and the regular stuff of class-based, parliamentary debate.

Under the usual format for debate, especially since 1979, the Conservatives advocate selectivity to concentrate resources on the poorest sections of society and efficiency in service delivery while Labour and to some degree the Liberal Democrats complain of cutbacks in the basic social rights of citizenship for all. But these are not only position issues. Under Butskellism, Conservative governments were keen to demonstrate their "one nation" credentials by advocating social welfare spending, as for instance in their housing program, and even in the 1980s and 1990s, Conservatives have reiterated such phrases as "the National Health Service is safe in our hands" to fend off Labour accusations that the government was shortchanging social welfare services with a long-term view to privatizing them.

In electoral terms, social welfare is an issue on which Labour has an advantage in public appeal because it normally places a higher priority on the issue.[17] In fact, the Conservatives managed to win elections in the 1980s and early 1990s despite the fact that Labour was perceived by the voters to be better on social welfare policy, especially in regard to maintaining the health service, and combating unemployment. The Conservatives feel that they have to avoid having social welfare issues become clear position (opposed) issues, if possible, because in such circumstances the damage to their electoral prospects could be considerable. Thus the Conservatives have backed away from bruited privatization schemes for education and health and have instead concentrated on making these services more efficient within the provision of state structure. Similarly, they have emphasized targeting of benefits rather than elimination of whole social welfare programs. Grants to support students in higher education, for instance, have been scaled back rather than eliminated.

Formation, Adoption, and Implementation

Health

Health care is perhaps the most notable feature of the British welfare state. The advent of the National Health Service in 1948 was an epic event, recognized around the world as a touchstone of the British welfare state, and subsequently the National Health Service has been studied carefully from a variety of perspectives.[18] It has become something of a sacred cow in Britain, with even Mrs. Thatcher disclaiming any intention to dismantle its basic provisions. In comparative perspective, however, the NHS is something of an anomaly. Although all Western democracies except the United States have a comprehensive public health-care system for all age groups, only the United Kingdom runs one directly, as a form of direct provision financed out of central government revenues. All of the others operate theirs on the basis of one form or another of social insurance, that is, one pays into the public treasury for benefits but the government does not directly provide for hospitals, equipment, personnel, treatment, and so on. Instead, the government or the individual contracts with private providers for services, which the government pays for out of the health insurance funds. The NHS, however, is a huge public enterprise; as noted previously, it is the second-largest government bureaucracy in Europe.

Arnold Heidenheimer, Hugh Heclo, and Carolyn Adams[19] have argued that, for all of its social welfare programs, the United Kingdom is similar to the United States in that there is a presumption of reliance on private enterprise and private resources, to be supplemented by public provision only when necessary. The direct provision of health care, as well as the still extensive public housing program, undercuts their generalization. In fact, Dunleavy[20] has argued that, if anything, British social policy has been more statist, than most countries, that is, in its direct provision of services rather than social insurance. In these two policies the United Kingdom central government has taken a more active role than in any other Western democracy. Partially, this is the result of early twentieth century investigations into the social conditions of the working-class population on this crowded island, such as those made by Seebohm Rowntree.[21] These reports led to calls for reform, aided by the growth of collectivist thought committed to a greater degree of basic social equality. Further aided by the publication of the

Beveridge Report on social welfare in 1942, health care and other social welfare issues, including housing, have continuously been on the governmental agenda ever since.

Also, in both housing and health care there is extensive reliance on local governments to administer the programs. Council (publicly built and subsidized) housing is administered, as the name indicates, by local councils, under guidelines supplied by the central government. The National Health Service is administered by regional district health authorities, which, in effect, means that whatever the equity aims of a centralized service there is variation from one district to another in health care provision, for instance in the availability of nonemergency surgery.

Direct central control over the health service in Britain gives the government several advantages. For one thing, it can directly determine the resources to be devoted to health care, except for those that private individuals are willing to pay for by taking out supplemental health insurance. The government determines how many hospitals will be built, how much money will be spent for heroic but rarely used and expensive technologies, such as CAT scans and kidney dialysis machines, and what fees physicians and other personnel will receive for their services. In Britain this has resulted in much smaller increases in health care costs than in other Western countries that rely more on market mechanisms. In fact, both Labour and Conservative governments have held down spending on the NHS by refusing to upgrade hospitals, buy new equipment, and hire more personnel to care for the increasingly aged population of the country.

Although the United Kingdom ranks well on most comparative indicators of health care provision, such as infant mortality rates and life expectancy,[22] the government's reluctance to invest in the National Health Service has made it subject to criticism for such practices as limiting access to kidney dialysis (ironically, this is the only procedure available to people under age sixty-two under the United States provision of Medicare for its aged population) and long waiting lists for elective surgery.[23] The most publicized incident of this variety was the so-called war of Jennifer's ear during the 1992 election campaign.[24] Furthermore, despite the centralized financing and regulation of the NHS, health care outcomes are still class related in the United Kingdom.[25] Nevertheless, the basic health care provision of the NHS remains strong and is popularly supported.[26]

The Conservative government's controversial reorganization of the National Health Service on the basis of an "internal market" for care in 1988 was also made possible by central government control over the delivery and financing of services. Its basic provisions are that individual care providers, including hospitals and physicians, can organize themselves according to their determination of the most efficient provision of services and that they are accountable to central authorities concerning how they manage their own budgets, although these budgets remain public funds. This is a method of providing greater accountability in the NHS, which necessarily will involve greater selectivity in what health care providers will supply to the public and how many citizens each will serve.

Although this policy does not necessarily follow the road to privatization, as various opposition groups have charged, it does involve more of a search by the consumers of health care for the services they need. It has also encouraged the development of private health insurance programs that offer expedited service.

The commitment of the government of the United Kingdom to public health care since 1948 can best be considered as a valence issue. All governments portray themselves as supporting the principle of a National Health Service based on need rather than ability to pay for services at the point of delivery, financed out of public funds. But this is an issue on which Labour, as the founder and guardian of the NHS, feels its has a presentational advantage over other parties.

Housing

Housing has been the social welfare issue in which the greatest changes have been wrought in recent years. The privatization boom under the Conservatives started with the sale of council houses to sitting tenants at huge discounts in the early 1980s. The popularity of these sales, even though taken up by only a minority of council tenants, encouraged further and larger privatization initiatives by the Conservative governnments of Thatcher and Major. As noted previously, Britain has been unusual in the amount of public housing that has been supplied. Even after the council-house sales, still fully 25 percent of the housing stock is public, down from 34 percent before the sales began. In addition to the reform proposals for improving the condition of the working class in urban areas through improved housing, further stimuli to house building have been the age and lack of modern amenities in much of Britain's housing stock and the destruction wreaked by German bombing in World War II. At the end of World War I, the coalition government, mainly composed of Conservatives but led by the Liberal Lloyd George, proposed a huge house-building program as part of its program for veterans in a "land fit for heroes." Similarly, the Conservative governments in the 1950s, led by Housing Minister Harold MacMillan, prided themselves on being able to build more houses than the previous postwar Labour government, many of which were built through public authorities. Yet by the early 1970s, housing amenities were still sufficiently lacking in some areas for there still to be more houses with television sets than indoor plumbing.[27]

British central government took measures to encourage private house-building, such as by allowing nonprofit housing associations to build and by providing a mortgage-interest tax-relief benefit for those investing in their own homes (currently this is worth up to thirty thousand pounds, only on one residence). But it was thought that private building could not keep up with the population growth in the twentieth century unless the government took a more direct hand. Furthermore, private rental availability did not keep up with demand. Thus governments of all political stripes engaged in the building, operation, and rental of housing, working through local government councils as the agent.

The first hints of change occurred under the Conservative government of Edward Heath in the early 1970s, when sales of council housing were encouraged. But the incentives (discounts) offered to purchasers were not that great and the program depended on the cooperation of local governments, many of them under Labour control, for its implementation. Such cooperation was only rarely forthcoming, and the number of houses sold was small.

There was a murmur of privatization of council houses in the 1979 Conservative Party platform but, given the modest results from a similar pledge by the Heath government, this did not occasion a great deal of commentary. As the program developed, however, the deep discounts proved an irresistible incentive to buyers, many of whom were the better-off among council-house tenants. The Conservatives considered that there would be a political reward for council-house sales as well, with personal property-owners more likely to develop a sense of individual responsibility for their investment and reward the Conservatives electorally for their good fortune. There does appear to have been a small electoral benefit for the Conservatives.[28] But privatization of council houses was only the first move in the developing Conservative program of shifting from producer-based subsidies to consumer subsidies. In the housing area, this meant moving from building houses, establishing a level of subsidized rents, maintaining the housing, and establishing eligibility criteria for council housing (which limited job and residential mobility) to allowing individual buyers to be responsible for their own abodes after purchase through a housing benefit.[29] The Conservatives were not nearly as successful with an early 1990s plan to encourage private associations to replace public housing authorities as major suppliers of rented accommodation and, as previously noted, there remains a substantial amount of council housing in Britain. But the Conservatives have severely restricted the building of public housing in the 1980s as well.

Accompanying these developments has been the growth of homelessness in the United Kingdom, especially in urban areas. As in the United States, there is considerable controversy about the causes of this phenomenon, revolving around the release from institutions of people suffering from mental incapacity, the consequences of government housing and social welfare policies, and problems of family breakups and lack of desire to work. The fact remains, however, that there has been an increase in the number of people either sleeping "rough" or joining mobile caravans of those who travel around the country with no permanent employment.

Housing, then, has been an issue that has moved from being a valence issue for much of the twentieth century (parties having similar goals) to a position issue (fundamental differences in goals) in the 1980s, with Labour criticizing the Conservative privatizations as providing less fairness in housing and, in effect, overly large government subsidies (through discounts) to council-house buyers. But, by the late 1980s and early 1990s, the new model Labour Party had become reconciled to the Conservative-dominated status quo in housing.[30] A future Labour government would not attempt to reclaim the sold council houses, although it probably would make a renewed effort to build public housing. The market would remain, however, the dominant mechanism of housing in Britain. In short, housing policy shows every sign of moving back toward a valence issue after its brief period as a position issue. Party differences in emphases will remain and the issue will doubtless be joined periodically in House of Commons debates, but the major period of partisan conflict is probably over (cf. Headey).

As the above account suggests, housing policy in twentieth-century Britain has been a matter of elite-led change, usually with considerable consensus on both goals and means, in response to what the elite has determined to be mass needs. There is little direct evidence that the mass public has forced its wishes on the elite through interest groups, petitions, demonstrations, or elections. In fact, housing, though frequently mentioned in election manifestos, has rarely captured the imagination of voters in campaigns.[31] The 1980s privatization proposals were also elite- rather than mass-driven.[32] Government housing policy is an issue that affects the lives of millions of Britons, but it is also one in which the elite has considerable freedom to act. The elite, however, acts with some view toward both meeting mass needs and drawing political benefits from the policy.

Education

Some of the continuing controversies over British educational policy were discussed in Chapter 2. Here again, British practices in education often differ from European norms, for better or worse. Unlike most continental countries, the well-off support their own nonsectarian private system of educational preparatory schools, the so-called public or fee-paying schools. Although less than 10 percent of the eligible population attends such schools, those so privileged provide a disproportionate number of leading political figures, especially in the Conservative Party. The presence of private fee-paying schools and selectivity in the state school system, along with the lack of apprenticeship job training for those who leave school at the minimum age and the relatively small share of the population that attends institutions of higher education, has led to questions about the appropriateness and efficiency of the educational system. As noted earlier, some "state-of-Britain" critics have laid the blame on the educational system, both in terms of its limited access and the content of the curriculum, for Britain's industrial and political decline. Other leftist critics have attributed Britain's ills to the class prejudice and social divisiveness that the educational system instills, even among those at the same level of education. The continued dominance of Oxford- and Cambridge-educated people in several areas of social and political life is one indication of this.

There has been continual government tinkering with educational policy. If the outcomes have still been unsatisfactory, it is not for want of having the issue on the agenda. Over the last century there has been a continual raising of the age at which students may leave school, and more resources have been poured into state schools as the population has expanded. Nevertheless, until the 1960s the basic structure and curriculum of the schools remained constant, with concentration on the traditional liberal arts in the early grades, accompanied by statewide examinations to separate children into the minority with academic abilities and the majority with technical or vocational abilities. Secondary education reflected this division, and entrance into higher education was therefore limited, although the government was willing to provide financial support for all domestic students attending institutions of higher education. Competition was keen to be accepted into the better universities for one's specialty, however.

This was a system that R. H. Turner[33] called sponsored mobility, in which a select number of working-class and lower-middle-class children were allowed to rise to higher levels through demonstrated ability on the exams, with scholarships. Education as an avenue for social mobility existed for the few, but not the many.[34] But through the 1960s, two-thirds of the population of the United Kingdom was working-class, and two-thirds of the school-age population left school at the minimum age allowed. Furthermore, as long as Britain was a first-rank industrial power, the problem of apprentice training could be left to individual firms, which often offered positions to the children of workers already employed by the firm and resident in the area. But in the postwar period, especially beginning in the 1960s, these comfortable certainties broke down.

The expansion of higher education, foreshadowed by the Robbins Report and implemented by the Wilson Labour government, was accompanied by a similar reformist zeal on the secondary educational level, embodied in the famous Circular 7/65, issued by the Department of Education and Science under Anthony Crosland. That administrative action mandated that all local educational authorities, under whose jurisdiction the state schools operated, were to switch from the use of educational tests that had separated students into grammar schools and secondary modern schools. They were to convert to comprehensive schools, in which all students would be educated, whatever their basic academic skills. Crucially, however, this did not mean that students in comprehensive schools would necessarily share the same classes, even for part of the day. They would be in the same building but still might be pursuing different courses of study. Nevertheless, "comprehensivization" was continued, not only under Labour but also under Conservative governments. At least until the late 1980s, there seemed to be no going back, however much right-wing critics might decry the "dumbing down" of the academically talented in the interests of social equality.

Despite the central government funding and setting of regulations for state education at all levels, the British educational system has been highly decentralized. Local educational authorities (LEAs), under the control of locally elected councils, actually administer educational policy under standards laid down by the central government. This has traditionally resulted in a considerable amount of diversity in the number and types of schools in a local authority area. Depending on the composition and attitudes of the LEA, curriculum content has differed as well. This became an issue in London and other urban areas in the 1980s when leftist Labour councils began to allow material designed to combat gender, racial, and sexual orientation discrimination into the schools, as well as sometimes deemphasizing competitive athletics. Parents and conservative (not always Conservative) critics complained that ideology was taking over the traditional educational goals. Even earlier, Labour Prime Minister James Callaghan in 1976 had indicated dissatisfaction with some of the results of the ten-year attempt to introduce more social equality into the schools. Traditional British "more is worse" thinking about education was beginning to reassert itself.

The third term of the Thatcher government saw the fruition of these reservations about the twenty-year direction of British educational policy in the form of the Education Act of 1988. This act seized on the British tradition of localism in education to move the system back toward traditional goals without doing away entirely with comprehensivation. It mandated, for the first time, a "national curriculum" to be taught in all schools, emphasizing the traditional subjects, complete with periodic examinations on those subjects. Furthermore, the act moved control of schools away from local education authorities and professional school staffs toward parents and headmasters (principals) by providing for schools to be self-governing. Such schools could opt out of local authority control in favor of having the parents, headmasters, and teachers be responsible for implementation of the central guidelines. This was also designed to provide for an internal "competitive market" of excellence within the state school system, resembling those in the health service and in the civil service more generally. Thus, as in several of the 1980s Conservative policy changes, there is increased centralization of operating rules combined with an increase in decentralization of organization, from local organizational control to an internal market. Critics have complained that this amounts to an overall centralization of the educational system in that local authorities have lost the power to gear schools toward local needs.[35]

Although the Conservative changes in the primary and secondary school systems have occasioned the greatest amount of attention and debate, there have also been changes taking place in both higher education and apprenticeship training. In higher education, the Conservatives aimed to introduce more competition and efficiency into the functioning of universities. Since the government controlled higher education funding both through the allocations of the University Grants Committee and the value of student aid (grants rather than loans, but the number of students supported is limited), it had the levers with which to implement its preferred policies. The result has been a proliferation of government-sponsored rankings of different universities and departments according to their teaching and research productivity (the bases on which these judgments have been made is highly disputed) and reallocations of government support based on these rankings. Polytechnics have also been upgraded into full-fledged universities to provide competition and increased attention to efficient use of faculty and staff, rather than accepting traditional justifications for academic organization and behavior. Many academics have decried these changes as resulting in more work for the same or less pay, and a number of them have voted with their feet, emigrating to the United States, Australia, or Canada. The Conservative government also attempted to wean academic institutions from the public purse, encouraging private fund-raising by universities on a scale hitherto associated with the United States. The University of Warwick in Coventry, which had been particularly successful in such endeavors for a long period of time predating the Thatcher government, has been lionized as the model for a successful academic institution.

Meanwhile, the value of direct government support of students in higher education has not kept up with inflation. Thus, students and parents are having to assume a higher proportion of the costs of higher education. British higher education is still selective. Even with the emphasis on universities attracting more students by economizing on costs, there are still more students seeking places in higher education than there are positions or government financial support for them. Britain still has one of the lowest percentages of students in higher education of any industrialized country.

On the other side of the equation, however, the loss of manufacturing jobs has led to massive youth unemployment and the involvement of the state, even under the Conservatives, in programs of training through quangos and contracts with private organizations.[36] German apprenticeship programs and the Swedish manpower retraining policy have often been cited as goals the British should emulate, but little has actually been done to bring that about. The disappearance of traditional industrial jobs on a massive scale in certain regions has led to a search for a government-induced policy to replace the former reliance on large private employers to provide whatever training was necessary and often a permanent job thereafter. This can also be considered part of the Conservative effort to reform the microeconomic supply side of economic policy in Britain. But so far the fragmentation of the British approach to education, along with a reliance on the market as a solution, has led to less than satisfactory results.

Despite its continuing importance on the British policy agenda, education has only rarely been a priority issue in election campaigns from a party perspective and even less frequently from the public's perspective.[37] The most sustained role education played in electoral politics, and that only in the broadest, most generic sense, was as part of the 1964–1966 Labour Party drive for a "white-hot, technological revolution," in conjunction with the Robbins Report on the need for expansion in higher education. This suggests that educational reform is not an issue that captures the public imagination, however much partisan, philosophical, and ideological aspects of education grip sections of the elite. Most of the critiques of the British educational system have emanated from elite critics, and their arguments are either ideologically or otherwise intellectually based. Many major education initiatives, including the famous Circular 7/65 mandating comprehensivation of the schools, have been administrative rather than legislative in nature. Although education has been in many ways a position issue, with partisan and class-based differences, it has rarely excited parliamentary passions the way the economy, trade-union regulation, health care, or other social welfare issues often do.

Although elites consider education an important policy issue, there is a broad central consensus that is fairly satisfied with how the British educational system works. Critics from the Left and Right may be allowed to tamper around the edges of the system when their preferred party is in power, but there has been no wholesale overhaul of the basic educational framework. Comprehensive schools are less inclusive than their counterparts in the United States and Sweden, the decentralist, academic elitist focus of the system has been maintained, and even post-1988 Conservative accountability is essentially a local option. Education is thus a recurrent issue on the political agenda, but one is that is not likely to be a major focus of public debate. In that sense, education, however important for the well-being of the country, is an elite and administrative issue in which debate is concentrated in particular policy networks.[38]

Social Security

The final issue to be considered under social welfare policy is the broadest in design, called social security in Britain. In the United States, social security focuses on Old Age, Survivors, and Disability Insurance (OASDI), and to be sure, the British conception includes those matters as well, but it also includes unemployment insurance, the child benefit, the Supplementary Benefit and income support for the low paid, disability and illness benefits, the housing benefit, assistance for those who care for the disabled and elderly, and payments for several other social support services, some of them often listed as part of "personal social services."[39] The personal social services (which include residential and nursing home care for the elderly) are also referred to as "community care," since they are functions of local government, even if financed and regulated by central government. (See Table 7.1.)

These constitute, of course, a major portion of what is conventionally understood by the term "welfare state." The programs have grown considerably in number, in number of citizens covered, and in cost since World War II. Today social security expenditures make up fully one-third of the government budget, or about 10 percent of total GNP and have risen every quarter since the Conservatives assumed office in 1979. There is not room to consider the large issue of why government has grown, especially in the social welfare field, but one contributing factor has been that society has become more urbanized and at the same time more atomized. The population is no longer tied so closely to primary or even secondary groups through marriage, common residence in an area, religion, union membership, or even education. As other collective groups have diminished in their capacity to provide for the social needs of their members, the gov-

TABLE 7.1   Social Security Benefits in Britain[a]

Benefit	Contributory (C) or noncontributory (NC)
Retirement pension	C
Widows benefits	C
Unemployment benefit	C
Sickness benefit	C
Statutory sick pay	NC
Invalidity benefit	C
Maternity allowance	C
Statutory maternity pay	NC
Noncontributory retirement pension	NC
War pension	C
Attendance allowance	NC
Disability living allowance	NC
Disability working allowance	NC
Invalid care allowance	NC
Severe disablement allowance	NC
Industrial injuries disablement benefit	NC
Industrial death benefit	NC
Income support	NC
Child benefit	NC
One parent benefit	NC
Family credit	NC
Housing benefit	NC
Community charge benefit	NC

[a]In some instance, there are several categories of aid within each benefit depending on age, dependencies, or assets of the recipient.
Source: Britain: An Official Handbook, 1994 (London: HMSO, 1993); Peter Catterall, ed. *Contemporary Britain: An Annual Review, 1990* (New York: Blackwell, 1990).

ernment has assumed growing responsibility. Labour governments, by and large, welcomed such government change, at least until the financial crises of the 1970s, as being part of the collective social responsibility that a caring, socialist government should willingly assume. Conservative governments have been somewhat more reluctant to assume these responsibilities and have often done so only on a selective basis, attempting to target aid to those most demonstrably in need rather than serving a broader range of the public. From the perspective of social welfare advocates, however, this leads to the humiliations of the "means test," whereby individuals and families have to demonstrate that they are sufficiently poor, disabled, and so forth in order to qualify for aid. The political and economic logic of coverage under social welfare programs is also in conflict. The economic logic favors the Conservative position: Minimize expenditure and concentrate resources on those most in need. The political logic, however, favors the Labour position of broad coverage through social insurance. However much "social solidarity" such an approach generates, it makes the programs more defensible politically because more people are covered and see the benefits. There is also a less invidious "welfare" aspect to the programs when they are covered under social insurance.

Since World War II British social security programs have tended to be of the social insurance variety. As these developed, the notion of a "social citizenship," meaning certain social rights to which all citizens were entitled, developed to complement the earlier ideas of legal and franchise citizenship rights.[40] It was this idea of social citizenship that the new Right and the Thatcher government set out to undermine, arguing that it had deleterious effects on the British economy and individual morality.[41] The policy, as opposed to the ideological attack, was piecemeal, however. The major mechanism was the much-touted Social Security Reform Act of 1986, which, in practice, turned out to be much less radical than it originally portended.[42] Pensions were cut back from their earlier earnings-related levels,[43] and other changes were made in an attempt to make programs more selective and thus less expensive to maintain. Even though this was a partisan-based bill, however, the Conservative government proved amenable to the arguments of moderate social collectivists in its own party, sometimes known as the "one nation" Tories.[44]

More generally, the supposedly radical, antisocial welfare governments of the 1980s made only small headway in cutting back the British government's commitment to such programs. There was some success in holding down the cost of programs and not allowing them to expand. But the aging of the population and the necessity for maintenance of a social welfare safety net during trying economic circumstances made the Conservative task prohibitive.[45] Unemployment rose to double digits after 1979, wreaking havoc with Conservative plans to control budgetary expenditures on a programmatic basis. In fact, many critics thought that the government's newly developed interest in manpower training was a direct result of the desire to get people on such training schemes off the unemployment rolls. Of course, unemployment benefits and other social insurance programs could in principle be cut back both in coverage and amount of benefits. Although the Conservatives managed some of this, there was much less of cutting than, say, in the contemporaneous Reagan administration in the United States. Instead, the Conservatives found themselves on the defensive for their supposed intention to limit benefits and privatize services. They fought back by describing what great defenders they were of Britain's basic social welfare provisions. Thus, while holding down any major expansion of social service commitments, the welfare state continued its growth largely unabated under a party containing some of its harshest critics.

Thus, for all of the partisan fire and heat over social security issues, there again appears to be an underlying consensus within the political elite about maintenance of the programs. The policies were developed through something of a bipartisan consensus, largely in the years following World War II,[46] and in effect, they have also been limited by a similar bipartisan consensus, especially after the IMF crisis of 1976 revealed the vulnerability of the British government under any party to international forces. Labour accepted IMF conditionality then, which meant limiting spending on social programs. The Conservatives have continued that tradition, with more rhetorical flourish.

Furthermore, being seen as the preferable guardian of social welfare programs by the electorate availed the Labour Party little over recent elections. It might be more beneficial if basic social welfare programs were thought to be under substantial threat, but heretofore they have not been. British public-sector spending remains moderate by comparative standards,[47] and so does the social welfare component of it. As Richard Rose[48] and Peter Taylor-Gooby[49] have pointed out, support for the British welfare state is well entrenched within the electorate. Although the support is not uncritical, it amounts to what Rose has called "two cheers." Governments tread warily in making major (synoptic) changes in programs generating such support; the Conservative government was frightened of performing radical surgery on the welfare state in the early 1980s. Incremental changes, however, are another matter, particularly if they can be treated as technical adjustments.[50]

Evaluation

Social welfare issues, then, present something of an anomaly among British policies. Although often the subject of partisan legislative debate and conflict in election campaigns, there has been an underlying continuity on policy in most areas when parties are in government. In short, this is an area in which policy inheritance[51] seems to count for a lot, as do basic demographic constraints and established expectations of the population. Although in some ways these issues appear to be classic position (opposed) issues, when examined more closely they have the characteristics of valence issues, those in which similar goals are espoused, even if the means chosen are different.

Despite all of the elite posturing on the issue, Britain over the years has moved from being a welfare state leader to a welfare state laggard. Partially, of course, that is due to its falling position, relatively speaking, among the world's economies. The country simply does not have the expanding economic resources in quantities sufficient to sustain welfare state leadership, at least while maintaining a conventional capitalist economy. But it is also true that most of the welfare state policy implementation has been incremental, in whichever direction it has gone. The right-wing Conservative attack on the welfare state was stymied in the 1980s in favor of selective cutbacks. Several studies, however, have found a widening gap in income between the rich and the poor since the Conservatives assumed office. All signs point to further incremental cutbacks or expansions, whatever the political coloration of governments, in the near future. Social citizenship, if not entirely rebuffed, has been resisted.

One indication of the reluctance to expand social entitlements is the refusal of the Conservative government to adopt the Social Chapter provisions of the Maastricht Treaty, the only one of the twelve European Union governments that has failed to do so. The Conservatives adopt a free-market view of Europe, not one in which the European Commission could step in to determine if British companies are meeting European-wide standards of minimum wages and working conditions for their employees. Interestingly enough, despite its many social welfare provisions, the United Kingdom has never adopted a countrywide minimum wage, one of few industrialized countries to be without one. This policy has been viewed as an interference with free collective bargaining. Adoption of the Social Chapter by the European Union does provide the opportunity for this international body to have an impact on the social policies of its member states, including Britain. A more leftist government in Britain would be more cooperative with the EU in social policies, but it might also selectively resist intervention of the Union on social welfare. Labour, after all, has been most adamant about wanting to keep control of the British economy out of the hands of the capitalist-oriented EC. Although adherence to the Social Chapter could represent the "thin edge of the wedge" for British social welfare policy, the class-oriented and British nationalist leaders of the country are unlikely to tolerate its intrusion very far into the society.

There is a further anomaly among these issues. They are mass issues in the sense that many people are affected by the policies adopted, and they are the subject of much partisan position taking and mass concern. Still, there is little evidence that these issues have been critical ones in terms of winning or losing elections. Furthermore, the relative consensus of parties when in government means that these are not issues of great public arousal and pressure on the government. In short, welfare-state issues seem to be ones on which the elite leads mass opinion. It is well to remember that the welfare state was not developed from mass demands, but rather from the initiatives of elites concerned about mass welfare.[52] Similarly, elites keep these issues to the fore in parliamentary debate and election campaigns, often by portraying alternative policies in starker terms than is justified. The public is concerned about these issues, but it rarely understands the technicalities of the issues sufficiently to be able to judge alternative party proposals competently. And unlike economic issues, social welfare issues are not critical voting matters. This is not to say that mass opinion is not important for policy on these issues. But as long as the parties contending for power do not transgress the broad limits of public opinion on these issues, they are probably safe from electoral recrimination. In that sense there is a "permissive consensus" supporting the broad principles of the welfare state, though without equally strong support for the details of policies. Thus elites are free to make changes in housing, health care, education, and social security, and they do so with regularity. These changes are elite-directed and as long as they do not appear to threaten the underlying principles will be tolerated by the masses. Hence the constant Conservative refrain under Mrs. Thatcher was that the "NHS is safe in our hands," even though the government was making changes in NHS organization and service delivery.

Since social-welfare issue positions are not critical to election outcomes, no strong messages about policy direction are being sent from the public to the elite. But there remain the broad opinion dikes, supportive of the basic concept of the welfare state, that no successful politicians in the postwar period have rechanneled. In short, there is a permissive consensus on these issues. It is not impossible to imagine an electorate aroused by a perceived threat to the welfare state fighting back at the polls. However, as long the basic principles are upheld, there is much elite room for maneuver.

John Hills's[53] survey of the postwar welfare state has given little credence to the idea that adversary politics has dominated the long-term social policy agenda, even under Margaret Thatcher.[54] Social welfare issues are rarely the subject of intraparty division on the floor of the House of Commons. But, as we have seen, they are not valence issues within the elite, at least in the particulars. Instead, for purposes of parliamentary debate and election campaigns, the elite treat these as position issues, highlighting partisan differences in approach and, to some degree, conflicting policies. In effect, what we have in this set of issues is a limited conflict within the generally agreed-on principles of the welfare state in the twentieth century. In policy classification terms, most of these issues would be considered sectorally fragmentated or regulatory politics.[55] The interesting question, and one that cannot be answered here, is whether without the firm anchor (two cheers) in public opinion, sections of the elite would fall into greater conflict than already exists, that is, whether the broad principles of the welfare state would come into question as well.

In contrast to the Reagan administration in the United States with which it is so often compared, the Thatcher government, for all of its individual responsibility and procapitalist rhetoric, never attempted major cutbacks on the welfare state, and its curbs on social-welfare spending tended to be couched in technical terms, for example, as in the Social Security Review of 1985, or in market efficiency terms, as in the housing, education, and health care reforms. These measures avoided full-scale assaults on the underlying principles of the welfare state. Selectivity, it was argued, was a means of delivering more services to those in need rather than limiting overall spending. The concept of "welfare scroungers" is much less a part of the lexicon of political debate in Britain than in the United States, where the continuing relevance of race suffuses social welfare issues.[56] But it also points to the importance of individualism and antistatism in the political culture of the United States, even as compared to other Anglo-American countries.[57] In the final analysis, British conservatism, even at its most individualist, does not challenge the necessity for the social welfare state. Nevertheless, the agenda of social welfare policy has changed over the years. Because of demographic trends and budgetary pressures, with perhaps a further nudge from the

European Community, there are likely to be further pressures on the welfare state. Neither its major enhancement nor its elimination is likely.

Notes

1. Richard Parry, "Social Policy," in *Developments in British Politics* 2, ed. Henry Drucker, Patrick Dunleavy, Andrew Gamble, and Gillian Peele (New York: St. Martin's Press, 1986).

2. David Judge, *Backbench Specialization in the House of Commons* (London: Heinemann, 1983); R. M. Punnett, *Front-Bench Opposition* (New York: St. Martin's Press, 1973).

3. B. Guy Peters, *European Politics Reconsidered* (New York: Holmes and Meier, 1991).

4. Peters, *European Politics Reconsidered,* p. 224.

5. Douglas E. Ashford, *The Emergence of the Welfare States* (Oxford: Basil Blackwell, 1986); Patrick Dunleavy, "The United Kingdom: Paradoxes of an Ungrounded Statism," in *The Comparative History of Public Policy,* ed. Francis G. Castles (Cambridge: Polity Press, 1989).

6. Dunleavy, "The United Kingdom: Paradoxes of an Ungrounded Statism."

7. Michael Hill, *The Welfare State in Britain* (Aldershot, England: Edward Elgar, 1993).

8. T. H. Marshall, *Social Policy* (London: Hutchinson, 1965).

9. Margaret Weir and Theda Skocpol, "State Structures and the Possibilities for 'Keynesian' Responses to the Great Depression in Sweden, Britain, and the United States," in *Bringing the State Back In,* ed. Peter B. Evans, Dietrich Rueschemeyer and Theda Skocpol (Cambridge: Cambridge University Press, 1985); Dunleavy, "The United Kingdom: Paradoxes of an Ungrounded Statism"; Arnold Heidenheimer, Hugh Heclo, and Carolyn Teich Adams, *Comparative Public Policy,* 3d ed. (New York: St. Martin's Press, 1990).

10. Dunleavy, "The United Kingdom: Paradoxes of an Ungrounded Statism."

11. Donley T. Studlar, Ian McAllister, and Alvaro Ascui, "Privatization and the British Electorate: Microeconomic Policies, Macroeconomic Evaluations and Party Support," *American Journal of Political Science* 34, no. 3 (1981):327–355; Chris Pierson, "Social Policy," in *Developments in British Politics* 4, ed. Patrick Dunleavy, Andrew Gamble, Ian Holliday, and Gillian Peele (New York: St. Martin's Press, 1993); Dunleavy, "The United Kingdom: Paradoxes of an Ungrounded Statism."

12. Harold Wilensky, *The Welfare State and Equality* (Berkeley: University of California Press, 1975).

13. Richard Rose, *The Territorial Dimension in Government* (Chatham, N.J.: Chatham House, 1982).

14. Richard Rose, *Understanding Big Government* (London: Sage Publications, 1984).

15. Albert Weale, "Social Policy," in *Developments in British Politics* 3, ed. Patrick Dunleavy, Andrew Gamble, and Gillian Peele (New York: St. Martin's Press, 1990).

16. Judge, *Backbench Specialization in the House of Commons.*

17. Richard Hofferbert and Ian Budge, "The Party Mandate and the Westminster Model: Election Programmes and Government Spending in Britain, 1945–1985," *British Journal of Political Science* 22, no. 1 (1992):151—182.

18. Harry Eckstein, *Pressure Group Politics* (London: Allen and Unwin, 1960); Rudolf Klein, *The Politics of the National Health Service,* 2d ed. (London: Longman, 1989).

19. Heidenheimer, Heclo, and Adams, *Comparative Public Policy.*

20. Dunleavy, "The United Kingdom: Paradoxes of an Ungrounded Statism."

21. Norman Furniss and Timothy Tilton, *The Case for the Welfare State* (Bloomington: Indiana University Press, 1979).

22. Andrew L. Shapiro, *We're Number One!* (New York: Vintage, 1992).

23. Thomas Halper, *The Misfortunes of Others* (Cambridge: Cambridge University Press, 1991).

24. Kenneth Newton, "Caring and Competence: The Long, Long Campaign," in King et al., *Britain at the Polls, 1992* (Chatham, N.J.: Chatham House, 1993).

25. Peters, *European Politics Reconsidered.*

26. Peter Taylor-Gooby, *Public Opinion, Ideology, and State Welfare* (London: Routledge and Kegan Paul, 1985).

27. Bruce Headey, *Housing Policy in the Developed Economy* (New York: St. Martin's Press, 1978).

28. N. J. Williams, J. B. Sewell, and F. E. Twine, "Council House Sales and the Electorate: Voting Behavior and Ideological Implications," *Housing Studies* 2, no. 4 (1987): 274–282; Pippa Norris, "Thatcher's Enterprise Society and Electoral Change," *West European Politics* 13, no. 1 (1990):63–78; Studlar, McAllister, and Ascui, "Privatization and the British Electorate: Microeconomic Policies, Macroeconomic Evaluations and Party Support"; Anthony Heath, Roger Jowell, and John Curtice, *How Britain Votes* (Oxford: Pergamon Press, 1985); Geoffrey Garrett, "The Political Consequences of Thatcherism," *Political Behavior* 14, no. 4 (1992):361–283; Helmut Norpoth, *Confidence Regained: Economics, Mrs. Thatcher, and the British Voter* (Ann Arbor: University of Michigan Press, 1992).

29. Heidenheimer, Heclo, and Adams, *Comparative Public Policy.*

30. Colin Hughes and Patrick Wintour, *Labour Rebuilt: The New Model Party* (London: Fourth Estate, 1991).

31. Hofferbert and Budge, "The Party Mandate and the Westminster Model: Election Programmes and Government Spending in Britain, 1945–1985"; Ian Budge and Denis Farlie, *Explaining and Predicting Elections* (London: Allen and Unwin, 1983); George H. Gallup, *The Gallup International Public Opinion Polls, Great Britain, 1937–1975*, Volume 1, 1937–1964; Volume 2, 1965–1975 (New York: Greenwood Press, 1976); George Gallup, *The International Gallup Polls: Public Opinion 1978* (Wilmington, Del.: Scholarly Resources, 1980).

32. Ian McAllister and Donley T. Studlar, "Popular Versus Elite Views of Privatization: The Case of Britain," *Journal of Public Policy* 9, no. 1 (1989): 157–178.

33. R. H. Turner, "Sponsored and Contest Mobility and the School System," *American Sociological Review* 25, no. 6 (1960):855–867.

34. Brian Jackson and Dennis Marsden, *Education and the Working Class* (London: Routledge, 1962).

35. Anthony Sampson, *The Essential Anatomy of Britain* (New York: Harcourt Brace and Company, 1993).

36. David Brian Robertson, "Labor Market Surgery, Labor Market Abandonment: The Thatcher and Reagan Unemployment Remedies," in *Political Economy: Public Policies in the United States and Britain,* ed. Jerold L. Waltman and Donley T. Studlar (Jackson: University Press of Mississippi, 1987); Richard Rose, *Lesson-Drawing in Public Policy* (Chatham, N.J.: Chatham House, 1993).

37. Budge and Farlie, *Explaining and Predicting Elections;* Gallup, *The Gallup International Public Opinion Polls, Great Britain, 1937–1975;* Gallup, *The International Gallup Polls: Public Opinion 1978.*

38. David Marsh and R.A.W. Rhodes, eds., *Implementing Thatcherite Policies* (Buckingham: Open University Press, 1992).

39. Neil Evans, "'A Caring Community'? Personal Social Services in the 1980s," in *Public Policy Under Thatcher,* ed. Stephen P. Savage and Lynton Robins (New York: St. Martin's Press, 1990); Francis McGlone, "Away from the Dependency Culture? Social Security Policy," in *Public Policy Under Thatcher,* ed. Savage and Robins; Jonathan Bradshaw, "Social Security," in *Implementing Thatcherite Policies,* ed. Marsh and Rhodes.

40. Marshall, *Social Policy.*

41. Desmond King, *The New Right* (London: Macmillan, 1987); Kenneth Hoover and Raymond Plant, *Conservative Capitalism* (London: Routledge, 1988).

42. Albert Weale, "Social Policy."

43. Gary P. Freeman, "National Styles and Policy Sectors: Explaining Structured Variation," *Journal of Public Policy* 5, no. 4 (1985):467–496; Pierson, "Social Policy."

44. Philip Norton and Arthur Aughey, *Conservatives and Conservatism* (London: Temple Smith, 1981).

45. Marsh and Rhodes, eds., *Implementing Thatcherite Policies.*

46. Richard Rose, *Do Parties Make a Difference?* (Chatham, N.J.: Chatham House, 1980); but see also John Hills, ed., *The State of Welfare* (New York: Oxford University Press, 1992).

47. Francis G. Castles, ed., *The Comparative History of Public Policy* (Cambridge: Polity Press, 1989); Richard Rose, *Ordinary People in Public Policy* (Newbury Park, Ca.: Sage Publications, 1989).

48. Rose, *Ordinary People in Public Policy.*

49. Taylor-Gooby, *Public Opinion, Ideology, and State Welfare.*

50. Bradshaw, "Social Security."

51. Jerold L. Waltman, "Changing the Course of Tax Policy: Convergent in Intent, Divergent in Practice," in *Political Economy: Public Policy in the United States and Britain,* ed. Waltman and Studlar; Rose, *Do Parties Make a Difference?*

52. Hugh Heclo, *Modern Social Politics in Britain and Sweden* (New Haven: Yale University Press, 1974); Furniss and Tilton, *The Case for the Welfare State.*

53. Hill, *The Welfare State in Britain.*

54. But see Hills, *The State of Welfare.*

55. Theodore J. Lowi, "American Business, Public Policy, Case Studies, and Political Theory," *World Politics* 16, no. 4 (1964):677–715; T. Alexander Smith, *The Comparative Policy Process* (Santa Barbara, Ca.: ABC-Clio, 1975).

56. Wilensky, *The Welfare State and Equality.*

57. Louis Hartz, *The Liberal Tradition in America* (New York: Harcourt Brace and Company, 1955); Seymour Martin Lipset, *Continental Divide* (New York: Routledge, 1989); Anthony King, "Ideas, Institutions, and the Policies of Government: A Comparative Analysis, Parts I and II," *British Journal of Political Science* 3, nos. 2 and 3 (1973):291–313, 409–423.

8

SOCIAL REGULATORY POLICIES: FROM PUBLIC MORALITY TO SOCIAL PERMISSIVENESS

SOCIAL POLICY INCLUDES two distinctive areas, those being social welfare policy, just covered in Chapter 7, and social regulatory policy, discussed here. Social regulatory policy refers to issues having to do with moral codes and other relationships among individuals and social groups that the state regulates to a greater or lesser extent.[1] These policies are not principally concerned with material resources, as policies of social welfare are. Instead, they involve laws regulating behavior, laws that do not usually involve material incentives. This is not to deny that there may be material costs and benefits associated with social regulations, for instance, they confer status preferments on people, but their principal focus is on social relationships, not economics.

Other observers have variously called social regulations "way of life," "emotive-symbolic," "moral code," or "civic" issues.[2] The names differ, but the content is much the same. These policies have to do with fundamental normative ways in which groups and individuals relate to each other and to the polity. Usually included are such issues as abortion, criminal justice (especially capital punishment), homosexuality, divorce, pornography, and national identity, especially when the latter is posed as a constitutional matter. One might argue that the European Union raises such concerns over group and individual identity, but for simplicity I have chosen to consider matters relating to the EU as mainly a foreign policy issue. Other issues such as immigration, race relations, and gender equality may be considered part of the social regulatory policy area, at least insofar as they involve moral and civil liberties dimensions rather than economics and income maintenance. Furthermore, government support of culture fits most readily, albeit somewhat uneasily, under social regulatory policy, if anywhere. Although hardly as rancorous as the debate in the United States over what types of art government subsidies will support, in Britain the government has chosen to support some forms of art over others and from ancient times has recognized a duty to regulate culture through the institution of official censorship, which determined what the public would be allowed to read, hear, and see.

The Agenda

Over the post–World War II period in particular the United Kingdom has been faced with several of these issues. They were highlighted in the "swinging sixties" when public questioning of traditional social behavior was in vogue, at least in liberal elite circles, and the political system responded by changing laws in several of these areas. Even if given less publicity than previously, some of these issues have not gone away, and not all political groups are satisfied with the decisions of the 1960s. The ban on capital punishment has periodically been challenged in Parliament, and there have been persistent attempts to amend the law on abortion in a more conservative direction. In 1994, there was also an attempt to lower the age of consent for homosexuality from twenty-one to sixteen, thus putting it on a par with that of heterosexuality in Britain and in line with laws in most other European countries, but the House of Commons rejected that age in favor of a compromise at age eighteen. The politics of social regulatory policy may be intermittent on the governmental agenda, but it never really completely disappears from the public agenda.

Actors

The political process on social regulatory issues is characterized by procedural unorthodoxy. As Alvin Cohan[3] has put it, civil liberties issues such as abortion are usually the concern of a small minority of the population, and those activists must struggle to get attention and support from a larger body of people. Often the majority may be hostile to any changes favoring a minority. Thus, instead of social regulatory issues being discussed and decided through "core mechanisms" of the polity, which in Britain would mean the cabinet and majority party in the House of Commons, proponents of social regulatory issues are often pushed into utilizing "peripheral mechanisms" in order to place their issues on the agenda and, perhaps, achieve resolution. Even when advocates of social regulatory issues are granted access to the core mechanisms, pursuing legislation in these policy areas may involve procedural unorthodoxies, such as extraordinary group pressure on the majority party, guillotine motions in the House of Commons, and referendums. Grappling with such issues does constitute "normal politics," at least initially. Over time, however, social regulatory issues may be redefined and placed on the agenda more readily through the usual channels. But some are rarely managed in this manner.

In Britain many social regulatory policies are declared "conscience issues," to be decided by a free vote in the House of Commons, that is, a vote on which the parliamentary parties do not demand unified party discipline from their members. In this fashion neither the governing party nor the opposition parties have to assume responsibility for policy on these issues. Sometimes a government may reluctantly enforce party discipline on a conscience matter,[4] but usually it is up to individual members of Parliament to vote by considering their consciences, their constituency interests, or whatever they think appropriate in the circumstances. Parties do not campaign on conscience issues, even though analyses of the votes on such policies usually show party affiliation to be either the first or second most important influence on MPs' behavior.[5] Nevertheless, in order for legislation on such issues to pass, the government of the day must be cooperative enough to allow parliamentary time for bills to be considered adequately.[6] Hence, governments and parties try to have it both ways, not taking political responsibility for conscience issues but sometimes implicitly favoring them. Thus the series of liberal reforms of social regulations in the mid-1960s on divorce, pornography, homosexuality, and abortion was not only encouraged by a Labour government willing to allow sufficient parliamentary time, but they were also largely supported by Labour and Liberal Party members, less so by Conservatives.[7]

Even if social regulatory policies are handled by more usual political processes, they often involve procedural unorthodoxies. In an attempt to generate some consensus about issues few may have thought about or about which considerable controversy exists, governments sometimes issue green papers (discussion papers) or white papers (statements of government intentions). This was the case with both immigration policy and the question of Welsh and Scottish devolution. Such documents may also be issued in other policy areas, for instance, as with the social security reform of the mid-1980s.

At other times, social regulatory issues may be forced on the governmental agenda by events or interest groups. This was the case with the first Immigration Control Bill in 1962, the product of internal group agitation in the Conservative Party, including a rare defeat for the party leadership on a motion at the 1960 Conservative Party Conference. In 1968 and 1972, the actions of African leaders in deporting British-passport-holding Asians in Kenya and Uganda, respectively, led to emergency consideration of immigration. The revival of violence in Northern Ireland in the late 1960s and early 1970s forced the House of Commons to rescind its formal agenda rule that, as part of devolved government, Northern Ireland matters were not to be discussed in the House. In short, it is often difficult either to put social regulatory policies on the governmental agenda or to keep them there. In addition to government and party resistance, there are often only a few members of Parliament willing to champion these issues,[8] and by the rules of the House, which allot over 90 percent of the available time to the government and Her Majesty's Loyal Opposition, the opportunities for private members to sponsor legislation or even to raise topics of their concern are relatively few.

Other procedural unorthodoxies also occur. For instance, if social regulatory issues become whipped votes, the strains within political parties are likely to be so great that party discipline in the division (voting) lobbies may break down. Social regulatory issues such as immigration, Northern Ireland, and the Scotland and Wales bills formed a large share of the votes on which Philip Norton[9] recorded increased parliamentary dissent in the 1970s, and such divisiveness sometimes even amounts to a rare government defeat in the House of Commons. A government defeat on the vote necessary to establish whether a Scottish or Welsh referendum on devolution had passed led to the government rescinding devolution legislation in 1979 after it had failed to receive the necessary 40 percent approval of the registered voting population in Scotland. That, in turn, led the eleven representatives of the Scottish Nationalist Party in the House of Commons voting against the Labour government in the confidence vote in March, 1979, which the government lost, by 310–311.[10] This is one of only two instances in the twentieth century in which a British government has been ousted by a motion of no confidence (the other being the Labour government of 1924). Sometimes the procedural unorthodoxies of social regulatory policy can lead to huge consequences.

Of the four referendums held in the United Kingdom up through 1994, three were held only in parts of the United Kingdom where national issues were under consideration—in Northern Ireland on the border issue (1972), and in Scotland and Wales (1978), separately, on devolved institutions.[11] The fourth—and only—United Kingdom–wide referendum was on British membership in the European Community in 1975, which, concerned as it was with the sovereignty question, bears some resemblance to characteristic social regulatory policy.

Most of the social regulatory policies fall under the implementation preserve of Home Affairs, an omnibus government department. Not only criminal procedures but also the prevention of terrorism and even immigration matters belong to Home Affairs. With a huge and multifaceted department to run, the home secretary does not usually set out strong positions on most social regulatory issues. On most conscience issues, the home secretary's position is only advisory for the House of Commons. But even on whipped votes the home secretary may not set out a clear, confident position. For instance, the home secretary in the first Labour government of the 1960s, Sir Frank Soskice, seemed confused by the various provisions of the 1965 Race Relations Bill.[12] On the other end of the scale, Home Secretary James Callaghan was one of the key figures in preventing the large-scale entry of Kenyan Asians into the United Kingdom in 1968, despite the pledges made to them as passport holders earlier.[13]

In some areas of social regulatory policy, such as race relations, there have been quangos (quasi-governmental agencies) set up to investigate particular problems and advise the government on them. The Commission for Racial Equality is a successor to two earlier government quangos, the Race Relations Board and the Community Relations Commission, and it has some statutory powers of fact-finding and attempting to reconcile disputants in this area.[14] Similarly, the Equal Opportunities Commission is concerned with monitoring the Sex Discrimination Acts of 1975 and 1986.[15] Quangos have come under attack, however, as being largely advocates for particular policy positions tied to interest groups and for interfering with the line-of-policy responsibility of government departments. In the social regulatory area, however, the policies of the Home Office itself have also been criticized as uncoordinated, especially in the race relations and immigration area.[16]

Formation, Adoption, and Implementation

As in other policy areas, discussion here focuses on a few policy areas, namely, abortion; immigration and race relations; devolution in Northern Ireland, Scotland, and Wales; criminal justice (law and order); capital punishment; regulation or promotion of culture; equal opportunities for women; and rights of homosexuals. These should provide an overview not only of policy development in these areas but also of the British political process at work.

Law and Order

Criminal justice covers a wide area and includes capital punishment, the oldest policy in which the unusual characteristics of social regulatory policy have been observed. The United Kingdom in the twentieth century has a low murder rate and relatively few violent crimes, especially by the standards of the United States.[17] Aside from Northern Ireland, the country lacks a traditional use of weapons in political confrontations, and strict firearms licensing for the ownership of both long guns and pistols is required. Although the carrying of guns by British police has increased in recent years, regular patrolmen still lack them. Perhaps because of the relatively few murders committed, the ones that do occur are often depicted in lurid terms by the popular press. Fictional murders, of course, have been a staple of British writing.

The British legal tradition emphasizes the common law and an adequate defense for all those accused, though their practices do not go to the lengths of the adversarial, individually based legal system in the United States.[18] People suspected of crimes can be held for long periods of time by the police, although in recent years greater restrictions have been placed on police behavior toward those not yet charged with crimes.[19] This is what is euphemistically known as "assisting police with their inquiries." In general, the legal system in Britain, which differs somewhat in Scotland for historical reasons and in Northern Ireland because of the need to combat terrorism, is more collectively oriented than in practically any other common-law country. This is so because there is no written constitution specifying unassailable individual civil liberties. In fact, there have been moves in recent years to provide either a full-scale written constitution or a more specific bill of rights, but so far the recent Conservative governments have deflected these concerns into the more bureaucratic channels of the Citizens' Charter.[20]

Traditionally, there has been wide allowance for individual behavior in the United Kingdom, political and otherwise. The assumption was that the rights of British subjects were a large residual category, that is, it was assumed that if the government had not legislated to prohibit certain behavior, either through Parliament or through administrative decree, then it was allowed. Among the more colorful examples of this are the activities at Speakers' Corner in Hyde Park in London and the general tolerance of eccentric behavior. This tolerance was part of the expanding of civil liberties in the United Kingdom in the eighteenth and nineteenth centuries. Nevertheless, British justice is swift, collective, and not inclined to allow individuals to escape penalties on the basis of technicalities or constitutional arguments. Trials are normally held within weeks of a criminal accusation, and few appeals are heard. The collective nature of the British legal system occurs in that the judges, as well as the attorneys, can question witnesses. Juries usually decide guilt or innocence; judges determine punishment. Changes to be made in the criminal law are usually not objects of great partisan controversy and routinely pass through Parliament.[21] Even the contentious Police and Criminal Evidence Act of 1984 was based on the report of a committee set up by the previous Labour government.[22] In 1994, however, there were mass demonstrations against legislation weakening a defendant's right to silence and giving police greater discrtionary power over meetings considered a potential threat to public order.

Law and order is always of concern to governments. The British approach to detecting and punishing crime is to put a lot of faith in individual police forces. Although the Home Office is responsible for law and order overall, the police, in fact, are treated as a professional force and are given a great deal of flexibility in deciding how to deal with matters in their areas of local jurisdiction. These jurisdictions are not coterminous with local government jurisdictions, further reducing police accountability to elected officials. The government is supposed to make the law; the police enforce it. Policy on law and order has been largely bipartisan. The Conservative Party has tended to emphasize law and order in its party pronouncements, to no particularly discernible effect except to improve police resources. Increasingly, however, deployment and practices of the police in such matters as controlling strikes and combating terrorism, especially spillovers from Northern Ireland to the mainland, have generated controversy as central government has assumed greater responsibility for police deployment and practices.

Recent Conservative governments have been generous with police pay and resources, not subjecting the police to the same public-sector pay restrictions as they did other government employees. Nevertheless, reported crime, including crimes of violence, has risen substantially in the same period, and the United Kingdom has one of the largest prison populations per capita in Western Europe. The Conservative answer to the spiraling crime problem was to bring forward a bill that gave enhanced powers to the police and prosecutors, including ending the unanimity rule for juries and making silence of the defendant in the courtroom an issue. Although this legislation generated controversy, Labour showed a tough attitude on criminal behavior, too.

The question of capital punishment, however, was different than with other amendments to criminal procedures. As with several other social regulatory issues, it aroused concerns about deep-seated moral principles about the sanctity of human life, the role of the state, and appropriate punishment to deter criminal behavior. James Christoph[23] was the first to detect the procedural anomalies that the debate over capital punishment in the 1940s and 1950s aroused and to suggest that these procedural unorthodoxies might also occur with other social regulatory issues. The maintenance of capital punishment as the ultimate punishment in British law was challenged by backbenchers, especially Labour and Liberal ones, through private members' bills from 1947 until its abolition as a form of punishment in the mid-1960s. Initiated by backbenchers, the capital punishment debate proceeded largely on the basis of free votes, as an issue of conscience, in the House of Commons. Only occasionally in the 1950s did the government step in, somewhat awkwardly, and demand a whipped vote. The eventual abolition of capital punishment came on a free vote in 1965, during the heyday of moral-reform legislation in Britain, and subsequent debates have also been settled by free votes.[24]

The issue continues to resonate, both among politicians and the public. Opinion polls have continued to show overwhelming public support for capital punishment, but it is difficult to hold parties responsible at elections for the free votes of their MPs.[25] Several cases that resulted in capital punishment, especially the controversial ones of the 1950s, have been the subjects of popular films or television programs (*Ten Rillington Place, Dance with a Stranger, Let Him Have It*). Thus, at least within public consciousness, and occasionally in the House of Commons, the issue rages on.

Abortion

Abortion has had a similar history of policy development, occurring but somewhat later than capital punishment. British abortion law was based on statutes passed in 1861 and 1929, limiting abortions to cases where birth might endanger the health of the mother, with no abortion allowed if the fetus could live outside the womb, which was considered to be after twenty-eight weeks.[26] In the 1960s, pressures arose to change the law to allow limited access to abortions.

There had, in effect, always been access to an abortion for those rich enough or desperate enough, but the practice was outside the law and condemned by respectable opinion. The abortion reformers of the 1960s wanted to legalize abortions uniformly while also limiting access. The original private members' bill that raised the issue was widely supported because of a common belief within the House of Commons that the law needed to be adjusted to accommodate the reality of abortion practices, especially in the wake of the discovery of fetal defects caused by the drug thalidomide in the early 1960s. But the exact language to be incorporated generated a great deal of controversy, abetted by the vociferous activities of pressure groups on both sides of the issue.[27] As with capital punishment, this was an issue that was understandable in principle by large sections of the public, and many people had strong opinions on the subject. With party discipline relaxed, the way was open for interest groups and individual members of the public to lobby members of Parliament. As with capital punishment, the judiciary did not play a major role in the abortion debate, unlike in the United States; this was a political decision, made by political bodies, most centrally the House of Commons.

Eventually the law that was passed in 1967 gave limited access to an abortion to a woman up to twenty-eight weeks pregnant. The permission of two medical doctors was necessary, but the procedure could be granted on either physical or social grounds. Because Britain was the first country in Western Europe to allow liberalized access to abortions, many people needing an abortion were drawn there from other countries with more restrictive policies, especially Ireland. Those who objected to liberalized access were free to pursue their goals through the political process, just as the abortion law reformers had been, since the right to have an abortion in the United Kingdom, unlike the United States, is not grounded in individual rights and constitutional law. There has been some response, however, in the form of a few legal challenges to sex education in the schools.[28] Periodically those wanting more restricted access to abortions have tried to lessen the period of pregnancy during which an abortion may be performed through private members' legislation, and these efforts have been occasions for more argumentation and free votes. Most recently, the period during which most abortions can be performed has been reduced to twenty-four weeks, but now there is no time limit on abortions involving fetal abnormality or serious permanent damage to the physical health of the pregnant woman. Even the long rule of what many observers saw as a Conservative government sympathetic to the demands of antiabortion campaigners has not resulted in a substantial change in the law.[29] Without the government assuming responsibility for changing the law, there was insufficient support from the backbenches alone to move the law in a significantly more restrictive direction.

Immigration and Race Relations

Policy development regarding immigration and race relations has been slightly different. There has never been a free vote on either an immigration control bill or a race relations bill, and these are not usually considered conscience issues. But they are issues of social regulation not tied to welfare concerns, except obliquely, and there have been unusual features in how they have been handled. Despite the fact that immigration control has foreign relations aspects as well, both the public and politicians have tended to think of it, certainly since the late 1950s, as principally concerned with domestic politics in the United Kingdom, namely, with how many and what kinds of people should be allowed into the country. As with other social regulatory issues, these were issues of "low politics" with which most powerful political figures were disinclined to intervene, except when pressed, as with Conservative Party leader Edward Heath's dismissal of shadow minister Enoch Powell for racist comments in 1968.[30] Nevertheless, there have been several immigration laws and regulations passed, most notably those of 1962, 1965, 1968 (the Kenyan Asians crisis), 1972 (the Ugandan Asians crisis), 1981, and 1990 (allowing limited immigration from Hong Kong before it returns to China in 1997). There have also been three separate race relations acts passed, in 1965, 1968, and 1976.[31]

Although all of these pieces of legislation were government-sponsored bills, there have been some unusual features. First, the immigration control question was not one that either major party wanted to put on the political agenda. Throughout the 1950s, as the growing postwar British economy brought more immigrant laborers and their families from the West Indies, India, and Pakistan (including those parts that became Bangladesh in 1971), there were periodic, usually brief discussions in cabinet about whether unfettered immigration should continue to be allowed. These deliberations were not known of until cabinet records became public information thirty years later.[32] In fact, it was agitation from backbenchers in the House of Commons, particularly those in the Conservative Party representing urban constituencies, that placed immigration control on the party agenda. This occurred first through motions to the Conservative Party's annual conference and eventually through the government's espousing immigration control in the Queen's Speech of 1961.[33] Similarly, the success of racially based appeals in the Smethwick constituency, and possibly in others, in the general election of 1964 made politicians wary of an aroused public that did not want further immigration and was uncomfortable with many aspects of the changing nature of urban life in Britain. Almost all of the nonwhite (or, in the British sense, "colored" immigrants, lived in urban areas).

The response was to adopt a two-pronged policy of increasingly stringent immigration controls, with occasional (and much disputed) exceptions on humanitarian grounds, and policies providing for government encouragement of racial tolerance domestically. The nonwhite immigrants to Britain were not "guest workers," who could legally be returned, but instead became full British citizens upon entry because of older ideals based on the concept of a unified, multiracial Commonwealth, in which even the citizens of independent Commonwealth countries could come freely and assume citizenship in the mother country. Once large numbers of nonwhite immigrants began arriving, however, the idea of Commonwealth unity took a back seat to domestic resentment about the intrusion of people considered unlike the natives.

There has been significant intraparty dissent on immigration bills. Liberals oppose stronger controls, thus the Kenyan Asians bill was rushed through the House of Commons in a week by a Labour government in 1968. Social conservatives oppose further loosening of admissions, as occurred with the Ugandan Asians in 1973 and Hong Kong residents in 1990.[34] In general, politicians have felt a considerable amount of public pressure to hold a firm line against further permanent immigration, as witnessed by the support for renegade Enoch Powell when he advocated not only immigration control but repatriation of immigrants already resident in the United Kingdom in 1968.[35]

Race relations bills have not generated the controversy that immigration control has, but the fact that three bills were passed in a little over a decade, in addition to legislation providing assistance to local government areas that have felt disproportionate impact from immigrant settlement, indicates the perceived difficulty of implementing effective legislation.[36] The passage of the initial Race Relations Act was particularly troubled, with the Labour government (sponsor of all three acts) reversing its own recommendations in some instances.

The United Kingdom has moved a long way from its characterization by scholars, as late as the 1960s, as a homogeneous society ethnically. Today it is a multicultural, multiracial, and multireligious society, especially in urban areas. Nonwhites, an increasing number of whom are native-born, make up approximately 5 percent of the total population. Among this 5 percent are a diverse number of groups ethnically and religiously. Although racial ghettos on the scale of the United States do not exist, this religious, ethnic, racial, and cultural diversity has led to significant conflict, ranging from thoughtless casual discrimination to beatings, riots, and the threat of death against British writer Salman Rushdie by Muslims following the commands of the mullahs in Iran. As the nonwhite population increases, retaining many of its previous cultural and religious tenets, these frictions may grow. This is another area of social regulatory policy that simmers in society, even if it is off the official political agenda temporarily.

Nationalism: Ireland, Scotland, and Wales

Even in the early 1960s the idea of Britain as an ethnically homogeneous society was suspect. Such a characterization ignored the multinational nature of the United Kingdom in Scotland, Wales, and Northern Ireland, overidentifying the whole state with the English sector, where 85 percent of the population resided.

The common notion that the United Kingdom was ethnically homogeneous, of course, indicates how much the distinctive background and concerns of Northern Ireland, Wales, and Scotland have traditionally been ignored in the unitary constitutional structure.[37] As Bulpitt[38] has argued, the constitutional arrangements were buttressed by an elite political culture (or statecraft as he calls it) that defined the particular concerns of the constituent parts of the United Kingdom as part of "low politics," not to be persistently and seriously pursued by politicians interested in high office, meaning achieving cabinet status. But despite, and perhaps because of, their relative neglect by the powerful, these issues have occasionally moved from their usual low politics status to burst upon the central political scence, at least temporarily. Once again, when this happens, procedural unorthodoxies result.

Northern Ireland is the longest-lasting and most difficult of these issues. As Roy Jenkins, British MP and cabinet minister, has said, among the many talents of the British there is lacking a capacity for dealing successfully with the problems of Ireland. Ireland moved from its earlier status as a discontented colony to become a principal domestic problem for the British government around the beginning of the twentieth century. The first demand was for home rule; the second, for independence, was backed by force of arms. Irish demands for home rule threw parliamentary institutions into crisis, leading directly or indirectly to such changes as government control over the parliamentary agenda and parliamentary time and weakening of the power of the House of Lords.

The Irish problem was not simply an issue of nationalist feeling and devolution of power, however. It was—and still is, as regards Northern Ireland—a multifaceted issue, concerning legal rights, social and economic discrimination, the functioning of political institutions, the place of majority rule and minority rights, internal and external security, foreign relations, and the relationship of that part of the country to the rest of the United Kingdom. Even with the granting of independence to twenty-six counties as the Irish Free State (later the Republic of Ireland) in 1922, the United Kingdom was unable to escape this morass of problems, although the politicians at Westminster managed to ignore the Irish problem for almost fifty years.

The Protestants in the north of Ireland were the descendants of colonists the British government had brought over, mainly from Scotland, to pacify the Irish rebels through example and force. They were not agreeable to becoming a 20-percent minority under Irish home rule in the United Kingdom, much less being part of an Irish Free State. When Irish home rule was due to be instituted before World War I broke out, the Protestants armed themselves and were prepared to fight to remain free of the dominance of Dublin. Later, in the peace agreement of 1921, the six Protestant-dominated counties in the northeastern part of the island, part of the traditional nine counties called Ulster, remained part of the United Kingdom. Although this decision avoided further immediate bloodshed in that part of Ireland, it led to a civil war between the fundamentalists of the Irish Republican Army, who wanted a unified thirty-two-county Ireland, and those who had signed the treaty with Britain.

In Northern Ireland, however, the effect of the events of the 1920s was to remove the issue of the province's constitutional status from the British political agenda for a half century, until the civil rights marches of the late 1960s and the violence visited upon the Roman Catholic marchers by their Protestant neighbors resurrected the issue.[39] During this time the Westminster Parliament left governance of the province in the hands of the two-thirds Protestant majority through a devolved government set up in Stormont Castle.

Thus a permanent majority, established on the basis of religion, nationalism, and constitutional conservatism, opposed a permanent minority, similarly based on religion, nationalism, and constitutional radicalism, that is, favoring a united Ireland. The irony was that both the elite and probably the masses in mainland Britain have consistently preferred a united Ireland as well, but they were stymied by the lack of agreement and the proclivities for violence among both groups in Northern Ireland.[40] On the one hand, Irish Protestants were ultranationalists, strongly identifying with a polity that did not reciprocate that loyalty. The Irish Republic, on the other hand, held to the hope of an eventual unification of Ireland but refused to endorse the use of violence to gain that end, even though some Irish leaders have sympathized with and been accused of covertly supporting the use of violence.

The devolved government in place in Northern Ireland, operated by Westminster-type rules, included no constitutional guarantees of civil rights.[41] Parliament and the cabinet in London effectively washed their hands of Northern Ireland. Ireland became almost exclusively a foreign policy issue, with the partial exception of the debate over its wish to leave the Commonwealth in 1949.[42] Various attempts to raise the issue of the governance of Northern Ireland in the Westminster Parliament were quashed by citing the rule that the domestic affairs of a devolved government were not a legitimate subject for the House of Commons. The violent clashes of the 1960s brought Northern Ireland to the fore, not only in the United Kingdom but worldwide. At that point the parliamentary rule excluding discussion of Northern Ireland was rescinded, to be followed in 1972 by the abolition of the Stormont government and the establishment of direct rule from London.

All of the various attempts to reconcile the disputants in Northern Ireland since 1972 have shared a common theme, namely, that the British government wants the two groups to find a means of living with each other without policing by the British army. That would allow the government of the United Kingdom to return to the status quo of pre-1972, that is, allowing Northern Ireland to look after itself, removed from the central British political agenda. The British government has pledged that it will never allow a change in the basic constitutional status of Northern Ireland without the consent of the majority of voters in the province, in other words, Northern Ireland will remain a part of the United Kingdom as long as the majority there prefers that status. This position was further endorsed by the "border poll" taken in Northern Ireland in 1972, even though most Catholics refused to take part in it. Despite a growing Catholic share of the population of the province (now 40 percent), it will be many years before Catholics approach majority status. It is also not entirely clear that, given the opportunity, Catholics would necessarily endorse a united Ireland.

As of 1994, all attempts at power sharing by mutual consent of the two groups within the province have failed, a consequence not only of mistrust between Protestants and Catholics but also of suspicion of the intentions of the British and Irish governments. The divisions are even more complicated than that, since there are differences within Catholic and Protestant opinion as well. Catholics, for instance, divide into peaceful and violent nationalists (with some who doubtless espouse any means possible) while Protestants differ on how much integration they want with the rest of the United Kingdom. But the various within-group differences ultimately lead to two considerations: (1) the status of the two groups within the province, and (2) whether the province itself is to remain within the United Kingdom or become part of Ireland.

Since 1972, the British government has poured massive funds for economic and social assistance into Northern Ireland in an attempt to generate conciliatory relations among the two groups. It has not dared to tamper, however, with the educational system, which is still based on sectarian lines.[43] The administration of justice has been severely questioned in the Northern Ireland context, with several practices traditionally associated with British justice—trial by jury, and ability to confront accusers—suspended in the atmosphere of terrorism and fear. There have been persistent rumors that the security forces in Northern Ireland have been allowed to "shoot to kill" without attempting to detain suspects first. The British reputation for justice has suffered on the mainland as well, with some major convictions of people accused of complicity in acts of IRA terrorism eventually being overturned by higher courts. Since 1969, over three thousand people have died from sectarian violence, not all that many compared with the murder rates of the United States, but a considerable proportion in a province of 1.5 million people. Few people have remained untouched by the violence, which exacerbates relations between Protestants and Catholics. The role of the British army has become increasingly controversial. Originally welcomed by the Catholic population as a protection against rampaging Protestant mobs, the army has turned into a long-term occupation force, resented by both sides for its interference with everyday life and suspected of acting arbitrarily in favor of the other side.

The policy of the British government toward Northern Ireland over the past twenty-five years has been motivated by the desire to bring about conditions for what Arend Lijphart[44] has labeled a "consociational" solution. That is, in contrast to the usual British majoritarian approach to constitutional matters (single-member districts, parliamentary majorities form governments, unitary rule, etc.), there has been a concerted attempt at power sharing—proportional representation in local and European elections in the province, a coalition executive, respect for minority rights, and other measures. The problem is not only that the British do not have much familiarity with such institutions or that the Protestant majority resents being told to share power with the Catholic minority. More fundamentally, the elite-mass divisions in Northern Ireland do not lend themselves to consociational solutions. When Protestant leaders, such as Terence O'Neil in the 1960s and Brian Faulkner in the 1970s, have shown themselves amenable to policies that involve improvement of the Catholic situation socially, economically, or politically, they have soon found themselves ex-leaders. Brian Faulkner, in fact, found his power-sharing executive, encouraged by the British government, deposed by what some have called the most successful general strike in the world, that engaged in by protesting Protestant workers in 1974.[45] Similarly, in the Catholic community, even those who argue for peaceful solutions to Northern Ireland's problems have done so through a nationalist lens—the long-term goal is Irish unification, not remaining within the United Kingdom. For a consociational solution to be viable, at least according to Lijphart's classic formulation, followers must trust their leaders to negotiate reasonable solutions to problems with other communally defined groups. Such trust does not exist between followers and leaders in Northern Ireland. Successful leaders must play to their followers' wishes, which means tilting toward the nonnegotiable.

The most recent initiatives on Northern Ireland involved the British government going over the heads of the disputants in the province to reach the Anglo-Irish Accord with the Republic of Ireland in 1985. Bitterly opposed by the Northern Ireland Protestants, whose protests were not nearly as successful as in 1974, the accord has been portrayed as an attempt at "coerced consociationalism" via an international agreement.[46] Although the accord does not change the constitutional status of Northern Ireland, it recognizes the interest of the Irish Republic of Ireland in the affairs of the province by providing for regular consultations with the Irish Republic about matters of mutual interest. This was followed by further Anglo-Irish collaborative efforts to generate all-party peace talks within the province in the mid-1990s. Cease-fires by both armed Catholic and Protestant groups led to increased hope of returning self-government to the province.

In short, despite many years of effort, the British have failed to convey habits of cooperation, pragmatism, and negotiation in good faith to the conflicting parties in Northern Ireland. Instead, the Northern Ireland Office in the cabinet, responsible for these attempts, is widely considered a graveyard for ambitious politicians. Given the lack of interest of the mainland public and politicians in the province, British central government would be only too pleased to return governance of the province to its inhabitants. But the short-term prospects for this are not favorable.

Scotland and Wales have also traditionally not received careful attention from British central government, except as part of more general social and economic policies. Indeed, treatment of Scottish and Welsh matters represents something of a paradox in British policy, especially on the Labour Party side.[47] Labour has often espoused the cause of devolution in these two provinces when in opposition, but it has been much less interested in pursuing such policies when in government. This changed to a degree in the mid-1970s when the Labour government, with key electoral bases in both areas at times of strong devolutionist and even separatist sentiment, spent a great deal of time and parliamentary effort in passing acts providing for devolution in both Scotland and Wales.[48]

But the task became complicated and eventually foundered because of breakdowns of party discipline in the House of Commons. First, the government had to impose a guillotine motion, a relatively rare procedure until the 1990s, to stop discussion on the bill and get a vote on final passage.[49] Then it had to accept amendments offered by one of its own backbenchers to provide for referenda on devolution, separately in Scotland and Wales (but not England), including a provision that more than 40 percent of the eligible voting population had to approve of the proposals before they would go into effect. Dissent on the Labour backbenches over this issue was considerable, with those who favored strong central provision of uniform social and economic benefits for all parts of the United Kingdom opposing devolution, even if they were from the affected provinces. The Welsh referendum failed overwhelmingly,[50] and the Scottish one failed narrowly because of the 40 percent rule.[51] When the legislation revoking the Scotland and Wales acts was laid before the House of Commons, it was approved, but the Scottish Nationalist Party members demanded a vote of confidence that defeated the Labour government, with all nationalist parties joining the opposition. Subsequently Labour in opposition once again espoused the cause of devolution.

The overriding problem, manifested clearly on the Labour side but also by the Conservatives, is political. Can a territorially compact country with a strong unitary tradition and an unwritten constitution afford to give a large degree of self-government to small, thinly populated provinces? There is more willingness to grant devolution to Northern Ireland because of the peculiar nature of the province by British mainland standards. But the experience of devolution in that province does not encourage similar experiments elsewhere in the United Kingdom. Indeed, the devolution debate in the 1970s led to several warnings, in the House of Commons and elsewhere, about the "slippery slope" of federalism and its dire implications for the British Constitution.[52]

Regionally based economic aid for areas in transition has been generally accepted, at least until the Thatcher government, and regionally equal provision of social service benefits is a stated goal, although sometimes not a reality. The legal and educational differences of Scotland and Northern Ireland can be accommodated because they are based on long practice and are, in the final analysis, also subject to the overriding authority of the Westminster government. But constitutional decentralization through devolution is much harder for the British political elite, even for representatives of those provinces, to accept. The elite would be only too happy to be rid of Northern Ireland, but Scotland and Wales have been more integrated into the United Kingdom through elite circulation, similar values, and congruent policies. Tampering with that arrangement is suspect.

William Miller[53] has compared the policy implications of the various nationalist movements in the United Kingdom. Welsh and, particularly, Scottish nationalist sentiment has been largely pacific, in contrast to the violence-prone groups in Northern Ireland. Of course, the violence in Northern Ireland has made British central government attentive to the problems of the province but has not necessarily led to policies desired by those espousing violence. Scottish nationalism has been extraordinarily peaceful, with petitions, marches, and electoral and parliamentary activity being the major vehicles for carrying the message. Welsh nationalism has tended more toward violence, although of a sporadic variety, such as the burning of vacation homes of English visitors to the province. Plaid Cymru, the Welsh nationalist party, has been only a tiny electoral force in comparison to the Scottish Nationalist Party. Plaid Cymru has never won more than 11 percent of the popular vote in Wales and three seats in the House of Commons, whereas the Scottish Nationalist Party has captured up to 30 percent of the vote and eleven seats (in the October 1974 general election). But the Plaid Cymru vote is better concentrated in a few constituencies, those in which the Welsh language is spoken (the language is spoken by only 30 percent of the population of the province). The major triumph of Welsh nationalism has been getting the British government to provide public services in Welsh, including devoting part of one television channel to the language. Special services by the central government to a regional area, however, are more readily granted than is the more politically threatening self-government through devolution.

Women's Rights

Equal rights for women is another policy area that falls under social regulatory policy. As in most countries of the Western world, there has been more attention paid to women's rights since the "second wave" of feminism in the 1960s.[54] Women's advocacy groups have been very active in the United Kingdom, although with mixed success.[55] Because the right to abortions has been discussed previously, the focus here is on British government policies pertaining to equal rights for women, which have concentrated on treatment in the workplace through such legislation as the Equal Pay Act of 1970, the Sex Discrimination Acts of 1975 and 1986, and the Employment Protection Act of 1975.[56] Again as in many other countries in the West, women have increasingly become a part of the workforce, both by necessity and by choice, but they tend to be concentrated in part-time, nonunionized, lower white-collar clerical occupations. By the early 1990s, Britain had one of the most economically active female populations among European Union countries, but was also a country that still had a relatively large wage gap between women and men.[57] But in line with developments elsewhere in the world, the greater numbers of women entering higher education and professional schools indicate that their overall employment status should be enhanced in the years ahead.[58]

As noted, the British government has dealt with women's rights in several separate pieces of legislation, most prominently the Sex Discrimination Acts of 1975 and 1986. The first act was modeled after equal opportunity legislation in the United States and British race relations legislation. It prohibited discrimination in employment, housing, education, and provision of goods and services, although without the aggressive enforcement mechanisms featured in the United States.[59] As relatively narrowly drawn legislation, it did not portend great social changes that would have aroused the hopes of some and the fears of others, as, for instance, the Equal Rights Amendment to the United States Constitution did. Thus there were no significant irregularities in the procedures used to legislate in this area. British entry into the European Community in 1973 was a major impetus toward equality legislation for women because of the EU commitment to gender equality as part of its social goals. Although Britain has moved to block other EU social initiatives in the Council of Ministers, it has so far not resisted these domestically.[60]

The 1975 act set up the Equal Opportunities Commission, a quango empowered to investigate charges of unfair labor practices based upon gender differences. But the Equal Opportunities Commission in practice has acted mainly as a cautionary body rather than serving as a major legal weapon for aggrieved women. British administrative practice rarely departs radically from legislative intent, not least because the doctrine of ultra vires adhered to by the courts does not allow much room for such departures. Despite occasional forays into judicial review,[61] the British judiciary itself is still overwhelmingly conservative in its interpretations and is unlikely to endorse positions not upheld by the legislature and the executive.

The government felt compelled to pass new legislation in 1986, which narrowly concerned equality in terms and conditions of work, to meet objections of the European Commission and the European Court of Justice. Thus, insofar as the issue of women's employment conditions is concerned, British membership in the EU may be the most important influence. As in the past, the United Kingdom can be expected, at least under Conservative governments, to try to block social initiatives, but it remains subject to the judgments of the European Court of Justice, a stronger source of judicial review than the British court system. Rights in employment and the abortion issue have been the "women's issues" most frequently on the official agenda. Obviously, women are also affected disproportionately by other government decisions, for instance, in social welfare policy. Although there has been agitation from the Left for the government to provide more nursery school places for working mothers, the Conservative governments resisted such pressures, despite Mrs. Thatcher's sympathy for it when she was minister of Education and Science in the early 1970s. Labour has pledged to create a Ministry for Women of cabinet rank; thus, women's concerns might receive more attention if Labour returns to power.

The implications of greater women's labor-force participation and increases in educational and professional credentials indicate that further changes may occur in the years ahead.[62] Educated and working women are more likely to support women's empowerment, which suggests that more women will be elected to the House of Commons and sit in the cabinet. Although the policy effects of having women members of Parliament have been limited by their small numbers and the role of party discipline thus far,[63] at least the first of these barriers may weaken, especially if there is a change in the electoral system.[64]

Homosexual Rights

Among the social reform legislation passed on free votes in the 1960s was the decriminalization of homosexual acts between consenting adult males (such acts between females had never been subject to legislation, supposedly partly because Queen Victoria could not conceive of them). The Wolfenden Committee Report of 1957 had recommended this, but the Sexual Offenses Act was not passed until 1967. Although it applied only to England and Wales, later legislation (1980 and 1982) extended it to Scotland and Northern Ireland as well. Despite this legislation, anomalies exist in government policy toward homosexuals. Tolerance of homosexual acts in private does not mean that the government is bound to allow homosexual behavior in all spheres of public life. As with legislation favorable to granting rights to women, nonwhites, and Catholics in Northern Ireland, policy is limited by what the legislature will enact and what the government will propose and enforce. There is no bill of rights or court pronouncements to rely on to extend broad protections for sexual minorities any more than for other minorities. The courts, as noted previously, are not inclined to draw inferences from legislation or move much beyond settled law.

In the case of homosexuals, their now-established right to be free of police harassment does not mean that they can rely on nondiscrimination in other aspects of life. Homosexuals have been treated more sympathetically in the popular arts, such as cinema and television. But there is no tolerance for declared homosexuals in the military, and proposals for same-sex government benefits and homosexual marriages had not been seriously considered as of 1994. Section twenty-eight of the 1988 Local Government Act wrote into law a proscription against using public funds to promote homosexuality; state schools were forbidden to teach that homosexuality was acceptable in family relationships.[65] This provision reflected socially conservative concern about "loony Left" Labour-controlled councils, especially in London, encouraging cultural permissiveness in this and other areas. Similarly, although the age of consent for heterosexuals is sixteen and is the same for lesbians, the 1967 act set the age of consent for male homosexuals at twenty-one. By 1994, the Conservative government allowed a free vote on an amendment to lower the age, but a motion to set the age at sixteen was defeated in favor of setting it at eighteen. Lacking access to the British courts on this issue, discontented petitioners for the lower level pledged to take the British government to the European Court of Human Rights.

Although Acquired Immune Deficiency Syndrome (AIDS) has disproportionately affected homosexuals in Britain, the disease has not spread as widely through the society as it has in the United States, where a flourishing drug culture in inner cities has also made it a minority racial concern. There are ten times as many AIDS cases per capita in the United States as in Britain, and twenty times more among U.S. blacks. In general, AIDS has been treated as a health issue in Britain rather than as one that raises questions about treatment of homosexuals.[66] For instance, the government has given financial compensation to hemophiliacs who have contracted the disease through contaminated blood products and has been willing to fund experimental programs on needle exchange. But there was considerable controversy over the government's education campaign about AIDS.[67] In short, in Britain homosexuals as a minority have not received rights as extensive as in many other countries, but the ones they do have are more secure from political attack than in the United States.

Cultural Policy

There are a host of matters included in any reasonable category called "cultural policy," ranging from government regulations for the mass media, discussed in Chapter 4, to laws concerning Sunday observance, only modified in the 1990s in the teeth of much parliamentary resistance. Government directly subsidizes different aritistic forms, including drama, through funding of the Royal Shakespeare Company and the National Theatre, and music, especially through various symphony orchestras. British culture is extended abroad through the British Council, which supports appearances by people and groups representing different areas of British life. Rarely have these government sponsorships been controversial, even though it has been reported that Mrs. Thatcher herself did not care for the modernist interpretations directed by Sir Peter Hall at the National Theatre. Such support for culture is part of the British tradition of state sponsorship of arts and entertainments.[68]

The institution of state censorship on moral grounds was also part of the accepted role of the state in cultural mentorship, regulating what was allowable in popular entertainments such as theatre, film, and literature. This role was severely compromised by the consequences of the trial concerning banning of *Lady Chatterley's Lover* in 1960. Theater censorship ended in 1959, and other censorship became limited under the Labour government in the 1960s and subsequently as well. Although the reduction of censorship powers did not occasion a great deal of controversy, it was a sign of how permissive Britain had become in the field of culture. Previously, many films and books had been banned, on grounds of violence as well as sexual content, including some that had either originated in or been widely distributed in the United States. Cinemas are licensed by local governments, which can also ban the showing of a film and enforce age limits for viewers based on ratings for content by an independent film board. There have been flurries of complaints over the cultural content and consequences of products of the "permissive society" (a phrase intended positively by Labour Home Secretary Roy Jenkins in the 1960s), including campaigns by Mrs. Mary Whitehouse over the depiction of sex in prime-time television and legislation in 1984 to regulate "video nasties," depicting sex and violence in graphic terms, at the flourishing videotape outlets.[69] But government policy on cultural content has become less geared toward restriction aimed at providing moral protection and more oriented toward lending financial support to group artistic activities. British artistic subsidies fall on the low end of the scale for industrialized countries, but not nearly as far below the mean as those in the United States.[70]

Evaluation

Most of the cases examined under social regulatory policy justify its characterization as a policy area in which the usual processes of policymaking do not apply. Only in the case of equal rights for women, basic law and order, and, to a degree, cultural policy do British political institutions operate normally, with the executive proposing the legislation and dominating the process from agenda setting to implementation. This suggests that some of the policies considered here bear a relationship to social welfare policy, at least in the minds and behavior of policymakers. It also suggests that a careful analysis of how political institutions work across a range of policies that are considered social regulatory is necessary in order to point out similarities and differences.[71]

In most of these other policies, unusual procedures abound. There have been free votes, referendums, guillotine motions, parliamentary dissents by backbenchers, government defeats on legislation, a successful vote of confidence against a sitting government, and mass pressures on a government to act against its stated preferences. Despite these various unusual procedures in the policy process, it is not fair to characterize these issues as solely a function of elitism or pluralism. They certainly do exhibit, however, a more democratic method of conflict resolution than is customary in Britain. These social regulatory issues allow interest groups, backbenchers, and latent but intense public opinion, among others, to take a larger role in the policy process than one would expect. Thus, even if some of these issues are largely the preserve of a minority of intensely interested individuals, and even if other such issues find the public to be largely hostile or indifferent to the outcome, airing of these issues is an example of pluralism at work in the British policy process. That process is open to a variety of influences, majority and minority, in these cases.

In allowing a more open conflict resolution to take place, however, the policy process may also serve larger elite interests. In the first place, the elite has structured the system to allow such resolutions to take place. Secondly, these are almost all issues on which the elites in the parties do not want their parties to run in general election campaigns. Most such issues are not even mentioned in party manifestos, and, even if they are, they usually are not emphasized.[72] Thirdly, without exception these issues form part of what Bulpitt[73] has called "low politics," issues that the elite would prefer to leave to local collaborating interests rather than forming part of the central political agenda, which tends to be reserved for foreign policy, economic policy, and social welfare.[74] The problem that arises for the elite is that these issues do not always lie dormant. At times they arouse such passions, either in active minorities or in the larger public, that they reach the central political agenda and must be confronted. But the elite nevertheless declines to make them a part of the ongoing agenda through incorporation into party platforms and the normal decisionmaking procedures of the executive and the legislature.

If the theorists of postmaterialism are correct, or perhaps even if they are not, then at least some social regulatory issues may become more prominent in the future as the politics of social identity expand and the politics of material scarcity contract.[75] But as pointed out in Chapter 4, heretofore Britain has been a laggard in developing postindustrial indicators and attitudes. If Britain develops constitutional structures that allow more popular input, then some of these issues may achieve a more permanent place on the governmental agenda because they would be entered on the public agenda by interest group agitation.

For the present, however, these issues are usually considered such a marginal part of British policy that, unless they are under active current discussion, they often are not even discussed in books on the policy process.[76] Yet they have an immense impact on the lives of ordinary people and should not be ignored. However much the political institutions are unprepared to deal with these issues on a regular basis and however much the elite would prefer to keep them marginal, their nontechnical, value-oriented nature makes them readily understood by ordinary people. They are an important part of British public policy.

The direction of outcomes for resolution of these issues has largely been deregulation, allowing more individual freedom at the price of restricting the role of the state in upholding traditional values. Yet this movement has not been universal across all issues considered here. In the provinces of immigration, law and order, and nationalism, in particular, traditional concerns for the welfare of the whole rather than that of individuals or national groups has held sway. But even in these areas, more consciousness has developed over minority concerns. It may be that the trend toward social permissiveness holds greater sway on those issues in which the minority is identified by practice and values rather than by ascriptive group identification.

Notes

1. Raymond Tatalovich and Byron W. Daynes, eds., *Social Regulatory Policy* (Boulder: Westview Press, 1988).

2. T. Alexander Smith, *The Comparative Policy Process* (Santa Barbara, Ca.: ABC-Clio, 1975); Christopher J. Hewitt, "The Power Structure of Britain" (Ph.D. diss. Brown University, 1970); Fred Frohock, *Public Policy: Scope and Logic* (Englewood Cliffs, N.J.: Prentice-Hall, 1979).

3. Alvin Cohan, "Abortion as a Marginal Issue: The Use of Peripheral Mechanisms in Britain and the United States," in *The New Politics of Abortion,* ed. Joni Lovenduski and Joyce Outshoorn (London: Sage Publications, 1986).

4. James B. Christoph, *Capital Punishment and British Politics* (Chicago: University of Chicago Press, 1962).

5. John R. Hibbing and David Marsh, "Accounting for the Voting Patterns of British MPs on Free Votes," *Legislative Studies Quarterly* 12, no. 2 (1987):275–297; David Marsh and Melvyn Read, *Private Members' Bills* (Cambridge: Cambridge University Press, 1988).

6. Peter Bromhead, *Private Members' Bills* (London: Routledge, 1956).

7. Peter Richards, *Parliament and Conscience* (London: Allen and Unwin, 1970); Bridget Pym, *Pressure Groups and the Permissive Society* (Newton Abbott, England: David and Clarks, 1974).

8. David Judge, *Backbench Specialization in the House of Commons* (London: Heinemann, 1983).

9. Philip Norton, *Dissension in the House of Commons, 1945–1974* (London: Macmillan, 1975); Philip Norton, *Dissension in the House of Commons, 1974–1979* (Oxford: Clarendon Press, 1980).

10. Denis Balsom and Ian McAllister, "The Scottish and Welsh Devolution Referenda of 1979: Constitutional Change and Popular Choice," *Parliamentary Affairs* 32, no. 4 (1980): 394–409.

11. Harry Lazer, "The Referendum and the British Constitution," in *Dilemmas of Change in British Politics,* ed. Donley T. Studlar and Jerold L. Waltman (London: Macmillan, 1984).

12. E.J.B. Rose et al. *Color and Citzenship* (New York: Oxford University Press, 1969).

13. David Steel, *No Entry* (London: Hurst, 1974).

14. Zig Layton-Henry, *The Politics of Immigration* (Boston: Allen and Unwin, 1984).

15. Elizabeth Meehan, *Women's Rights at Work* (London: Macmillan, 1985); Sally J. Kenney, *For Whose Protection?* (Ann Arbor: University of Michigan Press, 1993).

16. Jaqi Nixon, "The Home Office and Race Relations Policy: Co-ordinator or Initiator?" *Journal of Public Policy* 2, no. 2 (1982): 365–378; Marian FitzGerald, "Immigration and Race Relations—Political Aspect, no. 15," *New Community* 13, no. 1 (1986):265–271.

17. Philip Norton, *The British Polity,* 2d ed. (New York: Longman, 1991).

18. Norton, *The British Polity.*

19. David Robertson, "Preserving Order and Administering Justice: Other Faces of Government in Britain," in *The Developing British Political System: The 1990s,* ed. Ian Budge and David McKay (New York: Longman, 1993).

20. Richard Holme and Michael Elliott, eds., *1688–1988: Time for a New Constitution* (London: Macmillan, 1988).

21. Terence Morris, *Crime and Criminal Justice Since 1945* (New York: Basil Blackwell, 1989).

22. Stephen P. Savage, "A War on Crime? Law and Order Policy in the 1980s," in *Public Policy Under Thatcher,* ed. Stephen P. Savage and Lynton Robins (New York: St. Martin's Press, 1990).

23. Christoph, *Capital Punishment and British Politics.*

24. Hewitt, "The Power Structure of Britain"; Hibbing and Marsh, "Accounting for the Voting Patterns of British MPs on Free Votes."

25. George Gallup, *The International Gallup Polls: Public Opinion 1978* (Wilmington, Del.: Scholarly Resources, 1980); Richard Rose, *Politics in England,* 2d ed. (Boston: Little, Brown and Company, 1974).

26. Pym, *Pressure Groups and the Permissive Society;* Marsh and Read, *Private Members' Bills;* Cohan, "Abortion as a Marginal Issue: The Use of Peripheral Mechanisms in Britain and the United States"; Martin Durham, *Moral Crusades: Family and Morality in the Thatcher Years* (New York: New York University Press, 1991).

27. Pym, *Pressure Groups and the Permissive Society;* Marsh and Read, *Private Members' Bills.*

28. Durham, *Moral Crusades: Family and Morality in the Thatcher Years.*

29. Durham, *Moral Crusades: Family and Morality in the Thatcher Years.*

30. Jim Bulpitt, *Territory and Power in the United Kingdom* (Manchester: Manchester University Press, 1983); Jim Bulpitt, "Continuity, Autonomy and Peripheralisation: The Anatomy of the Centre's Race Statecraft in England," in *Race, Government, and Politics in Britain,* ed. Zig Layton-Henry and Paul B. Rich (London: Macmillan, 1986).

31. Rose, et al., *Color and Citzenship;* Layton-Henry, *The Politics of Immigration.*

32. Peter Hennessey, *Whitehall* (London: Secker and Warburg, 1989); Layton-Henry, *The Politics of Immigration.*

33. Paul Foot, *Immigration and Race in British Politics* (Harmondsworth, England: Penguin Books, 1965); Layton-Henry, *The Politics of Immigration.*

34. Derek Humphry and Michael Ward, *Passports and Politics* (Harmondsworth, England: Penguin Books, 1973).

35. Donley T. Studlar, "British Public Opinion, Colour Issues, and Enoch Powell: A Longitudinal Analysis," *British Journal of Political Science* 4, no. 2 (1974):371–381; Donley T. Studlar, "Policy Voting in Britain: The Colored Immigration Issue in the British General Elections of 1964, 1968, and 1970," *American Political Science Review* 72, no. 1 (1978):46–64.

36. John Edwards and Richard Batley, *The Politics of Positive Discrimination* (London: Tavistock, 1978); FitzGerald, "Immigration and Race Relations—Political Aspect, no. 15."

37. Bulpitt, *Territory and Power in the United Kingdom;* Anthony H. Birch, *Political Integration and Disintegration in the British Isles* (Boston: Allen and Unwin, 1977).

38. Bulpitt, *Territory and Power in the United Kingdom.*

39. Richard Rose, *Governing Without Census* (Boston: Beacon Press, 1969).

40. Richard Rose, Ian McAllister, and Peter Mair, *Is There a Concurring Majority About Northern Ireland?* (University of Strathclyde Studies in Public Policy No. 22 (Glasgow, 1978).

41. Richard Rose, "On the Priorities of Citizenship in the Deep South and Northern Ireland," *Journal of Politics* 38, no. 2 (1976):247–291.

42. Norton, *Dissension in the House of Commons, 1945–1974.*

43. Sabine Wichert, *Northern Ireland Since 1945* (New York: Longman, 1991).

44. Arend Lijphart, "Review Article: The Northern Ireland Problem—Cases, Theories, and Solutions," *British Journal of Political Science* 5, no. 1 (1975):83–106; Arend Lijphart, *Democracies* (New Haven: Yale University Press, 1984).

45. Samuel Finer, ed., *Adversary Politics and Electoral Reform* (London: Anthony Wigram, 1975).

46. Mary E. Kazmierczak, "British Policy and the Conflict in Northern Ireland" (paper presented at British Politics Group/American Political Science Association conference, Washington, D.C., 1993.

47. L. J. Sharpe, "The Labor Party and the Geography of Inequality: A Puzzle," in *The Politics of the Labor Party,* ed. Dennis Kavanagh (London: Allen and Unwin, 1982).

48. Richard Rose, *The Territorial Dimension in Government* (Chatham, N.J.: Chatham House, 1982).

49. Rose, *The Territorial Dimension in Government.*

50. David J. Foulkes, Barry Jones, and R. A. Wilford, eds., *The Welsh Veto* (Cardiff: University of Wales Press, 1983).

51. Balsom and McAllister, "The Scottish and Welsh Devolution Referenda of 1979: Constitutional Change and Popular Choice."

52. Vernon Bogdanor, *Devolution* (New York: Oxford University Press, 1979).

53. William Miller, "The De-Nationalisation of British Politics: The Re-emergence of the Periphery," in *Change in British Politics,* ed. Hugh Berrington (London: Frank Cass, 1984).

54. Vicky Randall, *Women in Politics,* 2d ed. (Chicago: University of Chicago Press, 1987).

55. Joyce Gelb, *Feminism and Politics* (Berkeley: University of California Press, 1989).

56. Gelb, *Feminism and Politics;* Kenney, *For Whose Protection?;* Meehan, *Women's Rights at Work;* Jeanne Gregory, *Sex, Race, and the Law* (London: Sage Publications, 1987).

57. David McKie, ed., *The Election: A Voter's Guide* (London: Fourth Estate, 1992), p. 152.

58. McKie, *The Election: A Voter's Guide,* p. 152.

59. Richard Rose, *Politics in England,* 5th ed. (Boston: Little, Brown and Company, 1989).

60. Kenney, *For Whose Protection?*

61. Jerold L. Waltman, "Judicial Activism in England," in *Judicial Activism in Comparative Perspective,* ed. Kenneth M. Holland (New York: St. Martin's Press, 1991); Robertson, "Preserving Order and Administering Justice: Other Faces of Government in Britain."

62. Lise Togeby, "Political Implications of Increasing Numbers of Women in the Labor Force," *Comparative Political Studies* 27, no. 2 (1994):211–240.

63. Pippa Norris, "Thatcher's Enterprise Society and Electoral Change," *West European Politics* 13, no. 1 (1990):63–78.

64. Pippa Norris, "Women's Legislative Participation in Western Europe," *West European Politics* 8, no. 1 (1985):90–101.

65. Durham, *Moral Crusades: Family and Morality in the Thatcher Years;* Philip Jenkins, *Intimate Enemies* (New York: Aldine De Gruyter, 1992).

66. Durham, *Moral Crusades: Family and Morality in the Thatcher Years;* Jenkins, *Intimate Enemies.*

67. Durham, *Moral Crusades: Family and Morality in the Thatcher Years.*

68. Robert Hewison, *In Anger: British Culture in the Cold War, 1945–1960* (New York: Oxford University Press, 1981); Robert Hewison, *Too Much: Art and Society in the Sixties, 1960–1975* (New York: Oxford University Press, 1987); Arthur Marwick, *Culture in Britain Since 1945* (London: Basil Blackwell, 1991).

69. Durham, *Moral Crusades: Family and Morality in the Thatcher Years.*

70. David Garnham, "Policy Cultures of Advanced Industrial Democracies" (paper presented at American Political Science Association conference, Washington, D.C., 1991).

71. Tatalovich and Daynes, eds., *Social Regulatory Policy.*

72. Ian Budge, David Robertson, and David Hearl, eds., *Ideology, Strategy, and Party Change* (Cambridge: Cambridge University Press, 1987); Donley T. Studlar, "The Influence of British Political Candidates on Public Attitudes Toward Immigrants," *Plural Societies* 10, no. 1 (1979):103–114.

73. Bulpitt, *Territory and Power in the United Kingdom.*

74. See also Judge, *Backbench Specialization in the House of Commons.*

75. Ronald Inglehart, *The Silent Revolution* (Princeton: Princeton University Press, 1977); Ronald Inglehart, *Cultural Shift* (Princeton: Princeton University Press, 1990); Ronald Inglehart and Paul R. Abramson, "Economic Security and Value Change," *American Political Science Review* 88, no. 2 (1994):336–354; Joseph I. H. Janssen, "Postmaterialism, Congitive Mobilization and Public Support for European Integration," *British Journal of Political Science* 21, no. 4 (October 1991):443–468.

76. A. Grant Jordan and Jeremy Richardson, "The British Policy Style or the Logic of Negotiation," in *Policy Styles in Western Europe,* ed. Jeremy Richardson (London: Allen and Unwin, 1982); Brian Hogwood, *Trends in British Public Policy* (Buckingham: Open University Press, 1992); Martin Burch and Bruce Wood, *Public Policy in Britain,* 2d ed. (London: Basil Blackwell, 1990).

9

CHANGE AND INSTITUTIONAL ADAPTATION IN THE UNITED KINGDOM

WHERE IS BRITAIN, THEN, in the middle of the 1990s? Has it changed radically over the past half century, or are the values, procedures, and behavior of the citizens and elites still much the same as they were fifty years ago? Change always seems more evident in the short run than in the long run. From the perspective of the 1990s, the privations and social and economic restructuring of the 1940s, the economic prosperity and complacency of the 1950s, the promised "white-hot technological revolution" of the 1960s, the fears of ungovernability and trade-union power of the 1970s, and the Thatcherite revival of individualism and private enterprise in the 1980s seem more ephemeral than they did at the time. Looking back, one can observe much continuity as well as much change. Mass attitudes have probably changed less than elite attitudes, but since elites have better access to the political agenda, the balance of thought or new trends in educated, politically influential circles is often taken to be the harbinger of things to come; sometimes it is, though sometimes only on a short-term basis.

Issues

The theoretical policy concerns outlined in Chapter 1 have aided understanding of agenda setting and policy directions in British politics. All policy areas are not handled the same way, even in the same country, and using a four-fold categorization developed by policy scholars helps in finding similarities and differences among policies, even if not all policies fit neatly into one of the categories. The elitism-pluralism distinction, even older than policy typologies, is related to it and also helps illuminate such other concepts as corporatism, party government, pluralistic stagnation, and adversary politics. Although the findings vary somewhat by policy category, in general much of British politics remains elitist in character, not so much from the lack of participation by actors but by the setting of the policy agenda, which, at least domestically, is largely in elite hands. Even when elites disagree about policy solutions, they usually agree about what the problems are and how to think about them (in class distributional terms). In short, there is an elite political culture, or statecraft.[1] Nonetheless, elite power to shape the agenda has decreased over the years, because of international factors and the perception of the country's decline from its former position of dominance economically and diplomatically. Within the agendas of different policy areas, however, there are a variety of actors, which leads to many areas being depicted as sectorally fragmented, or in British terms, as having policy networks active in particular sectors. Thus, as Hewitt[2] concluded in an earlier study, outcomes of particular issues may be pluralist in character, although usually still falling within the broader elite consensus. The problem is not so much pluralist stagnation as it is lack of appropriate resources and a disinclination to pursue focused implementation strategies over the long term. In other words, British government attempts to do a lot, constantly tinkering with how to carry out policies, not always for the better.

Although corporatism was oversold, party government and adversary politics have not been dominant modes of decisionmaking either. Parties are important, but many government problems and institutions are too intractable for party rhetoric to be readily translated into different policies. Considered as a whole, adversary politics is a minor rather than a major theme of British public policy. In some policy areas at certain times, for instance, in issues that concern housing, education, taxation, and trade unions, there is evidence of conflicting partisan goals and policies in government. But in other areas, such as foreign policy, the macroeconomy, and even social welfare policy broadly considered, changes of policy are not so closely tied to the partisan coloration of government. The social regulatory policy area has seen more formal bipartisanship, with the major parties either staking out similar positions on issues (immigration, Northern Ireland) or refusing to take party stands on issues (capital punishment, abortion, homosexual rights). There have also been more populistic pressures on these issues, usually in the form of public demonstrations and interest-group lobbying of MPs.

In the four policy areas discussed in this book, the continuities are as impressive, and perhaps more so, than the changes. Both the resources of the British economy and those available to the government have increased substantially throughout the century, and this must be borne in mind. In foreign policy overall, nevertheless, resources, including diplomatic and military ones, have increased by only a relatively small amount, if at all, which has limited capabilities. In foreign policy, aspirations have not changed as much as the ability to maneuver sufficiently in the international system to bring them about.[3] In other words, the policy space in which the United Kingdom has to move in foreign affairs has become more crowded, and its standing as a world actor has shrunk. Even if political elites no longer think of Britain as a great power, they often behave as if they assume little change in national status. The United States must be consulted on almost everything, of course, but Britain has often acted on its own in the foreign policy field, even in situations (the Falklands, the Maastricht Treaty) where caution would have suggested a more collaborative strategy. Few politicians, and indeed few members of the public, have embraced a "little England" perspective. Britain still holds that its moral authority as a democracy—twice a victor in the world wars, and a country with a proud history of worldwide influence—makes it a cut above most other countries in the world, even those with superior economic assets and alliances. There is some regret that the rest of the world does not march to the British drumbeat any longer, but there is no lack of willingness to stand up for positions British leaders prefer, even if major allies fail to come to their support. In short, British foreign policy has become more moderate and circumspect, in line with the country's position in the international system, but there has not been a sea change in the British approach to foreign policy. "Splendid isolation" is no longer possible. The postcommunist world, if it remains so, will further test Britain's ability to make foreign policies choices from opportunity rather than constraint.

In economic policy as well, the overriding goals have changed relatively little. Priorities among the four goals of economic growth, price stability, high employment, and a stable balance of payments have shifted many times, however, even within the same government. With a relatively declining share of industrial production and world trade and a dependence on international economic factors, the United Kingdom has had difficulty achieving an optimum mix among these four goals. Short-term success has never lasted very long, even for single goals. For a time in the middle to late 1980s, it appeared that the Conservative government had managed to arrest British decline. However, this boast quickly proved hollow in the late 1980s and early 1990s, when many of the symptoms of what has been called the "English disease" reappeared—low growth rates, balance of trade deficits, inflation, and lack of international investor confidence in the pound sterling. Thus in the 1990s, Britain has returned to stop-go policies, compounded by the decline of North Sea oil revenues and the dearth of state assets left to sell. The result was, in the Conservative budget for 1994, the largest tax increase in British history in order to cover a burgeoning deficit. This occurred only eighteen months after the Conservatives had chastised the Labour Party for its taxation plans in the 1992 campaign. The structure of the economy, especially concerning government ownership, industrialization, and trade-union strength may have changed considerably during the Thatcher and Major years, but the underlying problems did not.

With eyes firmly fixed on how competitors in Europe and elsewhere are doing, British governments of different political persuasions and techniques have been unable to arrest relative economic decline. The years ahead promise more economic challenges. The reformed Labour Party is bereft of ideas on how to bring about socialism, an ideology that is not favored by current international economic circumstances. Socialism in one country, working against the international economic tide, was tried unsuccessfully by the French Socialist Party in the 1980s. What the Labour Party promises today, if it gets back into government, is better management of the economy, particularly through selective investment in education and training, with more attention paid to collective social justice after years in which social inequality grew under the Conservatives. Thus, it appears that the subtitle of Peter Jenkins's book *The End of the Socialist Era*[4] may be correct, although how much this can be attributed to the Thatcher government is questionable. Undoubtedly, the long period of Conservative rule has damaged Labour's self-confidence and led the party to question accepted doctrines, particularly after the electoral failures of 1983 and 1987, with strongly socialist policies in the Labor Party program in certain areas. But the more market-based system of international trade and finance, allowing large-scale investment to be transferred rapidly among countries, has made it more difficult for the government of a country heavily exposed to the international economy to avoid going along with international trends in interest rates and macroeconomic policies. The Labour Party may also be forced into minority or coalition government, which would politically weaken its capacity to impose its own economic policy on the country.

Thus the international economic situation may have changed more than Britain's responses to it. Although the tribulations of enacting the Maastricht Treaty will probably delay the hoped-for economic and monetary union of the EU, the organization will continue to loom large in British economic policy. With Britain's trade ever more oriented toward Europe, Community decisions are important for Britain's future prospects. As of 1995, there appears to be no prospect for the United Kingdom to become a cooperative European to the extent that other countries in the Union want. There are still too many doubts about the economic worth and political purposes of the Union within British parties, and indeed within the British public, for the United Kingdom to become a wholehearted federalist. But the British economy by itself is not strong enough to stand far outside the common European policies, a tendency that will be reinforced as the Union enlarges. Thus the British economy still stands in jeopardy of the buffeting of international economic winds. The search for British economic stability and growth will continue in an environment in which old practices are increasingly ill-matched to address new realities.

Economic policy is intimately linked to British foreign policy, but it is even more closely tied to social welfare policy. As with other types of policies, British socioeconomic policy faces new challenges in a changing environment. Relative economic decline poses problems for maintenance and growth of the welfare state. Slow growth, high unemployment, interrupted work histories that affect contributory benefits, and an increasing proportion of elderly and single-parent families make it difficult to improve benefit levels without incurring taxpayer resistance. The Conservative move from paternalistic conservatism toward individualistic conservatism has allowed the party to meet this challenge by moving the agenda of socioeconomic policy toward selectivity in benefits for the neediest rather than growing benefits for all. The reduction of earnings-related old-age pensions in 1985 was one of the first forays into this area, and the reforms toward greater efficiency in health and education services are also part of this broad initiative. But just as welfare state expansion encountered limits, so too will reduction of social benefits. Shifting the agenda in this area will be more a case of incremental tendencies rather than wholesale attacks and slashing programs. Although single-party majority government with few constitutional checks, as is usually the case in Britain, is conducive to major changes in social entitlements,[5] there are also major dangers, such as electoral backlash. Furthermore, coalition or minority governments, more likely now than ever, encourage compromise. A slow erosion of the welfare state is more likely than major privatization of programs.

Social regulatory policy may also undergo changes, although there is likely to be considerable variation from one issue to another. On the one hand, broadened personal freedoms stemming from the moral reform legislation of the 1960s are unlikely to be significantly eroded. As new generations succeed older ones, they will assume these freedoms, and those who question them will suffer disproportionate loss from generational turnover. On the other hand, attempts to make social regulation adjustments of a more communal character, such as in law and order (excluding capital punishment), in race relations, in equal opportunities for women, and especially, in devolution of power to meet nationalist demands, are likely to encounter considerable debate and ferment. The legal role of the police is likely to be an issue up for continual redefinition, particularly if the movement for an established bill of rights makes much headway. In an increasingly fragmented social stucture, the rights of women and ethnic minorities could also be raised to formal agenda status occasionally, although the capacity of the British majoritarian polity to resist strong legal protection for minority interests is legion. Devolution, along with other constitutional-institutional questions, however, may become increasingly important, especially under a non-Conservative government.

If, as has been argued, there will be relatively little scope for innovation in economic, social welfare, or foreign policy, then constitutional-institutional questions may be major areas of political conflict. In the United Kingdom, with its unwritten British Constitution, any major legislated institutional change becomes a de facto constitutional question. In contrast, matters of executive flexibility, such as what departments and officials are in the cabinet or relations between cabinet ministers and the civil service, are not constitutional matters because they do not require parliamentary action. The areas of the Constitution that could be the subject of intense political controversy include the monarchy, the House of Lords, the electoral system, devolution, and a bill of rights. Central-local government relations are a perennial topic of reform. Notwithstanding recent agitation for a referendum on European Union matters, direct democracy is unlikely to proceed very far.

The monarchy, in spite of much speculation on its future, is unlikely to change in any significant way. Despite family embarrassments in the early 1990s, the monarchy has previously survived downturns in popular and political esteem. It would be a wrenching decision politically for politicians and the public to change to a different form of head of state. Although the monarchy is not as firmly entrenched in the political culture as has often been supposed, for the institution to be in danger of abolition there would have to be more incidents alienating the public and, more significantly, the politicians, from the institution itself, not only from individuals connected to the monarchy. Britain is not Australia, where the Labour prime minister (and Irish descendant) has called for the monarchy to be replaced as head of state.

An individual bill of rights, although more frequently espoused in Britain today, is also unlikely to make much headway. As people become less trusting of the police, the government, and the courts, increased demands for constitutionally entrenched protections have been voiced. Heretofore, however, no politically influential figure of either the Conservative or Labour Parties has come out in support of these initiatives. The leaders of these two parties are enamored of the flexibility that the current British Constitution affords. In general, there is a disinclination among political elites to entrench individual rights constitutionally, which would imply overriding parliamentary sovereignty and would also probably involve the courts in individual rights cases in a more signficant manner, including having them exercise the power of judicial review. The evidence of government deceit and abuse of individual rights would have to be much greater than the occasional cases raised today for such a reform to capture the imagination of political leaders. Only the Liberal Democrats seem especially interested in tying the hands of government, and they are likely to remain a distinct minority for the foreseeable future, even if they might succeed in forming part of a coalition government. If a change in the electoral system toward proportional representation occurred, however, the position of the Liberals would become more important since, like the Free Democrats in Germany, they could become the middle party essential to the formation of almost any government coalition.

A more likely reform is a change in the composition, or perhaps even the complete abolition, of the House of Lords. This institution is certainly an anomaly. Even the provocation of having the Lords temporarily block much of the Conservative government's legislation in the mid-1980s did not, however, lead the Conservatives to question its makeup. The Conservatives are not in favor of constitutional tinkering. If other parties come to power, however, Lords reform may occur. Any such change, however, would probably not mean an enhanced role for a reformed body. What Lijphart[6] has called "asymmetric bicameralism" will probably continue in Britain for the foreseeable future; it is more likely than complete abolition. Any attempt to change the Lords, however, would be fiercely resisted by traditionalists, especially Conservative traditionalists. Since the most likely replacement mechanism would be having regionally or locally elected representatives serve in the upper chamber, this would be further reason for resistance. British central government is loath to give up its control over subordinate units, even to the extent of compromising by giving them some role in central goverment policymaking.

Also likely to be the subject of constitutional reform is devolution of power to areas of the United Kingdom that are experiencing nationalist agitation. Scottish nationalism has been the most pacific of all such movements in the United Kingdom, and it has the fewest policy concessions to show for this reasonableness. Over the recent Conservative-dominant period, it has been the most anti-Conservative part of the United Kingdom electorally (considering the Ulster Unionists as basically sympathethic to the Conservatives). Although the Labour Party has dominated Scotland in partisan terms, there are significant pockets of Liberal Democratic and Scottish Nationalist strength as well. Both Labour and the Liberals have advocated creating a Scottish assembly and, either in power together or separately, they would be under pressure to deliver on this. How long even the Conservatives in government would be able to maintain a centralist position in the face of their declining prospects in Scotland is also questionable. Thus a serious attempt at devolution of power to Scotland is likely to occur. The last time this issue arose, in the 1970s, it convulsed the polity. The Labour government suffered defeats in the House of Commons and eventually the Labour government lost a vote of confidence in the wake of the Scottish referendum due to the refusal of the Scottish Nationalists to continue to support the government. There is no indication that a more comprehensive attempt at all-regional reform would be put forward by any party this time around. As before, enough political pressure may lead to an attempt to devise an ad hoc solution for Scotland and Wales. Major resistance to this constitutional change can be expected again.

Another area in which constitutional change is possible is in the status of Northern Ireland. In late 1993, there was a flurry of revelations and initiatives, including contacts with the provisional IRA and conferences with the Irish government, designed to create an opening for a permanent constitutional settlement in the province. This led to an IRA cease-fire in 1994, followed by a cease-fire by Protestant paramilitary groups. What the shape of that settlement would take, however, is not clear, and these activities may be yet another false dawn in a part of the United Kingdom that has seen many such over the course of the past few centuries. As the British have found out in places such as India, Israel, and Cyprus, promising self-determination of peoples in a society deeply divided by nationalism based on ethnicity or religion is fraught with difficulties. Undoubtedly most people and politicians on the mainland would welcome a permanent solution that would allow Northern Ireland to govern itself or to be incorporated into Ireland, thus relieving the British government of the tasks of armed peacekeeping there. The Labour Party has indicated that it favors withdrawal from Northern Ireland. The best that can reasonably be hoped for, however, is a slow process of accommodation under the watchful eyes of the governments of Ireland and the United Kingdom. Even that is far from certain.

Possibly the most far-reaching constitutional change is much nearer the formal governmental agenda. Before his unexpected death, Labour Party leader John Smith promised a referendum on the question of changing the electoral system if Labour forms the next government. It is debatable whether a Labour Party victorious in a general election would follow through on such a change. As the referendum on British membership in the European Community in 1975 indicates, however, Labor is more willing to consider referendums on issues that are divisive within the party than the Conservatives are. Although there have been persistent majorities recorded by public opinion polls in favor of a form of proportional representation, most likely the "single transferable vote," to replace the single-member district, simple plurality system, it remains to be seen how the referendum question would be framed, what positions the parties would take, and how receptive the public would be to the arguments put forward. The suspicion is that public opinion on such (heretofore) abstract questions is fragile and subject to large changes in the course of a referendum campaign. The Liberal Democrats, of course, would welcome a fairly phrased question on the electoral system, and the Conservatives would oppose it. Its chances of success might depend on the circumstances of the government that proposed it, that is, a majority Labour government would bring hope of future Labour single-party majorities and lead Labour partisans to discount the importance of changing the electoral system to prevent another long-term Conservative majority government based on a plurality of the voters. But a minority or coalition government would be more conducive to encouraging Labour to embrace electoral reform.

Electoral reform has been an issue in British politics before, for example after World War I, but it was the Liberals, ironically enough, who were opposed to it.[7] Despite the resistance to changing the electoral system by the two traditionally major parties, a constitutional change of the electoral system has been implemented in the 1990s in Japan, New Zealand, and Italy. So far, Britain has been a holdout for the unadulterated single-member district system, even to the point of being the only European Union country conducting elections for the European Parliament that is using it, except in Northern Ireland.

This is potentially the most far-reaching constitutional change of all, because altering the electoral system would most likely change the recruitment base of the House of Commons, allowing more women and minorities into the chamber, and it would also alter the partisan basis of British governments. Without single-party majority governments, many traditional practices and policies could no longer be taken for granted. The number of parties might increase, parties would have to think in terms of coalition governments, and ideological posturing would probably be reduced. Policies in some areas might change as well.[8] Recognition of this fact is undoubtedly a major factor keeping most politicians from embracing such a change.

Another constitutional question of a sort concerns the European Union, and this is also likely to be a continued source of political controversy in the United Kingdom. The EU involves two dimensions; one is constitutional, but the other is how the stucture and policies of the union affect British economic and social life. In the minds of some political leaders, these two issues are amalgamated. Strong central control by the European Commission and majority voting in the Council of Ministers would mean that the specifics of Britain's position are likely to be ignored; on the other hand, a more decentralized Union allowing individual states to pursue their own paths is more favorable to British interests, in this view. Even the strongest pro-EU opinions in Britain are voiced by hesitant federalists, except for the Liberal Democrats, who have not had to participate in actual decisionmaking in the EU.

Whatever form the European Union takes under the Maastricht Treaty and whatever expected enlargement occurs, the consequences of British membership will continue to be a major issue in British politics. The country has already made compromises in parliamentary sovereignty in order to enjoy the benefits of membership. Even though the immediate prospects are for a more decentralized, voluntary community than was envisioned in the original interpretations of the Maastricht Treaty, there will undoubtedly continue to be a struggle between those who see strengthened central institutions as the way for Europe to reconcile its internal differences and compete in the wider world and those who wish to preserve a larger measure of state sovereignty. Although a future government might reconcile Britain to the European Union, the more likely prospect is for a continuation of the party factionalism and suspicion of the EU that has characterized Britain's relations with the Community from its inception.

If the Cold War continues to stay buried, Britain may see its international security role diminish. Already, British defense forces are being substantially cut back. Lacking a focus of preparedness—a purpose the Soviet Union served for so long—the country may further trim its military commitments abroad. Although this would allow budget savings that could in principle be used for domestic purposes, it also might leave the British with less sense of international commitment in general. British international policies have usually been concerned with economic and military security. As previously noted, in military spending the United Kingdom is one of the most martial of industrialized states, and military endeavor is very much a part of the self-image of the country. Whether that type of commitment could be turned to more sanguine purposes in the international arena is questionable.

Whatever happens in the successor states of the Soviet bloc, Britain will remain concerned with military security in Europe and can be expected to contribute substantially to it, in arms and finance. Now Europe is not only its geographical neighbor but also its major marketplace. The British can be expected to respond militarily to any threats to Europe. But British entanglements in places further abroad will probably be trimmed further. The United Kingdom can still serve as a vital link between the United States and Europe; thus the Anglo-American special relationship may not disappear entirely. But in an international environment in which Britain, is, more than ever, an "ordinary country," it will find that it needs a more flexible foreign policy.

Institutions and Processes

The formal parliamentary institutions of the United Kingdom have changed little over the years, although there has been greater change in those institutions, such as local government and the civil service, that are not constitutionally grounded. As noted above, it would not be surprising to see significant constitutional revision in the years ahead. In Britain, however, discussion of constitutional change, which is carried on continuously, is often confused with openness to change. Elites who have been served well by the institutions that exist are reluctant to change them.

There are signs that the public is growing disenchanted with the performance of political institutions. Although some discontent is attributable to partisan factors, surveys indicate that over the last decade there has been a progressive loss of confidence in both political leaders and institutions in Britain.[9] This may be one of the forces, along with partisan dealignment, impelling members of Parliament to do more constituency service.[10] If this undermining of what has been called the civic culture continues, then the public may be more willing to tolerate calls for radical changes in institutions. But the initiatives would still have to come from politicians.

Although the comparison of elite values and mass values in Chapter 4 indicates that elites are, if anything, more tolerant and flexible in their values than masses, this does not necessarily translate into elite willingess to tamper with the fundamental political institutions of the country. Elites, after all, have a great deal immediately at stake in any institutional changes, and, for all of their willingess to consider various options, in the final analysis, it is not only values but position in the policy process that influences what politicians do.[11] As E. E. Schattschneider[12] pointed out, politicians have the power to shape public perceptions of issues.

The likely prospect is, therefore, that Britain will continue to be governed by a parliamentary system in a constitutional monarchy. Behaviorally, this means a restricted pluralism within a value consensus, not dissimilar from what Schumpeter envisioned a half century ago. Even if they cannot choose all of the issues, elites still set the characteristic style and tone of British politics. The narrow socialization processes mean that many members of the political elite know each other from an early age, and their controversies, while genuine, assume a familiar air. In the twentieth century these arguments have tended to focus domestically on questions of justice and opportunity between social classes. This is the stuff of Bulpitt's "high politics," the preferred agenda, along with foreign policy, of the political elite. Even if surveys show that the public has other issues, such as immigration, on its collective mind or that on other social issues, such as capital punishment, the elite is acting in ways that contradict the wishes of a majority of the public, there is a general permissive consensus that allows the elites to set most of the formal agenda most of the time. In short, Britain is not a populistic country. Low politics does intrude occasionally, but in a parliamentary system with usually a single-party government, the barriers are formidable concerning raising such issues when the elite does not want them to be.

Nevertheless, the vulnerability of the United Kingdom to foreign influences, even greater now that its international economic and military position is weaker, means that, in the larger sense, elites are less able to affect the direction of high politics issues. The increasing economic integration of Britain's medium-sized economy into the European Union is one indication of this process.

Even if political elites in Britain still largely set the agenda, does this mean that policy directions are consensual as well? This, of course, has been at the root of the discussion of how much Thatcherism has changed Britain. The short answer is that there is genuine ideological debate but that government policy response differences often fall short of the full range of the ideological debate. Not only is there a relatively narrow path to joining the political elite, but Parliament itself is an important socializing mechanism. Party disputes do not necessarily extend to the formal votes on legislation; the 1970s "adversary politics" argument has been overdrawn. Many policies are continuations from previous governments, even if the details may be changed somewhat. In fact, once a government with a coherent agenda has been able to serve in office long enough to implement it, such as the immediate postwar Labour government or the more recent Conservative ones, then not only that agenda but the direction of policy is likely to continue for some time. Thus the postwar Labour government inaugurated thirty years of Butskellite consensus about the economy and the welfare state, and the more recent Conservative governments have passed privatization and trade-union legislation that any future government would find hard to reverse comprehensively in a short time. Both of these governments, of course, had more than one term in which to bring about their reorientation of policies. Most governments are not that coherent in outlook or as long-lived in office.

Britain's status as a stable democracy, therefore, is dependent on its keeping political controversy and conflict within manageable proportions. Aside from the difficulties with Northern Ireland, it has generally managed to do so. There is an elite consensus about the political agenda, and even genuine differences in opinion about policy directions are often expressed more rhetorically than through actions in government. A restricted elite allows civilized discussion of alternatives, minimum political violence, and cohesive government. But increasingly, Britain has been less in control not only of its political agenda but also of its political direction. Relative economic and political decline has meant that the political elites are more subject to external forces, both domestically and internationally.[13]

But unlike traditionally small countries in Europe that have learned to be flexible enough to cope with international dependency through corporatist practices,[14] Britain has not given up the notion that it is a leader rather than a follower, and leaders, by definition, change their environment rather than bending to it. Thus, what has been identified as a characteristic postwar British practice in foreign policy—strategic defiance followed by tactical withdrawal[15]—is a product of elite tendencies toward assertion of Britain's interests and position, on the one hand, and eventual recognition of a weak position and a willingness to compromise, on the other. Policy directions in domestic policies have followed similar lines, strategic (ideological) defiance followed by retreat and moderation, in most instances. Party splits and electoral defeat, however, have sometimes been necessary to drive the point of moderation home to recalcitrant members of the political elite. In the final analysis, however, extremists like Enoch Powell and Tony Benn have been marginalized in the parliamentary parties. Mrs. Thatcher's government was more cohesive in its policy direction than most, but even its capacity to change the direction of the British society and economy was limited. Mrs. Thatcher showed that it was possible to depart from the postwar consensus and be reelected, and by doing so, as suggested earlier, it will have a long-term effect on policy directions. But one may question how influential even Mrs. Thatcher was in molding the longer-term agenda, as opposed to responding to her domestic and international environment. Britain's low and slow postwar economic growth pattern made it particularly vulnerable to experiencing some of the dislocations of the changing international economic environment in the 1970s. Other countries, even those with socialist governments, have followed the British lead in deregulation and privatization. Furthermore, the Conservatives did not come into office in 1979 with an entirely coherent program. The Thatcherite reorientation of policy direction was also made affordable by the abundance of North Sea oil, which allowed Britain to avoid budget deficits for a time.[16] Thus, one may question how far the Conservative governments went in actually changing the political agenda. That they reoriented policy directions for the medium term is less debatable. But overall, Thatcherism may have been less revolutionary than either its adherents or its critics claim.

Despite the formal constitutional flexibility of the British political process, a reluctance to change may inhibit its capacity to adapt to a changing environment. Frank Baumgartner and Bryan Jones[17] have shown that it is possible in the more decentralized polity of the United States to change the domestic political agenda by changing the images and venues of political issues. It is much more difficult to do this in the United Kingdom because the unwritten British Constitution pushes almost all issues toward the central level; hence the venue, ultimately, remains the same. If an issue is handled at a lower level, that is because of the preference of central authorities, who retain the capacity to take over the issue at any time. There is a shared elite reluctance to entrench the institutional capacity to deal with issues at lower levels; this may affect devolution proposals yet again, as it did in the 1970s. It is also difficult to change the image of issues, both because of the class rhetoric of the parties and established ideological positions of the printed media.

Ironically enough, British leaders have been in the forefront of calls for "subsidiarity" in the European Union, that is, allowing decisions to be made at levels of government lower than that of the EU, if possible. Politically, of course, the goal is to retain as much discretion for the British central government—but without necessarily applying the same principle within Britain. Adding the venue of the European Union to the British Constitution may aid in altering the agenda of British policy as well as its political processes. This has already taken place in the case of environmental policy, for instance, and may also occur in other policy areas, especially as interest groups increasingly lobby the EU for authoritative decisions. Changing the venue can change outcomes, too.

The United Kingdom centralization is being challenged from both above and below. The force of these challenges may result in substantial changes in the policy agenda and in issue processing, but there is a reluctance to concede much ground to them. The key issue is not whether Britain will allow either the EU or lower levels of government to make policy in certain areas, but whether this multilevel decisionmaking will be constitutionally entrenched. Only then will multiple venues of agenda access be possible. The same question also applies to such proposed domestic reforms as a new second chamber, a bill of rights, and encouragement of judicial review.

The fear of British policymakers, both political and bureaucratic, is that such a process would lead to deadlock and jurisdictional disputes. An examination of other countries provides considerable justification for such fears. But allowing multiple venues can also lead to compromise and consistent lines of policy, despite partisan differences. Indeed, the inconsistencies of British policy in some areas may be due less to adversarial politics on the grand scale than to partisan tinkering with policy, which renders it incoherent.[18]

The question remains whether a country so dependent on economic integration can resist social and political integration with other European countries. Similarly, Britain has largely been a holdout against decentralizing authority, a trend that has affected countries all over the world in the past twenty-five years. Meeting these twin demands might make Britain more capable of meeting the challenges of the next century, but resolution of these issues will not come easily.

Conclusion

The years ahead, then, are likely to bring further change to the United Kingdom. Most of the change that is on the horizon, however, is more clearly generated by social, economic, and international forces than by the internal political institutions and forces within the country. However much British leaders have attempted to retain great power status and keep Britain in charge of its own destiny, they have been more skillful in organizing well-managed retreats and compromises. The issues on the political agenda in Britain are often not of the leaders' own choosing. The question is how well a polity that is still, by most standards, a conservative one will cope with the changes beckoning in the twenty-first century.

In a country's affairs, there are eras of resiliency and eras of flexibility. Britain has been outstandingly resilient, both in the long-term building of liberal democratic institutions and in such short-term crises, relatively speaking, as World War II. In matters of flexibility, however, its response has not been as good. Despite the theoretical advantages of parliamentary institutions unbounded by a written constitution,[19] the country has often been slow to respond to changes in its external and internal environment. The slow responses to demands to grant increased suffrage and trade-union recognition and to the tribulations of the Great Depression,[20] and economic modernization are prime examples. This was not such a severe handicap when technology and communication were slower, but in the late twentieth century, lack of rapid adaptability has become a more serious problem, especially economically. With the changes occurring in human life spans, medical technology, and financial markets, among other things, governments will have to be increasingly flexible to meet the challenges posed by their changing environments. Whether the British government has gained enough adaptability, especially from the changes wrought by the recent Conservative governments, to be able to cope satisfactorily with a world that is increasingly out of its control remains a major question.

Notes

1. Robert D. Putnam, *The Beliefs of Politicians* (New Haven, Conn.: Yale University Press, 1973); Jim Bulpitt, *Territory and Power in the United Kingdom* (Manchester: Manchester University Press, 1983).

2. Christopher J. Hewitt, "The Power Structure of Britain" (Ph.D. dissertation, Brown University, 1970).

3. See Paul Kennedy, *The Rise and Fall of the Great Powers* (New York: Random House, 1987).

4. Peter Jenkins, *Mrs. Thatcher's Revolution* (Cambridge: Harvard University Press, 1989).

5. Paul D. Pierson and R. Kent Weaver, "Imposing Losses in Pension Policy," in *Do Institutions Matter? Government Capabilities in the United States and Abroad,* ed. R. Kent Weaver and Bert A. Rockman (Washington, D.C.: Brookings Institution, 1993).

6. Arend Lijphart, *Democracies* (New Haven: Yale University Press, 1984).

7. Vernon Bogdanor, *The People and the Party System* (Cambridge: Cambridge University Press, 1981).

8. Weaver and Rockman, eds., *Do Institutions Matter? Government Capabilities in the United States and Abroad.*

9. John R. Baker, Linda L. M. Bennett, Stephen E. Bennett, and Richard S. Flickinger, "Looking at Legislatures: Citizens' Knowledge and Perception of Legislatures in Canada, Great Britain, and the United States" (paper presented at International Political Science Association conference, Berlin, Germany, 1994).

10. Philip Norton and David Wood, *Back from Westminster* (Lexington: University Press of Kentucky, 1993).

11. Barbara J. Burt and Max Neiman, "Elite Belief Consistency and the Effect of Position in the Policy-Making Process," *Western Political Quarterly* 40, no. 1 (1987):121–136.

12. E. E. Schattschneider, *The Semi-Sovereign People* (New York: Holt, Rinehart and Winston, 1960).

13. Richard Rose, *Do Parties Make a Difference?* (Chatham, N.J.: Chatham House, 1980); Brian Hogwood, *Trends in British Public Policy* (Buckingham: Open University Press, 1992).

14. Peter Katzenstein, ed., *Between Power and Plenty* (Madison: University of Wisconsin Press, 1978).

15. David Sanders, "Relations with Outside Governments: Foreign and Military Policy," in *The Developing British Political System: The 1990s,* ed. Ian Budge and David McKay (New York: Longman, 1993).

16. Allen Schick, "Governments Versus Budget Deficits," in *Do Institutions Matter?* ed. Weaver and Rockman.

17. Frank R. Baumgartner and Bryan D. Jones, *Agendas and Instability in American Politics* (Chicago: University of Chicago Press, 1993).

18. Sven Steinmo, *Taxation and Democracy* (New Haven: Yale University Press, 1994); Patrick Dunleavy, "The United Kingdom: Paradoxes of an Ungrounded Statism," in *The Comparative History of Public Policy,* ed. Francis G. Castles (Cambridge: Polity Press, 1989).

19. Walter Bagehot, *The English Constitution* (London: Fontana, 1963); Kenneth Waltz, *Foreign Policy and Democratic Politics* (Boston: Little, Brown and Company, 1967).

20. Dennis Kavanagh, "Crisis Management and Incremental Adaptation in British Politics: The 1931 Crisis of the British Party System," in *Crisis, Choice, and Change,* ed. Gabriel A. Almond, Scott C. Flanagan, and Robert J. Mundt (Boston: Little, Brown and Company, 1973); Margaret Weir and Theda Skocpol, "State Structures and the Possibilities for 'Keynesian' Responses to the Great Depression in Sweden, Britain, and the United States," in *Bringing the State Back In,* ed. Peter B. Evans, Dietrich Rueschemeyer, and Theda Skocpol (Cambridge: Cambridge University Press, 1985).

Further Reading

THIS SECTION IS DESIGNED to provide some basic general sources on the topics covered in this book, in addition to the specific sources noted in the footnotes and bibliography. The standard political histories on Britain are the various editions of Alan Sked and Chris Cook, *Post-War Britain* (Harmondsworth, England: Penguin Books) and David Childs, *Britain Since 1945* (London: Ernest Benn). The annual editions of *Britain: An Official Handbook,* compiled by the Central Office of Information and published by Her Majesty's Stationery Office (HMSO) are an invaluable compendium of data and information on history, geography, economy, social life, culture, and public policies. There are several textbooks on British politics and government available, written from different intellectual perspectives. Particularly noteworthy for its extensive bibliographies are the fourth and fifth editions of R. M. Punnett, *British Government and Politics* (London: Heinemann, 1980, 1988). An annual bibliography of books on British politics is issued by the British Politics Group, currently administered by Donley T. Studlar, P.O. Box 6317, West Virginia University, Morgantown, West Virginia 26506-6317.

In recent years there has been much more concern with what is called "contemporary history" in Britain. Since 1990, Peter Catterall of the Institute of Contemporary British History has edited an annual yearbook of brief articles on British political, social, economic, and cultural affairs called *Contemporary Britain: An Annual Review* (New York: Basil Blackwell), with chronologies for each section. Longer-term perspectives on particular topics covered in this book (some of which are specifically cited) are provided by the series on postwar British history *Making Contemporary Britain,* published by Basil Blackwell since the late 1980s. Peter Hennessey and Anthony Seldon have edited an important reevaluation of postwar British governments, *Ruling Performance: British Government from Attlee to Thatcher* (New York: Basil Blackwell, 1987).

More recently, a competitor to the annual Basil Blackwell volumes has appeared, namely, *Focus on Britain,* edited by John Benyon and Barry McCormick (Chicago: Fitzroy Dearborn). There is also the series *Scottish Government Yearbook* (Edinburgh: various publishers). The Gallup polling organization periodically compiles a book, under various titles and authors, describing recent British public opinion. The annual publication *British Social Attitudes* (Aldershot, England: Gower) features more in-depth consideration of particular topics. Since 1991, the Elections, Parties, and Public Opinion section of the Political Studies Association of the United Kingdom has also published *British Parties and Elections Yearbook* (Ann Arbor: University of Michigan Press), an annual volume of scholarly articles and data focused on their concerns. David Butler's series of books with various coauthors on postwar British general elections (New York: St. Martin's Press) provides good summaries of political events between elections. More recently, a volume by Ivor Crewe and various coauthors, called *Political Communications* (Cambridge: Cambridge University Press), has been published after every election, too.

227

There are also several notable journals. *Contemporary Record* is the periodical of the Institute of Contemporary British History. *Political Studies* is the official journal of the Political Studies Association of the United Kingdom. In recent years, this journal has been publishing a series of articles on journals in other disciplines that are of interest to political scientists. *Parliamentary Affairs* provides descriptive pieces on political institutions. Both of these journals have comprehensive book review sections. The *British Journal of Political Science* publishes more behaviorally oriented articles. *Political Quarterly* focuses on contemporary policy issues. A more comparative viewpoint is the special province of *Government and Opposition*. *Teaching Politics* provides summary articles on political topics for teachers, as does *Politics Review* for students. There are also specialist journals for those interested in foreign policy, public administration, local government, social policy, and so on. Major newspapers and journals featuring political commentary are listed in Chapter 4 in the discussion on the media.

Bibliography

Aberbach, Joel D., Robert D. Putnam, and Bert A. Rockman. *Bureaucrats and Politicians in Western Democracies*. Cambridge: Harvard University Press, 1981.

Abrams, Mark, and Richard Rose. *Must Labour Lose?* London: Penguin Books, 1960.

Alderman, Geoffrey. *The Jewish Community in British Politics*. Oxford: Oxford University Press, 1983.

Alford, Robert, and Roger Friedland. *Powers of Theory*. Cambridge: Cambridge University Press, 1985.

Almond, Gabriel, and Sidney Verba. *The Civic Culture*. Princeton: Princeton University Press, 1963.

Alt, James E. *The Politics of Economic Decline*. Cambridge: Cambridge University Press, 1979.

Anderson, James. *Public Policymaking*. Boston: Houghton Mifflin Company, 1990.

————. "At the Pleasure of Parliament: The Politics of Local Reform in Britain." In *Dilemmas of Change in British Politics*. ed. Donley T. Studlar and Jerold L. Waltman. London: Macmillan, 1984.

————. *The Emergence of the Welfare States*. Oxford: Basil Blackwell, 1986.

Ashford, Douglas E. *Policy and Politics in Britain: The Limits of Consensus*. Philadelphia: Temple University Press, 1981.

Aydelotte, William. "Constituency Influence on the British House of Commons, 1841–1847." In *The History of Parliamentary Behavior*, ed. William Aydelotte. Princeton: Princeton University Press, 1977.

Bachrach, Peter, and Morton Baratz. "The Two Faces of Power." *American Political Science Review* 56, no. 4 (1962):947–952.

Bagehot, Walter. *The English Constitution*. London: Fontana, 1963.

Baker, David, Andrew Gamble, and Steve Ludlam. "More 'Classless' and Less 'Thatcherite': Conservative Ministers and New Conservative MPs After the 1992 Election." *Parliamentary Affairs* 45, no. 4 (1992):656–668.

Baker, John R., Linda L. M. Bennett, Stephen E. Bennett, and Richard S. Flickinger. "Looking at Legislatures: Citizens' Knowledge and Perceptions of Legislatures in Canada, Great Britain, and the United States." Paper presented at International Political Science Association Conference, Berlin, Germany, 1994.

Balsom, Denis, and Ian McAllister. "The Scottish and Welsh Devolution Referenda of 1979: Constitutional Change and Popular Choice." *Parliamentary Affairs* 32, no. 4 (1980): 394–409.

Barnes, Samuel H. et al. *Political Action*. London: Sage Publications, 1979.

Barnett, Corelli. *The Audit of War*. London: Macmillan, 1986.

Barnum, David, and John L. Sullivan. "The Elusive Foundations of Political Freedom in Britain and the United States." *Journal of Politics* 52, no. 3 (August 1990):719–739.

Baumgartner, Frank R., and Bryan D. Jones. *Agendas and Instability in American Politics.* Chicago: University of Chicago Press, 1993.

Bedarida, François. *A Social History of England, 1851–1975.* Trans. A. S. Forster. New York: Methuen, 1979.

Beer, Samuel H. *Britain Against Itself.* New York: W. W. Norton, 1982.

———. *British Politics in the Collectivist Age.* New York: Random House, 1965.

Benn, Tony. *Office Without Power: Diaries 1968–1972.* London: Hutchinson, 1988.

———. *Parliament, People, and Power.* London: Verso, 1982.

Birch, Anthony H. *The British System of Government.* 6th ed. Boston: Allen and Unwin, 1983.

———. *Political Integration and Disintegration in the British Isles.* Boston: Allen and Unwin, 1977.

Blank, Stephen. "Britain: The Politics of Foreign Economic Policy, the Domestic Economy, and the Problem of Pluralistic Stagnation." *International Organization* 31, no. 4 (1977): 673–721.

Bogdanor, Vernon. *Devolution.* New York: Oxford University Press, 1979.

———. *The People and the Party System.* Cambridge: Cambridge University Press, 1981.

Bradbeer, John. "Environmental Policy." In *Public Policy Under Thatcher,* ed. Stephen P. Savage and Lynton Robins. New York: St. Martin's Press, 1990.

Bradshaw, Jonathan, "Social Security." In *Implementing Thatcherite Policies,* ed. David Marsh and R.A.W. Rhodes. Buckingham: Open University Press, 1992.

Brand, Jack. *British Parliamentary Parties.* Oxford: Clarendon Press, 1992.

Brittan, Samuel. *Steering the Economy.* Harmondsworth, England: Penguin Books, 1971.

Bromhead, Peter. *Private Members' Bills.* London: Routledge, 1956.

Bronowski, J. *The Ascent of Man.* Boston: Little, Brown and Company, 1973.

Budge, Ian, and David McKay, eds. *The Developing British Political System.* 3d ed. New York: Longman, 1994.

Budge, Ian, and Denis Farlie. *Explaining and Predicting Elections.* London: Allen and Unwin, 1983.

Budge, Ian, David Robertson, and David Hearl, eds. *Ideology, Strategy, and Party Change.* Cambridge: Cambridge University Press, 1987.

Bulpitt, Jim. "Continuity, Autonomy, and Peripheralisation: The Anatomy of the Centre's Race Statecraft in England." In *Race, Government, and Politics in Britain,* ed. Zig Layton-Henry and Paul B. Rich. London: Macmillan, 1986.

———. *Territory and Power in the United Kingdom.* Manchester: Manchester University Press, 1983.

Burch, Martin. "Prime Minister and Whitehall." In (eds) *Churchill to Major: The British Prime Ministership Since 1945,* ed. Donald Shell and Richard Hodder-Williams. London: Macmillan, 1995.

Burch, Martin, and Bruce Wood. *Public Policy in Britain.* 2d ed. London: Basil Blackwell, 1990.

Burch, Martin, and Michael Moran. "The Changing British Political Elite, 1945–1983: MPs and Cabinet Ministers." *Parliamentary Affairs* 38, no. 1 (1985):1–15.

Burk, Kathleen, and Alec Cairncross. *Goodbye, Great Britain.* New Haven: Yale University Press, 1992.

Burt, Barbara J., and Max Neiman. "Elite Belief Consistency and the Effect of Position in the Policy-Making Process." *Western Political Quarterly* 40, no. 1 (1987):121–136.

Butler, David. *Governing Without a Majority.* London: Macmillan 1983.

Butler, David, and Anne Sloman. *British Political Facts, 1900–1979.* 5th ed. New York: St. Martin's Press, 1980.

Butler, David, and Austin Ranney. *Referendums.* Washington, D.C.: American Enterprise Institute, 1978.

Butler, David, and Dennis Kavanagh. *The British General Election of 1992.* New York: St. Martin's Press, 1992.

Butler, David, and Donald E. Stokes. *Political Change in Britain.* 2d ed. New York: St. Martin's Press, 1974.

Butler, David, and Gareth Butler. *British Political Facts, 1900–1986.* 6th ed. New York: St. Martin's Press, 1986.

Butler, David, and Richard Rose. *The British General Election of 1959.* New York: St. Martin's Press, 1960.

Butler, David, and Uwe Kitzinger. *The 1975 Referendum.* London: Macmillan, 1976.

Butt, Ronald. *The Power of Parliament.* 2d ed. London: Constable, 1969.

Byrd, Peter, ed. *British Defence Policy: Thatcher and Beyond.* London: Philip Allan, 1991.

———, ed. *British Foreign Policy Under Thatcher.* Oxford: Philip Allan, 1988.

Byrne, Tony. *Local Government in Britain.* 4th ed. London: Penguin Books, 1988.

Cain, Bruce, John Ferejohn, and Morris Fiorina. *The Personal Vote.* Cambridge: Harvard University Press, 1987.

Campbell, Angus, Philip Converse, Warren Miller, and Donald Stokes. *The American Voter.* New York: Wiley, 1961.

Castles, Francis G., ed. *The Comparative History of Public Policy.* Cambridge: Polity Press, 1989.

———. "The Dynamics of Policy Change: What Happened to the English-Speaking Nations in the 1980s." *European Journal of Political Research* 18, no. 4 (1990):491–513.

Catterall, Peter, ed. *Contemporary Britain: An Annual Review, 1990.* New York: Basil Blackwell, 1990.

———, ed. *Contemporary Britain: An Annual Review, 1991.* New York: Basil Blackwell, 1991.

———, ed. *Contemporary Britain: An Annual Review, 1992.* New York: Basil Blackwell, 1992.

Caves, Richard, and Lewis Krause. *Britain's Economic Performance.* Washington, D.C.: Brookings Institution, 1980.

Cawson, Alan. *Corporatism and Political Theory.* Oxford: Basil Blackwell, 1986.

Central Office of Information, *Britain, 1994: An Official Handbook.* London: Her Majesty's Stationery Office, 1993.

Champion, A. G., and A. R. Townsend. *Contemporary Britain: A Geographical Perspective.* London: Edward Arnold, 1990.

Childs, David. *Britain Since 1945.* London: Ernest Benn, 1979.

Christoph, James B. *Capital Punishment and British Politics.* Chicago: University of Chicago Press, 1962.

———. "Thatcher and Organizational Power." Paper presented at Midwest Political Science Association Conference, Chicago, 1990.

Clarke, Harold D., William Mishler, and Paul F. Whiteley. "Recapturing the Falklands: Models of Conservative Popularity, 1979–1983," *British Journal of Political Science* 20, no. 1 (1990):63–81.

Cloke, Paul, ed. *Policy and Change in Thatcher's Britain.* Oxford: Pergamon Press, 1992.

Cobb, Roger W., and Charles D. Elder. *Participation in American Politics: The Dynamics of Agenda Setting.* Baltimore: Johns Hopkins University Press, 1972.

Cohan, Alvin. "Abortion as a Marginal Issue: The Use of Peripheral Mechanisms in Britain and the United States." In *The New Politics of Abortion,* ed. Joni Lovenduski and Joyce Outshoorn. London: Sage Publications, 1986.

"Conservative Economics: Lord Wishful, Lady Rigorous." *Economist,* 24 October 1987, 23–26.

Cook, Chris. *A Short History of the Liberal Party, 1900–1984.* 2d ed. London: Macmillan, 1984.

Crafts, N.F.R., and Nicholas Woodward. *The British Economy Since 1945.* New York: Oxford University Press, 1991.

Crewe, Ivor. "Britain: Two and a Half Cheers for the Atlantic Alliance." In *The Public and Atlantic Defense,* ed. Gregory Flynn and Hans Rattinger. Lanham, Md.: Rowman and Littlefield, 1985.

———. "Is Britain's Two-Party System Really About to Crumble? The Social Democratic-Liberal Alliance and the Prospects for Realignment." *Electoral Studies* 1, no. 2 (1982):275–313.

———. "Has the Electorate Become Thatcherite?" In *Thatcherism,* ed. Robert Skidelsky. London: Chatto and Windus, 1988.

———. "How Labour Was Trounced All Around." *Guardian,* 14 June 1983.

———. "A Nation of Liars? Opinion Polls and the 1992 Election." *Parliamentary Affairs* 45, no. 4 (1992):475–495.

Crewe, Ivor, Bo Sarlvik, and James E. Alt. "Partisan Dealignment in Britain, 1964–74." *British Journal of Political Science* 7, no. 1 (1977):129–190.

Critchfield, Richard. *An American Looks at Britain.* New York: Doubleday Anchor Books, 1990.

Cronin, James. "The Historical Margaret Thatcher." In *Margaret Thatcher: Prime Minister Indomitable,* ed. Juliet L. Thompson and Wayne Thompson. Boulder: Westview Press, 1994.

Crosland, Anthony. *The Future of Socialism.* New York: Schocken Books, 1963.

Crossman, R.H.S. *Diaries of a Cabinet Minister.* 3 vols. London: Hamish Hamilton and Jonathon Cape, 1975, 1976, 1977.

Crossman, Richard. *The Myths of Cabinet Government.* Harvard: Harvard University Press, 1964.

Crynes, Shelly D. Day. "Agenda-Setting on Ethnic Issues: An Analysis of British Policy Towards Northern Ireland, 1968–1972." Master's thesis, Oklahoma State University, 1993.

Curtice, John, and Michael Steed. "Electoral Choice and the Production of Government in the United Kingdom: The Changing Operation of the Electoral System Since 1955." *British Journal of Political Science* 12, no. 2 (1982):249–298.

Dalton, Russell J. *Citizen Politics in Western Democracies.* Chatham, N.J.: Chatham House, 1988.

———. "Political Parties and Political Participation: Party Supporters and Party Elites in Nine Nations." *Comparative Political Studies* 17, no. 2 (1985):267–299.

Dalton, Russell J., and Robert Duval, "The Political Environment and Foreign Policy Opinions: British Attitudes Toward European Integration, 1972–1979," *British Journal of Political Science* 16, no. 1 (1986):113–134.

Dangerfield, George. *The Strange Death of Liberal England*. New York: H. Smith and R. Haas, 1935.

Darwin, John. *Britain and Decolonization: The Retreat from Empire in the Postwar World*. New York: St. Martin's Press, 1988.

Dockrill, Michael. *British Defence Since 1945*. Oxford: Basil Blackwell, 1988.

Dorfman, Gerald. *British Trade Unionism Against the Trade Unions Congress*. London: Macmillan, 1983.

Dowding, Keith. "Beyond Metaphor? Characteristic Explanation of Policy Networks." Paper presented at American Political Science Association conference, New York, 1994.

————. "Government at the Centre." In *Developments in British Politics* 4, ed. Patrick Dunleavy, Andrew Gamble, Ian Holliday and Gillian Peele. New York: St. Martin's Press, 1993.

Drewry, Gavin, ed. *The New Select Committees*. 2d ed. Oxford: Clarendon Press, 1989.

Dunleavy, Patrick. "Democracy in Britain: A Health Check for the 1990s." In *British Elections and Parties Yearbook 1991*, ed. Ivor Crewe, Pippa Norris, David Denver, and David Broughton. Hemel Hempstead, England: Harvester Wheatsheaf, 1992.

————. "The United Kingdom: Paradoxes of an Ungrounded Statism." In *The Comparative History of Public Policy*, ed. Francis G. Castles. Cambridge: Polity Press, 1989.

————. "The Urban Basis of Political Alignment: Social Class, Domestic Property Ownership and State Intervention in Consumption Processes." *British Journal of Political Science* 9, no. 4 (1979):409–443.

Dunleavy, Patrick, Andrew Gamble, Ian Holliday, and Gillian Peele, eds. *Developments in British Politics* 4. New York: St. Martin's Press, 1993.

Dunleavy, Patrick, and Brendan O'Leary. *Theories of the State*. London: Macmillan, 1987.

Durham, Martin. *Moral Crusades: Family and Morality in the Thatcher Years*. New York: New York University Press, 1991.

Eckstein, Harry. *Pressure Group Politics*. London: Allen and Unwin, 1960.

Edwards, John, and Richard Batley. *The Politics of Positive Discrimination*. London: Tavistock, 1978.

Epstein, Leon. *British Politics in the Suez Crisis*. London: Pall Mall Press, 1964.

Evans, Neil. "'A Caring Community'? Personal Social Services in the 1980s." In *Public Policy Under Thatcher*, ed. Stephen P. Savage and Lynton Robins. New York: St. Martin's Press, 1990.

Farnham, David. "Trade Union Policy, 1979–89: Restriction or Reform?" In *Public Policy Under Thatcher*, ed. Stephen P. Savage and Lynton Robins. New York: St. Martin's Press, 1990.

Finer, Samuel. *Pressure Group Politics*. London: Pall Mall Press, 1958.

————, ed. *Adversary Politics and Electoral Reform*. London: Anthony Wigram, 1975.

Fisk, Robert. *The Point of No Return: The Strike Which Broke the British in Ulster*. London: Andre Deutsch, 1975.

FitzGerald, Marian. "Immigration and Race Relations—Political Aspects, no. 15." *New Community* 13, no. 1 (1986):265–271.

Flickinger, Richard S. "British Political Parties and Public Attitudes Toward the European Community: Leading, Following or Getting Out of the Way?" In *British Parties and Elections Yearbook, 1994*, ed. David Broughton, David Farrell, David Denver, and Colin Rallings. London: Frank Cass, 1994.

Flickinger, Richard S., and Donley T. Studlar. "The Disappearing Voters? Exploring Declining Turnout in Western European Elections." *West European Politics* 15, no. 1 (1992):1–16.

Foley, Michael. *The Rise of the British Presidency.* Manchester: Manchester University Press, 1993.

Foot, Paul. *Immigration and Race in British Politics.* Harmondsworth, England: Penguin Books, 1965.

Foulkes, David, J. Barry Jones, and R. A. Wilford, eds. *The Welsh Veto.* Cardiff: University of Wales Press, 1983.

Frankland, E. Gene. "Does Green Politics Have a Future in Britain? An American Perspective." In *Green Politics One,* ed. Wolfgang Rudig. Edinburgh: Edinburgh University Press, 1990.

Franklin, Mark. *The Decline of Class Voting in Britain.* Oxford: Oxford University Press, 1985.

Franklin, Mark N., and Ed Page. "A Critique of the Consumption Cleavage Approach in British Voting Studies." *Political Studies* 32, no. 4 (1984):521–536.

Franklin, Mark, and Philip Norton, eds. *Parliamentary Questions.* Oxford: Clarendon Press, 1993.

Freedman, Lawrence H., and Michael Clarke, eds. *Britain in the World.* Cambridge: Cambridge University Press, 1991.

Freeman, Gary P. "Do Policy Issues Determine Politics? State Pensions Policy." In *Political Economy: Public Policies in the United States and Britain,* ed. Jerold L. Waltman and Donley T. Studlar. Jackson: University Press of Mississippi, 1987.

———. "National Styles and Policy Sectors: Explaining Structured Variation." *Journal of Public Policy* 5, no. 4 (1985):467–496.

Freyman, Jeffrey B. "Industrial Policy: Patterns of Convergence and Divergence." In *Political Economy: Public Policies in the United States and Britain,* ed. Jerold L. Waltman and Donley T. Studlar. Jackson: University Press of Mississippi, 1987.

Friedman, Lester, ed. *British Cinema and Thatcherism.* Minneapolis: University of Minnesota Press, 1993.

Friedman, Milton. *Capitalism and Freedom.* Chicago: University of Chicago Press, 1962.

Frohock, Fred. *Public Policy: Scope and Logic.* Englewood Cliffs, N.J.: Prentice-Hall, 1979.

Furniss, Norman, and Timothy Tilton. *The Case for the Welfare State.* Bloomington: Indiana University Press, 1979.

Gallup, George. *The International Gallup Polls: Public Opinion 1978.* Wilmington, Del.: Scholarly Resources, 1980.

Gallup, George H. *The Gallup International Public Opinion Polls, Great Britain, 1937–1975.* Volume 1, 1937–1964; Volume 2, 1965–1975. New York: Greenwood Press, 1976.

Gamble, Andrew. *The Conservative Nation.* London: Routledge, 1974.

———. *Britain in Decline.* 3d ed. London: Macmillan, 1990.

Gamble, Andrew, and S. A. Walkland. *The British Party System and Economic Policy, 1945–1983.* Oxford: Clarendon Press, 1984.

Garnham, David. "Policy Cultures of Advanced Industrial Democracies." Paper presented at American Political Science Association conference, Washington, D.C., 1991.

Garrett, Geoffrey. "The Political Consequences of Thatcherism." *Political Behavior* 14, no. 4 (1992):361–382.

Gefand, M. David, Martin Loughlin, and Ken Young, eds. "Half a Century of Municpal Decline 1935–1985." London and Winchester, Mass.: Allen and Unwin, 1985.

Gelb, Joyce. *Feminism and Politics.* Berkeley: University of California Press, 1989.

George, Stephen. *Britain and European Integration Since 1945.* New York: Basil Blackwell, 1991.

Goldsworthy, David. *Colonial Issues in British Politics, 1945–1961.* Oxford: Clarendon Press, 1971.

Grant, Wyn. *The Politics of Economic Policy.* London: Harvester Wheatsheaf, 1993.

Greenwood, David. "The Defense Policy of the United Kingdom." In *The Defense Policies of Nations: A Comparative Study,* ed. Douglas J. Murray and Paul R. Viotti. Baltimore: Johns Hopkins University Press, 1982.

Gregory, Jeanne. *Sex, Race, and the Law.* London: Sage Publications, 1987.

Guttsman, W. L. *The British Political Elite.* London: MacGibbon, 1963.

Gwyn, William B., and Richard Rose, eds. *Britain: Progress and Decline.* New Orleans: Tulane Studies in Political Science, 1980.

Hailsham, Lord. *Elective Dictatorship.* London: British Broadcasting Corporation, 1976.

Hall, Peter, ed. *The Political Power of Economic Ideas.* Princeton: Princeton University Press, 1989.

Halper, Thomas. *The Misfortunes of Others.* Cambridge: Cambridge University Press, 1991.

Halsey, A. H. *Change in British Society.* Oxford: Oxford University Press, 1982.

Harrop, Martin, ed. *Power and Policy in Liberal Democracies.* Cambridge: Cambridge University Press, 1992.

Harrop, Martin, and Margaret Scammell. "A Tabloid War." In *The British General Election of 1992,* ed. David Butler and Dennis Kavanagh. New York: St. Martin's Press, 1992.

Hartz, Louis. *The Liberal Tradition in America.* New York: Harcourt Brace and Company, 1955.

Hastings, Max, and Simon Jenkins. *The Battle for the Falklands.* London: Michael Joseph, 1983.

Headey, Bruce. *Housing Policy in the Developed Economy.* New York: St. Martin's Press, 1978.

Heath, Anthony, Roger Jowell, John Curtice. *How Britain Votes.* Oxford: Pergamon Press, 1985.

Heath, Anthony, Roger Jowell, John Curtice, Geoff Evans, Julia Field, and Sharon Witherspoon. *Understanding Political Change.* Oxford: Pergamon Press, 1991.

Heclo, Hugh. "Issue Networks and the Executive Establishment." In *The New American Political System,* ed. Anthony King. Washington, D.C.: American Enterprise Institute, 1978.

———. *Modern Social Politics in Britain and Sweden.* New Haven: Yale University Press, 1974.

Heclo, Hugh, and Aaron Wildavsky. *The Private Government of Public Money.* 2d ed. London: Macmillan, 1981.

Heidenheimer, Arnold, Hugh Heclo, and Carolyn Teich Adams. *Comparative Public Policy.* 3d ed. New York: St. Martin's Press, 1990.

Hennessey, Peter. *Whitehall.* London: Secker and Warburg, 1989.

Hennessey, Peter, and Anthony Seldon, eds. *Ruling Performance: British Government from Attlee to Thatcher.* Oxford: Basil Blackwell, 1987.

Hewison, Robert. *In Anger: British Culture in the Cold War, 1945–1960.* New York: Oxford University Press, 1981.

————. *Too Much: Art and Society in the Sixties, 1960–1975.* New York: Oxford University Press, 1987.

Hewitt, Christopher J. "Policy-making in Postwar Britain: A National-Level of Elitist and Pluralist Hypotheses." *British Journal of Political Science* 4, no. 2 (1974):187–216.

————. "The Power Structure of Britain." Ph.D. diss., Brown University, 1970.

Hibbing, John R., and David Marsh. "Accounting for the Voting Patterns of British MPs on Free Votes." *Legislative Studies Quarterly* 12, no. 2 (1987):275–297.

Hibbing, John R., and Samuel C. Patterson. "'Representing a Territory': Constituency Boundaries for the British House of Commons of the 1980s." *Journal of Politics* 48, no. 4 (1986):992–1005.

Hill, Michael. *The Welfare State in Britain.* Aldershot, England: Edward Elgar, 1993.

Hills, Jill. "Lifestyle Constraints on Formal Political Participation: Why So Few Women Local Government Councillors in Britain." *Electoral Studies* 2, no. 1 (1983):39–52.

Hills, John, ed. *The State of Welfare.* New York: Oxford University Press, 1992.

Hofferbert, Richard, and Ian Budge. "The Party Mandate and the Westminster Model: Election Programmes and Government Spending in Britain, 1945–1985." *British Journal of Political Science* 22, no. 1 (1992):151–182.

Hogwood, Brian. *Trends in British Public Policy.* Buckingham: Open University Press, 1992.

Holliday, Ian. "Organized Interests After Thatcher." In *Developments in British Politics* 4, ed. Patrick Dunleavy, Andrew Gamble, Ian Holliday, and Gillian Peele. New York: St. Martin's Press, 1993.

Holme, Richard, and Michael Elliott, eds. *1688–1988: Time for a New Constitution.* London: Macmillan, 1988.

Hoover, Kenneth, and Raymond Plant. *Conservative Capitalism.* London: Routledge, 1988.

Hughes, Colin, and Patrick Wintour. *Labour Rebuilt: The New Model Party.* London: Fourth Estate, 1991.

Humphry, Derek, and Michael Ward. *Passports and Politics.* Harmondsworth, England: Penguin Books: 1973.

Inglehart, Ronald. *Culture Shift.* Princeton: Princeton University Press, 1990.

————. *The Silent Revolution.* Princeton: Princeton University Press, 1977.

Inglehart, Ronald, and Paul R. Abramson. "Economic Security and Value Change." *American Political Science Review* 88, no. 2 (1994):336–354.

Jackson, Brian, and Dennis Marsden. *Education and the Working Class.* London: Routledge, 1962.

Jackson, Robert J. *Rebels and Whips.* New York: St. Martin's Press, 1968.

Janssen, Joseph I. H. "Postmaterialism, Cognitive Mobilization and Public Support for European Integration." *British Journal of Political Science* 21, no. 4 (October 1991): 443–468.

Jenkins, Peter. *Mrs. Thatcher's Revolution.* Cambridge: Harvard University Press, 1989.

Jenkins, Philip. *Intimate Enemies.* New York: Aldine De Gruyter, 1992.

Jogerst, Michael. *Reform in the Commons.* Lexington: University Press of Kentucky, 1992.

Johnston, R. J., C. J. Pattie, and J. G. Allsopp. *A Nation Dividing?* London: Longman, 1987.

Jones, Charles O. *An Introduction to the Study of Public Policy.* 3d ed. Monterey, Ca.: Brooks/Cole Publishing Company, 1984.

Jordan, A. Grant. "Iron Triangles, Woolly Corporatism and Elastic Nets: Images of the Policy Process." *Journal of Public Policy* 1, no. 1 (1981):95–123.

Jordan, A. Grant, and Jeremy Richardson. "The British Policy Style or the Logic of Negotiation." In *Policy Styles in Western Europe,* ed. Jeremy Richardson. London: Allen and Unwin, 1982.

———. *British Politics and the Policy Process.* London: Unwin Hyman, 1987.

Judge, David. *Backbench Specialisation in the House of Commons.* London: Heinemann, 1983.

Katzenstein, Peter, ed. *Between Power and Plenty.* Madison: University of Wisconsin Press, 1978.

Kavanagh, Dennis. "Crisis Management and Incremental Adaptation in British Politics: The 1931 Crisis of the British Party System." In *Crisis, Choice, and Change,* ed. Gabriel A. Almond, Scott C. Flanagan, and Robert J. Mundt. Boston: Little, Brown and Company, 1973.

———. "Opinion Polls and Elections." In *Democracy at the Polls,* ed. David Butler, Howard Penniman, and Austin Ranney. Washington, D.C.: American Enterprise Institute, 1981.

———. *Thatcherism and British Politics.* New York: Oxford University Press, 1989.

Kazmierczak, Mary E. "British Policy and the Conflict in Northern Ireland." Paper presented at British Politics Group/American Political Science Association conference, Washington, D.C., 1993.

Kennedy, Paul. *The Rise and Fall of the Great Powers.* New York: Random House, 1987.

Kenney, Sally J. *For Whose Protection?* Ann Arbor: University of Michigan Press, 1993.

Keohane, Robert. "The World Political Economy and the Crisis of Embedded Liberalism." In *Order and Conflict in Contemporary Capitalism,* ed. John Goldthorpe. Oxford: Clarendon Press, 1984.

Key, V. O. *Public Opinion and American Democracy.* New York: Knopf, 1961.

King, Anthony. "Ideas, Institutions, and the Policies of Government: A Comparative Analysis, Parts I and II." *British Journal of Political Science* 3, nos. 2 and 3 (1973):291–313, 409–423.

———. "Modes of Executive-Legislative Relations: Great Britain, France, and West Germany." *Legislative Studies Quarterly* 1, no. 1 (1976):37–65.

———. "Overload: Problems of Governing in the 1970s." *Political Studies* 23, no. 2 (1975):284–296.

———. "The Rise of the Career Politician in Britain—and Its Consequences." *British Journal of Political Science* 11, no. 2 (1981):249–285.

———. "What Do Elections Decide?" In *Democracy at the Polls,* ed. David Butler, Howard Penniman, and Austin Ranney. Washington, DC: American Enterprise Institute, 1981.

King, Desmond. *The New Right.* London: Macmillan, 1987.

Kirchner, Emil. "A Third Level of Government: Britain in the European Community." In *The Developing British Political System,* ed. Ian Budge and David McKay. London: Longman, 1994.

Kitzinger, Uwe. *Diplomacy and Persuasion.* London: Hudson, 1973.

Klein, Rudolf. *The Politics of the National Health Service.* 2d ed. London: Longman, 1989.

Koestler, Arthur, ed. *Suicide of a Nation?* New York: Macmillan, 1964.

Kogan, David, and Maurice Kogan. *The Battle for the Labour Party.* London: Fontana, 1982.

Krammick, Isaac, ed. *Is Britain Dying?* Ithaca: Cornell University Press, 1979.

Layton-Henry, Zig. *The Politics of Immigration.* Boston: Allen and Unwin, 1984.

Lazer, Harry. "The Referendum and the British Constitution." In *Dilemmas of Change in British Politics,* ed. Donley T. Studlar and Jerold L. Waltman. London: Macmillan, 1984.

Lewis-Beck, Michael S. *Economics and Elections.* Ann Arbor: University of Michigan Press, 1988.

Lijphart, Arend. *Democracies.* New Haven: Yale University Press, 1984.

———. "Review Article: The Northern Ireland Problem—Cases, Theories, and Solutions." *British Journal of Political Science* 5, no. 1 (1975):83–106.

Lipset, Seymour Martin. *Continental Divide.* New York: Routledge, 1989.

Loughlin, Martin, M. David Gelfand, and Ken Young, eds. *Half a Century of Muncipal Decline, 1935–1985.* London: Allen and Unwin, 1985.

Lowi, Theodore J. "American Business, Public Policy, Case Studies, and Political Theory." *World Politics* 16, no. 4 (1964):677–715.

Lynn, Jonathon, and Antony Jay. *Yes, Minister: The Complete Diaries of a Cabinet Minister.* London: British Broadcasting Corporation, 1984.

McAllister, Ian, and Anthony Mughan. "Attitudes, Issues and Labor Party Decline in England, 1974–1979." *Comparative Political Studies* 18, no. 1 (1985):37–57.

McAllister, Ian, and Donley T. Studlar. "Bandwagon, Underdog, or Projection? Opinion Polls and Electoral Choice in Britain, 1979–87." *Journal of Politics* 53, no. 3 (1991):720–741.

———. "The Electoral Geography of Immigrant Groups in Britain." *Electoral Studies* 3, no. 2 (1984):139–150.

———. "Region and Voting in Britain, 1979–1987: Territorial Polarization or Artifact?" *American Journal of Political Science* 36, no. 1 (1992):168–199.

———. "Popular Versus Elite Views of Privatization: The Case of Britain." *Journal of Public Policy* 9, no. 1 (1989):157–178.

McCombs, Maxwell E., and Donald L. Shaw. "The Agenda-Setting Function of the Mass Media." *Public Opinion Quarterly* 36, no. 2 (1972):176–187.

McCormick, John. "Environmental Politics." In *Developments in British Politics* 4, ed. Patrick Dunleavy, Andrew Gamble, Ian Holliday, and Gillian Peele. New York: St. Martin's Press, 1993.

McGlone, Francis. "Away from the Dependency Culture? Social Security Policy." In *Public Policy Under Thatcher,* ed. Stephen P. Savage and Lynton Robins. New York: St. Martin's Press, 1990.

McKenzie, Robert T. *British Political Parties.* 2d ed. New York: St. Martin's Press, 1963.

McKenzie, Robert T., and Alan Silver. *Angels in Marble.* Chicago: University of Chicago Press, 1968.

McKie, David, ed. *The Election: A Voter's Guide.* London: Fourth Estate, 1992.

Marsh, Alan. "The Silent Revolution, Value Priorities, and the Quality of Life in Britain." *American Political Science Review* 69, no. 1 (1975):21–30.

Marsh, David. "Industrial Relations." In *Implementing Thatcherite Policies,* ed. David Marsh and R.A.W. Rhodes. Buckingham: Open University Press, 1992.

Marsh, David, and Melvyn Read. *Private Members' Bills.* Cambridge: Cambridge University Press, 1988.

Marsh, David, and R.A.W. Rhodes, eds. *Implementing Thatcherite Policies.* Buckingham: Open University Press, 1992.

Marshall, T. H. *Social Policy.* London: Hutchinson, 1965.

Marwick, Arthur. *Culture in Britain Since 1945.* London: Basil Blackwell, 1991.

Meehan, Elizabeth. *Women's Rights at Work.* London: Macmillan, 1985.

Meier, Kenneth J. *Politics and the Bureaucracy.* 3d ed. Pacific Grove, Ca.: Brooks/Cole Publishing Company, 1993.

Michelmann, Hans J. "Britain and the European Community." In *Dilemmas of Change in British Politics,* ed. Donley T. Studlar and Jerold L. Waltman. London: Macmillan, 1983.

Middlemas, Keith. *Politics in Industrial Society.* London: Andre Deutsch, 1980.

Miller, William L. "The De-Nationalisation of British Politics: The Re-emergence of the Periphery." In *Change in British Politics,* ed. Hugh Berrington. London: Frank Cass, 1984.

————. *Electoral Dynamics in Britain Since 1918.* London: Macmillan, 1977.

————. *Media and Voters.* Oxford: Clarendon Press, 1991.

————. "What Was the Profit in Following the Crowd? The Effectiveness of Party Strategies on Immigration and Devolution." *British Journal of Political Science* 11, no. 1 (1981):15–38.

Milner, Helen. "Maintaining Commitments in Trade Policy." In *Do Institutions Matter?* ed. R. Kent Weaver and Bert A. Rockman. Washington, D.C.: Brookings Institution, 1993.

Minkin, Louis. *The Labour Party Conference.* 2d ed. Manchester: Manchester University Press, 1980.

Moon, Jeremy. *Innovative Leadership in Democracy.* Aldershot, England: Dartmouth, 1993.

Moore, Barrington. *Social Origins of Dictatorship and Democracy.* Boston: Beacon Press, 1967.

Morgan, Kenneth. *The People's Peace.* New York: Oxford University Press, 1990.

Morris, Jan. *Farewell the Trumpets.* New York: Harcourt Brace Jovanovich, 1978.

Morris, Terence. *Crime and Criminal Justice Since 1945.* New York: Basil Blackwell, 1989.

Mosley, Paul. "Economic Policy." In *Developments in British Politics* 2, ed. Henry Rucker, Patrick Dunleavy, Andrew Gamble, and Gillian Peele. New York: St. Martin's Press, 1988.

Moss, Robert. *The Collapse of Democracy.* New Rochelle, N.Y.: Arlington House, 1976.

Muller, William D. *The Kept Men? The First Century of Trade Union Representation in the House of Commons, 1874–1975.* London: Harvester Press, 1977.

Nairn, Tom. *The Breakup of Britain.* 2d ed. London: New Left Books, 1981.

Neustadt, Richard E. *Alliance Politics.* New York: Columbia University Press, 1970.

————. "Whitehouse and Whitehall." *Public Interest* 2, no. 1 (1966):55–69.

Neustadt, Richard E., and Ernest R. May. *Thinking in Time.* New York: Free Press, 1986.

Newton, Kenneth. "Caring and Competence: The Long, Long Campaign." In King et al., *Britain at the Polls, 1992.* Chatham, N.J.: Chatham House, 1993.

————. "Do People Read Everything They Believe in the Papers? Newspapers and Voters in the 1983 and 1987 Elections." In *British Elections and Parties Yearbook 1991,* ed. Ivor Crewe, Pippa Norris, David Denver, and David Broughton. London: Harvester Wheatsheaf, 1992.

Nicholson, Max. *The System: The Misgovernment of Modern Britain.* London: Hodder and Stoughton, 1967.

Nixon, Jaqi. "The Home Office and Race Relations Policy: Co-ordinator or Initiator?" *Journal of Public Policy* 2, no. 2 (1982):365–378.

Norpoth, Helmut. *Confidence Regained: Economics, Mrs. Thatcher, and the British Voter.* Ann Arbor: University of Michigan Press, 1992.

Norris, Pippa. "Thatcher's Enterprise Society and Electoral Change." *West European Politics* 13, no. 1:63–78.

———. "Women's Legislative Participation in Western Europe." *West European Politics* 8, no. 1 (1985):90–101.

Norris, Pippa, and Joni Lovenduski. *Political Representation and Recruitment.* Cambridge: Cambridge University Press, 1994.

———. "Women Candidates for Parliament: Transforming the Agenda?" *British Journal of Political Science* 19, no. 1 (1989):106–115.

Northedge, F.E.S. *Descent from Power: British Foreign Policy, 1945–73.* London: Allen and Unwin, 1974.

Norton, Philip. *The British Polity.* 2d ed. New York: Longman, 1991.

———. "Choosing a Leader: Margaret Thatcher and the Parliamentary Conservative Party, 1989–90." *Parliamentary Affairs* 43, no. 2 (1990):249–257.

———. *Dissension in the House of Commons, 1945–1974.* London: Macmillan, 1975.

———. *Dissension in the House of Commons, 1974–1979.* Oxford: Clarendon Press, 1980.

———. "'The Lady's Not for Turning,' but What About the Rest? Margaret Thatcher and the Conservative Party, 1979–89," *Parliamentary Affairs* 43, no. 1 (1990):41–58.

Norton, Philip, and Arthur Aughey. *Conservatives and Conservatism.* London: Temple Smith, 1981.

Norton, Philip, and David Wood. *Back from Westminster.* Lexington: University Press of Kentucky, 1993.

Nossiter, Bernard. *Britain: A Future That Works.* Boston: Little, Brown and Company, 1978.

Nugent, Neil. "The European Dimension." In *Developments in British Politics* 4, ed. Patrick Dunleavy, Andrew Gamble, Ian Holliday, and Gillian Peele. New York: St. Martin's Press, 1993.

Oakland, John. *British Civilization.* London: Routledge, 1989.

Olson, Mancur. *The Rise and Decline of Nations.* New Haven: Yale University Press, 1982.

Parry, Geraint, George Moyser, and Neil Day. *Political Participation in Britain.* Cambridge: Cambridge University Press, 1992.

Parry, Richard. "Social Policy." In *Developments in British Politics* 2, ed. Henry Drucker, Patrick Dunleavy, Andrew Gamble, and Gillian Peele. New York: St. Martin's Press, 1986.

Pennock, J. Roland. "Agricultural Subsidies in England and America." *American Political Science Review* 56, no. 3 (1962):621–633.

Peters, B. Guy. *European Politics Reconsidered.* New York: Holmes and Meier, 1991.

Pierson, Chris. "Social Policy." In *Developments in British Politics* 4, ed. Patrick Dunleavy, Andrew Gamble, Ian Holliday, and Gillian Peele. New York: St. Martin's Press, 1993.

Pierson, Paul D., and R. Kent Weaver. "Imposing Losses in Pension Policy." In *Do Institutions Matter? Government Capabilities in the United States and Abroad,* ed. R. Kent Weaver, and Bert A. Rockman. Washington, D.C.: Brookings Institution, 1993.

Pollard, Sydney. *The Wasting of the British Economy.* 2d ed. London: Macmillan, 1984.

Punnett, R. M. *British Government and Politics.* 4th ed. London: Heineman, 1980.

———. *British Government and Politics.* 5th ed. Chicago: Dorsey Press, 1988.

———. *Front-Bench Opposition.* New York: St. Martin's Press, 1973.

Putnam, Robert D. *The Beliefs of Politicians.* New Haven: Yale University Press, 1973.

———. *The Comparative Study of Political Elites.* Englewood Cliffs. N.J.: Prentice-Hall, 1976.

Pym, Bridget. *Pressure Groups and the Permissive Society.* Newton Abbott, England: David and Clarks.

Randall, Vicky. *Women in Politics.* 2d ed. Chicago: University of Chicago Press, 1987.

Ranney, Austin. *Pathways to Parliament.* Madison: University of Wisconsin Press, 1965.

Rasmussen, Jorgen. *The British Political Process.* Belmont, Ca.: Wadsworth, 1993.

————. "Is Parliament Revolting?" In *Dilemmas of Change in British Politics,* ed. Donley T. Studlar and Jerold L. Waltman. London: Macmillan, 1984.

Rasmussen, Jorgen, and James M. McCormick. "British Mass Perceptions of the Anglo-American Special Relationship." *Political Science Quarterly* 108, no. 3 (1993):515–541.

Rhodes, R.A.W. "Policy Networks: A British Perspective." *Journal of Theoretical Politics* 2, no. 2 (1990):293–317.

Richards, Peter. *Parliament and Conscience.* London: Allen and Unwin, 1970.

Richardson, Jeremy, ed. *Policy Styles in Western Europe.* London: Allen and Unwin, 1982.

Riddell, Peter. *The Thatcher Decade.* New York: Basil Blackwell, 1989.

Ripley, Randall B. *Policy Analysis in Political Science.* Chicago: Nelson-Hall, 1985.

Ripley, Randall B., and Grace Franklin. *Congress, the Bureaucracy, and Public Policy.* 5th ed. Pacific Grove, Ca.: Brooks/Cole Publishing Company, 1991.

Robertson, David. "Preserving Order and Administering Justice: Other Faces of Government in Britain." In *The Developing British Political System: The 1990s,* ed. Ian Budge and David McKay. New York: Longman, 1993.

Robertson, David Brian. "Labor Market Surgery, Labor Market Abandonment: The Thatcher and Reagan Unemployment Remedies." In *Political Economy: Public Policies in the United States and Britain,* ed. Jerold L. Waltman and Donley T. Studlar. Jackson: University Press of Mississippi, 1987.

Rose, E.J.B. et al. *Color and Citizenship.* New York: Oxford University Press, 1969.

Rose, Richard. "Comparative Policy Analysis: The Programme Approach." In *Comparing Pluralist Democracies,* ed. Mattei Dogan. Boulder: Westview Press, 1988.

————. *Do Parties Make a Difference?* Chatham, N.J.: Chatham House, 1980.

————. *Governing Without Consensus.* New York: Oxford University Press, 1969.

————. "Inheritance Before Choice in Public Policy." *Journal of Theoretical Politics* 2, no. 2 (1990):263–291.

————. *Lesson-Drawing in Public Policy.* Chatham, N.J.: Chatham House, 1993.

————. "On the Priorities of Citizenship in the Deep South and Northern Ireland." *Journal of Politics* 38, no. 2 (1976):247–291.

————. *Ordinary People in Public Policy.* Newbury Park, Ca.: Sage Publications, 1989.

————. *Politics in England.* 2d ed. Boston: Little, Brown and Company, 1974.

————. *Politics in England.* 5th ed. Boston: Little, Brown and Company, 1989.

————. "Still the Era of Party Government?" *Parliamentary Affairs* 26, no. 2 (1983):282–299.

————. *The Territorial Dimension in Government.* Chatham, N.J.: Chatham House, 1982.

————. *Understanding Big Government.* London: Sage Publications, 1984.

————. "Ungovernability: Is There Fire Behind the Smoke?" *Political Studies* 27, no. 3 (1979):351–370.

Rose, Richard, and Dennis Kavanagh. "The Monarchy in Contemporary Political Culture." *Comparative Politics* 8, no. 4 (1976):548–576.

Rose, Richard, and Derek W. Urwin. "Social Cohesion, Political Parties and Strains in Regimes." *Comparative Political Studies* 2, no. 1 (1969):7–67.

Rose, Richard, and Ian McAllister. "The Loyalties of Voters." London: Sage Publications, 1990.

Rose, Richard, Ian McAllister, and Peter Mair. *Is There a Concurring Majority About Northern Ireland?* University of Strathclyde Studies in Public Policy No. 22. Glasgow, 1978.

Rudig, Wolgang, and Philip D. Lowe. "The Withered Greening of British Politics." *Political Studies* 34, no. 2 (1986):262–284.

Rudolph, Joseph R., Jr. "Energy Policy in the United States and Britain." In Jerold L. Waltman *Political Economy: Public Policies in the United States and Britain,* ed. Jerold L. Waltman and Donley T. Studlar. Jackson: University Press of Mississippi, 1987.

Rush, Michael, ed. *Parliament and Pressure Groups.* Oxford: Oxford University Press, 1990.

Sabatier, Paul A., and Hank C. Jenkins-Smith, eds. *Policy Change and Learning: An Advocacy Coalition Approach.* Boulder: Westview Press, 1993.

Saggar, Shamit. *Race and Politics in Britain.* London: Harvester Wheatsheaf, 1992.

Sampson, Anthony. *The Anatomy of Britain.* London: Hodder and Stoughton, 1962.

———. *The Anatomy of Britain Today.* New York: Harper Colophon Books, 1965.

———. *The Changing Anatomy of Britain.* New York: Random House, 1982.

———. *The Essential Anatomy of Britain.* New York: Harcourt Brace and Company, 1993.

———. *The New Anatomy of Britain.* London: Hodder and Stoughton, 1971.

Sanders, David, "Relations with Outside Governments: Foreign and Military Policy." In *The Developing British Political System: The 1990s,* ed. Ian Budge and David McKay. New York: Longman, 1993.

Sanders, David, Hugh Ward, David Marsh, and Tony Fletcher. "Government Popularity and the Falklands War: A Reassessment." *British Journal of Political Science* 17, no. 3 (1987):281–313.

Sanderson, John B. "The National Smoke Abatement Society and the Clean Air Act." *Political Studies* 9, no. 2 (1961):236–253.

Sarlvik, Bo, and Ivor Crewe. *Decade of Dealignment.* Cambridge: Cambridge University Press, 1983.

Savage, Stephen P. "A War of Crime? Law and Order Policy in the 1980s." In *Public Policy Under Thatcher,* ed. Stephen P. Savage and Lynton Robins. New York: St. Martin's Press, 1990.

Savage, Stephen P., and Lynton Robins, eds. *Public Policy Under Thatcher.* New York: St. Martin's Press, 1990.

Schattschneider, E. E. *The Semi-Sovereign People.* New York: Holt, Rinehart and Winston, 1960.

Schick, Allen. "Governments Versus Budget Deficits." *Do Institutions Matter?* In ed. R. Kent Weaver and Bert A. Rockman. Washington, D.C.: Brookings Institution, 1993.

Schmitter, Philippe. "Still the Century of Corporatism?" *Review of Politics* 36, no. 1 (1974):85–131.

Schumpeter, Joseph. *Socialism, Capitalism, and Democracy.* 3d ed. New York: Harper Colophon Books, 1962.

Schwartz, Nathan. "Housing Policy: Coverging Trends, Diverging Futures." In *Political Economy: Public Policies in the United States and Britain,* ed. Jerold L. Waltman and Donley T. Studlar. Jackson: University Press of Mississippi, 1987.

Searing, Donald D. "A Theory of Political Socialization." *British Journal of Political Science* 16, no. 3 (1986):341–376.

————. *Westminster's World.* Cambridge: Harvard University Press, 1994.

Sedgemore, Brian. *The Secret Constitution.* London: Hodder and Stoughton, 1980.

Self, Peter, and Herbert Storing. *The State and the Farmer.* 2d ed. London: Allen and Unwin, 1971.

Seyd, Patrick, and Paul Whiteley. *Labour's Grassroots.* Oxford: Clarendon Press. 1992.

Seymour-Ure, Colin. "Managing Media Relations: The Prime Minister and the Public." In *Churchill to Major: The British Prime Ministership Since 1945,* ed. Donald Shell and Richard Hodder-Williams. London: Macmillan, 1995.

Shanks, Michael. *The Stagnant Society.* Harmondsworth: Penguin Books, 1961.

Shapiro, Andrew L. *We're Number One!* New York: Vintage, 1992.

Sharpe, L. J. "The Labor Party and the Geography of Inequality: A Puzzle." In *The Politics of the Labor Party,* ed. Dennis Kavanagh. London: Allen and Unwin, 1982.

Shell, Donald. *The House of Lords.* 2d ed. Hemel Hempstead, England: Harvester Wheatsheaf, 1992.

Shell, Donald, and Richard Hodder-Williams. *Churchill to Major: The British Prime Ministership Since 1945.* London: Macmillan, 1995.

Shonfield, Andrew. *Modern Capitalism.* New York: Oxford University Press, 1965.

Sked, Alan, and Chris Cook. *Post-War Britain.* 3rd ed. New York: Penguin Books, 1990.

Smith, Michael, Steve Smith, and Brian White, eds. *British Foreign Policy.* London: Unwin Hyman, 1988.

Smith, T. Alexander. *The Comparative Policy Process.* Santa Barbara, Ca.: ABC-Clio, 1975.

Spanier, John, and Eric M. Uslaner. *American Foreign Policy Making and the Democratic Dilemmas.* 5th ed. Pacific Grove, Ca.: Brooks/Cole Publishing Company, 1989.

Stanworth, Philip, and Anthony Giddens, eds. *Elites and Power in British Society.* Cambridge: Cambridge University Press, 1974.

Steel, David. *No Entry.* London: Hurst, 1969.

Steiner, Jurg. *European Politics.* 2d ed. New York: Longman, 1991.

Steinmo, Sven. *Taxation and Democracy.* New Haven: Yale University Press, 1994.

Studlar, Donley T. "British Public Opinion, Colour Issues, and Enoch Powell: A Longitudinal Analysis." *British Journal of Political Science* 4, no. 2 (1974):371–381.

————. "Elite Responsiveness or Elite Autonomy: British Immigration Policy Reconsidered." *Ethnic and Racial Studies* 3, no. 2 (1980):207–223.

————. "The Influence of British Political Candidates on Public Attitudes Toward Immigrants." *Plural Societies* 10, no. 1 (1979):103–114.

————. "Policy Voting in Britain: The Colored Immigration Issue in the British General Elections of 1964, 1968, and 1970." *American Political Science Review* 72, no. 1. (1978):46–64.

Studlar, Donley T., and Ian McAllister. "A Changing Political Agenda? The Structure of Political Attitudes in Britain, 1974–1987." *International Journal of Public Opinion Research* 4, no. 2 (1992):148–176.

————. "Protest and Survive? Alliance Support in the 1983 British General Election." *Political Studies* 35, no. 1 (1987):39–60.

Studlar, Donley T., Ian McAllister, and Alvaro Ascui. "Privatization and the British Electorate: Microeconomic Policies, Macroeconomic Evaluations and Party Support." *American Journal of Political Science* 34, no. 4 (1990):1077–1101.

Studlar, Donley T., and Susan Welch. "Mass Attitudes on Political Issues in Britain." *Comparative Political Studies* 14, no. 3 (1981):327–355.

Tant, A. P. *British Government: The Triumph of Elitism*. Brookfield, Vt.: Ashgate Publishers, 1993.

Tatalovich, Raymond, and Byron W. Daynes, eds. *Social Regulatory Policy*. Boulder: Westview Press, 1988.

Taylor-Gooby, Peter. *Public Opinion, Ideology, and State Welfare*. London: Routledge and Kegan Paul, 1985.

Thomas, Hugh. *The Establishment*. London: Blond, 1959.

————. *The Suez Affair*. London: Weidenfeld and Nicolson, 1966.

Togeby, Lise. "Political Implications of Increasing Numbers of Women in the Labor Force." *Comparative Political Studies* 27, no. 2 (1994):211–240.

Tomlinson, Jim. *British Macroeconomic Policy Since 1940*. London: Croom Helm, 1985.

Turner, R. H. "Sponsored and Contest Mobility and the School System." *American Sociological Review* 25, no. 6 (1960):855–867.

Tyrrell, R. Emmett, ed. *The Future That Doesn't Work*. Garden City, N.Y.: Doubleday Books, 1977.

Vogel, David. "Representing Diffuse Interests in Environmental Policymaking." In *Do Institutions Matter?* ed. R. Kent Weaver and Bert A. Rockman. Washington, D.C.: Brookings Institution, 1993.

Wald, Kenneth D. *Crosses on the Ballot*. Princeton: Princeton University Press, 1983.

Walker, Jack L. "Setting the Agenda in the U.S. Senate: A Theory of Problem Selection." *British Journal of Political Science* 7, no. 4 (1977):423–445.

Waltman, Jerold L. "Changing the Course of Tax Policy: Convergent in Intent, Divergent in Practice." In *Political Economy: Public Policies in the United States and Britain*, ed. Jerold L. Waltman and Donley T. Studlar. Jackson: University Press of Mississippi, 1987.

————. "Judicial Activism in England." In *Judicial Activism in Comparative Perspective*, ed. Kenneth M. Holland. New York: St. Martin's Press, 1991.

————. "The Strength of Policy Inheritance." In *Political Economy: Public Policies in the United States and Britain*, ed. Jerold L. Waltman and Donley T. Studlar. Jackson: University Press of Mississippi, 1987.

Waltman, Jerold L., and Donley T. Studlar, eds. *Political Economy: Public Policies in the United States and Britain*. Jackson: University Press of Mississippi, 1987.

Waltz, Kenneth. *Foreign Policy and Democratic Politics*. Boston: Little, Brown and Company, 1967.

Ward, Hugh, with David Samways and Ted Benton. "Environmental Policy." In *Developments in British Politics* 3, ed. Patrick Dunleavy, Andrew Gamble, and Gillian Peele. New York: St. Martin's Press, 1990.

Weale, Albert. "Social Policy." In *Developments in British Politics* 3, ed. Patrick Dunleavy, Andrew Gamble, and Gillian Peele. New York: St. Martin's Press, 1990.

Weaver, R. Kent, and Bert A. Rockman, eds. *Do Institutions Matter? Government Capabilities in the United States and Abroad*. Washington, D.C.: Brookings Institution, 1993.

Webb, Paul. *Trade Unions and the British Electorate*. Aldershot, England: Dartmouth, 1992.

Weir, Margaret, and Theda Skocpol. "State Structures and the Possibilities for 'Keynesian' Responses to the Great Depression in Sweden, Britain, and the United States." In *Bringing the State Back In*, ed. Peter B. Evans, Dietrich Rueschemeyer, and Theda Skocpol. Cambridge: Cambridge University Press, 1985.

White, Brian C. "British Foreign Policy: Tradition and Change." *In Foreign Policy in World Politics*, ed. Roy C. Macridis. 8th ed. Englewood Cliffs, N.J.: Prentice Hall, 1992.

Whiteley, Paul. "Economic Policy." In *Developments in British Politics* 3, ed. Patrick Dunleavy, Andrew Gamble, and Gillian Peele. New York: St. Martin's Press, 1990.

———. *The Labour Party in Crisis.* New York, Methuen, 1983.

Whiteley, Paul, Patrick Seyd, Jeremy Richardson, and Paul Bissell. "Thatcher and the Conservative Party." *Political Studies* 42, no. 2 (1994):185–203.

Whitty, Geoff. "The Politics of the 1988 Education Reform Act." In *Developments in British Politics* 3, ed. Patrick Dunleavy, Andrew Gamble, and Gillian Peele. New York: St. Martin's Press, 1990.

Wichert, Sabine. *Northern Ireland Since 1945.* New York: Longman, 1991.

Wiener, Martin J. *English Culture and the Decline of the Industrial Spirit, 1850–1980.* Cambridge: Cambridge University Press, 1981.

Wilensky, Harold. *The Welfare State and Equality.* Berkeley: University of California Press, 1975.

Wilks, Stephen. "Economic Policy." In *Developments in British Politics* 4, ed. Patrick Dunleavy, Andrew Gamble, Ian Holliay, and Gillian Peele. New York: St. Martin's Press, 1993.

Williams, John H. P. "Britain and the European Community: Maverick or Insider?" Paper presented at British Politics Group/American Political Science Association conference, Washington, D.C., 1993.

Williams, N. J., J. B. Sewell and F. E. Twine. "Council House Sales and the Electorate: Voting Behaviour and Ideological Implications." *Housing Studies* 2, no. 4 (1987):274–282.

Wilson, H. W. *Pressure Group.* London: Secker and Warburg, 1961.

Wolf, T. Phillip. "Seats for Cheats: Reapportionment in the House of Commons." Paper presented at American Political Science Association conference, New York, 1978.

Worcester, Robert M., ed. *Public Opinion Polling: An International Review.* New York: St. Martin's Press, 1983.

Wright, Peter. *Spycatcher.* New York: Viking, 1987.

Wybrow, Robert J. *Britain Speaks Out, 1937–1987.* London: Macmillan, 1989.

Zahariadis, Nikolaos. *Markets, States, and Public Policy: Privatization in Britain and France.* Ann Arbor: University of Michigan Press, 1995.

About the Book and Author

THIS THOUGHTFUL INTRODUCTION to British politics explores a country undergoing a painful transition as the twenty-first century approaches. Informed throughout by a comparative public policy perspective, this book surveys British policy, institutions, and behavior since World War II. Donley Studlar analyzes challenges facing contemporary Britain and suggests the likely official responses in areas ranging from constitutional change to foreign policy. Considering issues such as domestic economic and social welfare policy, Studlar also looks at noneconomic regulation of individual behavior and group relations—especially as it applies to minorities. Weaving together a wealth of material, Studlar assesses the future course of Britain at a crucial time in its development.

Donley T. Studlar is Eberly Family Distinguished Professor of Political Science at West Virginia University. Since 1994, he has served as executive secretary of the British Politics Group.

Index

Abortion, 12, 80, 187, 188, 189, 193, 194, 202, 203, 213
Acheson, Dean, 1
Acquired Immune Deficiency Syndrome (AIDS), 205
Act of Settlement (1701), 38–39
Act of Succession, (1701) 61
Act of Union, (1706) 20
Adams, Carolyn, 170
Aden, 122
adversary politics, 5, 11, 71, 157, 213, 222
advocacy coalitions, 9
Africa, 24, 118, 122, 189
agendas, 115, 133, 177, 188, 189, 195, 203, 206, 207, 222, 223, 224
agenda setting, 8, 9, 20, 77, 79, 106, 107, 133–134, 166–168, 188
agriculture, 22, 46, 85, 112, 113–114, 119, 150, 153
Algeria, 118
Alliance of Liberals and Social Democrats, 44, 86, 87, 98
Almond, Gabriel, 72–73
American Revolution, 39–40
Americas, 118
Anatomy of Britain, The, 3
Angles, 19, 28
Anglo-American, 127
Anglo-American special relationship, 6, 112, 125, 221
Anglo-Irish Accord, 200
Anglo-Saxons, 28
Angola, 119
Anne, Queen, 39
Anonymous Empire, 79
Antarctica, 24
Arab, 138
Archbishop of Canterbury, 30, 41
arenas of power, 8
Argentina, 122, 123, 126
army, 198, 199
aristocracy, 22, 23, 27, 37, 38
Asia, 24, 25, 29, 118, 126, 189
Aswan High Dam, 120
Atlantic Alliance, 126, 127, 141
Attlee, Clement, 90, 125, 140, 145, 151, 159, 166
Australia, 24, 25, 55, 77, 119, 120, 156, 177, 217

Backbenchers, 45, 51, 52, 59, 69, 97, 116, 122, 123, 193, 195, 201, 206
Bagehot, Walter, 4, 37

Bangladesh, 29, 139, 195
Bank of England, 82, 134, 135, 136
Baptists, 18
Barnett, Corelli, 8
Battle of Britain, 25
Baumgartner, Frank, 223
Beeching, Richard, 152
Beer, Samuel, 11
Belgics, 19
Belgium, 29, 111, 112, 125
Benn, Tony, 68, 145, 157, 223
Berlin, 126
Beveridge Report, 166, 171
Beveridge, William, 166, 167
Bevin, Ernest, 125, 141, 149
bill of rights, 6, 192, 216, 217, 224
Bill of Rights (1689), 38–39
Birmingham, 29
Black Rod, 41
Black Wednesday, 114, 135
Blair, Tony, 89, 97, 145
Boundary Commission, 92–93
Breton Woods, 26
British Broadcasting Corporation (BBC), 10, 75–76, 145
British Coal, 84
British Council, 205
British Election Studies, 72
British Empire, 24, 107
British Nationality Act, 122
Brussels, 109, 111, 117,
Brussels Pact, 125
Buckingham Palace, 41
Bulpitt, Jim, 10, 69, 197, 207, 222
Bundebank, 82, 114, 160
bureaucracy, 52, 55, 56–59, 70, 110, 116, 135, 157, 168, 192, 216
Burke, Edmund, 70
business, 17, 27, 80, 81, 82, 85, 156
Butler, David, 145, 149
Butler, R.A.B., 90, 142
Butskellism, 90, 142, 157, 166, 169, 222
by-elections, 71, 87

C-SPAN, 2
Cabinet, 113, 116, 121, 134, 195

Cabinet ministers, 34, 37, 39, 41, 45, 47, 49, 50, 51–56, 61, 97, 108, 110, 113, 216
Cabinet Office, 53, 56
Calais, 17
Callaghan, James, 122, 138, 176, 190
Cambridge, 137, 174
Campaign for Nuclear Disarmament, 109, 125, 126
Canada, 24, 25, 118, 119, 125, 141, 177
capital punishment, 80, 98, 187, 188, 191, 193, 194, 213, 216
capitalism, 23, 113, 138
Caribbean Sea, 24
Castle, Barbara, 53
Celts, 19, 28, 86, 116
Central African Federation, 118
Central Office, 94
Central Policy Review Staff, 57, 141
censorship, 188, 205
Chancellor of the Exchequer, 57, 90, 96, 97, 135, 142, 154
Channel Four, 175
Channel Tunnel, 154
Charles I, King, 38
Charles II, King, 38
Charter 88, 68
China, 24, 123, 195
Christoph, James, 193
Churchill, Winston, 90, 106, 117, 151
Church of England, 2, 10, 18, 22, 23, 30, 39, 42, 56
Church of Scotland, 18
Circular 7/65, 175, 177
Citizen's Charter, 59, 192
City of London, 10, 82, 134, 135, 140
civil liberties, 188
civil rights, 198
Civil service. See Bureaucracy
class, social, 23, 27, 30, 31, 46, 62, 67, 86, 87, 88, 90, 93, 94, 95, 98, 148, 150, 178, 182, 224
Clause IV, 133, 143
coal miners, 148
Cohan, Alvin, 188
Cold War, 4, 12, 59, 123, 126, 127, 128, 220
Commission for Racial Equality, 191
Committee of Permanent Representatives (COREPOR), 109, 111, 117
Common Agricultural Policy, 5, 113, 114, 119, 153
Commonwealth, 12, 38, 40, 106, 107, 108, 111, 112, 118, 119, 120, 125, 127, 196, 198
Commonwealth Immigrants Act of 1962, 118
Commonwealth of Independent States, 168
Communism, 23, 25
community charge, 48, 70
Community Relations Commission, 191
comprehensive schools, 32, 175, 177–178,
Confederation of British Industry, 82, 135
Conservative, 5, 6, 7, 12, 20, 21, 27, 28, 33, 42, 43, 44, 45, 46, 47, 48, 57, 58, 59, 60, 61, 68, 73, 75, 76, 77,

78, 80, 81, 82, 83, 84, 86, 87, 88, 89, 90, 91, 93, 94, 97, 98, 110, 111, 112, 113, 114, 115, 116, 117, 118, 119, 120, 121, 125, 126, 127, 128, 133, 134, 135, 138, 139, 140, 141, 142, 143, 144, 145, 146, 148, 149, 150, 152, 153, 154, 155, 156, 157, 158, 159, 167, 169, 171, 172, 173, 174, 175, 176, 177, 178, 179, 181, 182, 189, 192, 193, 195, 201, 203, 204, 214, 215, 216, 217, 218, 218, 219, 222, 223, 225
consociationalism, 199, 200
Constitution, 4, 6, 7, 8, 36–63, 68, 69, 73, 98, 187, 198, 199, 201, 216, 221, 223, 224, 225
Cornwall, 19
corporatism, 10, 57, 80, 81–83, 154, 213
Council of Economic Advisers, 135
council housing, 173, 174
Council of Ministers, 109, 110, 111, 116, 206, 220
Criminal justice, 12, 187, 191, 192
Cromwell, Oliver, 38
Crosland, Anthony, 138, 175
Crossman, Richard, 37, 53, 55
culture, 2, 17, 188, 191, 205–206
cultural policy, 205–206
Cyprus, 118, 218
Czechoslovakia, 126

Daily Express, 76
Daily Mail, 76
Daily Mirror, 76
Daily Star, 76
Daily Telegraph, 76
Dance with a Stranger, 193
Declaration of Independence, 20
decolonization, 117–123
defense, 93, 106, 107, 108, 115, 117, 123–127, 128, 220
Defense Department, 108, 122, 135
Defense and Overseas Policy Committee, 108
de Gaulle, Charles, 112
democratic deficit, 110, 117
Denmark, 27, 115
devolution, 5, 6, 20, 48, 60–61, 63, 69, 90, 98, 116, 189, 190, 197, 198, 201, 202, 216, 217
Dickens, Charles, 23, 149
Disraeli, Benjamin, 95
divorce, 187, 189
Dover, 17
Downing Street, 57
Dublin, 21, 197
Dunleavy, Patrick, 91, 152, 170

Eastern Europe, 12, 28, 115, 125, 128
Economics, 5–8, 12, 22, 23, 24, 25–29, 31, 49, 69, 73, 80, 82, 83–84, 88, 91, 93, 108, 112–116, 117, 119, 121, 128, 132–164, 165, 178, 188, 195, 201, 207, 213, 214, 215, 223, 225
Economist, 76, 113, 139, 142
Eden, Anthony, 121
Edinburgh, 17

education, 26, 30, 31–33, 67–68, 93, 139, 167, 168, 170,
    174–178, 194, 199, 213, 216
Education Act (1944), 32
Education Bill of 1988, 167, 176
Education and Science Department, 135, 168, 175, 204
Edward VIII, King, 40
Egypt, 24, 120, 121, 122, 123
elections, European, 110, 154, 200
elections, general, 41, 43–44, 46, 48, 50, 51, 73, 78, 79,
    90–94, 113, 117, 121, 126, 141, 147, 148, 156, 158
elective dictatorship, 5, 157
electoral system, 6, 44, 71, 74, 86, 204, 217, 219
elite ideology, 116
elite values, 221
elites, 66–72, 73, 94–98, 112, 113, 115, 118, 120, 121,
    174, 178, 181, 182, 197, 198, 200, 201, 207, 212,
    213, 221
elitism-pluralism debate, 10, 11, 66, 127, 168, 213
Elizabeth I, Queen, 20, 38
Elizabeth II, Queen, 40
emigration, 29
Employment Department, 97, 135
Employment Protection Act of 1975, 202
End of the Socialist Era, The, 215
Energy Department, 97, 135
energy policy, 144, 150–154
Engels, Friedrich, 23, 149
England, 16, 17, 18, 30, 33, 38, 60, 61, 86, 156, 204
English Channel, 17
English Civil War, 38
English Constitution, The, 4
English disease, 214
English Revolution, 22, 24
environment, 80, 85, 135, 144, 150–154, 168
Episcopalians, 18
Equal Opportunities Commission, 191, 203
Equal Pay Act of 1970, 202
Equal Rights Amendment, 203
Essay on the Principle of Population, 30
establishment, the, 10
ethnic groups, 28–31, 75, 119, 196, 197, 216
Eton 32, 67
Eurocrats, 110
Europe, 16, 18, 19, 25, 28, 30, 31, 40, 116, 117, 119, 121,
    125, 126, 128, 141, 142, 153, 167, 168, 182, 188,
    193, 194, 215, 220, 221
European bank, 115
European Commission, 6, 109, 110, 111, 114, 147, 203,
    220
European Community, see European Union
European Convention on Human Rights, 62
European Council, 109
European Court of Human Rights, 205
European Court of Justice, 62, 109, 111, 203
European Free Trade Association (EFTA), 112, 115
European Intergovernmental Conference, 113
European Monetary Union, 114, 135

European Parliament, 89, 109, 110, 114
European Union 2, 3, 4, 5,6, 9, 12, 27, 45, 47, 48, 52, 62,
    85, 88, 91, 98, 105, 106, 108, 109, 111–117, 119,
    122, 125, 127, 128, 134, 135, 136, 144, 147, 150,
    153, 154, 155, 158, 160, 182, 184, 187, 190, 202,
    203, 215, 217, 219, 220, 222, 224
Exchange Rate Mechanism, (ERM), 114, 115,
executive, 6, 17, 37, 39, 45, 51–56, 79–80, 96, 108, 109,
    127, 200

Falklands, 105, 107, 108, 120, 121, 122, 125, 126, 214
family relations, 31, 34
Farouk, King, 120
fascism, 25, 80
Faulkner, Brian, 200
Federal Reserve Bank, 82
feminism, 33, 202
feudalism, 21
finance, 10, 17, 80, 81, 82, 85, 113, 133, 134, 215, 225
Financial Times, 76
Finer, Samuel, 79
Fiscal policy, 137
Foot, Michael, 43
Foreign and Commonwealth Office, 51, 96, 97, 108,
    109, 111
Foreign Office, 51, 109, 121, 122
foreign policy, 4, 5, 6, 8, 9, 10, 12, 18, 19 24, 25, 69,
    105–131, 133, 187, 207, 213, 214, 215, 222
foreign relations, 195
Foreign Secretary, 125, 149
France, 16, 17, 18, 19, 20, 25, 27, 31, 69, 71, 111, 112,
    114, 115, 118, 120, 121, 125, 133, 151
Franklin, Grace, 132, 165
Free Democrats, 217
free votes, 81, 189, 193, 194, 195, 204, 206
Friedman, Milton, 138
frontbenchers, 45, 96
Fulton Report, 58

Gaitskell, Hugh, 90, 142, 143, 144
gender, 12, 33–34, 203
gender equality, 187
General Agreement on Tariffs and Trade (GATT), 105,
    134
General Strike, 27, 98
George III, King, 40
George V, King, 41
Germany, 16, 18, 19, 24, 25, 27, 29, 31, 82, 111, 112,
    114, 115, 126, 128, 133, 136, 172, 177, 217
Ghana, 118
Gibraltar, 122
Gladstone, William, 20
Glasgow, 17, 29
geography, 12, 16–21
Gorbachev, Mikhail, 127
Gold Coast, 118
Government. See Executive

Government Communications Headquarters, 55
Grant, Wyn, 133
Great Depression, 25, 26, 137, 138, 139, 155, 225
Greater London Council, 60
Great Reform Act (1832), 46
Greece, 25, 125
Green Party, 154, 189
Group of Seven Industrialized Countries, 3, 105, 155
Guardian, 76
guns, 191

Hall, Peter, 205
Harrow, 32, 67
health policy, 168, 170–172
Heath, Edward, 53, 112, 116, 140, 148, 149, 159, 172, 195
Heidenheimer, Arnold, 170
Helco, Hugh, 170
Henry VIII, King, 19, 22, 38
Heseltine, Michael, 82
Hewitt, Christopher, 121, 213
higher education, 32–33, 68, 167, 169, 170, 176, 203
Hills, Jill, 95
Hills, John, 183
Hindus, 117
Hitler, Aldoph, 19, 25
history, 12, 19–34
history of public policy, 8
Hobbes, Thomas, 22
home office, 57, 96, 97, 190, 191, 192
home rule, 20, 21
homosexuality, 80, 187, 188, 189, 191, 204–205, 213
Hong Kong, 105, 123, 195, 196
honors list, 41, 56
Hooker, Richard, 39
House of Commons, 4, 20, 21, 22, 36, 39, 41, 42–51, 52, 56, 58, 63, 67, 68, 69, 70, 75, 81, 84, 85, 86, 89, 92, 96, 108, 109, 112, 115, 116, 121, 122, 123, 158, 168, 169, 174, 183, 188, 189, 193, 194, 195, 196, 198, 201, 204, 218, 219
     members, 6, 20, 44, 46, 47, 48, 59, 70, 79, 94–95, 97, 108, 189, 193
     procedures, 47–51, 63, 81, 85
     Question Time, 1, 49, 50, 52, 54, 70
     Select Committees, 50, 51, 52, 54, 59, 108, 169
     Speaker, 45, 68
House of Lords, 2, 5, 6, 20, 21, 22, 23, 36, 37–43, 45, 49, 51, 52, 56, 61, 62, 63, 68, 90, 97, 98, 108, 197, 217
housing policy, 168, 171, 172–174, 213
Hungary, 121, 126

ideology, 5, 71, 874, 85, 88, 95, 223
immigration, 28–29, 30, 34, 70, 93, 118, 187, 189, 190, 195–196, 207, 213
Imperial, 24, 108, 118, 119, 121, 123, 128
Independent, 76
Independent Television, 75–76

India, 24, 25, 29, 107, 117, 139, 195, 218
Individual rights, 4,5, 37, 39, 192, 194, 217
industrial policy, 144–147
Industrial Relations Act, 81
Industrial Relations Bill, 53
Industrial Revolution, 21, 22, 23, 24, 26, 29, 148
Institute of Directors, 82
interest groups, 10, 11, 26–27, 79–85, 108–109, 115, 116, 122, 206, 207, 213
International Monetary Fund, 26, 90, 105, 138, 143, 159, 181
Iran, 29, 122, 151
Iraq, 125, 126
Ireland, 3, 17, 19, 20, 21, 25, 29, 30, 31, 194, 197, 198, 199, 200, 219
Irish, 217, 218
Irish Republican Army (IRA), 98, 198, 199, 218
Islam, 29
Israel, 120, 121, 122, 143, 218
issue network, 9
Italy, 25, 27, 111, 133, 219

James I, King, 20, 38
James II, King, 30, 38
James IV, King, 20
Japan, 25, 26, 27, 128, 135, 219
Jenkins, Peter, 215
Jenkins, Roy, 197, 206
Jews, 28, 30
John, King, 22
Jones, Bryan, 223
Judge, David, 70
judicial review, 203, 217, 224
judiciary, 61–63, 109, 111, 194, 203, 205
justice, 199

Kennedy, Paul, 128, 129
Kenya, 118, 189
Kenyan Asians, 191, 195, 196
Keynes, John Maynard, 137
Keynesian economics, 136, 137, 138, 142
Kinnock, Neil, 98
Kipling, Rudyard, 24
Korean War, 125
Kuwait, 125, 126

Labor, 29, 81, 139, 156
Labour party, 5, 6, 7, 26, 28, 32, 33, 37, 42, 43, 45, 47, 48, 52, 55, 60, 61, 63, 67, 69, 71, 72, 73, 74, 78, 80, 81, 83, 84, 86–94, 95, 97, 98, 109, 110, 112, 115, 117, 120, 123, 124, 125, 126, 127, 128, 133, 134, 136, 138, 142, 143, 144, 145, 146, 147, 148, 149, 150, 152, 154, 157, 158, 159, 160, 166, 169, 171. 172, 173, 176, 177, 179, 181, 189, 190, 192, 193, 196, 201, 204, 205, 206, 214, 215, 217, 218, 219, 222
Lady Chatterley's Lover, 205

Latin America, 126
Law Lords, 42, 61–62, 115
law and order policy, 191–193, 206, 207
Lawson, Nigel, 57
League of Empire Loyalists, 109
legal system, 38, 40, 61–63, 77, 191–193
legislative process, 48–49
Let Him Have It, 193
Lib-Lab Pact, 71
Liberal Party, 4, 6, 20, 21, 42, 44, 46, 48, 71, 86–91, 98, 113, 116, 120, 137, 166, 172, 189, 193, 196, 219
Liberal Democrats, 44, 78, 87, 88, 91, 93, 94, 95, 97, 98, 169, 217, 218, 219, 220
Lijphart, Arend, 199, 200, 218
Little Englanders, 115, 126, 214
Liverpool, 17, 29
Lloyd George, David, 21, 172
local educational authorities (LEAs), 175, 176
local government, 60, 63, 92, 168, 171, 192, 196, 204, 206, 217
local management committee, 94
Locke John, 39, 43
Lome Convention, 119
London, 17, 24, 28, 76, 126, 135, 152, 156, 176, 197, 204
Lord Chancellor, 61
Lowi, Theodore, 8, 10, 123, 132, 165
Luxembourg, 27, 112, 125

Maastricht Treaty, 5, 9, 47, 48, 108, 110, 113, 114, 115, 127, 160, 182, 214, 215, 220
Macmillan, Harold, 80, 111, 112, 121, 125, 141, 146, 172
Magistrates' Courts, 62
Magna Carta, 22, 36, 38
Mainland Britain, 16, 28, 86, 193, 198, 199, 200, 201
Major, John, 34, 45, 47, 53, 59, 96, 113, 153, 167, 172, 214
majority rule, 4, 37
Malaysia, 118, 122
Malthus, Thomas, 30
Malvinas, 122
Marshall Plan, 25, 141
Marx, Karl, 23, 85, 149
Marxism 10, 23, 119, 137
masses, 66–67, 72–74, 98, 113, 115, 174, 182, 198, 212, 221
Masterpiece Theater, 1
Mau Mau, 118
McCormick, John, 153
media, 40, 55, 74–79, 109, 123, 205, 224
Methodism, 18, 23
MI5, 54
MI6 (Secret Service), 54, 55
Middle East, 125, 151
Middle East War, 83, 143
Miller, William, 202
military, 10, 19, 24, 25, 59, 121, 123, 168, 204, 213, 220, 221

ministers, 135, 168
Ministry of Agriculture, Fisheries, and Food, 154
Ministry for Women, 204
minorities, 219
monarchy, 5, 19, 20, 22, 23, 30, 36–42, 45, 56, 59, 61, 68, 74, 92, 120, 217, 221
monetarism, 138, 143
monetary policy, 135–136, 137, 139
Moore, Barrington, 22
moral issues, 8
moral reform, 216
Mozambique, 119
Murdock, Rupert, 77
Muslims, 117, 196

Napoleonic Wars, 24
Nasser, Gamal Abdel, 120
National Economic Development Council, 80, 82
National Executive Committee, 83, 89, 145
National Health Service, 61, 78, 165, 167, 169, 170, 171
national identity, 187
National Theatre, 205
National Union of Mineworkers, 84
nationalism, 121, 196–202, 207
nationalist movements, 202
nationalist parties, 6, 18, 61, 86, 90, 116, 120, 197, 199, 200, 216
nationalities, 12, 18, 98
nationalization, 73, 133, 143, 144, 145, 146, 147, 158
natural resources, 21, 105
Nazi party, 29
Nazi-Soviet Pact, 25
Netherlands, 16, 27, 30, 112, 125
New International Economic Order, 119
New Society, 77
New Statesman, 77
New Statesman and Society, 77
New Zealand, 25, 119, 219
newly industrialized countries (NIC), 138, 143, 159
newspapers, 10, 68, 76–77, 78, 79
Next Steps program, 52, 57, 59
Nigeria, 118, 119
Nile River, 120
Nobel Prize, 27
nonwhites, 204
Nordics, 28
Normans, 19, 21, 28
North Atlantic Treaty Organization (NATO), 3, 12, 18, 105, 107, 123, 125, 126, 141
North Sea oil, 17, 21, 26, 83, 143, 151, 152, 155, 214, 223
Northcote-Trevelyan Report, 58
Northern Ireland, 3, 16, 17, 18, 20, 21, 29, 30, 45, 60, 61, 62, 63, 69, 70, 93, 98, 109, 189, 191, 192, 193, 196, 197, 198, 199, 200, 201, 202, 204, 213, 218, 219, 222
Northern Ireland Office, 135, 168, 200

Norton, Philip, 190
Norway, 17, 152, 156
Nuclear Nonproliferation Treaty of 1964, 125
Nuclear Test Ban Treaty of 1962, 125

Observer, 76
Office of Management and Budget, 135
Official Secrets Act (1911), 55, 77–78
Old Age, Survivors, and Disability Insurance (OASDI), 178
Olson, Mancur, 11
Ombudsman, 58
O'Neil, Terence, 200
Operation Sea Lion, 19
Orders in Council, 53
Oregon, 16
Organization of Petroleum Exporting Countries (OPEC), 143
Orkney and Shetland, 17
Orwell, George, 149
Ottoman Empire, 24
Owen, David, 42
Oxbridge, 32, 94
Oxford, 174

Pacific Ocean, 128
Pakistan, 29, 117, 139, 195
Palace of Westminster, 41
Palestine, 24, 118
Parliament, 18, 20, 21, 30, 38–40, 41, 43, 44, 48–49, 50, 51, 52, 53, 55, 56, 58, 61, 62, 63, 67, 68, 69, 70, 85, 92, 93, 107–108, 115, 127, 135, 150, 151, 154, 157, 169, 182, 190, 192, 194, 197
parliamentary sovereignty, 2, 6, 36, 45, 46, 59, 62, 217
party government, 213
party leaders, 96–97
party platforms, 168
party whips, 47
Pearl Harbor, 25
Peers, Hereditary, 42, 97
Peers, Life, 42
Permanent Representation to the European Communities, 117
Plaid Cymru, 18, 202
pluralistic stagnation, 11, 213
pluralism, 221
Poland, 28, 29, 126
Police and Criminal Evidence Act of 1984, 192
policy community, 9
policy typologies, 8, 9
Policy Unit, 57
political behavior, 66–98
political culture, 12 , 66–74, 197, 217
political parties, 5, 7, 18, 41, 44, 45 46, 46, 47, 50, 55, 56, 71, 73, 85–91, 92, 94–97, 98, 108, 109, 112, 113, 121, 122, 123, 133, 157, 174, 189, 219, 222
political recruitment, 50–51, 67, 70, 94–97
political socialization, 67–74

Pollard, Sydney, 139, 156
polytechnics, 33
popular sovereignty, 39, 43–44, 98
population, 16, 17, 18, 28–31, 152, 178
pornography, 187, 189
postmaterialism, 73, 207
Powell, Enoch, 43, 195, 196, 223
Presbyterianism, 18, 30
Prescott, John, 89
Presidency of the Council of Ministers, 109, 111
president of the European Union, 110
presidentialization of British politics, 37, 54
press secretary, 57
pressure groups, 194
prime minister, 39, 40, 41, 43–45, 49, 51–56, 61, 121, 134
primogeniture, 22
Private Eye, 77
Private Office, 56
private schools, 32
privatization, 146, 150, 158, 170, 172, 174
Privy Council, 39
Protestantism, 30, 39, 197, 198, 199, 200
public opinion, 1, 108, 111, 115, 116, 120, 121, 123, 127, 134, 145, 147, 149, 151, 157, 158, 167, 174, 194, 195, 200, 206
public opinion polls, 79, 108, 112, 193, 219
public (fee-paying) schools, 32
Putnam, Robert, 11, 71

Quangos, 57, 191, 203
Queen's Counselors 40
Queen's Speech 41, 45, 168, 195
Question Time, 127

race, 12, 70, 75, 95, 120, 191, 195, 196, 205
race relations, 187
Race Relations Bill, 195, 190
Race Relations Board, 191
radio, 76, 78
Reagan, Ronald, 139, 180, 183
redistricting, 92–93
referendum, 45, 47, 71, 98, 106–107, 111, 112, 113, 116, 189, 190, 201, 206, 217, 218, 219
Reformation, 22
Regency Act (1707), 30
regional aid, 116, 146
regional economic differences, 28, 70
regional voting, 93
religion, 30, 38, 41, 98, 198
Renaissance, 22
Republicans, 18, 68
Restoration, 38
Rhodesia, 107, 118, 119, 120, 126
Ripley, Randall, 132, 165
Robbins Report, 177
Roman Catholicism, 18, 20, 21, 22, 30, 38, 39, 198, 199, 200, 204
Romans, 19

Rose, Richard, 49, 68, 74, 117, 157, 181
Rose, Richard, and Ian McAllister, 74
Rose, Richard, and Derek Urwin, 98
Rothschild, Lord, 141
Rowntree, Seebohm, 170
Royal Commissions, 57
Royal Prerogative, 53
Royal Shakespeare Company, 205
Rudolph, Joseph, 151
Runnymede, 22
Rushdie, Salman, 29, 196
Russia, 18, 19, 28, 37

Sampson, Anthony, 3
Saxons, 28
Scandinavia, 19
Schatteschneider, E.E., 221
Schumepter, Joseph, 73, 91
Scotland, 3, 5, 16, 17, 18, 19, 20, 28, 30, 33, 38, 45, 48,
    60, 61, 63, 69, 73, 76, 86, 92, 152, 156, 190, 191,
    192, 196, 197, 200, 201, 202, 204
Scottish nationalism, 218
Scottish Nationalist Party, 18, 190, 201, 202
Scottish office, 135, 168, 189
Searing, Donald, 67
secrecy, 37, 53, 54–55, 56, 57, 58, 77, 106, 125, 127
security services, 54–55
Sex Discrimination Act of 1975, 191, 202, 203
Sex Discrimination Act of 1986, 202, 203
Sexual Offenses Act, 204
sexual orientation, 12
shadow cabinet, 45, 55, 97
Single European Act, 110, 114, 153
Smethwick, 195
Smith, John, 89, 219
Smith, T. Alexander, 132, 165
Smoke Abatement Act of 1956, 154
Social Chapter, 113, 116, 182
Social Democratic Party, 42, 73, 87, 88, 113, 126
social policy, 115, 150
social regulatory policy, 8, 12, 74, 85, 187–211, 213,
    216
Social Security department, 97, 166, 168, 180
Social Security policy, 178–181
Social Security Reform Act of 1986, 180
Social Security Review of 1985, 183
social services, 135
social spending, 136
social welfare policy, 7, 8, 12, 69, 74, 84, 91, 165–186,
    187, 206, 207, 213, 215
Socialism, 4, 87, 88, 89, 113, 120, 133, 134, 138, 143,
    153, 215
Soskice, Frank, 190
South Africa, 107, 118, 119, 120, 126
Southern Africa, 120
Soviet Union, 3, 12, 18, 25, 29, 121, 125, 126, 127, 128,
    220
Spain, 18, 20, 123

Speaker's Corner, 192
Spycatcher, 55
stages of public policy, 9, 106, 111–129, 136–150,
    170–184, 191–208
Stalin, Joseph, 25
Statute of Westminster, 25
Statutory Instruments, 53, 54
Steinmo, Sven, 157
Stokes, Donald, 145, 149
Strasbourg, 110
strike, 200
Succession to the Crown Act (1705), 30
Suez, 107, 120, 121, 122, 123, 125, 126, 151
Suffragettes, 4, 33
Sun, The, 76
Supplementary Benefit, 165, 167, 178
Sweden, 27, 137, 155, 156, 178
Swedish, 177
swinging sixties, 188

Taylor-Gooby, Peter, 181
tax policy, 48, 70, 136, 137, 139, 144, 154–155, 168, 213,
    214
television, 74–75, 78–79, 92, 109, 142, 202, 204,
    206
Ten Rillington Place, 193
terrorism, 62, 109, 190, 192, 199
Thames River, 17, 154
Thatcher, Margaret, 10, 28, 34, 45, 48, 53, 54, 57, 59, 60,
    63, 72, 81, 82, 83, 90, 94, 97, 110, 113, 114, 116,
    118, 122, 123, 127, 134, 136, 138, 139, 141, 143,
    146, 148, 149, 153, 155, 156, 159, 167, 168, 172,
    176, 177, 180, 183, 201, 203, 205, 215, 223
Thatcherism, 1, 12, 26, 73, 212, 222, 223
theories of public policy, 7–13
Third World, 119, 123, 126
Three Mile Island, Pennsylvania, 151
Times, 76, 115
Today, 76
Tomlinson, Jim, 139
Trade Disputes Act, 81
Trade and Industry Department, 97, 135
trade unions, 5, 24, 27–28, 31, 71, 73, 80, 81, 82, 83–84,
    88, 89, 97, 116, 136, 139, 140, 144, *147, 148–150,
    158, 178, 212, 213, 214, 225
Trades Union Congress, 83, 149
Transportation Department, 135, 150
Treasury, 51, 97, 108, 134, 1358
Treaty of Versailles, 25
Trident, 125
Turkey, 125
Turner, R.H., 175
turnout, 92, 93, 110, 116

Uganda, 119, 189
Ugandan Asians, 195, 196
Ulster Unionists, 21, 218
ungovernability, 5, 11, 81, 143, 212

Unilateral Declaration of Independence (UDI), 118
unitary state, 59
United Nations, 105, 118, 119, 123, 126, 128
United States, 12, 18, 19, 24, 25, 30, 32, 39, 42, 49, 50,
    51, 54, 55, 56, 57, 69, 71, 74, 75, 77, 78, 79, 82, 107,
    111, 112, 119, 120, 121, 122, 123, 124, 125, 126,
    133, 135, 136, 137, 138, 139, 141, 149, 154, 155,
    156, 170, 171, 177, 178, 180, 183, 191, 194, 196,
    199, 203, 205, 206, 214·
University Grants Committee, 176
University of Chicago, 138
Universities, 10, 32–33, 68, 94
    Buckingham, 32
    Cambridge, 32, 58, 68
    Durham, 32
    London, 32
    Open, 33
    Oxford, 32, 58, 68
    Warwick, 177
    Urbanization, 16, 22, 23, 30, 46, 153, 157

values, 2, 12, 67–74, 98
Verba, Sidney, 72–73
Victoria, Queen, 24, 204
Victorian, 145
Vietnam, 118, 126
V.O. Key, 158
vote of confidence, 41, 45, 46, 47, 49, 190, 206
voting, 5, 33, 46, 92–93, 133

Wales, 3, 5, 16, 17, 18, 19, 28, 30, 33, 45, 48, 60, 61, 63,
    69, 73, 86, 92, 156, 190, 191, 196, 197, 200, 201,
    202, 204, 218
Walters, Sir Alan, 57
welfare state, 123
Welsh office, 135, 168, 189
West Indies, 29, 139, 195
West European Union, 125
white-hot technological revolution, 7, 87, 143, 177, 212
Whitehouse, Mary, 206
white paper, 189
Wiener, Martin, 156
William of Saxony, 19
King William and Queen Mary, 30, 38
Wilson, Harold, 7, 33, 53, 63, 112, 113, 140, 149, 175
Windscale, 151
Winter of Discontent, 5, 84, 98, 140, 144, 148, 158
Wolfenden Committee Report, 204
women, 10, 33–34, 46, 80, 89, 95, 191, 194, 202–204,
    206, 216, 219
World War I, 19, 21, 24, 25, 29, 86, 88, 107, 137, 151, 197
World War II, 3,4, 27, 29, 90, 105, 107, 117, 125, 133,
    139, 141, 152, 156, 167, 178, 180, 188, 225

Yes, Minister, 56
Yes, Prime Minister, 56
Yugoslavia, 125

Zimbabwe, 107